CHRISTOPHER

All good wishes,

14.2.06

THE EXCAVATION OF THE ROMAN FORT AT RECULVER, KENT

The Report on the programme of excavations from 1959–1969 on this major Roman military site, half destroyed by coastal erosion. The work, both research and rescue, dealt with the fort's defences, two gatehouses, eleven internal buildings, minor structures and over 25,000 finds.

By

BRIAN PHILP FSA

With main contributions by :

> Richard Reece
> Joanna Bird
> Kay Hartley

TENTH RESEARCH REPORT IN THE KENT MONOGRAPH SERIES
(ISSN 0141 2264)
(ISBN 0947831-24-X)

Published by:
Kent Archaeological Rescue Unit,
Roman Painted House, New Street, Dover, Kent CT17 9AJ

2005

Dedicated to

Anne and Harold Gough
for their help and support
over five decades
and to
all the CIB volunteers

Printed in Great Britain by Henry Ling Limited, at The Dorset Press, Dorchester DT1 1HD

The Unit is greatly indebted to **THE COUNCIL FOR KENTISH ARCHAEOLOGY, THE KENT ARCHAEOLOGICAL TRUST and AND THE AUTHOR** for help in financing the cost of this publication.

CONTENTS

CHAPTER VI   THE EXCAVATED OBJECTS

CHAPTER VII   DISCUSSION

REFERENCES

INDEX

PLATES

LIST OF FIGURES

LIST OF PLATES

ABOUT THIS REPORT

This Report is the 10th in the Kent Monograph Series, which started in 1968 and has now covered sites at Faversham, Hayes, Darenth, Polhill, Dover (three volumes), Farningham, Otford, Keston (Reports I and II) and Orpington. It largely follows the pattern set by the earlier volumes and as before all proceeds from sales go towards preparation, printing and publication costs, or into a reserve fund for subsequent volumes. Further Reports are already in preparation.

The Report deals mainly with an 11-year programme of extensive excavation inside the Roman fort at Reculver, from 1959–69, but also including some work carried out from 1952–8. The work was undertaken by the Reculver Excavation Group, whilst minor work since 1970 has been under taken by the Kent Archaeological Rescue Unit, both directed by the writer. Details of the excavation programme and post-excavation work are given below (p. 4).

As with previous Reports in this series, footnotes have been excluded and the bibliographical references, numbered throughout the text, are listed at the back. These show as numbers placed in brackets and prefixed by the letters Ref. (e.g. Ref. 47). The illustrated finds are numbered progressively, this time prefixed by the letters No. or Nos., so as to eliminate recurring numbers and thus avoid confusion. References in the text to drawn sections and layers are shown in brackets, prefixed by the letters S. and L., respectively (e.g. S.H, L.18).

CHAPTER I

INTRODUCTION

(A) THE SITE

The site of Reculver (NGR.TR.2269.2369) lies on the north coast of Kent about three miles east of Herne Bay and about nine miles north-east of inland Canterbury (Fig. 1). It broadly marks the mouth of the Thames Estuary, here about 20 miles wide, at a point where it flows into the North Sea. The overall site was occupied in the late-Bronze/early-Iron Ages and then throughout the whole historic period. The major Roman fort here occupied a very low outlying hill of Thanet Sand, which had a central high-point of only 34 ft. O.D. Here the ground sloped away on the west, south and east sides by some 15–20 ft.

The soft underlying Thanet Sand has suffered from very considerable sea erosion since Roman times and about half the Roman fort and much more of the overall archaeological site has now been totally destroyed (Plates I–II). To the west the land dips twice before rising to over 100 ft. well before it reaches Herne Bay. To the east, at least in Roman times, there was a wide tidal channel later known as the Wantsum (Fig. 2). This silted massively in the post-Roman period, partly as a by-product of the coastal erosion, and is today low-lying marshland, mostly farmed and lined with drainage dykes. This wide channel defined the Isle of Thanet and joined the English Channel near present-day Pegwell Bay. Near the south end of the channel lay the major Roman base at Richborough, which in its later military history must have worked in concert with the fort at Reculver.

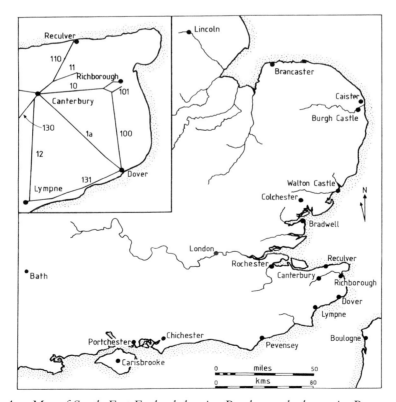

Fig. 1.   *Map of South-East England showing Reculver and other major Roman sites.*

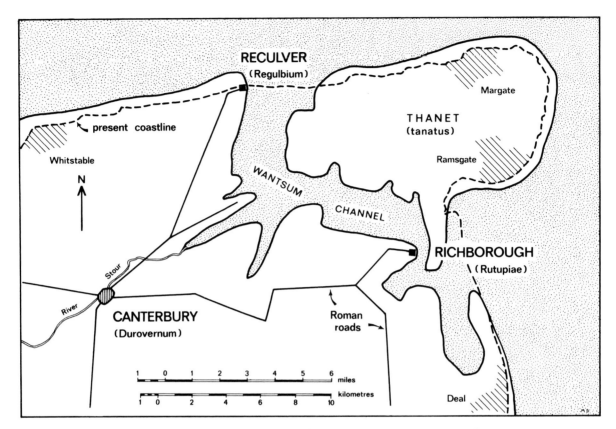

Fig. 2.   *Map of North-East Kent showing conjectured Roman Coastline.*

Today the site of Reculver is dominated by the towers of St. Mary's Church (Plate III), which was itself planted in the centre of the ruined Roman fort in the 7th century A.D. The substantial medieval settlement, recorded in early documents, has been progressively destroyed by sea erosion and today only the King Ethelbert public-house, five houses and several hundred caravans occupy the surviving areas. Whilst the permanent population now numbers about twenty people, this increases to over 1,000 at the height of the holiday season. This coastal location remains very exposed and only massive sea-walls prevent more erosion that by now would have destroyed what little remains of Reculver. Even so, storms from the north-east are particularly damaging and very severe storms still threaten the north tower of the ruined church.

Of special interest, in topographical terms, is a fine estate map of 1685 (Fig. 3), when at least 120 yards of land still survived north of the church. This also shows a narrow inlet (not included here) extending diagonally inland for about 260 yards. If extended it roughly strikes an outcrop of firm rock about 1,200 yards seawards of the present cliffs (Fig. 4). This outcrop is now known as the Black Rock, a strip about 100 m. in length which is exposed at some low Spring Tides. The 1685 map describes the inlet as **"a place anciently for a harber of ships, called now The Old Pen"**, which strongly suggests a local tidal inlet existing some decades earlier. The projection of this inlet to the Black Rock creates, with the sea to the north and wide eastern channel, a headland with water on three sides. Such a major topographical feature could certainly help explain the likely derivation of the Celtic name REGULBIUM as Great (Ro) Headland (GULBIO) as suggested in 1979 (Ref. 89). The Roman fort can be seen to control access to such a headland and it also helps to limit the area of the discoveries by the Rev. J. Battely in the late-17th century (see p. 12).

The coastal erosion has clearly been very rapid, but calculatios based on written accounts since Leland produce varying annual rates. The matter is further complicated for it is unlikely to have

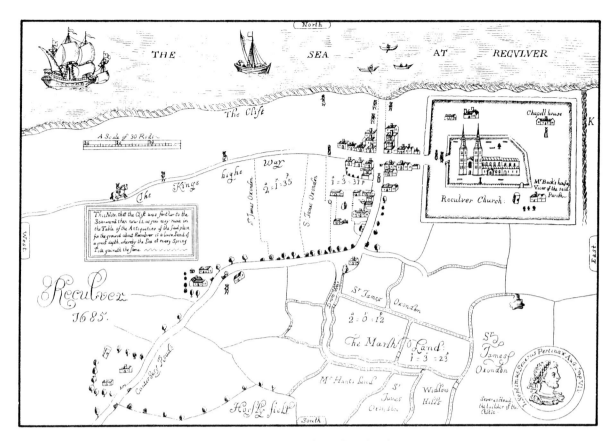

Fig. 3.   *Estate map of Reculver dated 1685.*

occurred at a constant rate, depending mostly on variations in regional land submergence. Historically, rates of 1–3 yards per annum have been suggested, which if constant, would place the Roman shore-line about 1–3 miles further north. This is largely the figure suggested in a study published in 1971(Ref. 83), again based on uncertain accounts, but also by extending tographical profiles offshore. With the considerable uncertainties involved it is at present best to suggest that the Roman coastline was nominally one mile offshore and generally in the vicinity of the Black Rock.

Certainly, in late Roman times the site was connected to the Roman road-network which covered most of Roman Britain and it was linked to Canterbury (*Durovernum Cantiacorum*), a distance of about ten Roman miles. It must be certain that the Roman fort had a supporting harbour, probably a natural feature improved by quays and jetties. So far this has not been found. Possible areas are (the Old Pen considered) north-west and north of the fort, both now destroyed. Equally, the south and east areas are possible where substantial evidence could yet survive. The wide tidal Channel on the east side is perhaps the best candidate as this offered the most convenient and protected area, linking access through the East Gate of the fort. Much would, however, depend on the precise levels in Roman times, now much masked by large-scale silting, dykes and agriculture.

(B) THE EXCAVATION PROGRAMME

The ongoing excavations at Reculver cover a span of over 50 years. Three broad phases of work are represented. An initial phase of rescue-work (1952–7) on the foreshore west of the fort revealed

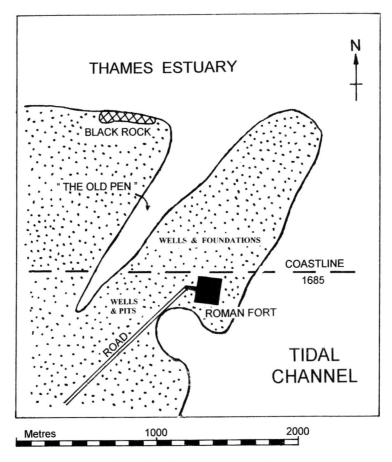

Fig. 4. *Map of Reculver showing conjectured Roman Coastline.*

twelve Roman wells, pits and other features was fully published by 1958 (Refs. 1 and 2). This early work, directed by the writer assisted by a few friends, led to the formation of the Reculver Excavation Group in 1957. The core of the Group, mostly fit young men, all dedicated and enthusiastic amateur archaeologists, was soon joined by others, both local and from other parts of Kent. Notable additions were Harold and Anne Gough and members of the West Kent Archaeological Group. Each year from 1957 until 1969 (13 seasons) the Reculver Group carried out a programme of evaluation-trenching, or area-excavation, across much of what survived of the fort (Refs. 3–9). The excellent results obtained form the basis of this Report (Fig. 5).

The outline results of this work were published in a series of booklets (of which the 10th edition was published in 1996) sold on the site and elsewhere at a nominal price. These were specifically identified as being designed for the general public, though this was totally misunderstood by one critical researcher in 2002 (Ref. 71). The main programme of work was interrupted in June, 1970 when the whole Reculver team, joined by other Kent groups, moved to Dover to undertake urgent large-scale rescue-excavations in the centre of the town. There, three Roman forts were soon located, substantially excavated and preserved from certain destruction (Refs. 10–11). Major excavations by the Kent Archaeological Rescue Unit, formed in 1971 from the combined forces of the Reculver, West Kent and other groups, continued in central Dover for the next 30 years with spectacular success (Refs. 12–15). The third and continuing phase of work at Reculver (1970–2005), by the Kent Archaeological Rescue Unit., has been on a smaller scale, but covered both the fort and a much wider area (Ref. 16). This phase of work will be covered by a subsequent Report.

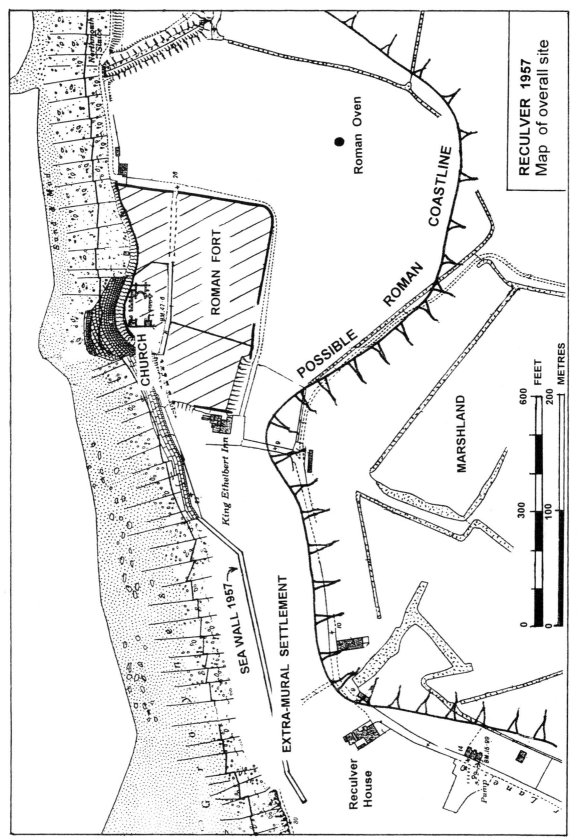

Fig. 5. *Map of Reculver showing Roman Fort and adjacent area (1957).*

Of the four acres of the Roman fort surviving, considerable parts were covered (in 1957) by the houses and gardens of both the original and new Coastguard Stations and also the church and churchyard. This only left about two acres of the fort available for excavation and a selective programme of work was devised at the start and always approved by the Ministry of Public Building and Works in advance. This combined both rescue and research work, as required, with the latter involving long exploratory trenches (much later described as evaluation interventions) conforming to a basic grid across open areas. These trenches were mostly confined to a 4 ft. width and were supplemented by area-excavations at selected points. The programme as devised at the outset aimed to examine the forts defences, the internal buildings and roads and the two surviving gatehouses. In all, the 1300 linear feet of trenches, the area-excavations and trial-holes, the excavations covered a total area of about 1700 sq. yds., or perhaps only 8% of the surviving area of the fort and thus only 4% of the original area. By far the greater part was left untouched, though of this it should be noted that the central area has been greatly reduced by various agencies.

All the site drawings and records were completed using imperial measurements and these are used in the text and on the drawings, though metric scales have been added. The major sections were numbered progressively through the years and these numbers are retained here (Sections 1–40). Inevitably, the quality of the drawings varied depending on the skills of those available at any time and this may be reflected in this publication. Generally this was done to a good standard and the detail accurate. One problem encountered was the difficulty of plotting precisely some of the east trenches where the area was covered with very dense vegetation (since cleared). The plans and sections were mostly drawn at a scale of 1 inch to 2 ft. (1/24), but sometimes this was increased to 1 inch to 1 ft. (1/12) where extra detail was needed. The overall plans were then produced to a scale of 1 inch to 10 ft. (1/120) and related to a 100 ft. fixed grid. The soil deposits were recorded by individual layer numbers (hence layers 1–95) and all coins and special objects were recorded in key-finds registers, all by years. The site O.D. levels are held in the site archive.

The detailed programme of work, actually started in 1957 and had dealt with 13 specific sites up until 1969. These are listed below together with the numbered major sections.

				Sections
Year	1	1957	North-east Cliff	1–2
	2	1958	South-west corner of fort and south ditch	3
	3	1959	East Defences and *Via Quintana*	4
	4	1960	Central Area and test-holes (Principia)	5–7
	5	1961	East Area. Barracks Nos.1 & 2 (Trenches A–D)	8–11
	6	1962	East Area. Barracks Nos. 1 & 2	–
			East Ditches of Fort	12
			Fortlet Ditches	13
	7	1963	South Area – SW Building (Trenches A–D). Box J and JH	14–16
			Cistern and Corn-drying Oven	17–18
	8	1964	Repair to East Wall	19
			Fortlet Ditches	20
			South Gate and Allotment Area	21–24
	9	1965	Bath House and Officers Quarters	25–27
			North-east Cliff	
	10	1966	West Area. Barracks and North-east Cliff	28–30
	11	1967	East Gate and *Via Quintana* (training)	31–34
	12	1968	East Area. Barracks Nos. 1 & 2	35–37
	13	1969	ChurchSite	
			North East Area. Timber-framed Building (Trenches A–D)	38–40

The total period of excavation probably covered more than 300 working days. The small-scale autumn, winter and spring projects (not listed) mostly involved a team of 4–5 people, but the large-scale summer operation often had a daily team of 20–30. In all, a total in excess of 5,000 working days was recorded and none paid. At a basic current daily rate, this would today have cost over £150,000, excluding the management, technical staff and material costs. The team varied from year to year, but the core team had good excavational skills developed on West Kent sites. Many of the other volunteers had little or no previous experience, but their good level of fitness, their flexibility, enthusiasm and rapid learning helped most make useful contributions. Some continued with archaeological work and some others even made it a career. The results were generally good and a large amount of important information, both relating to Reculver and the wider Roman coastal defence system, obtained. In addition, over 25,000 artefacts were recovered, including over 620 coins, half of which were neatly stratified. About 1,000 individual soil deposits (now contexts) were recorded and over 1,000 photographs taken. These, together with 40 large-scale plans and sections and also the annual registers, form the overall site-archive.

The overall programme of work at Reculver, which started in 1952 and still continues in a small way, has always been carried out with very limited financial resources. It is still largely supported by private individual effort and over the years has generated a large body of skilled and semi-skilled excavators. In many ways the larger excavations of the 1960s pioneered group excavations elsewhere and led to the formation of the Kent Archaeological Rescue Unit in 1971. That Unit has subsequently carried out over 700 projects and also produced the largest volume of excavation and related reports ever produced in Kent by a single organisation (Ref. 31).

As the work continued inside the Roman fort various problems were progressively (and inevitably) revealed. It became clear that the fort had been constructed upon a low hill with its central point roughly occupying the centre of the hill. Certainly, the ground fell away on the three surviving sides. Post-Roman land use and some soil erosion has resulted in the central area (south of the surviving churchyard wall) being severely reduced. Hence it seems clear that only deep foundations and cut features will have survived there. A large central area, perhaps 300 x 250 ft., is thus likely to have been reduced in this way. Beyond this area the stratification and structures mostly survive to an ever increasing depth to a point inside the fort walls where it can attain a depth of 6–9 ft. Clearly, the fort wall has acted as a retaining wall, though along much of the south side the pressure of the soil has pushed the wall outwards.

It also gradually became clear that some of the larger walls of the internal buildings had been constructed on deep foundations. Unusually, these took the form of layers of rolled beach pebbles alternating with thick bands of soil. The soil was that removed from the foundation-trench and thus identical to the sides and bottom of the trench and this made location very difficult, especially in hot dry weather. It is possible that some deeply buried pebble foundations were not seen in the early years. Similarly, the fill of any water-pipe trenches, also derived from the identical underlying soils, may have masked their lines. Only on the West Site, excavated in 1966, was one certain line detected and this only following the discovery of a pair of iron water-pipe collars. It seems no surface water was available and it may be that this pipeline and perhaps others were fed from cisterns, or wells.

The same problem of location also applied to all the Fortlet ditches, but to a lesser extent, where these were found under the later stone fort. Most had silted progressively over many decades and thus their fills closely matched the soils through which they had been cut. The ultimate remedy was to water the excavation at dusk and sheet over with plastic, thus emphasising any contrast between buried soils. In addition, it is also possible that the linear trenching method may have missed certain types of non-continuous features.

It is also clear that parts of the site have been cut by medieval pits and World War II defences and pits. Even so, these could contain significant Roman material. The church area is likely to have suffered from many hundreds of grave-cuts, both within the church and churchyard, but it is possible that some trace of Roman structures and deposits survives. A stone-lined well, found near the centre in 1923 and only partly emptied, was not examined in 1960 and could be either of Roman, or later, date. It is sealed by a slab of concrete. Significantly, perhaps, it appears to occupy the north-east corner of the courtyard of the *principia*.

Of very special interest, however, was the discovery of ten infant-burials and several Roman coins directly associated with Roman walls. Whilst infant-burials are common on Roman sites, three of those at Reculver were found in direct association with the foundation pebbles of the West Building. Others were found inserted into the centre of the wall of the East Barrack No. 1 and in the internal north-west corner of the same building (Room A). There can be little doubt that the first four were foundation deposits and were all discovered largely by chance. The probability is that several, or many, others remain to be found as 99% of the masonry located was left intact. Several coins appeared to have been inserted into the clay walls. These were again chance discoveries for the walls were not removed and the coins only revealed during the cleaning process.

As regards the excavation funding, the basic material costs each year were mainly covered by the proceeds from the sale of publications, lecture fees and donations on site. These totalled about £400 (today about £4,000). The Ministry of Public Building and Works provided some tools and the use of two wooden huts from 1964, largely through the kindly interest of Andrew Saunders (then Chief Inspector) and also Stuart Rigold. All the other tools and equipment were provided by the Group and all travel and accommodation costs were met by the individuals concerned.

As regards the post-excavation costs, the raising of the substantial funds involved was a major problem. The most likely source, English Heritage, eventually agreed in 1998 to assist under its "back-log publication" programme. It provided about £5,000 for Stage I, which entailed the quantification of the large artefact collection. This work was completed on target, with three times the amount of work done than was anticipated. Sadly, English Heritage took a year to refund the final costs, which caused obvious cash-flow problems. Stage II, which involved the sensible consolidation of the total written archive, was rejected by English Heritage as it did not conform to its MAP II model. This bureaucratic adherence to what was always claimed to be a flexible model, the repetitive and sometimes contradictory meetings and the endless delays meant that this very important project had to be abandoned. The archaeological section of English Heritage, it seems, needs radical reform imposed by a new broom with a very long handle.

In spite of this major setback, limited alternative funds were gradually obtained so that the post-excavation programme could resume. This shortfall caused the deletion of several aspects of a total report and thus no detailed fabric analysis of the large pottery collection could be attempted. Nor has a detailed study of the building-materials been carried out, whilst the animal bones and mollusca were anyway of very limited value.

Happily, more constructive sources were at hand and the following contributions are gratefully acknowledged most notably that of Howard Davies.

Kent Archaeological Trust	£3,250
Kent Archaeological Society	£3,000
Howard Davies	£2,500
Association for Roman Archaeology	£600
Canterbury Archaeological Society	£500
Richard Reece	£500 (contra)
C. B. A. South-east	£450

Hanson Aggregates	£300
Herne Bay Records Society	£200
J. Clubb Ltd.	£100
Millbrook Garden Centre	£50

These extra contributions eventually totalled over £10,000 and allowed a reduced post-excavation programme to be completed. Even then, the K.A.R.U. had to add another £1,000 from its limited reserves and the author had to work unpaid for the final fifteen months. The total cost of printing and distribution had to be met jointly by the Unit and the author.

(C) ACKNOWLEDGEMENTS

The large programme of work represented by this Report, both excavation and post-excavation analyses, is the result of very substantial efforts by many people. These are gratefully acknowledged here, though it is not possible to mention everyone by name.

The excavation team over the 11 main years (1959–69) totalled about 150 people, including many who were only able to work for a single year. All were volunteers and the majority had little or no previous archaeological experience. Only the main core-team, which had worked extensively on rescue sites in West Kent had good excavation skills, but most had a good level of fitness, accepted strict site discipline and enjoyed the work. Whilst the main excavations were carried out in the summer, minor excavations continued at intervals throughout the years, including the great freeze of 1962–3.

The main core-team, all of whom worked for more than 80 days were Mrs. Anne Gough, Ms. Edna Mynott, Mrs. Nellie Roberts; Messrs. Alan Casement, Roy Casement, Gerald Cramp, Harold Gough, Jonathan Horne and Arthur Lewington. Of these Harold Gough acted as Deputy throughout, Gerald Cramp as supervisor on the West site in 1966 and John Swale was responsible for many of the early site drawings.

The main support team consisted of Mrs. Doris Howe, Misses Janet Banks, Frances Brennan, Anita Gaunt, Pat Goldsmith, Marianne Last, Amanda Steele, Michelle Thomas and also Messrs. Andrew Appleby, David Bartlett, Howard Davies, David Ellwood, Derek Garrod, Ray Gierth, Graeme Horner, Harry Howe, Mike Kellaway, Peter Knivett, Andrew Norris, Alan Rice, Harold Robinson, Richard Wattenbach and Norman White.

In addition, good support was given by Misses Christine Blackett, Frances Lloyd, Dawn Marshall, Diana Phillips and Paula Smithson; and Messrs. Frank Barnes, Roger Campbell, Gerald Clewley, Alan Gidlow, Rupert Goodhart, Cedric Hart, Brian Kewell, Karl Lardner, Martin Montagne, Bill Ramsey, Ernest Salter and Christopher Terry.

As regards the long programme of post-excavation analysis, the following are acknowledged for their special work: Maurice Chenery, John Swale, Gerald Clewley and Mike Weaver for the finished plans and sections, Gemma Bates, Gerald Clewley, Katherine Smith, Graham Welstead and Wendy Williams for the illustration of the objects and Pam Barrett, Claire Wright and Debbie Cooper for the type-setting and proof-reading. In addition, Les Murrell has continued his good work on checking the text and identifying many errors and omisions. Of specialist help Joanna Bird has kindly reported on the samian ware; Ralph Merrifield and Richard Reece on the coins; Kay Hartley on the mortaria, Brenda Dickinson on the samian stamps and Martin Henig on a gemstone. Maurice Chenery has written up the small-finds catalogue, Mike Bennett the coarse pottery catalogue, whilst the author has commented briefly on the wall-plaster, glass and some buildings materials.

Finally, the whole project always had the support of Norman Cook, director of the Museum of London; Dennis Hicks, Ministry of Works custodian at Reculver and Stuart Rigold of the Ministry of Public Building and Works.

In addition, Professors Sheppard Frere, Sir Ian Richmond and Jocelyn Toynbee offered expert advice. To everyone concerned the writer records his sincere thanks, though sadly only the younger people involved will be able to receive it!

CHAPTER II

EARLY RECORDS AND DISCOVERIES

The absence of the name of Reculver (*Regulbium*) by name in the Antonine Itineraries need not be significant in itself, for the routes taken by the Itineraries varied both in length and direction and were never totally inclusive. In addition, with the Channel ports of Dover (*Dubris*) and Richborough (*Rutupiae*) being more suitable for Continental departures from Britain, Reculver was rather tucked away on the Thames Estuary.

The first mention of Reculver occurs in the *Notitia Dignitatum* an impressive list of civil and military commands thought to have been originally compiled at the end of the 4th century. Only four medieval copies of it have survived. The *Notitia* lists nine Roman forts by name, all under the command of the Count of the Saxon Shore, and this clearly relates to the series of extant Roman stone forts along the South East coasts from the Wash to the Solent. In fact, twelve forts can now be identified on the coast and of these eight can be reconciled with the *Notitia Dignitatum* list whilst the others remain uncertain. The relevant entry for Reculver reads

Tribunis cohortis primae Baetasiorum Regulbio
The Tribune of the first Baetasian cohort, at Regulbium

This famous auxiliary cohort seems to have been raised from the Brabant area in the first century and to have gained Roman Citizen status thereafter, perhaps for valour in the campaigns in Scotland. It certainly garrisoned the fort at Maryport (Ref. 17), on the Cumberland coast, in the later 2nd century and carefully buried five of its altars nearby, which named two of its commanders. It had previously served on the Antonine Wall, both at Barhill (Ref. 18) and Balmuildy (Ref. 19). The next mention of Reculver comes in the Anglo-Saxon Chronicles (Ref. 20), under the date A.D. 669 when **"Basa the monk priest was given land at Reculf by to build a minster thereon"**. It must have been about then that the early Saxon church was built in the centre of the Roman fort. Several late-Saxon charters and grants followed (Ref. 21) and by A.D.1086 the Domesday Survey records (Ref. 22).

"In Roculf Hundret. The Archbishop himself holds Roculf. It is assessed at 8 sulungs. There is land for 30 ploughs. On the demesne are 3 ploughs; and 90 villeins with 25 bordars have 27 ploughs. A church is there and 1 mill worth (de) 25 pence, and 33 acres of meadow, and woodland (to render) 20 swine and 5 salt-pans worth (de) 64 pence and 1 fishery. In all (*totis valentiis*) this manor was worth T.R.E. 14 pounds; it was worth a like amount when received; it is now worth 35 pounds. The Archbishop has (from it) 7 pounds and 7 shillings more than this".

Clearly, Reculver was then a Hundred in its own right, with the church and lands still held by the Archbishop, though the monastic status had probably gone following earlier Danish raids. The fishery and five salt-pans reflect the coastal location and it is likely that Reculver was a substantial settlement in medieval times with dozens of houses and a much enlarged church, the two twin towers having been added at about the end of the 12th century. Records more directly relevant to Roman Reculver start with John Leland (1530–7) who recorded (Ref. 23).

"Reculver, ii. myles and more be water, and a mile dim. by land, beyownd Heron, ys fro Cantorbury v. goode myles and stondeth withyn a quarter of a myle, or little more, of the se syde. . . . . . The hole precinct of the monastery appereth by the old walle; . . . . . . Ther hath bene much Romain mony fownd abowt Reculver.

Clearly, the fort was then visible with its walls serving as a precinct boundary for the church. His mention of the sea being "**a quarter of a mile or a little more**" can only be a rough guide for his calculation that Canterbury was only five miles away (actually nearer nine miles) suggests he had unusually long strides! A distance of about 600 yards in about 1535 thus seems more likely. From then on the advance of the sea on the settlement can be traced with some certainty. A map of about 1600 shows the church and fort complete, but only a distance of about 180 yards from the cliff edge to the fort.

The excellent estate map of 1685 (Fig. 3) shows less land north of the fort, highlights the constant erosion and even offers Septimius Severus as the builder of the Roman fort. The fort walls, churchyard walls, church and vicarage were all then intact and a wide gap at the centre of the west wall of the fort clearly provided the main access. Some 30 houses are shown mostly centred on a cross-roads opposite the fort entrance of which one arm continues westwards and is described as The Kings Highe Way. The main text reads:-

"**Neer the church of Reculver was once an ancient towne (but now demolished, except a small village of houses yet standing). Anciently, there was a Mint, or coynage for Roman money, being then under that empire; for in the days of Severus, emperor of Rome (being 1480 years since), built here a castle, which he fortified against the Britains, the foundations yet to be seene about the church (like the figure on this plott, about 10 acres of land) neer a mile distance then from the sea . . . . .**"

The Rev. J. Battely (who died in 1708) records that part of the north wall of the fort had been undermined by the sea in his time. It is clear from Battely's account (Ref. 24) that important structures and many objects were then being uncovered by the sea. He records brick substructures and arches and also vestiges of mosaic flooring, probably representing a hypocausted structure outside the north wall of the fort. He also records 'cisterns' 10–12 ft. deep, lined with oak-stakes and planks and bottomed with puddled clay. These were probably shallow wells, broadly similar to those found by the present writer west of the fort in 1952–7. Importantly, Battely also lists many coins from the site including several British, several of Tiberius and Nero being fresh and unworn and also early Saxon coins. Other Roman coins included denarii of Severus, Julia Domna, Caracalla, Geta, Elagabalus and Carausius. He also referred to coins of most emperors from Julius Caesar to Honorius. In addition, he lists other important objects and also stamps on five samian vessels and a mortarium.

By 1780, when William Boys produced the first full plan (Ref. 25), the north-west corner of the fort and most of the north wall had already gone. Another plan in 1785, shows that about 38ft. of cliff had gone in just five years. The north-east corner must have followed soon after. In 1790, Edward Hasted added more detail and repeated that the fort had been built by the Emperor Septimius Severus. He wrote:

"**The (fort) walls on three sides are very visible, but the fourth, towards the north, has been very lately, nearly all of it, destroyed by the falling of the cliff down on the sea shore, where vast fragments of it lie...... The ancient town............as far as a place called the Black Rock, seen at low-water mark, where tradition says, a parish church once stood..... ...the village....... is so close to it (the sea), as to be washed by the waves, and the church itself is only a few rods from it. At present it is only a small mean village, of five or six houses, situated a small distance westward from the church, and inhabited mostly by fishermen and smugglers .....it was feared in a few years it (the church) would have been wholly destroyed, til very lately such quantities of beach have been thrown up by the waves, so as to form an unexpected, though very sure, natural bulwork**"

As the church appeared doomed the parishioners on a majority vote of one arranged its substantial demolition, but in 1809 Trinity House bought the two towers as a navigational aid and built a very effective protective stone apron. This prevented the sea destroying the church, but the extensive erosion continued to the west. Hence, today, the church still protected by its frequently repaired apron, is left standing on a small projecting headland which dramatically dominates some 30 miles of the North Kent coast.

The early efforts of John Battely were applauded by Roach Smith in 1850 in his study of Richborough, Reculver and Lympne (Ref. 21). He also bemoaned the fact that large numbers of other artefacts must also have been lost from Reculver in subsequent decades and that Battely's fine example "**is seldom followed**". In 1877 George Dowker carried out a minor excavation behind the east wall of the fort and wrote more extensively about the church, which he described as Roman (Ref. 26). In 1923 a well, accidentally discovered inside the fort by a villager, was cleared to a depth of 15ft. 9in. by Major Gordon Home. This was 3ft. 4in. in diameter and built of flint rubble 1ft. 2in. thick with footholes on both sides. No significant finds were made in it. In 1927 (Ref. 27) the Major had workmen digging diagonal trenches near the south wall of the fort and located a substantial wall 24ft. in length, 3ft. 4in. thick, above a concrete floor with roof tiles and painted plaster. He also made a cut against the inside face of the south wall of the fort and probed a possible South Gatehouse. The work was not continued and little ever published.

In 1932, Mortimer Wheeler summarised all the early discoveries and some later work in his grand survey of Roman Kent in the Victoria County Histories (Ref. 39). Finally, Mr. F. H. Thompson carried out the first controlled excavation behind both the south and west walls of the fort which produced some important details (Ref. 28). By the early part of the 20th century the 200 ft. section of the west cliff nearest the fort had been protected by massive concrete walls though the east cliff was left exposed. The cliffs further west were, however, still being eroded and after World War II Roman features and objects were still being revealed after severe storms and notably after the Great Storm of January, 1953. The objects were variously collected in a random way and seldom recorded. Only on the arrival in April, 1952 of a (slightly anonymous) young man did proper recording begin and a programme of rescue-work and large-scale excavation start, that was to continue without a break for the next 53 years. Much of that work forms the subject of this Report.

CHAPTER III

THE EXCAVATED STRUCTURES

(A) THE DEFENCES AND GATEHOUSES

The earliest detail of the fort dates from about 1780 when William Boys made his survey (Ref. 25). The walls then survived largely intact on all four sides to a maximum height of 10 ft. The ground-level inside was (as now) level with the top of the walls. Boys' plan shows the fort as measuring 570 x 585 ft. internally and these are the only dimensions taken whilst the north-east corner of the fort was still intact. The walls then enclosed an area of a little more than 7½ acres. Later surveyors made it 565 x 565 ft. Measurements taken during our extensive programme of excavations suggested the internal east-west width to have been about 582 ft. The work also suggested that the fort had been laid out with some precision with the South Gatehouse being positioned at the centre of the south side. If the surviving East Gatehouse was also centrally placed then an internal north-south width of 560 ft. can be estimated. In about 1805 a Mr. R. Freeman (Ref. 29) examined fragments of the fort wall, then recently collapsed onto the beach, finding them to be at least 9 ft. in thickness.

In 1877, George Dowker, another noted Kent archaeologist, excavated a small trench behind the east wall of the fort near to the centre of the east side. He wisely chose a spot where a few external facing stones survived. He was able to conclude that the wall had been 10 ft. wide at its base and reduced by two internal offsets to about 8 ft. (Ref. 26). In 1927, Major Gordon Home made another cut, this time against the south wall some yards east of the central South Gatehouse. This confirmed the presence of the two internal offsets and also located part of an internal bank (Ref. 27). Finally, in 1951, F.H. Thompson dug a substantial trench against both the west and south walls (Ref. 28). Both trenches revealed the internal offsets and confirmed the presence of an internal bank. The larger trench, against the south wall, revealed the bank to be at least 29 ft. in length and that it sealed a distinctive mortar-mixing layer, directly relating to the construction of the fort wall. This in turn sealed a substantial pre-fort soil containing a small amount of Iron Age and mid-first century A.D. pottery.

In 2002, after the final sea defences were completed, the Unit carried out a measured survey of what still survived of the Roman fort walls. The north wall had been totally removed by the sea around 1700 and the northern sections of both east and west walls severely truncated. Only a short section of the west wall now survives for a length of about 128 ft. (39 m.), largely behind the King Ethelbert Inn. Large parts of this have tilted forward and are now supported by four modern buttresses. The south-west corner has largely gone, but a damaged stub and part of a small internal foundation, perhaps a stair-base, excavated by the Group in 1958 (Ref. 4), remain buried.

As regards the (inland) south wall, a major section about 162 ft. (49.40 m.) in length has been removed from its junction with the south-west corner. This section lies adjacent to the only access road into Reculver and it seems likely that this facilitated the large-scale removal of masonry at this point. Indeed, the medieval palace at Ford lies only about two miles from Reculver and it is generally supposed that much of the stone used there had come from Reculver. If so, this section was clearly the most accessible.

A poor section of the south wall, some 109 ft. (33.20 m.) in length consisting of a mixture of flint, sandstone and ragstone survives west of the South Gatehouse, where there is now a 48 ft. (14.70 m.) gap, caused by more robbing. East of the Gatehouse the wall survives well for the rest of its length (Plate IV), here some 285 ft. (87m.) to a point of projection with the east wall. This section of the south wall is generally 6ft. (2m.) high and exhibits clear coursing set in a hard cream-white mortar containing small black, grey and brown pebbles. The coursing clearly lifts towards a high point, though this is exaggerated by the wall having tilted forward. This section of fort wall also aligns marginally inwards towards the South Gatehouse and this is shown on most published surveys. This section is principally constructed of large flints (perhaps 90%) with largely random Kentish Ragstone rubble (9%) and occasional other rocks (1%). It is just possible that some of the protruding flints here may have formed part of the external facing, though elsewhere this was ragstone.

The east wall is by far the most complete and a total projected length of 457 ft. (139.40m.) survives, excluding a gap of 20 ft. (6 m.) at the site of the East Gatehouse. The wall on this side survives to a maximum height of about 8 ft. 6 in. (2.5 m.), some 14 courses high and thus averaging about 8 in.(18 cm.)per course, including a generous layer of white mortar. It is again very largely constructed of large flints (95%), with occasional ragstone rubble (4%) and other stone (1%). The mortar and coursing largely matches that along the south wall, but here about 60 of the external facing stones survive in small patches (Plate V). These are all of Kentish Ragstone and measure 4–8 in. (10–20cm.) in length and 4–6in. (10–16 cm.) in width. Their depths into the wall cannot easily be determined, but are likely to have been about 9–12 in. (25–30 cm.). The east wall seems to align at about 15 degrees east of magnetic north. Some 144 ft. (43.80 m.) south of the centre of the East Gatehouse is a large repair in the upper part of the fort wall and about 12 ft.(3.70 m.) in width (see p. 20). Many of the flints in the upper section of the east wall have been laid at an angle of about 45 degrees. The ground-level inside the wall is mostly 10ft. (3 m.) high above the present outside level, which itself has been reduced since Roman times.

As regards the interior of the fort, this contained two terraces of cottages during the time of the main excavations. The smaller, which stood in the north-east sector of the fort, backing onto the sea, is claimed to be the oldest coastguard cottages in the country and was constructed in the early 19th century. The larger, which stood in line with the church towers facing Herne Bay, were certainly coastguard cottages and built about 1885. These included six large houses and a look-out post, the latter strangely behind the towers and thus not providing a complete view of the coast. This unusual arrangement may have been condemned by the occasional mariner in distress, but perhaps applauded by the busy local smugglers. Presumably the architect involved had a family or business connection with the latter or may anyway have been familiar with the opening lines of the Ingoldsby Legends (The Smuggler's Leap).

The older cottages were pushed over the cliff in 1969 as part of the new sea wall operations and the more recent cottages were demolished in 1988 when the site was restored by the Kent Archaeological Rescue Unit on behalf of English Heritage. This now leaves the whole site clear and down to grass. The church ruins clearly stand at the highest point of the site and overlook the central area, some 170 ft. (50 m.), now largely flat, but sloping gently to the south. On the east side some 200 ft. (60 m.) of ground gradually falls away towards the marsh. The larger area on the west side, some 230 ft. (70 m.) drops sharply towards the access road into Reculver.

No. 1 THE EAST WALL AND THE *VIA QUINTANA* (Fig. 6)

An important part of the programme to examine the fort's defences, was a section through the east wall of the fort and the adjacent internal arrangements. This was done in 1959 when a single trench, 4ft. wide, was excavated at right-angles to the east wall of the fort for an internal distance of 150ft. (Section 4). The exact position of the 1959 east-west trench was partly determined by the need to avoid dense bushes and so a position 102–106ft. from the estimated internal face of the south wall of the fort was selected. This trench exposed the inside face of the fort wall, revealed a wide Rampart Bank, located a major internal road (the *Via Quintana*) and other features. These are described below (**A–E**).

(A) THE FORT WALL

Although the external face of the east wall had been completely robbed here, a substantial core nearly 8 ft. wide, set in hard white mortar, had survived. In detail, some 15 courses of the wall remained to an internal height of about 8 ft. 3 in. This vertical height was divided into three zones, separated by two internal offsets as first noted by George Dowker in 1877. The bottom three courses (1 ft. 6 in.) were of flint and the wall had a surviving width of about 7 ft. 9 in. at this level. Above this the wall had been offset inwards about 1 ft. and continued upwards another eight courses (4 ft. 3 in.). Seven of these were of flint and one of ragstone. At that point the internal face was reduced by another internal offset, also 1 ft. wide, before continuing for another four courses, one ragstone and three of flint. The upper three courses of flints had been laid at about 45 degrees. The two offsets reduced the surviving thickness of the fort wall here to about 3 ft. 6 in. including a slight batter in the upper section. Large worn beach pebbles are known to lie under the wall here, representing a broad foundation, but these could not be reached in 1959.

(B) THE MORTAR MIXING LAYER (L.22)

A very distinct and hard layer of white mortar was found running from the internal face of the fort wall and traced for a distance of nearly 50 ft. westwards. It rested directly on the pre-fort soils, was largely constant, but humped over a low mound of soil about 10 ft. from the internal wall face. It seems certain that this low mound was thrown up by the fort builders when digging the wide foundation-trench for the east wall. Significantly, this mortar layer joined the fort wall about six courses above its base and clearly over which some soil had been pulled back over the bottom offset.

There can be no reasonable doubt that this extensive layer represents the area over which the mortar for the fort wall was mixed and carried. The layer was mostly 1 in. thick, but at about 16–24 ft. from the wall it increased to about 3 in., almost certainly where the main mortar-mixing took place. A similar mortar-mixing layer, always inside the fort wall, has been noted at a number of other points.

(C) THE RAMPART BANK (L.9, 10, 18–21)

The inside face of the fort wall, including the two offsets, was entirely encased in a massive dump of dense orange clay, mixed occasionally with brown clay and minor deposits. This extended internally, slightly uphill, for a distance of 48 ft. and totally sealed the mortar-mixing layer. It was clearly formed of dumped clay coming in from the west side in very large quantities. It tapered away to nothing at its west end, but for the first 25 ft. it still survived 6 ft. deep and was originally higher. Indeed, if the same angle of slope was maintained then the Bank would have risen about 10 ft. up the internal face of the fort wall, but probably not more. An intermediate stage in the dumping process seems to be marked by a thin band of mussel shells (L.24) sandwiched between two dumps of orange clay. This band must have been deposited by the men building the fort.

The dumped clay was largely sterile, but did contain occasional potsherds. Of special interest are a mortarium rim (No. 184) and a decorated wall sherd of a fine Rhenish ware beaker (No. 176). Both appear to date from the end of the second century and clearly relate to the fort-construction period. A large medieval pit (Pit 12 L.7) had been cut into the Rampart Bank in the 13th or 14th centuries and a slit-trench (Pit 11)had been dug just inside the fort wall during World War II.

(D) THE *VIA QUINTANA* (Plates IX –X)

The trench, by some chance, cut directly along the centre of a major Roman metalled road inside the fort. There can be little doubt, by its position relative to the Headquarters Building found the following year, that this was the *Via Quintana* forming part of a standard military layout.

The road metalling (L.3) began about 40 ft. from the inside face of the fort wall and thus covered the last 8 ft. of the tail of the Rampart Bank. It was traced to a point 125 ft. from the fort wall, hence over a distance of 85 ft., but slight traces were detected beyond this point. It was constructed with shingle and pebbles varying in depth from 3–15 in., being particularly deep between 70–102 ft. from the fort wall. In the deepest area many stone boulders, some very large indeed, had been buried with the pebbles (Plate X). These may have been unsuitable for building purposes and were incorporated into the road area to make up its volume. Two small additional trenches were also dug, north and south of the main east-west trench, at a point about 110ft. from the fort wall. These picked up the edges of the road and indicated a width of 17–18 ft. Only a small amount of pottery was recovered from the metalling (Nos. 10–11).

The road had been cut into the top of a continuous layer of sandy loam (L.4), surviving 4–9 in. thick, which just covered the tail of the Rampart Bank and sealed the pre-fort construction soils (L.6) along most of the rest of the trench. It contained small amounts of domestic rubbish, including potsherds (Nos. 1–9), oyster shells, Roman roof tile, small fragments of painted *opus signinum* and one large fragment of mortar with faint cream and red paint on it. This layer clearly represents the primary phase of occupation (Period I), that was soon superseded by the road. Whilst this road appeared to be largely uniform in construction, it is likely that the easternmost 15–20 ft. really formed part of the *Intervallum* Road circuit known to be in this position elsewhere inside the fort. If so, then the *Via Quintana* proper would have started perhaps 55–60 ft. from the fort wall.

(E) OTHER FEATURES

The Roman sequences were cut through by two World War II slit-trenches and two large medieval pits. One (Pit 12 L.7) of the latter cut the Rampart Bank and the other (Pit 18 L.17) lay close to the west end of the trench.

The Roman road metalling (L.3) was cut through in two places by small late-Roman pits. One (Pit 13 L.27) at 65 ft. from the fort wall was roughly circular and had a diameter of about 3 ft. 9 in. It was about 3 ft. deep and had steep sides and a flat base. Its sides were stained black which may have been traces of a wooden lining. Its loam filling contained potsherds, animal bones, tile fragments and also part of a tile stamped with the letter C (No. 448) clearly part of C IB. The second pit, at 110 ft. (Pit 14 L.11) was about 3 ft. 9 in. in diameter and 3 ft. deep with vertical sides and a flat base. Its filling of black loam contained domestic rubbish, including a crushed bronze bowl (KF.56) and a single illegible Roman coin (Coin No. 59-30). The two pits were similar in character, size and date and seem to have been dug in the fourth century when the *Via Quintana* was already buried by domestic rubbish. Their function is not clear. A fragment of a clay lamp (No. 453) was found in Pit 15 (L.16).

The Dating Evidence

In addition to the two potsherds from the Rampart Bank and the contents of the pits, a substantial collection of artefacts was also recovered during the 1959 excavation. This included 31 coins (Table A) and two large groups of pottery. The small group of potsherds, including five samian sherds, from beneath the road (L.4) appear to date from the late 2nd century or early 3rd century. Only two coins were found in direct association with the road metalling (Coin Nos. 4 and 25). One was of Gallienus (A.D. 260–8) and the other of Tacitus (A.D. 275–6). More significantly, the extensive layer of grey – black loam (L.5) immediately above the road contained 11 coins, nine samian sherds, a large group of coarse pottery (Nos. 12–27), a pipe-clay figurine (No. 457), a fragment of a stone inscription (No. 442), showing parts of four letters and part of a bronze bracelet (No. 311). The coins included one each of Valerian II (A.D. 253–5), Victorinus (A.D. 268–70) and Claudius II (A.D. 268–70) and two of Tetricus I (A.D. 270–3), two barbarous radiates (A.D. 270–90) and four illegible.

A deep deposit of black loam (L.2) was found along much of the trench and appeared to seal all of the grey–black loam (L.5). This contained another nine coins, another large group of pottery (Nos. 28–45) and two bronze bracelets (Nos. 306–7). The coins include one of Gallienus (A.D. 260–8), two each of Claudius II (A.D. 268–70) and Tetricus (A.D. 270–3), a barbarous radiate (A.D. 270–90), Carausius (A.D. 290–2) and two illegible. Finally, the disturbed topsoil deposits produced seven more coins including two of Claudius II (A.D. 268–70), one of Tetricus II (A.D. 270–3), a barbarous radiate (A.D. 270–90), two of Allectus (A.D. 293–6) and an Urbs Roma (A.D. 330–45).

Context	Coin Nos. (1959)	Emperor	Date	Exc. Code
Pit 14, in Road	30	Illegible	3–4 C	11
Road Metalling	25	Gallienus	260–8	3
	4	Tacitus	275–6	3
Soil on Road	11,16,21,22	Illegible	3–4 C	5
	13	Barbarous Radiate	270–90	5
	15	Victorinus	268–70	5
	17	Barbarous Radiate	270–90	5
	18	Valerian II	253–5	5
	20	Claudius II	268–70	5
	23,24	Tetricus I	270–3	5
Soil Over Deposit 5	1, 31	Illegible	3–4 C	2
	7	Claudius II	268–70	2
	8	Barbarous Radiate	270–90	2
	9	Gallienus	260–68	2
	10	Claudius II	268–70	2
	12	Tetricus II	270–73	2
	14	Tetricus I	270–73	2
	29	Carausius	290–2	2
Unstratified	2	Tetricus II	270–73	1
	3	Urbs Roma	330–45	1
	5,6	Claudius II	268–70	1
	19,28	Allectus	293–96	1
	27	Barbarous Radiate	270–90	1
Medieval Pit	26	Medieval		17

Table A. Coins from the *Via Quintana* area (1959)

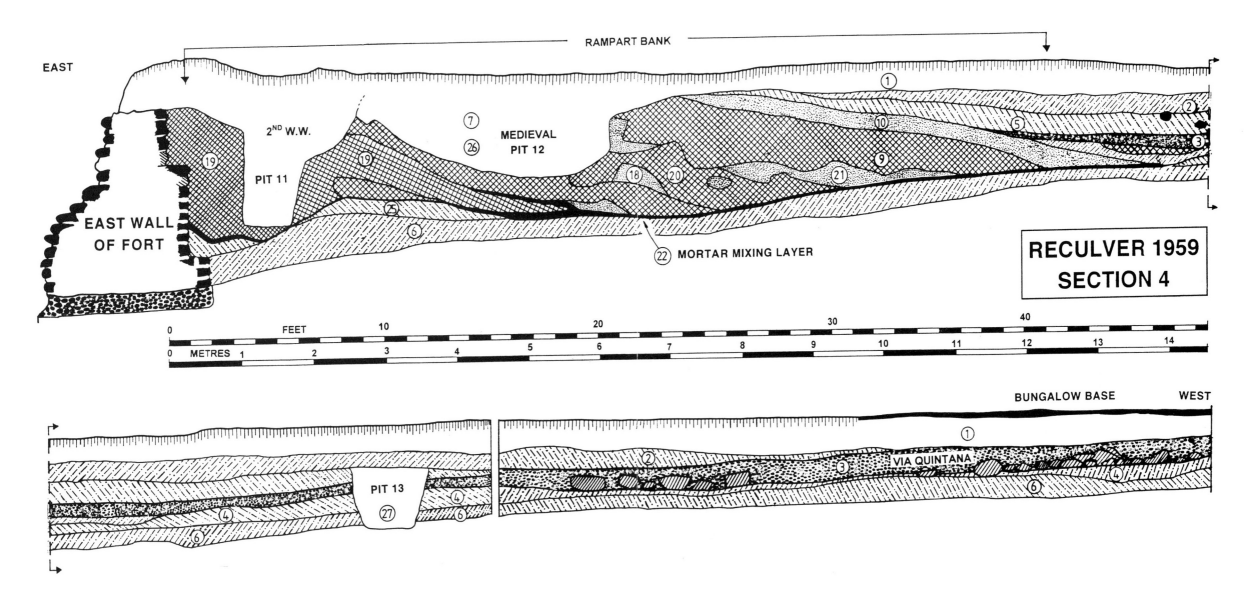

EAST

RAMPART BANK

① ②

⑦

2ND W.W.

MEDIEVAL
PIT 12

⑩

⑤

⑬

⑲

⑲

⑧

⑳

⑨

③

⑲

PIT 11

⑱

㉑

EAST WALL
OF FORT

㉕

㉒ MORTAR MIXING LAYER

⑥

RECULVER 1959
SECTION 4

0   FEET   10   20   30   40

0   METRES   1   2   3   4   5   6   7   8   9   10   11   12   13   14

BUNGALOW BASE   WEST

①

②

VIA QUINTANA

③

PIT 13

④

④

㉗

⑥

④

⑥

⑥

Fig. 6.   *Reculver 1959. Section 4 along the* Via Quintana.

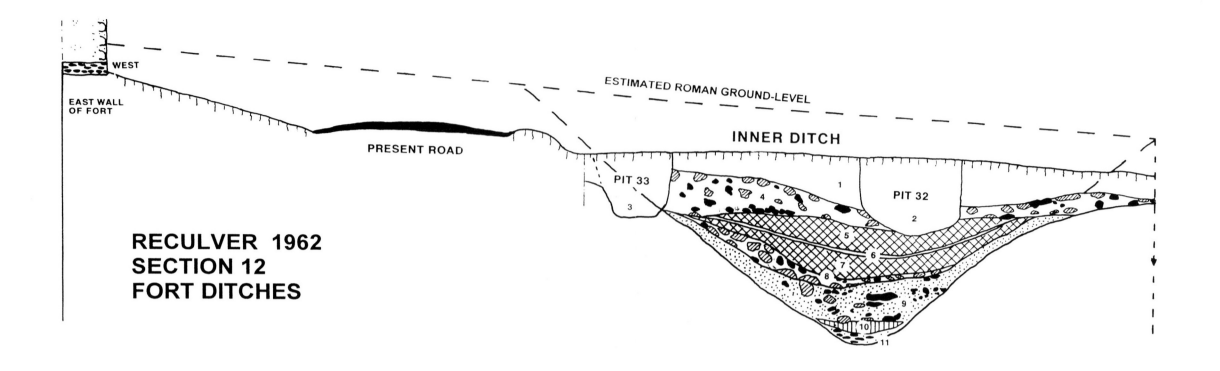

RECULVER 1962
SECTION 12
FORT DITCHES

WEST

EAST WALL OF FORT

ESTIMATED ROMAN GROUND-LEVEL

PRESENT ROAD

INNER DITCH

PIT 33

PIT 32

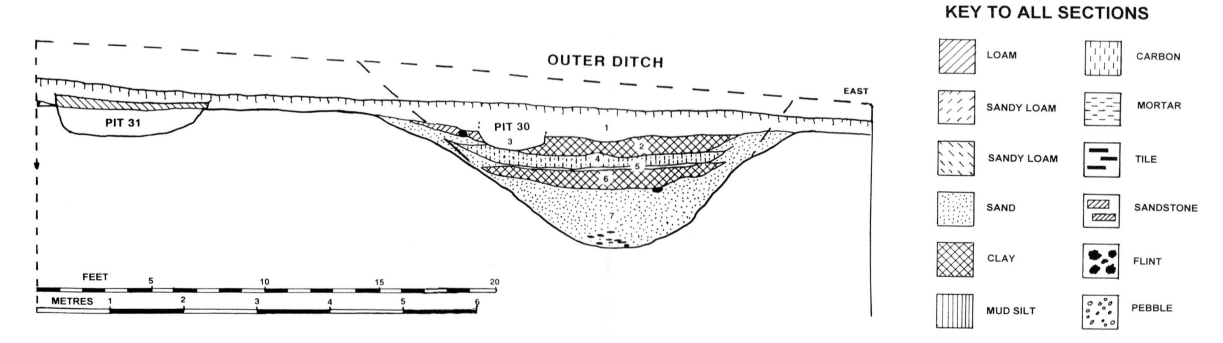

OUTER DITCH

EAST

PIT 31

PIT 30

FEET

METRES

KEY TO ALL SECTIONS

▨	LOAM	▦	CARBON
▨	SANDY LOAM	▤	MORTAR
▨	SANDY LOAM	▬	TILE
⣿	SAND	▨	SANDSTONE
▩	CLAY	⬤	FLINT
▥	MUD SILT	◌	PEBBLE

Fig. 7.   *Reculver 1962. Section 12 across East Ditches.*

The two coins found in association with the surface of the metalling suggest that it was not laid down before about A.D. 275, but the somewhat mobile nature of the pebbles makes this inconclusive. It does seem clear, however, that the road was rapidly buried by soil and domestic rubbish in the period A.D. 270–290. Similarly, a secondary layer of soil and domestic rubbish on top of this contained coins of a similar date. It seems significant that of the twenty coins from these two layers, all date from the second half of the 3rd century and none is 4th century. The majority are likely to have been minted between A.D. 268–90. Even the topsoil above produced similar coins, though this time including two of Allectus yet only one of 4th century date.

An immediately adjacent area, some 40 x 10 ft. in extent, was excavated on the south side of the *Via Quintana* in 1967 as a training programme at about Datums 82–92 from the inside face of the east wall of the fort. This produced a similar sequence of soil deposits, no masonry, another 25 coins (see Table B) and a mortarium (No. 199). The same lower loam, effectively sealing the *Via Quintana*, produced another seven coins, one of Claudius II (A.D. 268–70), a radiate (A.D. 260–80) and the rest illegible. The upper loam, again sealing the lower, contained another five coins, this time one each of Tetricus (A.D. 270–3), Octacilia Severa (A.D. 238–59) and Carausius (A.D. 286–93) and two barbarous radiates (A.D. 270–90). The unstratified or unrelated deposits included seven coins of the 3rd century and four coins of the 4th century. These largely conform with the coins from the 1959 excavation.

Context	Coin Nos. (1959)	Emperor	Date	Exc. Code
Lower Loam	40	Illegible	3–4C	111
	41, 45, 56	Illegible	3C	111
	46	Claudius II	268–70	118
	42	Radiate	260–80	112
	43	Illegible	3–4C	112
Upper Loam	18	Carausius	286–93	104
	24, 29	Barbarous Radiate	270–90	104
	28	Tetricus I	270–3	104
	39	Otacilia Severa	238–59	110
Unstratified & Other Deposits	15	Early 3C – Denarius	200–40	101
	25	Tetricus I	270–3	101
	54	Radiate	270–90	101
	38	Illegible	3C ?	101
	16	Constantine I	320–4	101
	17	House of Constantine	330–48	102
	19	Claudius II	268–70	106
	31	Tetricus I	270–3	106
	30	House of Constantine	330–60	106
	20	Medieval farthing		105
	22	Constans	345–8	105
	32	Radiate	260–90	105
	34	Allectus	293–6	105

Table B. Coins from *Via Quintana* (Training) Area (1967)

No. 2   REPAIR TO THE EAST WALL (Fig. 8)

As part of the programme of work covering the fort's defences a large masonry repair in its east wall, about 149–161 ft. from the centre of the East Gate, was examined in April, 1964. This repair had first been noted in 1957 by the writer when both Roman and medieval construction dates were considered possible (Plate VI).

The work was confined to a single trench, about 10 x 8 ft. in area, behind only the southern half of the visible repair. This soon established that the original fort wall only survived to a height of about 4 ft. and that it had been removed above this level, probably for a width of 10–12 ft. The gap so created had subsequently been blocked by the insertion of a much narrower wall of masonry, this about 4 ft. 6 in. wide at its base, but tapering internally to about 3 ft. 8 in. This insertion (or repair) had been built flush with the outside face of the fort wall and still survives to a height of about 3 ft. 6 in. above the original fort wall. A large Roman oven had been built in the recess behind the narrower repair and excavation revealed deposits to a total depth of about 10 ft. (Fig. 8. Section 19 and Plate VII).

In detail, a very deep layer of topsoil (L.1) sealed much of the fort wall and also an extensive layer of rubble (L.4) containing flints, sandstone and pebbles. This general layer sealed a short stub of a foundation (L.5), about 2 ft. 5 in. wide and projecting into the excavation by about 2 ft. 6 in. It was constructed with flints, but its function is difficult to gauge. It did, however, cut into a deep layer (L.6) of burnt clay which represented the collapsed superstructure of a large Roman oven.

The oven had been constructed on a bed of flat sandstone blocks about 2 in. thick and a thin layer of pebbles covered by orange clay (L.7) some 3–7 in. deep. The latter created a circular oven, of which only about half was in the trench with the other half extending northwards and thus unexcavated. This would have been about 6 ft. in diameter and its floor surface was baked hard and black due to severe heat. The floor was covered with the collapse of the burnt clay superstructure, which was some 9–12 in. in total thickness. The oven deposits close to the fort wall had been cut into by a shallow trench (L.2), containing medieval pottery, mostly filled with loam, but with crumbled mortar (L.3) at its base.

The oven was constructed on top of a deep layer of black loam (L.10) containing a small amount of domestic rubbish, some 1 ft. 3 in. in depth and extending over the reduced section of the original fort wall. The layer had also formed up against the inside face of the later repair and clearly both it and the oven above partly occupied the recess left at the rear of the repair. Both must therefore date to a period after the repair was completed and as the associated potsherds were of Roman date then it seems certain that the repair was a late-Roman structure.

In detail, the repair consisted of an irregular mixture of large sandstone blocks and flints bonded in a white mortar containing many cockle shells, in sharp contrast to the original fort wall below. In particular its external facing stones were an odd mixture of blocks of different sizes and this contrasts sharply with the neat ashlar of the fort wall elsewhere. That the facing survived here may be due to the poor quality of the blocks used, which may have been regarded by later stone-robbers as unsuitable material. The original fort wall was again neatly coursed, mostly built of flints and ragstone, set in a hard white mortar containing small grits. The fort wall survived seven courses high at the bottom of the repair, but stood 14 courses on the south side of it. Again the bottom internal offset, about 13 in. wide, was noted and also the second internal offset some 4 ft. 4 in. above the first. The fort wall survived for a base width of 8 ft. 6 in. and clearly only the facing stones had been removed. This suggests that the original width had been about 9 ft. 3 in.

The soil beneath the oven changed in character and consisted of a grey-black loam (L.11) containing scattered lumps of yellow clay and was generally 2 ft. in depth. Part of this layer also

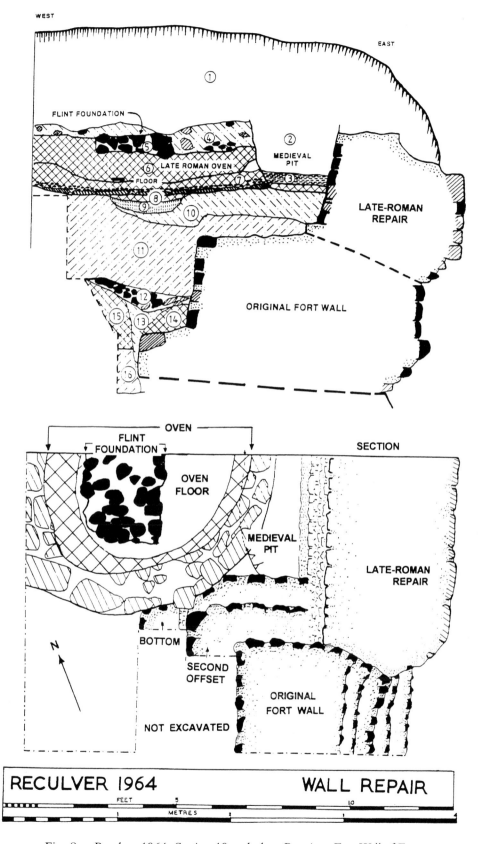

Fig. 8.   *Reculver 1964. Section 19 and plan. Repair to East Wall of Fort.*

covered the top of the original fort wall and extended down its internal face. The clay lumps suggest that it was part of the original Rampart Bank and it seems likely that part of this layer was pushed forward to level just after the repair was completed. Whatever its interpretation this layer clearly sealed a dump of flints and rubble (L.12), a loosely filled void (L.13), the orange clay (L.14 and L.15) all deposited in the early stages of the construction of the fort wall. These sealed the pre-fort sandy loam (L.16).

No. 3 THE RAMPART BANK (Figs. 6 and 31)

The presence of an internal bank behind the fort wall was always a strong possibility, as these occur frequently at other Roman military sites in Britain. Whilst it is likely that George Dowker cut marginally into the bank in 1877 (Ref. 26), it was Gordon Home who first identified it in his small excavation against the south wall in 1927 (Ref. 27). There he found the bank overlying a distinctive mortar-mixing layer which lead directly to the fort wall. The first controlled examination of the bank came in 1951 when Mr. F.H.Thompson cut two trenches against the south and west walls. His published section (Ref. 28) shows 29 ft. of bank behind the south wall and the whole Bank sat directly on the mortar-mixing layer, again leading back to fort wall. The Rampart Bank consisted of a series of large dumps of clay and sand all lying at an angle of about 30 degrees from the horizontal. It had a maximum depth of about 6 ft., but clearly had been higher and indeed longer than the trench excavated. A band of mussel shells marked an intermediate stage in the construction of the bank. The pre-fort soils contained a small amount of prehistoric pottery.

The first complete section to be recorded through the Rampart Bank was made in October, 1957 when the newly formed Reculver Excavation Group selected the exposed East Cliff section as its first priority. Strangely, earlier excavators had never targeted this constantly threatened part of the Roman fort. The work in 1957 was largely confined to dressing-down and recording about 100 ft. of the cliff westwards of the east wall of the fort. The results were clearly important and were published in 1959 (Ref. 3).

The Rampart Bank was then traced for about 40 ft. and consisted of dense layers of dark and light brown clay to a depth of at least 5 ft. Significantly, the bank lay on top of a large Roman oven (then Oven I) about 6 ft. in diameter. This in turn sealed the upcast soil from the foundation-trench of the fort wall and also a small pile of rolled flints intended for the actual foundations. The oven walls had been built of sandstone blocks and its floor of flat bricks, each some 11 x 13 in. Charcoal and ash from the oven had been raked out to the west and this both sealed and was sealed by clear traces of the mortar-mixing layer relating again to the construction of the fort wall. As stated in 1959, there can be little doubt that this oven was constructed by the workmen building the east wall of the fort.

The Rampart Bank also contained a band of soil containing mixed domestic rubbish (First Rubbish Layer) and this was initially dated A.D. 160–200 (Key Deposit II). A small pit had also been dug into the tail of the bank and this, too, was initially dated A.D. 160–200 (Key Deposit III). Another band of soil containing domestic rubbish (Second Rubbish Layer) was found dumped on the bank (Key Deposit VI) and finally another layer of charcoal, ash and domestic rubbish (Key Deposit VII) sealed the tail of the bank and also part of the Intervallum Road. This contained pottery of late-second to early-third century date and a coin (No. 1957–2) of Elagabalus (A.D. 219–22).

The pre-fort soils beneath the bank were found to contain a light scatter of flint-tempered pottery of Iron Age date. In addition, part of a later Roman sub-structure was located cut into the top of the Rampart Bank just 8–16 ft. from the fort wall and directly above Oven I. It is now clear that this was the base of another large oven (examined as Oven II in 1965–6, see below) and that the charcoal and ash layer then found covering the tail of the Rampart Bank (Key Deposit VI) was almost certainly the rake-back from this oven. The pottery sealed within the Rampart Bank was redated to A.D. 200–25.

The next complete excavation of the Rampart Bank was carried out by the Group in 1959 during its ongoing programme of work. Then, a trench 150 ft. in length was dug at right angles to the east wall of the fort (p. 16) and this not only examined the fort wall and cut through the complete bank, but also ran up the centre of the *Via Quintana* (Section 4 and Plate VIII). The bank had a total width of 48 ft. and attained a maximum height of 6 ft., though again this originally would have been higher. The bank also sealed another mortar-mixing layer along its entire length. In detail, it had been constructed of large dumps of orange clay, with occasional brown clay and minor deposits. Yet again a thin band of mussel shells lay within the rampart which, apart from fragments of two pottery vessels, was largely sterile. The pottery includes a mortarium rim (No. 184) and part of a fine Rhenish beaker (No. 176), both of late-second century date. The tail of the rampart was sealed by a metalled road.

In 1963, small sections of the Rampart Bank behind the south wall of the fort were revealed (p. 49 Trenches A and B). In 1964, traces of the same Rampart Bank were revealed on each side of the South Gatehouse (p. 32). Also, in 1964 the tail of the same bank was found on the Allotment site (p. 53). In 1966, a section of the tail of the Rampart Bank behind the west wall of the fort was also located (p. 89).

In March, 1965 and March, 1966 the exposed East Cliff section, only dressed-back in 1957, was subject to a major excavation ahead of sea-wall construction (p. 64). The Rampart Bank was examined in depth confirming its width there as about 40 ft. and its construction of thick bands of dumped clay. This time the mortar-mixing layer extended under the full length of the Bank (Fig. 31, Section 25). What was left of Oven I was then excavated and another high-level oven (Oven II) recorded, cut into the top of the bank. The latter had been badly cut through by World War II army trenches, but it was from the floor of this structure that two complete Roman tiles stamped with the letters C IB (No. 445) had been rescued in 1960. In the Bank was a coin (No. 66–8) of Marcus Aurelius (A.D. 150–60) and pottery which included a samian Form 33 stamped MATERNVS, dated A.D. 160–80 (No. 223, Stamp No. 7).

Finally, in 1967, the substantial excavation of the East Gatehouse (p. 37) revealed a large section of the Rampart Bank enclosing the north side of the guardroom. Again the bank consisted of large dumps of orange and brown clay some 5 ft. high and extending back from the fort wall for a minimum of 22 ft. The bank was largely sterile, but a coin of Commodus (A.D. 180–92) was found sealed beneath it. The bank had been cut by a large pit which contained three coins, the latest of Allectus (A.D. 293–6), and in turn the bank sealed the pre-fort soils containing prehistoric sherds and also a small ditch.

Thanks to the work from 1951–1967, it is now clear that a substantial Rampart Bank was constructed behind the east, south and west walls of the Roman fort. It is highly likely that this was constructed behind the missing north wall as well. The two complete sections cut through the Bank, in 1959 and 1965–6, were both on the east side. These showed the bank sloping up to the fort wall, with the width of 40–48 ft. and a surviving maximum height of 6 ft. It is likely that originally the bank extended higher up the inside face of the fort wall.

In all sections where the Rampart Bank has been seen, it has consisted of large layers of dumped clay and sands, most lying at an angle. These were largely sterile, except for the substantial rubbish deposits found on the East Cliff site, and are likely to represent material dug from the two defensive ditches outside the fort wall. If so, considerable volumes of soil were either carried through the Gatehouses after completion, or at an earlier stage when sections of the wall were unfinished. It is also possible that soil taken from any terracing or levelling inside the fort, or even foundation-trenches, could have been dumped behind the fort wall. Apart from prehistoric pottery the only objects found under the Bank were the potsherds found in 1959 and the coin found in 1967. It seems likely that several more remain to be found, though their future discovery will largely be a matter of chance.

Only on the East Cliff site in 1957 and 1965–6 was a structure found within the Rampart Bank. There a large oven (Oven I) had been built by the men constructing the fort, but soon abandoned and buried by dumped clay. This was later replaced by another large oven (Oven II) directly above it and cut into the top of the bank. Two tiles stamped C IB came from the floor of this oven and clearly relate to the garrison of the fort, almost certainly deposited by the builders.

No. 4 THE DEFENSIVE DITCHES (Fig. 7)

The great majority of Roman forts in Britain had deep defensive ditches, either single or multiple, positioned outside the main defensive walls. Two were most commonly provided and their function was to give added depth to the defences and prevent large formations of attackers from quickly reaching and scaling the walls.

An aerial photograph of Reculver, taken in 1920 (Aerofilms Ltd., Ref. 531) when the area on the east and south sides of the fort were open farmland, shows a faint pair of dark lines parallel to the fort walls. These appeared to be the fort ditches. In 1948 the sea washed away some of the brushwood protection of the seawall close to the east wall of the fort. The exposed area was seen by Harold Gough who detected the deep fill of the inner ditch (Ref. 28).

In 1958, the Reculver Excavation Group cut a 75 ft. trench (Section 3) across the line of the south ditches some 135 ft. from the south-west corner of the fort (Ref. 4). The area was then part of a garden allotment. Only an inner ditch was then located, being at least 4 ft. deep and 25 ft. wide. No clear trace of an outer ditch was seen, but what then appeared to be two shallow drainage ditches seemed to have helped drain this very low-lying area and thus avoid the inner defensive ditch being flooded.

Finally, in 1962 the first complete section (Fig. 7, Section 12) was excavated through the fort ditches on the east side about 122 ft. south of the centre of the East Gatehouse. The trench lay about 30 ft. north of the Repair to the fort wall (p. 20) on what is still the Council owned caravan site. A 3 ft. wide trench was cut at right-angles to the fort wall, beginning just 21 ft. from its external face and extending for a distance of 62 ft. Both the inner and outer ditches were then found, largely as suggested by the earlier air photograph. Both were V-shaped in section. As found, the inner ditch was 24 ft. wide and 9 ft. deep and its inner lip lay just 21 ft. from the face of the fort wall. The two ditches were separated by an inter-ditch berm just 16 ft. wide, whilst the outer ditch was 19 ft. wide and 6 ft. 6 in. deep. The ditches were cut by four shallow pits (Pits 30–33), probably relating to military activity in World War II.

Both ditches contained an impressive succession of deposits. The inner ditch contained a layer of orange-grey loam with a band of worn beach pebbles (L.11) at its base, sealed by a dense black mud-silt (L.10). The former are similar to the pebbles from the foundation-trench of the fort wall and the latter probably formed when the ditch flooded. Above, was a grey loam of progressive silt (L.9), some 2 ft. thick, which contained fragments of ragstone probably from the fort wall. This was in turn sealed by a dense layer of ragstone and flints (L.8), again similar to the fort wall and perhaps indicating a degree of collapse.

Whilst all the deposits described above may be regarded as occurring naturally, the next three deposits (L.5–7) were clearly thrown down. These attain a maximum depth of 2 ft. 6 in. which, allowing for post-Roman slump, largely filled the ditch at this point. The new upper and lower layers here consisted of dense orange-brown clay (L.5 and 7), whilst the layer between consisted of grey-black loam with animal bones (L.6). These were in turn sealed by a layer of brown loam (L–4) containing ragstone, tile, mortar and flints, probably representing the post-Roman decay of the fort wall.

In detail, it is important to note that the general land-surface outside the walls of the fort has been reduced by ploughing and surface erosion to below the level of its foundations. Where the ditch section was excavated, about 3 ft. of soil has gone and this has an impact on the ditch sizes. Allowing for a general truncation here of roughly 2 ft. it is possible to suggest that the berm in front of the fort wall had been about 18 ft. wide. In the same way the inner ditch is increased in width to about 28 ft. and its depth to about 11 ft. The interditch berm is then reduced to about 14 ft. and the outer ditch is increased to about 20 ft. in width and 8 ft. in depth. These are likely to be typical dimensions, though those on the surviving west side could be different due to the different topography. It is also possible that the ditches were marginally deeper than shown due to the close similarity between the lower primary fill and the natural soils through which the ditches were cut.

The outer ditch contained a broadly similar sequence of deposits though, predictably, without the ragstone wall tumble as this ditch was 60 ft. from the fort wall. The primary silt (L.7) was 3 ft. deep and again contained a scatter of beach pebbles. There was no mud silt as in the inner ditch, but the two broad bands of dumped clay (L.2 and 6) were again present. These, too, sandwiched a thick band of black charcoal (L.4) and also a thin band of grey-black loam (L.5) containing a small amount of domestic rubbish. These four layers represented a dump fill some 2 ft. 6 in. deep which, again allowing for slumping, largely filled the ditch.

Very few artefacts were recovered from either ditch fill. The only critical dating evidence was a single coin (No. 287) of Gallienus (A.D. 258–68) found in the domestic rubbish (L.5) in the outer ditch. Elsewhere at Reculver, these coins occur almost exclusively in deposits of the late-third century. On its merits alone, this suggests that both ditches had partly silted and were deliberately filled at this point sometime around A.D. 300.

In 1965, a shallow pipe-trench was dug by workmen at right-angles across the line of the south ditches at a point 25 ft. east of the centre-line of the South Gatehouse. This was recorded by Harold Gough who located the tops of what must have been two ditches. The inner ditch was at least 15 ft. wide, the outer ditch about 16 ft. wide, but the interditch berm was some 20 ft. The full depths were not reached and the exact profiles remain unclear, but again considerable truncation must have taken place. The inner ditch contained more ragstone blocks, presumably derived from the south wall of the fort. This extra information helps confirm the presence of two ditches on at least part of the south side.

No. 5 THE SOUTH GATEHOUSE (*PORTA DECUMANA*) – (Figs. 9–11 and Plates XI–XIII)

This site was excavated in 1964 as part of the programme of work examining the defences of the fort. Its location was soon identified for it marked the centre of the south side and also the only opening in the 450 ft. of surviving south wall. It had been noted by Major Gordon Home in 1927, when small trenches were dug around the masonry, but not recorded in detail.

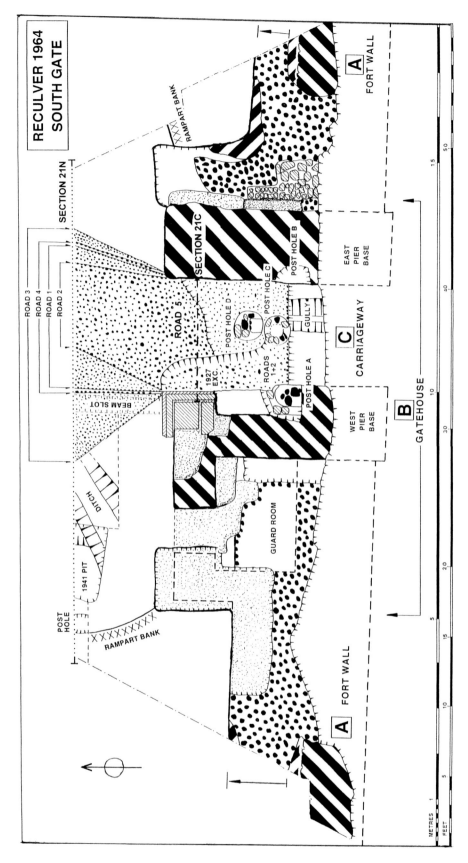

Fig. 9. *Reculver 1964. Plan of South Gatehouse.*

The actual site now occupies the central part of a steep soil bank, in all nearly 20 ft. high, where the internal area of the fort overlooks the Council caravan-site set at the lower level. This dramatic change of level is not natural, but it is caused in part by the remnant of the fort wall retaining the dumped clay Rampart Bank and later soils. The effect is exaggerated in front of the wall where the soils have been reduced by 3–5 ft. by erosion and farming activity.

The excavated area was trapezoidal in plan (Fig. 9) with the smaller, north side being about 35 ft. wide and the eroded south side some 55 ft. It was generally 20 ft. in north-south width and this covered the surviving masonry and some 8ft. of soil on the north side (Fig. 11, Section 21N). At the latter, the stratified deposits were mostly 8 ft. deep, increasing to about 11 ft. at one point. From there the deposits had been truncated by the slope and ran away to nothing only about 16 ft. to the south. Three east-west sections were recorded across the Gate and associated roads and another on a north-south axis. Over 100 tons of soil were removed, but only about half replaced as some of the Gate area was subsequently consolidated and left open for public viewing. The various structural elements located are described below (**A–E**). This site also produced a series of small-finds in bronze (Nos. 316, 320, 329, 385), bone (Nos. 238, 240, 358), a pottery spindle-whorl (No. 411) and a flint scraper (No. 456). The general late-Roman deposits also contained 23 sherds of samian ware, including Forms Curle 21, 31(2), 32, 33, 45, Walters 79 and Ludowici (4) and also a mortarium (No. 196).

(A) THE FORT WALL

Only the badly robbed ends of the fort wall, located about 46 ft. from each other, were located within the area excavated. Of that on the west side only a width of about 4 ft. survived and this has slumped forward about 5 ft. A large area of the foundation pebbles here had, however, survived *in situ* and this produced a clear outline some 20 ft. long and still 4–6 ft. wide. Similarly, on the east side the wall stub was only about 4 ft. wide and had slumped forward about 3 ft. Again the foundation pebbles survived and covered an area about 10 ft. in length and 6 ft. in width, thus showing the original *in situ* arrangement.

(B) THE GATEHOUSE

The excavation revealed that the Gatehouse had occupied an area of about 30 ft. in east-west length and a minimum width, as surviving, of 12 ft. It comprised, as the East Gatehouse did when excavated in 1967, of two unequal masonry masses separated from each other by a space about 7 ft. 3 in. wide. The masonry mass on the east side (East Pier Base), of which only the flint and mortar foundation survived, was about 5 ft. wide and 11 ft. in length, though clearly it had been longer (probably about 16 ft.). The Gatehouse had occupied the whole width of the fort wall and also projected internally by about 6 ft., where extended pebble foundations suggest that the fort wall had returned alongside it with a width of 4 ft. This extra feature is likely to have been functional and steps leading up to the rampart walk are the most attractive possibility.

The masonry mass on the west side (West Pier Base) was much larger, probably some 16 x 16 ft. originally, for it contained a single guard-room which was also partly within the thickness of the fort wall. Whilst most of the superstructure had been robbed, part of the north wall of the guard-room and three blocks of the adjacent internal gate jamb had survived (Plate XI).

In detail, the guard-room measured internally about 8 ft. in length and had been wider than 4 ft. It seems certain that it matched the corresponding room in the East Gate and that its original internal size would have been about 8 x 6 ft. No trace of a floor was found, though a slight layer of mortar may represent the mortar dropped when its walls were built. The only surviving (north) wall remained to a height of 2 ft. 9 in. and included traces of 11 courses of flat bricks. It was 3 ft. in width and rested on a much broader concrete foundation over pebbles. The latter sealed a rectangular slot, now soil filled, but of uncertain function.

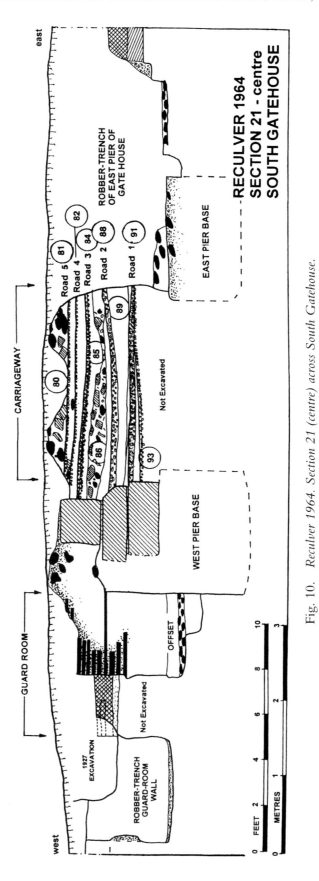

Fig. 10. *Reculver 1964. Section 21 (centre) across South Gatehouse.*

The three surviving blocks provided the only evidence of architectural detail of the actual Gatehouse arch (Fig. 10. Section 21C). A very large grey-brown sandstone block, some 3 ft. 2 in. x 2 ft. 5 in. and 1ft. 4 in. deep, formed the base of the arch and rested directly on the mortared flint foundation. On this sat an even larger grey-brown sandstone block, some 3 ft. 2 in. x 3 ft. 8 in. and 1 ft. 2 in. high. This had been neatly chamfered on the exposed north and east sides, where the tooling marks could clearly be seen. This was in turn capped by a large, rectangular, greensand block some 2 ft. 8 in. x 1 ft. 9 in. and 1 ft. 10 in. high (Plate XIII). This must be the base block of the actual arch over the carriageway, with its surface pitted by fine tooling. It suggests that the whole arch had been built of similar greensand blocks to produce a decorative effect. It must represent the only arch block left *in situ,* of any of the fort's original gates though the church towers may incorporate others removed in the 12th century.

(C) THE CARRIAGEWAY

The Gatehouse was clearly designed to enclose a single carriageway effectively about 8 ft. 6 in. in width, increasing to about 11 ft. 6 in. within recesses, though the actual foundations were less. The metalling survived for only about 10 ft. within the Gatehouse, but was traced northwards for another 7 ft. to the vertical face of the excavation. From here it certainly extended northwards where it was detected in the 1960 and 1963 excavations and can now be identified as the *Via Decumana*, providing essential access from the South Gate to the *Intervallum* Road, the *Via Quintana* and the back of the Headquarters Building.

In detail, the surviving west block of the Gatehouse showed that its central section was recessed inwards by about 1 ft. 9 in. thus reducing the effective width of the main West Pier from 5 ft. to about 3 ft. 3 in. This recess had a minimum length of about 6 ft. and the corresponding feature on the identical East Gate suggests that this would have been about 7 ft. in total length. It seems certain that a matching recess would have existed on the destroyed east side. The effect of two recesses would be to exaggerate the two responds, at each end of the carriageway, thus forming solid rectangular buttresses which must have carried the arches over the gate.

In addition to the masonry structure, there was evidence of at least four large post-holes, clearly associated with the carriageway. These were largely at the centre of the Gatehouse and seem to represent door-posts for the main gate. These are described below.

Post-hole A – The socket for a large post, about 9 in. sq., containing flint and mortar packing was found cut into the recess within the west side of the Gatehouse. This was about 1 ft. 10 in. x 1 ft. 6 in. in size and had cut away part of the original masonry to a depth of at least 1 ft. On closer examination this post-hole seems to have replaced an original post (later removed) held in a carefully constructed post-hole built neatly in the recess. Only three sandstone blocks, representing the original packing of this, survived. Two phases of post construction seem to be represented.

Post-hole B – Another socket, in a corresponding position to Post-Hole A, was found in the surviving foundation on the east side of the Gatehouse. Most of the detail had been destroyed, but it is clear that this too had been cut into the original masonry and thus probably represents a secondary phase. Posts A and B were probably no more than 8 ft. 8 in. apart.

Post-hole C – A largely complete circular pit for a post-hole was found at the centre of the carriageway roughly in line with Post-holes A and B. It was about 2 ft. 2 in. in diameter and its packing of ragstone, flints and Roman tile on all sides supported a rectangular post-pipe 8 in. sq. The post-pipe ran the full depth of the post-hole which was 3 ft. 1 in. deep from the surface of Road 2 which sealed the packing. It seems clear that this post relates to the original Road 1.

Post-hole D – The outline for another pit for a post-hole, probably 2 ft. in diameter, was found just 5 in. north of Post-hole C and again in the centre of the carriageway. This contained the outline of a rectangular wooden post about 9 in. sq. that was packed with sandstone and flint on its north side. This post-hole had been cut through the metalling of Road 2 and is likely to have replaced post-hole C which was sealed by the same road. Hence, again, two phases seem to be represented.

All four post-holes must have held large upright posts and those within the lateral recesses (Posts A and B) probably held the main entrance doors to the Gatehouse. It seems likely that these opened inwards into the respective recesses, which would comfortably take a door 4 ft. 6 in. in width. This arrangement suggests two equal doors, as opposed to a large single door, but the function of the two central posts is not fully understood. It maybe that they were inserted simply to divide the carriageway, or better still to offer firm extra support for the doors when fully closed. Either way, two phases of construction are implied.

The Metalling (Figs. 10 and 11)

An examination of the metalling within the Gatehouse revealed a sequence of a dozen largely horizontal deposits which covered a vertical height of about 3 ft. 6 in. and mostly represented successive roads. Allowing for a primary surface (L.93), mainly of stone chipping's and gravel, five actual roads were identified (Figs. 10 and 11, Sections 21N and 21C). The lowest road (Road 1 – L.91 and 98) covered the full width of the carriageway and butted to the large base stone of the arch. It consisted of a 3–4 in. layer of compacted pebbles and gravel, which was traced to the north face of the excavation where its width had increased to about 10 ft. 8 in. This was covered by a layer of silty loam (L.26, 89, 100) which contained a coin (Coin No. 23) of about A.D. 270. This was in turn sealed by another compacted gravel road (Road 2 – L.52, 65, 88) which butted to the side of the chamfered block of the arch. This road contained six coins (Coin Nos. 16, 20–22, 24 and 27), two of the late-third century, one of Crispus (A.D. 317–26) and two illegible. This road decreased in width and at the vertical north soil section at the edge of the excavation was reduced to only 6 ft. 2 in.

Context	Coin Nos. (1964)	Emperor	Date	Exc. Code
Road I	25	Illegible	270–90	91
Loam Layer	23	Barbarous Radiate	270–90	89
Road II	16	Illegible	3–4C	65
	20	Barbarous Radiate	270–90	88
	21	Illegible	3–4C	88
	22	Illegible	3–4C	88
	27	House of Constantine	320–30	65
	24	Illegible	3–4C	65
Loam Layer	26	Claudius II	268–70	87
	14	Illegible	3–4C	–
Rubble	15	Illegible	3–4C	31
	17	Barbarous Radiate	270–90	68
	18	Illegible	3–4C	64
Unstratified	1, 2	Carausius	287–93	1
	13	Illegible	3–4C	54
	19	Constantinopolis	330–45	1

Table C. Coins from the South Gatehouse area (1964)

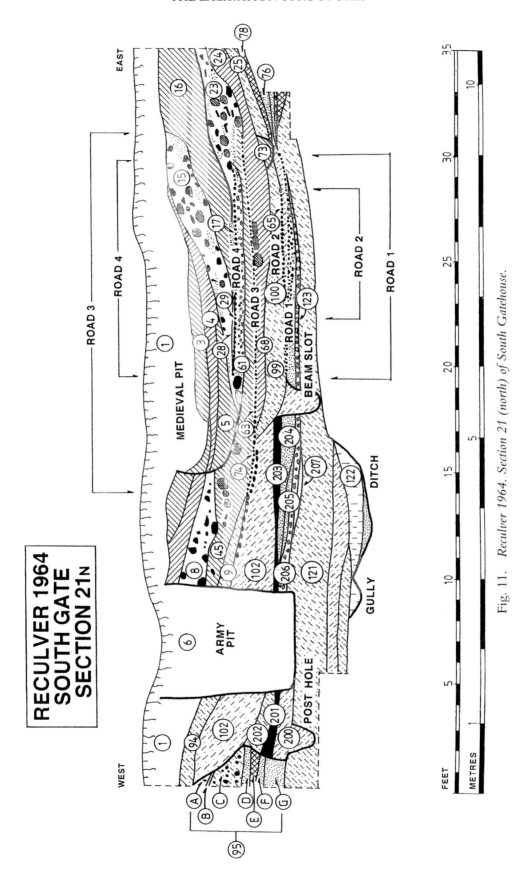

Fig. 11. *Reculver 1964. Section 21 (north) of South Gatehouse.*

Another deep layer of silty loam (L.87 and 99) formed next and this produced a single coin (Coin No. 26) of Claudius II (A.D. 268–70). The top of this was then sealed by a deep layer of rubble, 4–12 in. deep (L.85, 86, 55, 68, 31, 64), upon which another road (Road 3 – L.63, 74 and 84) had been constructed. This seems to represent a major operation, which included pebbles rammed down, in two layers under the arch and pushed the level half way up the greensand block increasing the road width to about 17 ft. at the north face of the excavation.

The rubble contained four coins (Coin Nos. 14, 15, 17, 18), three illegible and a barbarous radiate of c. A.D. 270. This was sealed by another substantial layer of black loam, containing domestic rubbish (L.83, 30, 62) before another road (Road 4 – L.82, 29, 61) was laid over it, this time based on poor quality *opus signinum* (L.61). This lifted the road-level another 4 in. inside the Gatehouse, but at the north section the width was reduced to only 10 ft. 8 in. Within the Gatehouse part of another road (Road 5 – L.81) was recorded, but this expired before the north section and is here regarded as a repair to the underlying road. Rubble (L.80) covered this upper surface, except at the north face where a large post-medieval pit had removed the later deposits. The soils above produced a mortarium (No. 202) from Oxfordshire, dated A.D. 240–300.

(D) THE RAMPART BANK

Only slight traces of the Rampart Bank, known to back the fort wall, were found on both the east and west sides and the edges were ill-defined. These consisted of dumped clays and loams which capped the pre-fort construction soils. A small feature (L.200) near the north-west corner (Section 21N) seems to represent a post-hole, or slot, which seems to have held a vertical post, which helped retain a series of dumped soils (L.95 A–G), clays, sands and pebbles. The sandstone chippings (L.123, 206, 207) of the fort construction period covered the base of the void east of the vertical post, which were soon covered by layers of charcoal and soil (L.203–5). A horizontal slot, 1 ft. 2 in. wide, 2 ft. deep, with vertical sides and a flat base, was next dug northwards from the sides of the arch. This may have contained a wooden sleeper-beam which seems to have retained the soils forming in the void. Roads 1 and 2 respected this slot, behind which a large dump of soil (L.102) up to 3 ft. deep seems to have later helped complete the west side of the Rampart Bank.

(E) THE PRE-FORT FEATURES

The underlying soils were found constantly across much of the site, generally 5–12 in. in depth, but increasing on the west side (North Section). There a shallow gully and a small ditch (L.122), the latter running north-east/south-west was traced for 6 ft. The fill of this produced a small amount of pottery of late-first century date, including a samian Form 18 of Flavian date and a stamped Form 18 (Stamp No. 11) by Vitalis (A.D. 65–90), but the function and extent of this ditch are not known. It seems likely that any south-west continuation of it will have been destroyed by the considerable ground-reduction outside the fort wall.

No. 6 THE EAST GATEHOUSE (*PORTA PRINCIPALIS DEXTRA*) – (Figs. 12–14 and Plates XIV–XVI)

This site was excavated in 1967 as part of the programme of work examining the defences of the fort. Its location was easily determined for its site marked the central point in the east wall of the fort and even now remains the only gap in the surviving 450 ft. of that wall. The present tarmac path passes through the site of the East Gatehouse and it seems likely that this has remained the only entry-point on this side since Roman times. An area about 36 x 32 ft. (128 sq. yds.) was

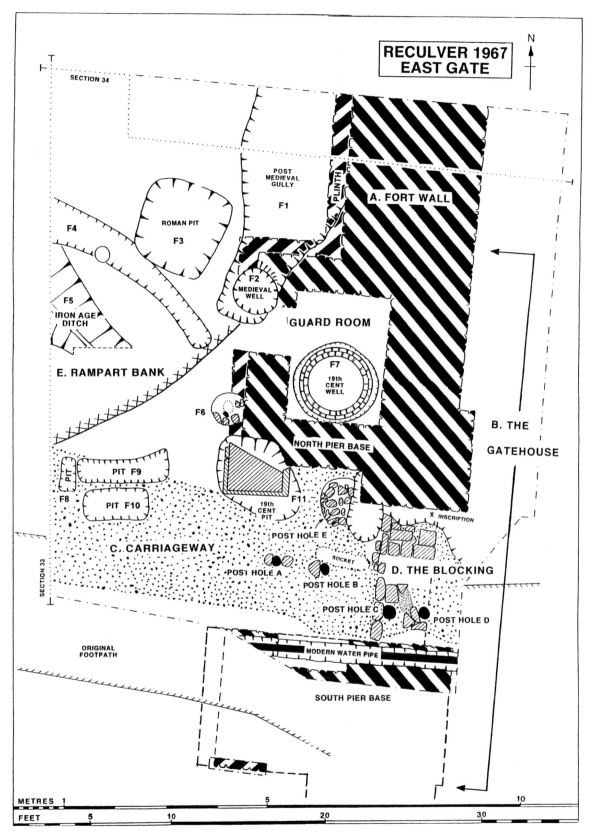

Fig. 12.   *Reculver 1967. Plan of East Gatehouse.*

substantially excavated in 1967 and recorded (Sections 31 and 33/34). A large chamfered sandstone block, found standing on edge by the path, largely matched one built into the South Gatehouse and had clearly been moved from nearby.

The excavation produced only a small quantity of artefacts by Reculver standards, but pottery apart it included only eight stratified coins, two brooches and a small fragment of an inscription (No. 441). The latter was found in 1965 in disturbed soils at the front of the Gatehouse and it is possible that this had formed part of a commemorative tablet placed on the structure, as at the Roman fort at Carpow. The fragment is the top left-hand corner on which is a large, well-cut letter T. Other fragments could yet survive nearby beyond the limits of the excavation. The various structural elements located are described below (A–E) and other features listed in the following table.

Feature No.	Type	Period	Deposit	Notes
1	Gully	20th Century	2	Cuts across fill of F2
2	Well	Medieval	3,4	Abortive
3	Pit	Roman	16, 27, 28, 37	Contained coins Nos. 48, 49, 52
4	Gully	Post-Roman	30	Cuts top of Rampart Bank
5	Ditch	Pre-historic	–	Progressive silt, no finds
6	Post-hole	Roman	19	Sandstone packing
7	Well	19th Century	34	Cuts centre of Guard-room
8	Pit	Undated	–	Shallow, cuts Roman road
9	Pit	"	–	" " " "
10	Pit	"	–	" " " "
11	Well	19th Century	21	Abortive

Table D. Features on the East Gatehouse Site (1967)

(A) THE FORT WALL

A good section of fort wall survives on each side of the Gatehouse, that on the south side appearing to survive to its full width of about 10 ft. This includes three courses of external ragstone facing, including the bottom two offset courses. The latter reduces the wall thickness to about 9 ft., the core of which consists of flint and ragstone rubble and still survives some 10–12 courses high.

The section of fort wall north of the Gatehouse was exposed for a distance of about 10 ft. This included a short length of the external bottom plinth, just one course high and built of ragstone ashlar blocks. The second course of ashlar blocks seems to represent the actual external face which probably extended upwards for about 15–25 ft. If so, this produces a wall thickness of about 8 ft. which increases to 10 ft. with the inclusion of the basal plinths on both the inside and outside. Again, the core mostly consists of flint and occasional ragstone rubble, laid in horizontal courses of which a maximum of eight survive at this point.

(B) THE GATEHOUSE (Fig. 12)

The work revealed that the Gatehouse had occupied an area about 33 x 15 ft. overall, comprising two unequal masonry masses separated from each other by a space about 8 ft. 6 in. in width. The masonry on the south side (South Pier Base) appears to have been solid and it occupied the full

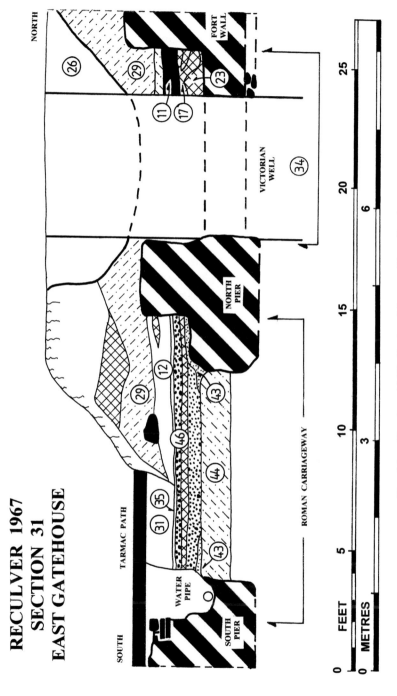

Fig. 13.   *Reculver 1967. Section 31 across East Gatehouse.*

width of the fort wall and also projected about 5 ft. internally. Its overall dimensions were thus about 16 ft. x 9 ft. Its south-west corner incorporated at least five courses of flat bricks, but it was not possible to examine these in detail for this corner lay outside the main area of excavation. The masonry on the north side (North Pier Base) was larger, about 16 ft. x 16 ft. and contained the only guard-room which sat partly within the fort wall and partly projected internally. The guard-room seems to have had no certain floor and it may have contained a wooden stair giving access to the upper part of the Gatehouse and the adjacent rampart walk. The Gatehouse probably rose 5–10 ft. above the fort wall, which itself may have been 15–20 ft. high and surmounted by crenellations. Externally, the entrance would have appeared to have been off-centre of the complete Gatehouse. The guard-room chamber and its side walls all sat on a massive flint and mortar foundation, which extended about 1 ft. on the west and north sides thus matching the bottom internal offset of the fort wall. In detail the guard-room was rectangular and measured internally 8 ft. 2 in. x 6 ft. Its walls were mostly 2 ft. 6 in. in width and survived to a height of 3 ft. 2 in. above the base. The single doorway, on the west side, was about 3 ft. wide. The external size of the guard-room was about 13 ft. 6 in. x 8 ft. It had clearly formed an integral part of the fort wall and was constructed of large flints set in a pebbly white mortar. Courses of large fragments of brick, many 12 in. wide and two 17 in. in length, lined the doorway of the guard-room.

The masonry pier on the south side of the Gatehouse mostly lay under the tarmac path and could not be examined. Its whole north side was located, however, but this had been severely cut along its length by a trench containing a steel waterpipe. Enough survived to show that it had contained a shallow recess about 2 ft. deep, near its centre. The face of this contained two flat tiles and it is likely that the recess matched the surviving one on the north side, which had a length of about 7 ft. The large buttresses so created on each side of the recesses probably supported large arches over the carriageway.

The only architectural detail surviving was the large chamfered block found standing upright by the path. It is now clear that this large block was once positioned horizontally at the south-west corner of the guard-room. Here it had originally rested on a larger sandstone block that remained *in situ* and measured about 4 ft. 3 in. x 3 ft. The chamfered block measured about 3 ft. 9 in. x 3 ft. and was about 8 in. in thickness, with the chamfer being only on the south and west sides. It is now clear that the latter was lifted from its position in Victorian times when an attempt was made to excavate a well shaft. This work, which smashed part of the upper wall of the actual guard-room, was abandoned when the larger underlying stone was revealed and an alternative well (F.7) then dug nearby, but straight through the guard-room chamber!

(C) THE CARRIAGEWAY (Fig. 13)

The Gatehouse clearly enclosed a single metalled carriageway, effectively just 8 ft. 6 in. wide, but increasing to about 12 ft. 6 in., within the central recesses. The metalling survived over most of the area excavated, here a length of about 26 ft., where it consisted of small pebbles in a sandy matrix and 2–4 in. in depth. This extended into the recesses, to the front of the Gatehouse and internally, where no doubt it increased its width and where it can be identified as the *Via Principalis*. It had been cut into by several small pits of uncertain date, but also incorporated four small and one large post-holes. Two of the smaller ones (PH A and B) were on the central axis of the carriageway and seem to have held posts 6–8 in. in diameter. These appear to form an integral part of the metalled road and may have sub-divided the carriageway into two equal parts at some stage. Two more smaller ones (PH C and D), about 8–10 in. in diameter and cut into the metalling, were found under the later blocking. Their function is not known. A single large post-hole (PH E) was found in the recess on the north side of the carriageway, was about 2 ft. 8 in. in diameter and packed with sandstone rubble. This cut in from a higher level and it also cut the metalling by 5 in. It could have held a large rectangular upright post, on which a single door some 9 ft. wide could have been fixed. If so, such a door would have opened inwards and be fixed open onto the wider face of the north respond. When closed it could have been stopped and secured on the inside of the south recess, but in the absence of direct evidence this remains uncertain.

The stratification here was confined to an optimum depth of 3 ft. 3 in. The underlying sandy loam (L.10) represents the pre-fort levels and this was sealed by a band of gravel and pebble (L.8) some 4–6 in. deep and localised patches of sandstone chippings (L.9). Both these deposits overlapped the actual masonry foundations and are likely to have been formed during the fort-construction period. These were capped by a 3 in. layer of yellow clay (L.7) upon which was placed the final metalling (L.6). The surface of this produced two coins (Coin Nos. 53 and 55) both corroded, but of 3rd–4th century date, in a thin band of black loam (L.5). This was in turn sealed by a deep layer of grey-green loam and rubbish (L.4) of Roman date. All the soil above this was disturbed.

(D) THE BLOCKING OF THE CARRIAGEWAY

It seems clear that the East Gate of the fort had later been deliberately blocked by the construction of a wall across its external end. This had been built in line with the external facing and mostly on top of the metalling (L.6). Only some 20 medium sized sandstone blocks remained of the inserted wall, the rest having been robbed away with the bulk of the Gatehouse.

In detail, slight traces of speckled white mortar were found in association with the blocks, which generally only survived 1 ft. above the metalling. A continuous line of sandstone blocks appeared to mark the west face of the blocking wall, though these were set into the road and could represent an earlier feature. The rest of the surviving blocks had been built against this line to give a total width of 3 ft. 6 in. One group of five large blocks on the north side seem to represent a defined structural element, but this is more likely to have been caused by differential robbing. If structural, then these could represent a door jamb, perhaps flanking a small pedestrian door created in the blocking.

(E) THE RAMPART BANK

A large section of the Rampart Bank was revealed in the excavated area as earlier excavations on the east side of the fort had indicated it would. It occupied the north-western third of the area examined and encased the inside face of the fort wall and the north wall of the guard-room. It extended along the entire north side of the excavation for some 22 ft, was clearly much more extensive and had a maximum depth of 5 ft.

In detail it consisted of dumps of soils, mostly orange and brown clays (L.3–16), tipped in sloping layers across the site and spilling across the concrete base of the guard-room. Most of the soils were clean and devoid of finds and the clays in particular looked freshly dug. Some layers (L.13–16) could represent upcast from the foundation-trenches of the Gatehouse and others (L.4 and 12) may have been generated by the digging of the fort's external ditches nearby. The bank also included a band of black charcoal (L.8 and 10) which may have come from an adjacent oven. This, too, had spilled into the guard-room and not been removed. These deposits produced four sherds of samian ware, including Forms 31(2) and 37, all of late 2nd – early 3rd century date.

Of special interest was a single coin (Coin No. 23) of Commodus (A.D. 180–92) that was found in the dumped soil at the base of the rampart. This may have been dropped by the builders of the fort. Clear evidence of the familiar mortar-mixing floor, associated with the fort-construction period, was found along the west side of the excavation. This lay above a small pre-Roman ditch and beneath the dumped soils forming the Rampart Bank.

Context	Coin Nos. (1967 Reg)	Emperor	Date	Site code
Base of Rampart	23	Commodus	180–92	14
Pit in Rampart	48	Allectus	293–6	16
	49	Radiate	270–90	27
	52	Severus Alexander	222–35	28
On Road Metalling	53, 55	Illegible	3–4C	46
Soils Sealing Metalling	21	Claudius II	268–70	13
	50	Illegible	3–4C	13
Unstratified and Other Deposits	9	George III	1797	1
	10	Counter France	15C	1
	11	Gallienus	260–8	1
	12, 47	Illegible	–	1, 39
	13	Tetricus I	270–3	1
	14	House of Constantine	335–45	1
	26	Illegible	3–4C	1
	27	Tetricus II	270–3	1
	51	Barbarous Radiate	270–90	1

Table E. Coins from East Gatehouse Area (1967)

The bank sealed the pre-fort land surface (L.18) and also a thin layer of greensand chippings (L.17) dropped by the workmen building the Gatehouse. The chippings must represent the final dressing of the large greensand blocks that had once lined the main arch over the carriageway. The bank also sealed part of the small pre-historic ditch (L.19–21) which was detected near the north-west corner of the excavation, but not followed. The bank had been cut into by several features, with perhaps the only significant one being a large Roman pit. This was sub-rectangular in plan, some 5 ft. 11 in. x 5 ft. 6 in., with nearly vertical sides, a largely flat base and a depth of about 4 ft. It contained a succession of dumped soils, Roman domestic rubbish and pottery (Nos. 46–52) and three coins (Coin Nos. 48, 49 and 52). These were of Severus Alexander (A.D. 222–35), Allectus (A.D. 293–6) and a radiate (A.D. 270–90). This pit, whose function is not clear, was probably dug and filled at the end of the third century. The small amount of domestic rubbish found on this site included only 14 sherds of samian ware, including Forms 30, 31(2), 32, 36, 37(2), 38, 45 and Luduwici, all Antonine – 1st half 3rd century.

No. 7 THE NORTH AND WEST GATEHOUSES (*The Porta Praetoria and Porta Principalis Sinistra*) – (Figs.70–72)

In common with the great majority of Roman forts in Britain, particularly those of 2nd or early-3rd century date, it must be certain that Reculver was originally provided with four gatehouses. Those on the south and east sides survive and have been excavated, the South Gatehouse in 1964 (p. 25) and the East Gatehouse in 1967 (p. 32).

The gatehouses on the north and west sides have long since been removed by the rapid sea erosion of the past few centuries. The fort was still complete about 1700, but the north-east corner

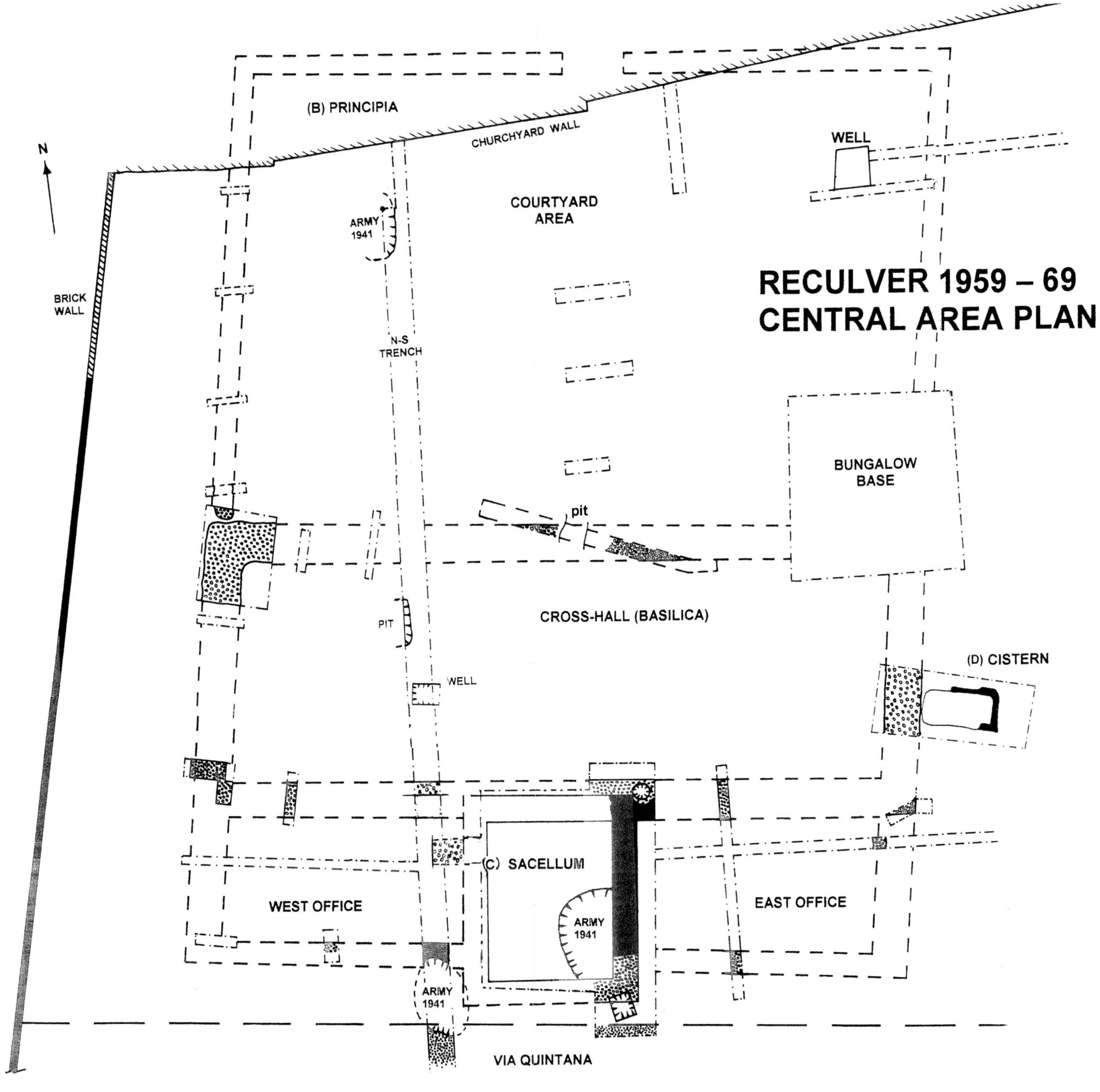
RECULVER 1959 – 69
CENTRAL AREA PLAN
N
(B) PRINCIPIA
CHURCHYARD WALL
WELL
COURTYARD
AREA
ARMY
1941
BRICK
WALL
N-S
TRENCH
BUNGALOW
BASE
pit
CROSS-HALL (BASILICA)
PIT
(D) CISTERN
WELL
(C) SACELLUM
ARMY
1941
WEST OFFICE
EAST OFFICE
ARMY
1941
VIA QUINTANA

Fig. 15. *Reculver 1960–1. Plan of Central Area.*

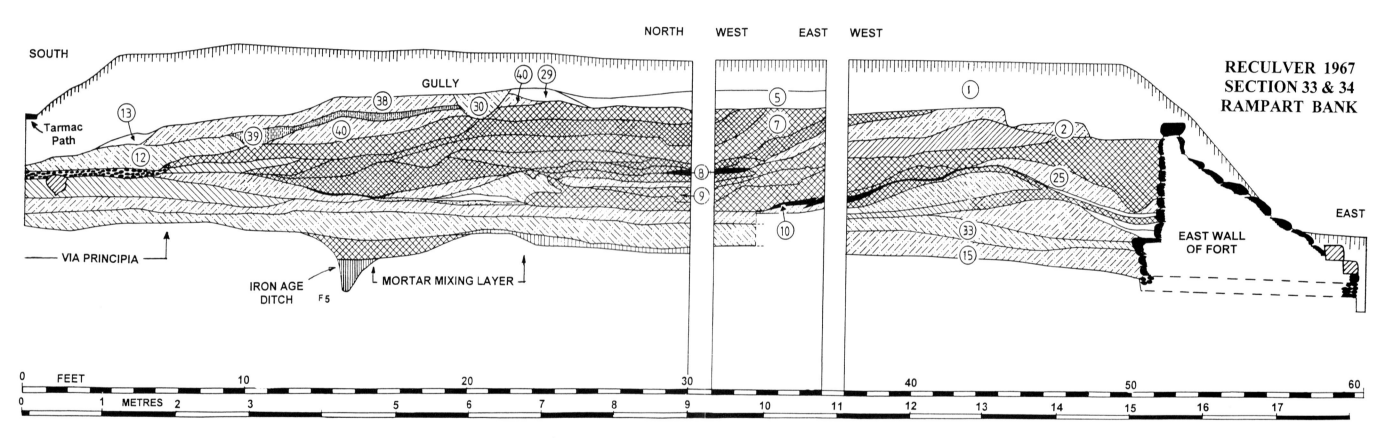

SOUTH

NORTH WEST EAST WEST

RECULVER 1967
SECTION 33 & 34
RAMPART BANK

Tarmac
Path

GULLY

EAST

EAST WALL
OF FORT

VIA PRINCIPIA

IRON AGE
DITCH
F5

MORTAR MIXING LAYER

| 0 | FEET | 10 | 20 | 30 | 40 | 50 | 60 |

| 0 | 1 METRES 2 | 3 | 5 | 6 | 7 | 8 | 9 | 10 | 11 | 12 | 13 | 14 | 15 | 16 | 17 |

Fig. 14.   *Reculver 1967. Sections 33 and 34 through Rampart Bank, East Gatehouse.*

had gone by 1708. It would have been in the following years that what remained of the North Gatehouse would have crashed down onto the beach. The sea had reached to within five yards of the north tower of the church by 1806 and it must have been about then, or slightly later, that the West Gatehouse was destroyed. No details of either have survived.

With the East and South Gatehouses centrally placed and both fitting in with a well-established road pattern, it must be that the West and North Gatehouses were also centrally placed. That on the north side would have been lined up on the central axis of the fort and thus facing (internally) the *principia*. It can therefore be identified as the *Porta Praetoria,* the main gate of the fort. It would have straddled the *Via Praetoria,* which itself would have led back into the fort to join the *Via Principalis* at right-angles in the long-established manner. What is less certain is the form of this, the principal gatehouse. It could have matched the very similar East and South Gatehouses, both about 30–33 x 15 ft., but it is possible that it was built on a larger scale, perhaps with a pair of matching guard-rooms, or even with twin portals.

Exactly this arrangement was employed by the *Classis Britannica* at Dover in the second century (Ref. 50). There, very extensive work by the Kent Archaeological Rescue Unit over many years, both in discovery and excavation, revealed the defences and internal buildings in some detail. The North, West and East Gatehouses all had double portals and square towers. Only the main *Porta Praetoria* on the east side, facing the quays and harbour, was treated differently and provided with impressive drum-towers of unusual form. Dover, as the Gateway to Roman Britain, anyway had a special role in welcoming leading officials to Roman Britain. It had a large tidal harbour, flanked by an impressive timber-framed sea wall, together with two large masonry lighthouses on the adjacent cliffs. Clearly, Dover was a high-status naval port and town in the second century sporting the *Classis Britannica* fort, a large military bath-house and the now-famous Roman Painted House, identified as a *mansio* of Mediterranean quality (Ref. 30). Both the bath-house and the Roman Painted House were also excavated by the K.A.R.U. in its extensive programme of excavation from 1970–2005, which still continues.

As regards the lost West Gatehouse at Reculver, it is certain that this would have marked the west end of the *Via Principalis* and can thus be identified as the *Porta Principalis Sinistra*. From here it also served a major metalled road leading from the fort, part of which was observed and recorded by the author in 1957. This road was the fort's main link with the countywide road network, via *Durovernum Cantiacorum,* now Canterbury.

It thus had a major function and was probably more important than either the East or South Gatehouses, which faced the tidal estuary or its inlets. Even so, it is difficult to gauge its size. It is more likely that it matched its opposite East Gatehouse, though it is still possible that its form was larger due to its importance.

CHAPTER IV

THE EXCAVATED STRUCTURES

(B) THE INTERNAL BUILDINGS AND ROADS

No. 8 THE CENTRAL AREA (*PRINCIPIA*) – (Figs. 15–19)

The excavations of 1957–1959 had suggested that the internal layout of the fort was much more planned than that of the great majority of other forts of the Shore-fort defensive system. Accordingly, the 1960 programme of work was directed at the large open central area south of the medieval church where any Headquarters Building might have been. Apart from some very limited and unrecorded trenching in 1927, the area had never been examined. The aim of the 1960 work was to locate structures and stratigraphy, to assess the survival and quality and to recover dating evidence. Two long trenches, each 4 ft. wide, were laid out at right angles to each other, one north–south and 188 ft. in length and the other east–west and 77 ft. 6 in. in length. In the event both largely cut the axes of the Headquarters Building, though not centrally, but certainly including the most critical area.

(A) THE STRATIFICATION, MINOR FEATURES AND ROADS (Fig. 17)

In detail, the longer north–south trench (Section 5) began about 10 ft. from the stone boundary wall which now retains the footpath and formed the south wall of the churchyard. No stratification survived in the northern 110 ft. (actually Datums 40–150 ft.) of the trench, where natural clay was mostly encountered at a depth of only 10–12 in. Only cut features seem to have survived here and apart from modern intrusions only a possible Roman well and a square pit were found. The pit was found on the west side of the main trench (at Datum 84–91 ft.) and was about 7 ft. x 1 ft. (min.) in plan and only about 1–2 ft. deep. It contained (L.100) potsherds of Roman date, but was not further explored. The well (at Datum 76 ft.) was largely 4 ft. square in plan and only 9 ft. 9 in. deep and appears to have been abandoned due to the soft sand through which it had been excavated. Its fill of sandy loam may represent the replacement of soil, but a broad band of sand and loam, with charcoal and burnt soil had been tipped in from the south side when it was half filled. This may have been derived from an adjacent oven or hearth. The top of the shaft had partly been consolidated with fragments of tile on end and small sandstone blocks, all compacted into the upper fill. The shaft itself produced two bone pins, part of a bone comb (Nos. 342–3), a bone needle (No. 291), other objects (Nos. 302, 342) and a coin (No. 60–9) of Tetricus (A.D.270–3), near the top edge. Clearly, this shaft could not have been consolidated much before about A.D. 300.

Horizontal stratification seemed to start at about Datum 40 ft. and continued southwards for 78 ft. to the end of the trench (actually at Datum -38 ft.) where its depth had steadily increased to about 3 ft. This suggests that the northern part of this large area had been reduced by various agencies, but that the southern downhill part has been progressively buried. This in turn indicates that the slope of the hill was greater in the prehistoric and Roman periods than at present where the gradient is about 1 in 40. As regards the stratified (south) end of the trench beyond the Headquarters Building, a number of features and deposits deserve comment.

The fort-construction level was marked at the extreme south end of the trench (Datums -35 to -38 ft.) by a mortar-mixing layer. This was flanked by a thin band of pebble about 13 ft. wide.

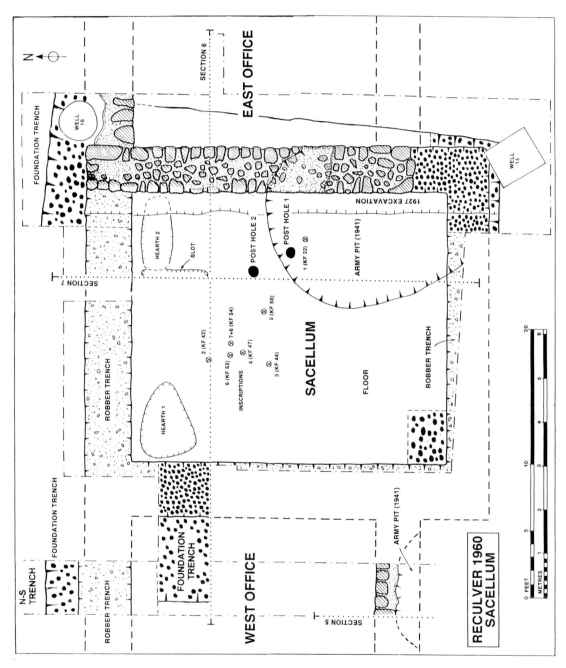

Fig. 16. *Reculver 1960. Plan of Sacellum.*

(Datums -22 to -35 ft.) which corresponds with the *Intervallum* Road that should flank the tail of the Rampart Bank behind the south wall of the fort. After an interval of 31 ft. another primary pebble band, barely 2–3 in. deep, was traced for another 16 ft. (Datums -9 to -25 ft.) where it was cut by a large Army Pit dug in 1941. This pebble band aligns well with the *Via Quintana* found in 1959 some 180 ft. to the east and it clearly flanked the back wall of the *sacellum*. It is thus certain that it represents the continuation of the *Via Quintana*.

Both layers of metalling were sealed by a deposit of grey-black loam (L.14), some 6–20 in. deep, which contained some rubble, fragments of tile, domestic rubbish, several small-finds, including various bronze (Nos. 303, 312, 430, 431), bone (No. 345) and iron (No. 423) objects. This also included eleven samian ware sherds, mostly of 3rd century date, coarse pottery and two coins (Coin Nos. 60–11, 17), one of Severus Alexander (A.D. 227) and the other of Postumus (A.D. 260–68). This layer was partly sealed by a layer of crumbled mortar (between Datums -18 to -34 ft.), perhaps laid down to form a localised compacted surface. This layer contained a fragment of pink granite and iron objects (Nos. 426, 432, 433). This was in turn sealed by an extensive deposit of black loam, some 6–12 in. deep, which covered the southern 63 ft. of the trench (between Datums +25 and –38 ft.). This also contained domestic rubbish and four more coins (Coin Nos. 5, 6, 10,19), two of the late-third century and two minted about A.D. 320–4. Finally, a substantial layer of rubble, including tile, sandstone blocks, white mortar and domestic rubbish formed over a distance of about 37 ft. (between Datums -12 to -49 ft.). This may represent a demolition layer largely confined to the area of the Headquarters Building. No coins were recovered from this layer, which appears extensive, but another 16 samian sherds were recovered, including Forms Curle 23(2), 30, 36, 37(No. 218), 38 and 45.

Another rectangular pit was also located on the east side of the north–south trench (between Datums -12 to -16 ft.). It was 4 ft. 2 in. north–south, at least 2 ft. 6 in. wide, had vertical sides, was 1 ft. 10 in. deep and had a flat base. Its grey loam and charcoal filling was sealed by a band of orange clay and it contained a small amount of Roman pottery. In further detail, the shorter east–west trench (Fig. 18, Section 6) also encountered natural clay at a depth of only about 12 in. along much of its length where any horizontal stratigraphy had been removed. Again, only cut features had survived, most notably a 28 ft. wide cut made in the Roman period for the construction of a sub-basement forming the Central Office of the Headquarters Building (see below).

(B)   THE HEADQUARTERS BUILDING (*PRINCIPIA*) (Fig. 16)

The two main trenches were later supplemented by a series of about 20 small trenches aimed at locating the continuations of foundations already located. This work produced the tentative outline of a very large rectangular structure, probably about 130–140 ft. in north–south length and about 104 ft. in overall east–west width. There can be little doubt that this represents the principal Roman building inside the fort and from its position there can be no doubt that this was the Headquarters (*principia*). No floors seem to have survived anywhere and these must have been removed, or reduced, since Roman times. Indeed, apart from the east wall of the Central Office sub-basement (*sacellum*) almost no masonry seems to have survived and this is likely to have been removed by later building-work elsewhere, most notably for the adjacent church of St. Mary's. Happily, the broad foundations of worn beach pebbles (Plate XVII) had mostly survived and it is from these that the outline plan has been produced. From this it seems clear that three major divisions of the Headquarters Building can be identified, as the Courtyard, the Cross-hall and the offices. A deep tank, or Cistern, was also located outside the east wall of the Cross-hall and fully excavated. All these structures are described below:

(1) THE COURTYARD

This was a largely standard component of a Roman military Headquarters and almost invariably occupied the front area. Unfortunately, this area at Reculver has suffered the greatest ground-reduction and only slight traces of the pebble foundations were found. These suggest an overall area about 104 ft. x 70–80 ft., with the unknown north wall assumed to flank the projected *Via Principalis*. The internal area is likely to have been about 98 x 67– 77 ft. No internal divisions were sought, though a narrow portico on three sides and a central, northern entrance are likely. The narrower pebble foundations, mostly about 3 ft. wide, located here suggest that this division was of a single storey in height. Significantly, perhaps, a stone-lined well, found in 1923 and at least 16 ft. deep, plots out near the north-east corner of the courtyard and could be Roman. It contained no significant finds, but could also be medieval, or later, in date.

(2) THE CROSS-HALL (*BASILICA*)

The series of small trenches also revealed the foundations and outline of the large central division of the Headquarters. There can be little doubt that this was the great Cross-hall so familiar in *principia* in both auxiliary forts and legionary fortresses. At Reculver the overall dimensions were 104 ft. x 40 ft. which, allowing for walls reduces to about 95 x 31 ft. internally. Again only the foundations, some patchy, were located, but those at the north-west corner (Plate XVII) were substantial. There they were 6 ft. wide and 6–12 in. deep. Their greater breadth suggests a two, or even three, storey structure above ground. A Cross-hall of this form may be identified as a *basilica*, due to its form, here perhaps supported by internal piers of which some slight trace could yet survive.

(3) THE OFFICES

The rear division of the fort, as outlined by a small amount of masonry and areas of foundation pebbles, was about 104 x 25 ft. overall. Allowing for walls this reduces to about 96 x 20 ft. internally. By analogy with other Roman forts this equates with a range of offices, mostly three or five in number, invariably with a central *sacellum*, or strong-room. A large *sacellum*, in the form of a sub-basement, and two large side offices, appear to complete the rear division of the Headquarters Building at Reculver. The *sacellum*, at least, may have been two storeys in height.

The main 1960 east-west trench cut through the West Office and located its robbed east wall, but not its west wall. The adjacent minor trenches suggested an internal length of about 35 ft. The main 1960 north–south trench (see above) picked up a remnant of its south wall and the robber-trench of its north wall. The width between these was 18 ft. 4 in. and an effective internal width of about 20 ft. seems likely. No related stratification was found and not much more can be said other than that it was probably entered from a north doorway linking it with the adjacent Cross-hall.

The outline of the foundations of the east room was partly revealed by the four small trenches dug after the main 1960 excavation had found its west wall, which it shared in common with the *sacellum*. These suggested a size largely similar to that of the large West Office, roughly 20 x 35 ft. internally. Again no related stratigraphy seems to have survived and more than this cannot be said. Presumably it, too, was entered by means of a north doorway linking it with the Cross-hall.

(4) THE STRONGROOM AND *SACELLUM* (Figs. 18 and 19, Sections 6 and 7 and Plates XVIII–XIX)

This large room occupied the major part of the 1960 excavation. The area was marginally extended in October, 1961 resulting in the almost total excavation of the room. In 1960, the initial trench, running east–west and 4 ft. wide, located the surviving east wall and an area about 32 x 26 ft. (92 sq. yds.) was then opened up for examination. Both the main east–west axis (Section 6) and the north–south axis of the room (Section 7) were recorded and are published here. Only about 60% of the original area remained undisturbed, with medieval stone-robbing, a narrow trench dug in 1927 and a large pit dug by the military in 1941 having removed the rest.

The undisturbed pre-Roman natural soils were mostly encountered at a shallow depth of only about 12 in. on all sides of the underground room and it seems clear that virtually all the horizontal archaeological stratigraphy here has been removed. This is likely to have been caused by cultivation and soil erosion on this slightly sloping site, over many centuries. Centrally, the stratification survived to a total depth of about 4 ft. and it was at once clear that this room, although heavily robbed, had formed a sub-basement some 4–5 ft. deeper than the conjectured floor-levels that must have once existed in the adjacent rooms.

Of the structure of the room itself, only a 24 ft. length of the massive east wall and a single stone of the south wall (near the south-west corner) had fortuitously survived. This is almost certainly the wall located in 1927 (p. 13) and indeed a narrow trench found following its west face had removed the related stratigraphy. The east wall survived up to six courses high (2 ft. 6 in.) and was faced with squared sandstone blocks held in a white mortar. It was 3 ft. 5 in. wide, with a small internal offset over a compact foundation of worn beach pebbles, mostly about 8 in. in depth. The other three walls had been carefully removed by stone-robbers and the largely vertical robber-trenches were clear on all sides. These indicated that all the walls had been about 3 ft. 5 in. in width. The upper fill of the robber-trenches mostly contained a mixture of grey-brown loam and scattered stone fragments, probably representing backfill. The lower fill (L.3) largely consisted of mortar fragments left behind during the stone removal process. Beneath the fill were the same beach pebble foundations, though these were not examined throughout. These varied from about 6–9 in. in depth. Medieval pottery fragments, of 12th century date, were also recovered from the fill of the robber-trenches and it seems likely that this extensive robbing took place about A.D. 1180–1200 probably when the two large towers were added to the nearby St. Mary's church. About 75 ft. of Roman masonry had been removed from the underground room and this would have yielded some 30 cu. yds. of stone, even if the walls then only stood to existing ground-level.

The surviving masonry and the robber-trenches show that this room had been rectangular, internally some 20 ft. in east-west width and 23 ft. 10 in. in north–south length, thus covering an area of about 54 sq. yds. It had been constructed within a much larger pit dug into the natural clay, the steep sides of which were found on the west, north and east sides. These were clear on the shorter east–west axis (Section 6) and suggest that the excavated pit was probably about 36 x 36 ft. in area. The section also shows that once the foundations and the lower parts of the walls had been constructed within the pit, the external voids were then filled. This included dumped soils (L.8), over mortar droppings (L.9), over more dumped soils (L.10) and discarded flints (L.11). The soils here were probably derived from the original excavation of the pit dug for the room. It is now clear that this sub-basement room had been the underground strongroom of the headquarters (*principia*), above which had been the shrine (*sacellum*) of the garrison.

Internally, the room had been very substantially robbed. Only a thin skin of white mortar (L.7), showed where any finished floor had been removed. At the south–west corner a small piece of *in situ* concrete, 3 in. in thickness, survived. This overlapped a small offset on the only surviving stone block and sat over a pebble base. A north–south slot some 4 ft. 8 in. wide and 6 in. deep was found close to the north–east corner. Its purpose is not clear, but it may have supported a wooden-plate set in the floor. Nearby were two circular post-holes, each about 9 in. in diameter and about 2–3 in. deep and these appear to have been set in the floor. Again, their function is not clear, though a partition or stairs are possibilities.

In spite of the extensive robbing and other intrusions, about 60% of the stratification within the room remained intact, though both the 1927 and 1941 activity had cut through it to floor-level. A small pocket of orange clay (L.6) was found by the west wall, but otherwise the entire area was covered with a primary deposit mostly 6–12 in. deep. This consisted of a grey-brown loam (L.19 and L.21) containing fine mortar, sand, painted plaster, domestic rubbish and other objects. Included in the latter were eleven fragments (Nos. 1–8 on the plan) of two stone inscriptions, 21 coins (see Table F), coarse pottery (Nos. 53–69), a samian Form 33 (Stamp No. 9) by Saturninus (No. 228)

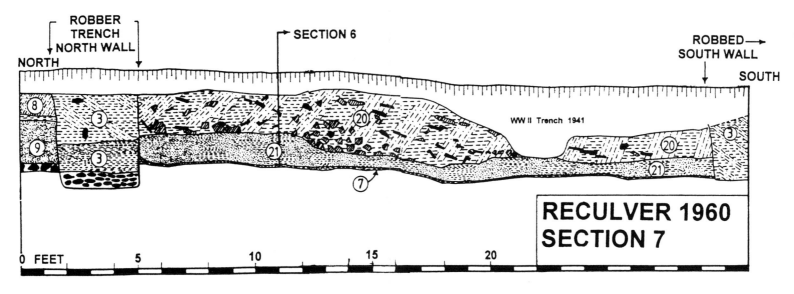

Fig. 19. *Reculver 1960. Section 7 across* sacellum *(N–S).*

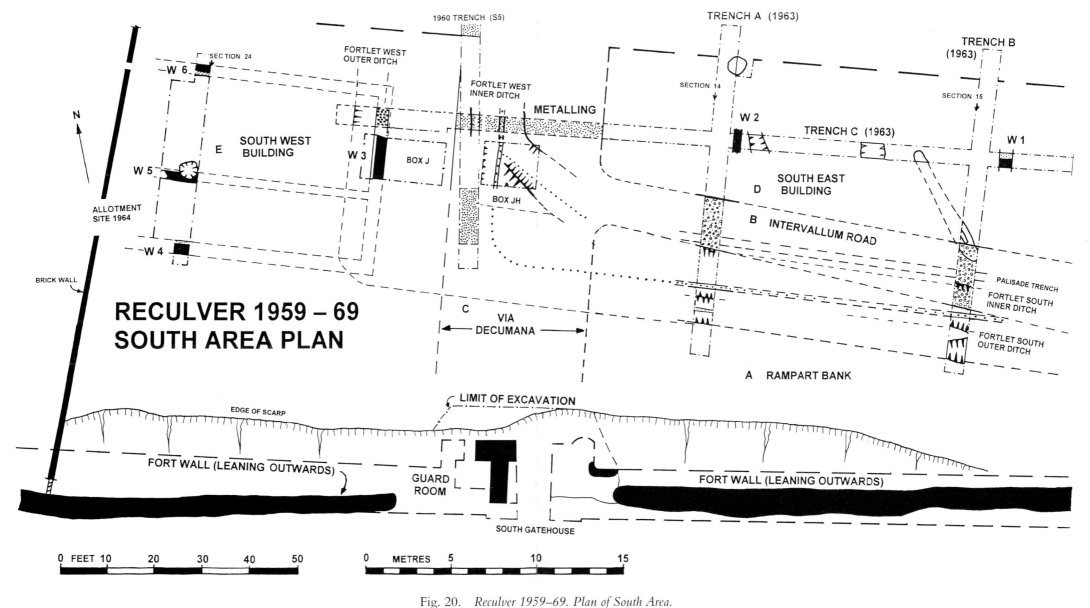

Fig. 20. *Reculver 1959–69. Plan of South Area.*

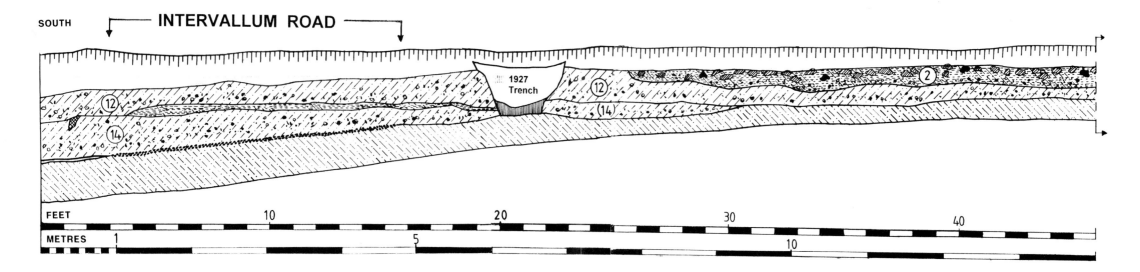

SOUTH
INTERVALLUM ROAD

1927
Trench

② ⑫ ⑭ ⑫ ⑭

FEET 10 20 30 40
METRES 1 5 10

Fig. 17.   *Reculver 1960. Section 5 across Principia (N–S).*

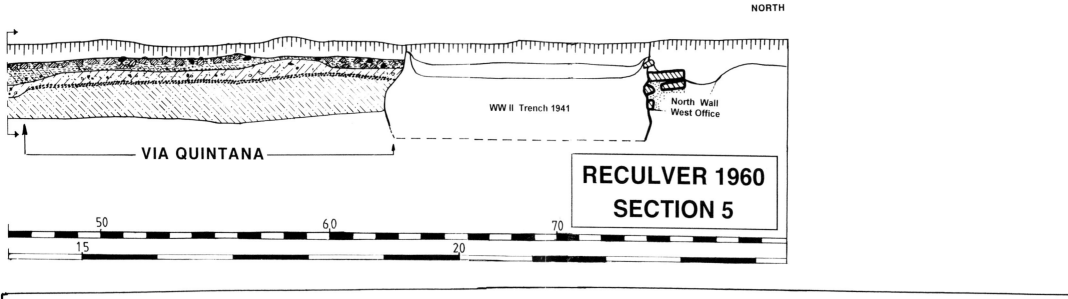

NORTH

VIA QUINTANA

WW II Trench 1941

North Wall
West Office

**RECULVER 1960
SECTION 5**

50 60 70
15 20

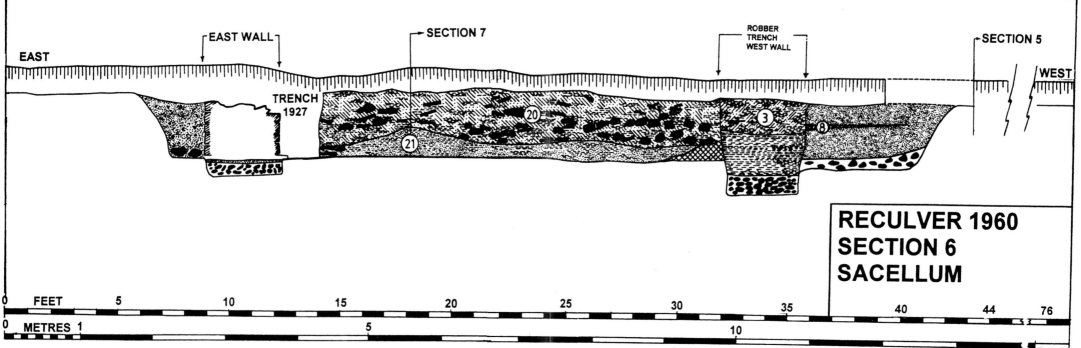

ROBBER
TRENCH
WEST WALL

EAST WALL SECTION 7 SECTION 5

EAST WEST

TRENCH
1927

⑳ ③ ⑧
㉑

**RECULVER 1960
SECTION 6
SACELLUM**

FEET 0 5 10 15 20 25 30 35 40 44 76
METRES 0 1 5 10

Fig. 18.   *Reculver 1960. Section 6 across sacellum (E–W).*

Context	Coin Nos. (1960)	Emperor	Date	Exc. code
Well Shaft	9	Tetricus II	270–3	10
Grey-Black Lm.-Period I	11	Severus Alexander	227	14
	17	Postumus	260–8	14
Black Lm.- Period II	10	Allectus	293–6	12
	5	Constantine I	320–4	12
	6	Victorinus	260–70	7
	19	Constantine I	320–4	7
Primary Deposit in Sacellum	29	Antoninus Pius	138–61	21
	25	Marcus Aurelius	161–80	21
	36	Severus Alexander	222–35	21
	22, 35	Gallienus	260–8	21
	1,23, 26, 28, 33	Claudius II	268–70	21
	31, 32	Tetricus	270–3	21
	15	Tetricus	270–3	19
	24	Postumus	259–73	21
	27	Diocletian	284–96	21
	34, 37	Carausius	286–93	21
	13	Constantine I	320–4	21
	30	Constantine II	330–5	21
	18, 20	Illegible	3–4 C	21
Secondary Rubble Deposit in Sacellum	21	Postumus	260–8	6
	3, 12	Constantine I	320–4	6
	14	Constantine II	324–6	20
Robber Trench in Sacellum	8	Septimius Severus	200–1	3
	7	Magnentius	350–1	3
Pre-Fort Layer	16	Marcus Aurelius	155–65	15
Unstratified	4	Constantine I	320–4	1
	2	Charles I	1634–6	1

Table F. Coins from the *Principia* Area (1960)

and several small-finds (Nos. 304, 384, 386–9, 417–9, 439). These included six iron arrowheads, a bronze corner-plate and a lead clamp. This primary layer sealed two small areas of burnt brushwood in the north–west and north–east corners, shown as possible hearths on the plan.

The two inscriptions are of outstanding importance for the site and one, the most complete (Fig. 73), is of paramount interest to Shore-fort studies. It may well be the most important single find from the whole length of 350 miles of coastline that the forts defended. It was effectively a commemorative tablet of the Headquarters Building for it records the construction of both the *Aed[em]* and *basilica*, the *sacellum* shrine and Cross-hall, respectively. It names the *co[n]s[ularis]* of that year as *Rufinus* and one *[For]tunatus*, probably the fort commander. Both inscriptions are discussed below (p. 210) and were probably originally mounted on the walls of the *sacellum*.

The coins include two of the 2nd century, one of the earlier 3rd century and 14 of A.D. 260–93. Two certainly date from A.D. 320–35. A total of 280 painted wall plaster fragments (Group A) were found well scattered and not articulated and reveal a range of at least eight colours and suggest a series of lined panels, but no non-linear decoration (Fig. 66, 462). No plaster was found *in situ*, but a small concentration of fragments by the robbed west wall may indicate how it was decorated. The rest probably came from the upper walls of the *sacellum*. The whole deposit seems to represent a substantial decay, with the floor having been removed, the plastered surfaces damaged or weathered, the dedicatory inscriptions smashed and the room no longer fulfilling its original function. This deposit could not have formed before A.D. 330 and more probably about A.D. 340–55.

The secondary layer (L.3, 6 and 20) was generally 18–30 in. deep and completely sealed the primary deposit. Its brown loam fill contained a large amount of building rubble, including hundreds of roof tile fragments, sandstone blocks, *opus signinum* fragments, tufa, box-flue tiles (No. 479) and some domestic debris, including two mortaria (not illustrated) and another 112 fragments of similar wall-plaster. It also included another four coins and five samian sherds, mostly of Antonine, or later, date. The coins date from A.D. 268 and again indicate that this deposit could not have formed before about A.D. 326. In appearance, this deposit seems to represent an advanced period of decay of at least part of the building. The large number of roof tile fragments in the upper part of this layer (Plate XVIII) could have been from a collapsed roof.

The only other features of interest were two wells, both roughly on the line of the east wall of the *Sacellum*. That at the north end (Well 16), cut through Roman foundations, was circular with a diameter of 3 ft. It was excavated to a depth of 9 ft. 6 in. but the bottom was not reached. It had a series of footholds cut into its side, opposite each other in pairs, at intervals of about 1 ft. 8 in. Its filling of brown loam contained medieval pottery and roof tile. Clearly, this well was dug when no Roman masonry was visible and it is likely that it would need to be at least 20–30 ft. deep to have produced water.

The other well (Well 15), at the south end of the east wall, also cut through part of the Roman foundations and again clearly no wall was then visible. It was rectangular in plan, 3 ft. 4 in. east–west and 4 ft. 4 in. north–south. It was excavated to a depth of 9 ft. 8 in. which appeared to be the bottom. It may have been abandoned after hitting soft sand. Its largely sandy fill contained a few sherds of medieval pottery.

(C) THE WATER CISTERN (Fig. 21 and Plate XX)

In 1962, a trial-trench picked up the south-east corner of a large underground structure and this was substantially excavated in 1963 (Box GC). It was rectangular in plan, with its main east-west axis touching the external foundations of the east wall of the Cross-hall of the Headquarters. It appeared to have two phases and was certainly cut on its north side by two shallow medieval pits (not shown) and a small post-medieval ditch.

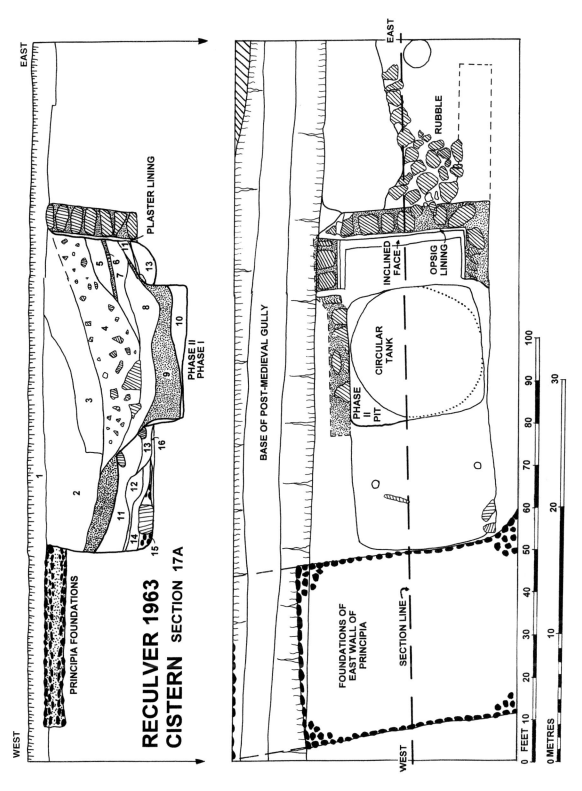

Fig. 21. Reculver 1963. Plan and Section17A of Cistern at side of Principia.

Its first phase appears to have been a neat oblong pit, about 10 ft. x 4 ft. 6 in., with vertical sides, a flat base and about 4 ft. deep. Three masonry walls, constructed of sandstone blocks held in white mortar and 9 in. wide, were then constructed on the south, east and north sides. These were cut into the sides of the original pit, thus increasing the overall size to about 11 ft. 6 in. x 6 ft., but about 9 in. shallower. The walls were carefully inclined outwards and rendered internally with a pale pink-white *opus signinum,* about 1–2 in. in thickness.

The east wall, 4 ft. 6 in. wide and 3 ft. high, survived complete, but only short stubs of north and south walls remained. Both of the latter had certainly been robbed, but for an uncertain distance. No trace of a west wall was detected and it seems likely that this would have been close to the Cross-hall foundations. Two circular stake-holes, each about 3 in. in diameter and 1 ft. deep, were found in the western area, but their function is not clear. The related stratification (L.11–16) within the pit included a mass of worn pebbles (L.15), which may have fallen from the foundations nearby and also mortar (L.12) which could have been derived from a robbed west wall. The rest was largely dumped clay and it seems all these layers formed after the original structure had been largely robbed. Its inclined walls, lined surfaces and subterranean construction, all suggest this was a large water storage cistern, perhaps even to take roof-water from the adjacent Cross-hall.

A second phase of construction was detected, perhaps carried out soon after the partial demolition of the original tank. The original structure and the dumped soils within it were then cut through by another rectangular pit, this time about 4 ft. 8 in. x 4 ft. 5 in. and probably 5 ft. deep. This had a flat base and mostly vertical sides. On examination it was found to contain a circular area 4 ft. 6 in. in diameter, clearly showing a socket which had originally held some large container or tank. It seems likely that this would have been of metal or wood, of which no trace survived. The angles of the pit behind this circular outline had been packed with clay and sandstone. Two cupped-shaped indentations, $1\frac{1}{2}$ and $2\frac{1}{2}$ in. wide and touching, were noted in the clay packing and these may represent hoops or bands around the circular tank. It seems likely that this second feature was another cistern to hold surface water and, although deeper, its capacity was less.

After the circular container had been removed, the socket and the rest of the structure were completely filled (L.2–10). Of special interest was a large deposit (L.9) of crushed red brick and tile chippings clearly thrown into the open void. This material must represent an unused pile of chippings previously prepared for inclusion in an *opus signimum* mortar, but never used. The final layers (L.2–3) were of sterile yellow-brown clay, probably dug from nearby. The only finds recovered were fragments of three coarse pottery vessels (Nos. 70–2) and small fragments of lead and bronze pipe (No. 452), the latter perhaps remnants of the actual cistern. The pottery seems to be of 3rd century date.

In the area some 60 ft. wide east of the *principia,* only very slight traces of Roman structures or stratification appear to have survived. Pits of various dates do occur and also the masonry foundations of the vicarage attached to St Mary's church. The latter appears on maps of 1685, 1781 and 1880, but it was demolished some time before 1922.

No. 9 THE SOUTH AREA (*RETENTURA*) – (Figs. 20, 22 and 23 and Plate XXI)

The excavations of 1959 and 1960 seemed to show clearly that the *Via Quintana* passed at the rear of the Headquarters Building and thus defined a narrow division between it and the south wall of the fort. Accordingly, in 1963 a series of three long evaluation trenches (Trenches A–C) was excavated to test this area to assess the extent and quality of what might survive. A very long trench (Trench C) running east–west for 156 ft. and mostly 3 ft. wide was laid out some 75 ft. from the south wall of the fort and about 40 ft. south of the Headquarters Building. This was crossed at right-angles by two more trenches (Trenches A and B) each 68 ft. in length, 4 ft. wide and 50 ft. apart, designed to connect with both the *Via Quintana* and the Rampart Bank behind the fort wall. Two additional squares (Boxes J and JH) were later opened up near the west end of the east-west trench. Part of this area was further examined in 1964, when a wide trench, mostly 43 x 8 ft., was dug in a small allotment close to the brick boundary wall flanking the west side of the area.

This work revealed that most of the north-eastern part of this South Area had been reduced to below Roman level and that no trace of the *Via Quintana* survived. Shallow horizontal stratigraphy was picked up along most of the east-west trench where, it reached a depth of about 2 ft. at the western end. It also survived along the southern two-thirds of the north-south trenches, where due to the original steeper slope, it attained a maximum depth of about 4 ft., at the extreme south ends. Several walls, roads, ditches, pits and other features were located and are described below (**A–E**). Of special interest were four Roman ditches, which underlay the fort construction deposits and formed the south-west corner of the mid-first century Fortlet. This is described separately below (p. 192).

(A) THE RAMPART BANK (Figs. 20 and 22)

Both trenches A and B located the northern end of the large Rampart Bank that was known to exist behind the south wall of the fort. This showed as a dump of yellow, orange or brown clay, loam and sand, largely sterile and directly sealing the pre-Roman soils. It generally tapered away about 45 ft. from the wall and had a maximum depth of nearly 4 ft. (L.60–62, 75–6). The soils over the tail of the Bank (L.55) contained domestic rubbish including a mortarium (No. 192) of 4th century date.

(B) THE *INTERVALLUM* ROAD (Figs. 20 and 22)

In Trench A, a thin band of pebble (L.12), some 10 ft. wide was located directly on the pre-Roman soils and flanked the tail of the Rampart Bank. On its merits this appears to be the predicted *Intervallum* Road and indeed a broadly similar layer was found in Trench B, some 13 ft. wide, though marginally nearer the fort wall and encroaching slightly on the Rampart Bank. These two sections, if fully representative, suggest that this perimeter road was here about 40–55 ft. from the back of the fort wall.

(C) THE *VIA DECUMANA* (Fig. 20)

Trench C picked up two layers of pebble metalling, running north-south one above the other, exactly behind the *sacellum* and in line with the adjacent South Gatehouse. There can be little doubt that these can be identified as the *Via Decumana,* normally running from the rear gate of a fort and joining the *Via Quintana,* which is exactly what it does at Reculver. In detail, the Lower Metalling (L.70) was traced for about 27 ft. (Datums -4 ft. to +23 ft.) and consisted of a thin band of pebble, perhaps 1–2 in. deep. This lay directly on the pre-fort soils, but seems to have settled into an underlying ditch (L.48 and L.57), which produced a samian Form 18. A substantial layer of loam and rubbish (L.28) had formed into the hollow so created and on this the Upper Metalling (L.27) was laid down over a slightly wider area and moved nearly 4 ft. to the east.

The surface of the lower road produced an illegible coin (Coin No. 26) and the top road two more coins (Coin Nos. 8 and 25), both barbarous radiates (A.D. 270–90) and an iron stylus (No. 429). The rubbish in the soil between the roads produced five more coins (Coin Nos. 14, 20–22, 30), two illegible, one of Hadrian (A.D. 117–38) and two more radiates, a bone pin (No. 235), a

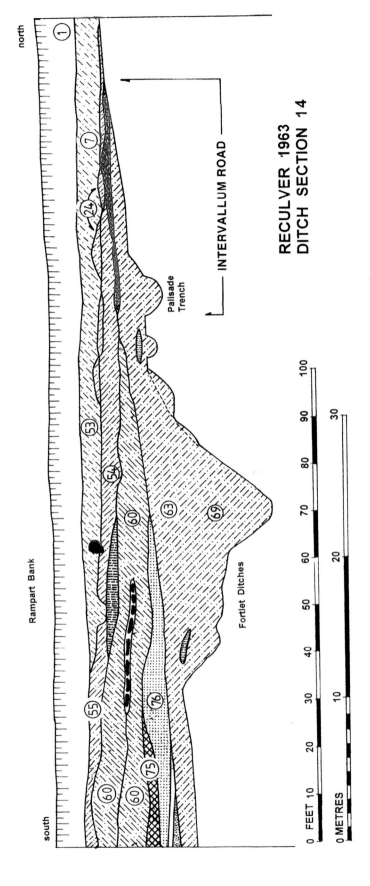

Fig. 22. *Reculver 1963. Section 14 across South Area (Trench A).*

shale bracelet (No. 404), six samain sherds mostly dating to the first half of the 3rd century and coarse pottery (Nos. 76–85).

Four minor features relating to this road require comment. The earlier was a long irregular gully (L.73, L.100), which was cut into the pre-fort deposits (Datums 27–40 ft. in Trench C) to a maximum depth of 13 in. and sealed by the lower metalling. It contained black loam, charcoal and domestic rubbish and a single coin (Coin No. 27) of Antoninus Pius (A.D. 138–61). It probably relates to the fort construction period and may reflect a nearby hearth, or oven.

Nearby (Datums 19 and 25 ft. in Trench C) were two substantial post-holes, one cutting the Lower Metalling and both sealed by the Upper Metalling, thus both relating to Period I. Both were circular, about 29–35 in. in diameter, 12 or 20 in. deep and contained stone packing. They were 5 ft. 6 in. apart, but their function is uncertain. Two small areas of disturbed pebble metalling, one in Trench A and the other in Trench C, each about 10–12 ft. wide were found just under the topsoil. These are effectively undated, but a late-Roman date is just possible though the likelihood is that these are post-Roman. The Upper Metalling was sealed by a general black loam deposit (L.26, 33, 40–41) which contained domestic rubbish, including four samian sherds, Forms 31, 33 and 38 of Antonine-3rd century date, a pottery counter (No. 451) and a bronze stylus (No. 382). This was inturn sealed by a final layer of black loam with some bands of rubble (L.39) and shell (L.25). These contained more domestic rubbish, a bronze fitting (No. 393) and a bone pin (No. 232).

(D) THE SOUTH-EAST BUILDING (Fig. 20)

The area east of the *Via Decumana* should logically have contained a Roman military building, but it was soon clear that in contrast with some other areas inside the fort, very little evidence was revealed here by the three evaluation trenches (A–C). Only two possible walls were located, both crossing north-south, in the long Trench C. The first (W1 at Datum 116 ft.) consisted of a disturbed mass of sandstone blocks. These were confined to a width of about 2 ft. 6 in. and a depth of 20–30 in. They were associated with several beach pebbles and the whole group resembles a section of a Roman wall typical of many elsewhere inside the fort, though here badly disturbed.

The second wall (W2 at Datum 59 ft.) also consisted of a series of disturbed sandstone blocks, this time just 1 ft. 10 in. wide. There were no obvious traces of corresponding east-west walls in either Trenches A or B and all that can be said is that the two possible walls were about 56 ft. apart. If these are walls and they relate to a single building then a length of 60–100 ft. is possible and a width of 20–25 ft. likely. This would fit within the *Via Quintana* and the *Intervallum* Road, but would then indicate very substantial robbing. Other possibilities occur. One is that the two possible walls are not representative and that no masonry building was ever constructed here. Another is that only a timber-framed building had existed here. Either way, the apparent absence of horizontal stratigraphy relating to structures must be significant.

The area east of the *Via Decumana*, did contain some mixed loam deposits representing the Roman military occupation of the fort. This ranged from 1–20 in. in depth and contained domestic rubbish and light building debris. This included six coins (Coin Nos. 4, 7, 11, 18, 19 and 23) and pottery, which included twelve samian ware sherds, Forms Ritterling 12, 31, 37, 43, 45(2), Walters 79 and Ludowici (3). All date from the late-2nd – 1st half of the 4th centuries, with the coins mostly being radiates of A.D. 270–300. Another 13 coins came from unstratified or unrelated deposits, of which nine are 3rd century, one 4th century, one an illegible 3–4 century and two medieval tokens (see Table G).

(E) THE SOUTH-WEST BUILDING (Figs. 20 and 23 and Plates XXII – XXIII)

The area west of the *Via Decumana* was also likely to contain a large masonry building and indeed a Roman sandstone block wall (W3), typical of many others inside the fort, was found near the

Context	Coin Nos.	Emperor	Date	Exc. Code
Rear Division 1963				
Lower Road	26	Illegible	3–4C	70
Upper Road	8, 25	Barbarous Radiate	270–90	27
Between Roads	14	Hadrian	117–38	28
	21	Radiate	260–90	28
	30	Illegible	3–4C	28
	16	Barbarous Radiate	270–90	28
	17	Gallienus	260–8	28
	20	Barbarous Radiate	270–90	59
	22	Illegible	3–4C	59
Gully under Roads	27	Antoninus Pius	138–61	73
General Black Soils	7	Claudius II	268–70	15
	11, 23	Illegible	3–4C	39
	18	Tetricus I	270–3	53
	19	Tetricus I	270–3	46
	4	Barbarous Radiate	270–90	7
Clay Wall – South-West Building	13	Hadrian	117–38	80
Unstratified and unrelated	1	Tetricus II	270–3	1
	2	Allectus	293–6	1
	10	Radiate	260–90	1
	12	Barbarous Radiate	270–90	1
	15	Valentinian	364–75	1
	29	Carinus	282–4	1
	31	Illegible	3–4C	1
	6	Tetricus II	270–3	4
	9	Barbarous Radiate	270–90	38
Allotment Site 1964				
In wall collapse	10	Radiate	260–90	42
Black Loam	5	Tetricus I	270–3	13
	6	House of Constantine	350–60	13
North-South Gully	8	Valens	364–78	35
Unstratified and unrelated	7	Barbarous Radiate	270–90	36
	9	Tetricus I	270–3	40
	11	Illegible	3–4C	47
	12	Tetricus II	270–3	48

Table G. Coins from the South Area (1963) and the Allotment Site (1964)

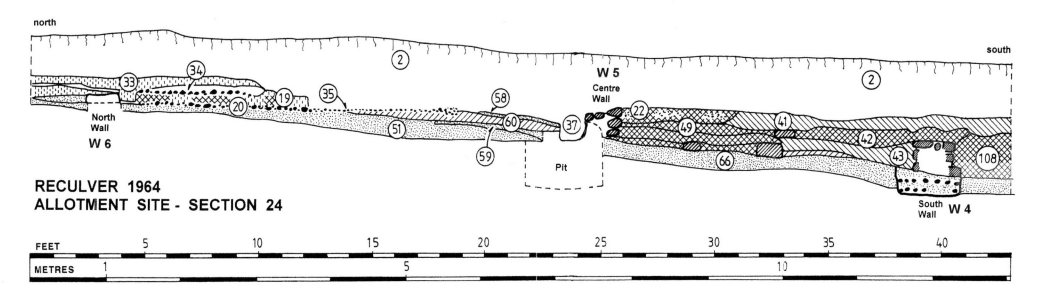

north

south

W 5
Centre
Wall

North
Wall

W 6

Pit

South
Wall W 4

RECULVER 1964
ALLOTMENT SITE - SECTION 24

FEET		5		10		15		20		25		30		35		40	

METRES	1		5		10	

Fig. 23.   *Reculver 1964. Section 24 across S. W. Building (N–S). Allotment Site.*

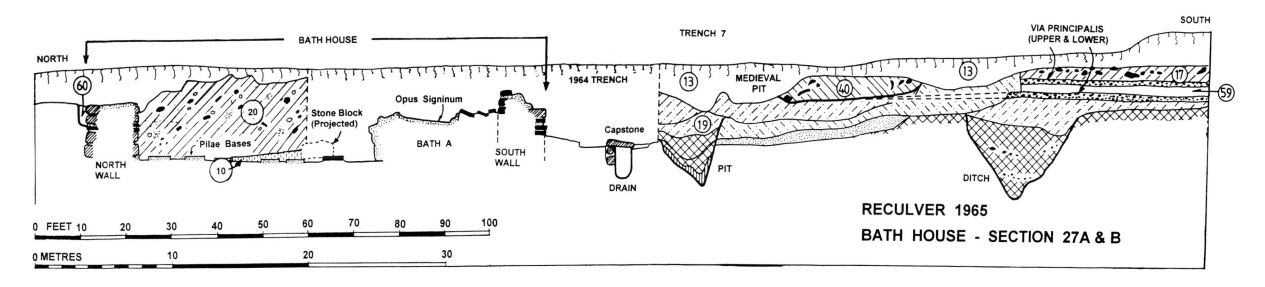

BATH HOUSE

TRENCH 7

VIA PRINCIPALIS
(UPPER & LOWER)

SOUTH

NORTH

1964 TRENCH

MEDIEVAL
PIT

Opus Signinum

Stone Block
(Projected)

BATH A

Pilae Bases

SOUTH
WALL

Capstone

PIT

DITCH

NORTH
WALL

DRAIN

RECULVER 1965
BATH HOUSE - SECTION 27A & B

0	FEET 10	20	30	40	50	60	70	80	90	100

0 METRES	10	20	30

Fig. 24.   *Reculver 1965. Section 27 across Bath House and* Via Principalis *(N–S).*

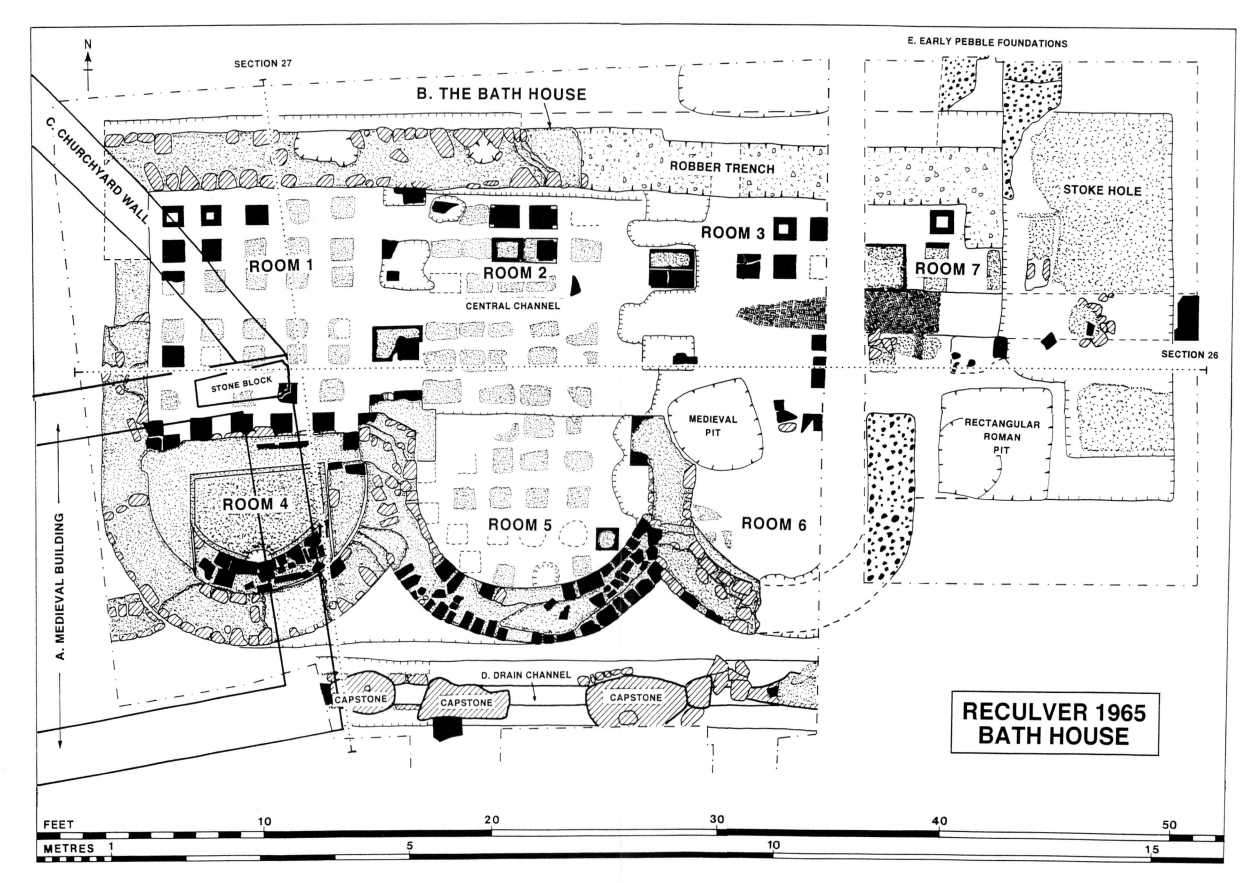

N

SECTION 27

E. EARLY PEBBLE FOUNDATIONS

B. THE BATH HOUSE

C. CHURCHYARD WALL

ROBBER TRENCH

STOKE HOLE

ROOM 3

ROOM 1

ROOM 2

ROOM 7

CENTRAL CHANNEL

SECTION 26

STONE BLOCK

A. MEDIEVAL BUILDING

MEDIEVAL PIT

RECTANGULAR ROMAN PIT

ROOM 4

ROOM 5

ROOM 6

D. DRAIN CHANNEL

CAPSTONE

CAPSTONE

CAPSTONE

RECULVER 1965 BATH HOUSE

FEET   10   20   30   40   50

METRES 1   5   10   15

Fig. 25.   *Reculver 1965. Plan of Bath House.*

extreme west end of Trench C. This was also traced in the adjacent Box J where a combined north-south length of 14 ft. was recorded. This lay about 11–15 ft. west of the edge of the *Via Decumana* and it must surely represent the east end of a building. It had been partially cut by a trench dug in 1927 and consisted of disturbed sandstone blocks over a foundation of pebbles. It was 2 ft. 5 in. wide and scattered rubble on its outer (east) side could represent its partial demolition. A coin (Coin No. 63–13), recovered from the top of the wall, was of Hadrian (A.D. 134–8).

On its (west) internal side was a succession of thin deposits, totalling just 9 in. in depth, which seemed to represent floors and repairs. A primary orange clay was overlaid by a thin band of *opus signinum*, overlaid by more orange clay, in turn overlaid by a thin band of plaster, including some painted red. These were extended westwards by a chalk floor, but all other higher deposits had been disturbed. A larger north-south trench (43 x 8 ft.) dug in an old allotment area in 1964, about 40 ft. further to the west revealed three more walls, all on an east-west axis, which probably relate to the wall found in Trench C. If so, a building at least 50 ft. in length and up to 40 ft. in width is suggested, though two periods seem to be indicated.

Of the three walls then found the north wall (W6) and centre wall (W5) seem to be contemporary and represent the primary structure. Although damaged, both had been built of sandstone blocks set in orange clay and each was 2 ft. 2 in. in width. They were about 19 ft. 6 in. apart and thus the building had an overall width of about 23 ft. 10 in. The sloping ground of the original hillside had been levelled up by a thick dump of clay (L.60) into which the centre wall had been cut. The inner area had been largely floored with a thin band of pebbles (L.20) ending short of the centre wall. The latter had been faced internally with a thin rendering of mortar, of which only a small vertical area survived. The floor was sealed by layers of ash (L.19) and mortar-plaster (L.58), after which a small area of a possible later floor (L.34) seems to have been inserted.

The third wall (W4) was located further south and appears to represent a wall added to the original structure as a second phase. It was also 2 ft. 2 in. in width and three courses of sandstone blocks set in clay had survived. This wall rested on a foundation some 9 in. wider, consisting of two layers of pebbles carefully laid between compacted sand. This seemed to contrast with the original foundations, but closely resembles the Period II foundations on the east side of the fort. The new wall increased the width of the building from nearly 24 ft. to a total of about 38 ft. 6 in. It seems to have been cut into the tail of the Rampart Bank, though this is not entirely certain. The upper part of the wall (L.42) seems to have collapsed to the north at some later time. The whole building was then finally sealed by some mixed darker soils (L.22, 41) and several black loams (L.10–13) all badly disturbed by the digging of the allotment, but producing some coarse pottery (Nos. 73–5).

Only eight coins (see Table G) were found on the Allotment site. One (Coin No. 10) a radiate of A.D. 260–90 was found in the clay of the collapsed wall. Two more (Coin Nos. 5 and 6) came from the overlying soils and one (Coin No. 8) came from a later north- south gully. The rest were unstratified. Small-finds from the Allotment Area included bronze and bone objects (Nos. 305, 313, 348, 374, 380).

No. 10 THE BATH HOUSE SITE (Figs. 24 and 25 and Plates XXIV–XXVI)

As part of the programme to explore the surviving internal area of the fort, a series of additional trial-holes was also dug at selected points. In 1964 one of these targeted a dense area of bushes on the north side of the central tarmac path and immediately east of the churchyard wall. This struck part of a curving Roman wall and in August–September, 1965 the bushes were cleared and an area, about 48 x 27 ft., largely excavated (Boxes 1–6). Additional trenches (Boxes 7–19) were also excavated then and in the adjacent areas in October, 1966. This work revealed a substantial masonry Bath House and other features. These are described below (**A–F**).

(A) THE MEDIEVAL STRUCTURE

Part of a small rectangular masonry structure was found at the extreme west end of the area and partly built directly above the west apsidal bath (Room 4) of the Bath House. About 10 ft. of this structure lay within the excavation and the rest appeared as a crop-mark in the mowed grass within the churchyard to the west. From this it appears that it was an isolated structure about 21 ft. x 15 ft. 9 in. overall. Its walls were mostly 2 ft. 2 in. wide and the internal area about 16 ft. x 11 ft. 3 in.

In detail, the walls revealed were constructed of flints and sandstone blocks set in white mortar containing pebbles. The floor consisted of a thin layer of similar mortar that was only 1 ft. below the existing grass. This rested on a bed of flints some 4–5 in. thick. The inside faces of the walls had been plastered with a thin layer of white mortar. A maximum of five courses of stonework survived where its east wall sat directly on the Roman walls and floor of the apse. In contrast, its north-east corner lay over the soft fill of the robbed *hypocaust* and a large stone block, some 48 x 15 x 10 in., had been laid to support the corner.

It seems highly significant that the churchyard wall on the north-east side of the church was aligned on the east end of this building. It seems likely from this that the building pre-dates this section of churchyard wall and that it probably stood as an isolated structure about 50 ft. from the south-east corner of the church itself. Its high floor-level suggests that it was medieval, or later, but no finds were recovered from it. The ground-level inside the churchyard is still some two feet higher, as often elsewhere, than the surrounding ground outside on the east side.

(B) THE BATH HOUSE

The complete outline of a heavily robbed Roman masonry building was found running parallel to the central *Via Principalis* and only about 20 ft. north of its centre-line. It also lay roughly midway from the *Intervallum* Road on the east side and the conjectured *Via Praetoria* to the west. It consisted of seven rooms, all hypocausted, including three apsidal baths along the south side. It can be identified as a small Bath House built, unusually, inside the Roman fort (see Discussion p. 222). The suggestion (Ref. 84) that part of this structure could have been reconstructed to form a bapistry attached to the adjacent church, is attractive but totally unsupported by any evidence from the excavations.

Its overall length, running east-west, was 39 ft. and its width was 21 ft. 6 in. including the apses. The building clearly sat within a marginally larger excavation for part of its foundation-trench, about 6–9 in. wide, was found along the north side. The vertical cuts for its east side and part of its south side were also found. The walls subsequently survived on the south, west and part of the north sides mostly some 5–7 courses high. These were constructed of sandstone blocks, both roughly squared and rounded boulders, with a double course of bricks, mostly *tegulae*, sandwiched between them. The longer lateral walls were 24–28 in. in width whilst the shorter end (west) wall was only 24 in. suggesting that the side walls took the thrust from the roof in the normal way.

The internal room sizes are given below:-

	East-West	North-South	*Pilae*
Room 1	10 ft.	9 ft. 4 in.	30
Room 2	9 ft. 6 in.	9 ft. 7 in.	30
Room 3	7 ft. 8 in.	9 ft. 0 in. (estimated)	12
Room 4 – W Apse	9 ft. 6 in.	7 ft. 4 in.	24
Room 5 – C Apse	10 ft. 1 in.	7 ft. 2 in.	24
Room 6 – E Apse	7 ft. 6 in.	7 ft. 0 in. (estimated)	20
Room 7	2 ft. 6 in.	8 ft. 3 in.	10

From these it seems clear that the internal width was divided into two unequal parts, the three larger rooms on the north side being mainly square, whilst the three on the south side were not. A possible seventh room probably had a specialised function.

It is clear that the building had been constructed about 2 ft. below contemporary ground-level so that the hypocausts would fit neatly below normal floor-level. This also helped retain the heat within what was effectively a sub-basement. The stoke-hole had been at the east end, but this was heavily robbed. The system had a main east-west flue channel running up the centres of Rooms 1, 2 and 3. This was mostly 12–15 in. wide and it passed through the walls dividing the rooms, almost certainly under a curved or corbelled arch about 2 ft. high, though only the bases of tiled piers survived. The heat from the stoke-hole passed along the central channel and then circulated in all directions through a series of narrow channels, created by isolated stacks of *pilae* tiles in each room. The *pilae* continued into Rooms 4, 5 and 6 so that the heat reached every part of the building.

Room 1

Room 1 originally had 30 *pilae* (6 rows of 5) of which seven survived, mostly only 1–2 tiles high, all 11 in. square. The mortar pads marking the bottom of the robbed *pilae* were clear in the other 23 cases. Only in the extreme north-west corner did one *pila* survive three courses high and here the third tile was about $7\frac{1}{2}$ in. square, whilst at least two others showed imprints of the same size. The central flue opening, linking with Room 2, was 23 in. wide and the pier-bases each side about 25 x 19 in. These were flanked by smaller openings 15–17 in. wide, thus leaving the two attached end-responds at 10 in. each. This arrangement provided three openings, all originally arched, between the two rooms. The *pilae* in Room 1 were clearly aligned on these openings so that there were two rows of ten closely spaced *pilae* each side of the central flue, whilst the outer two rows of *pilae* filled the remaining space.

Room 2

It seems that the corresponding Room 2 had also been provided with 30 *pilae,* though only four remained in part, with the other 26 being revealed as mortar pads. Unlike Room 1, all 30 had been based on complete *tegulae* tiles, aligned east-west and measuring 15 x 10 in. Only in one place did five courses of tile survive and here the lower two were *tegulae* and the upper three *pilae* tiles about $7\frac{1}{2}$ in square. The openings in the wall joining it with Room 3 were largely similar to those linking with Room 1, though partly damaged by robbing.

Room 3

The masonry of this smaller room was almost totally robbed out, but the bases of three *pilae* survived as did the imprints of three others. It seems likely that the original pattern was of four rows of three *pilae,* 12 in all. One *pila* survived two tiles high and this matched the arrangement in Room 1.

Room 4   (Plate XXV)

This was the most complete room surviving in the Bath House and this could reflect the fact that it was largely buried beneath the medieval masonry building. The walls of the apse survived intact to a maximum height of about 3 ft. 4 in. (10 courses) above the foundations externally and at least seven courses internally. All the sandstone courses were 4–5 in. high and there were two layers of tile at the third and fourth courses from the base. A drain-hole was revealed near the base of the wall.

The original apse had contained a pillared hypocaust and the first line of *pilae*, four in line with the responds, survived two courses high. As in Room 1 these were all 11 in. square. The only other *pilae* visible were parts of two more stacks flanking the responds and part of the second row, which survived eight courses high (about 18 in.). Beyond these the hypocaust had been filled with mortared stone blocks and rubble when a later cold-bath had been inserted. It seems likely that the hypocaust here had originally contained about 24 *pilae* to match the arrangement in the identical Room 5.

The original apse (Phase A) was lined internally with a thin layer of *opus signinum* plaster and it seems likely that this was the side of a bath occupying the whole apse area as far as the side responds. If so, it would have been 9 ft. 9 in. x 5 ft. 4 in. and D-shaped in plan, probably with a deep step between the responds to separate it from Room 1. Clearly, the original floor had been destroyed when the later alterations were carried out, but the survival of parts of at least two rows of *pilae* shows that it was originally heated.

Subsequently, (Phase B) the hypocaust was partially destroyed and infilled with sandstone blocks, tile fragments and layers of *opus signinum*. Little if any soil was included. All sides of the original apsidal bath were then blocked-in with an 18 in. wide wall of mortared sandstone blocks and tiles to create a smaller sub-rectangular cold-bath some 6 ft. 1 in. x 5 ft. 4 in. This was given its own rendering of red *opus signinum,* of which only patches survived. The new floor, only about ½ in. thick, was also of *opus signinum.* It used the same drain outlet as in Phase A.

Later still (Phase C), the south side of the inserted cold bath was blocked in with a tiled step, about 16 in. wide and 11 in. high. It was built of sandstone blocks and tiles, this time set in a sandy grey-white mortar. This reduced the bath to about 6 ft. x 3 ft. 11 in. and produced a six-sided plan. Again it was rendered with *opus signinum* on its face and provided with a similar floor only ½ in. thick. The floor-wall joint was sealed by a quarter-round moulding about 2 in. x 2 in. A new drain-hole was constructed within the inserted south step and this cut through the two earlier floors.

Room 5

The walls and responds of this room only survived mostly two courses high and in one place up to four courses. It matched the apse in Room 4 and formed an integral part of it. No *pila* remained *in situ*, but the mortar pads of 13 survived and the sockets of another seven were detected. In all it seems that about 24 would have been required to support the floor adequately. All appear to have been standard *pilae* tiles about 11 in. square. The suspended floor must have supported a heated bath (since robbed), probably the same size as the apsidal bath in Room 4. A coin (Coin 65–2) of Julia Mamaea (A.D. 222–35) appeared to come from the wall of this room.

Room 6

Only the outline of about half of this apsidal room had survived extensive robbing, but what remained showed it to be an integral part of the original structure. Apart from its smaller size it was otherwise similar to Rooms 4 and 5. Its *hypocaust* had been totally robbed out, but a pattern of

15 *pilae* was faintly indicated. These must have supported a suspended floor which in turn held a shallow heated bath, probably the full size of the apse, much as surviving in Room 4.

Room 7

This small room was squeezed between the east wall of Room 3 and what is taken to be the end wall of the Bath House. It appears to straddle the central flue channel at a point where the heat would have been the most severe. Its floor had been clearly suspended, for the remains of two *pilae* survive and the imprint of two more, in *opus signinum,* were located. It is likely that this narrow room held a large tank of water which, when heated, supplied hot water through pipes to the baths in the apses on the south side. No trace of any tank or pipes had survived.

The Stoke-Hole

It seems certain that the whole hypocaust system was supplied by heat from the east end for it was only here that evidence of a stoke-hole was found. The central flue channel serving Rooms 1–3 and 7 all originated at the east end where the channel was worn into the underlying clay and filled with ash and carbonised wood. This led into a rectangular area, about 11 x 7 ft., which had traces of a robbed-out mortar floor. No other details seem to have survived. This is here regarded as the original stoke-hole, which clearly cut through the earlier pebble foundations.

The stratification within the Bath House largely consisted of rubble and soil (L.20) representing the final demolition of the structure. This was generally 2–3 ft. deep and effectively sealed the ruins of the building. It also sealed a thin layer of black charcoal (L. 10) that was found over the base of the hypocausts, which represented the residue from the fires heating the system. The demolition had been fairly thorough with the whole structure above ground having been removed and half the walls beneath the ground, almost all the floors and almost all the *pilae*. The debris contained 548 fragments of painted wall-plaster (Group B, Fig. 67). Over 200 of these consisted of a thick layer of *opus signinum* plaster, badly stained, but painted with tones of black and orange-yellow. Many fragments had a secondary layer of *opus signinum* attached to them and mostly had a backing of white, overpainted with double medallions in red (Nos. 463–4), or a backing of yellow with a double medallion painted in black (Nos. 465–6). the former seems to have enclosed a floral design. Other fragments have been painted varying colours and tentatively suggest both curved and linear (No. 467) patterns. One fragment seems to show part of a column base (No. 471). Some of the secondary painted plaster exhibited deep chisel cuts, clearly intended to provide a keying for a third layer. Only seven fragments had a third layer intact and this was painted in white, red and orange. It seems probable that the Bath House, in all or in part, had been replastered at least twice during its period of use. Significantly, or not, the apsidal bath in Room 4 had also undergone two structural changes. Just possibly these changes coincided with the replastering of the Bath House itself.

Of special interest were many fragments of box-flue tiles, none complete, which had carried the hot air up inside the walls from the underfloor hypocaust in the normal way. At least two types seem to be represented (Nos. 475–78) including fragments with marginally tapered sides and these are clearly hollow voissoirs, which must represent a vaulted roof, or roofs, within the Bath House. It is possible that all the rooms and baths were vaulted. A total of 22 coins was found in association with the Bath House and Officers Quarters (see Table H). The general soil deposits on this site produced comparatively little pottery, but included twelve sherds of samian ware (No. 206), Forms 27, 31(3), 37, 43 and 45, mostly of Antonine – early 3rd century date.

As regards the hypocausts, it seems clear that the seven rooms together originally had a total of about 160 *pilae*. Each of these must have contained about 15 tiles (about 2 ft. high), hence about 2500 *pila* tiles would have been needed to complete the system. Each column of *pilae* would have

Context	Coin Nos. 1965	Emperor	Date	Exc. Code
Bath House				
Wall of Apse Room 5	2	Julia Mamaea	222–35	
Rubble to South	8	Tetricus I	270–3	4
Soil by Drain	9	Constantius II	345–8	33
	10	House of Constantine	350–60	33
	11	Constans	345–8	33
	12	Magnentius	350–3	33
Silt by Drain (under L.33)	15	Magnentius	350–3	48
	18	Constantine I	310–17	48
	19	Allectus	293–6	48
	20	Claudius II	268–70	48
Between Roads	17	Carausius	286–93	59
Officers Quarters				
On floor Room C	22	Septimius Severus	193–211	67
Rubble over robbed hypocaust (Room A)	3	Constantine I	310–17	16
	4	Gallienus	260–8	16
	6	Illegible	3–4C	16
	7	Severus Alexander	222–35	16
	13	Theodosius I	388–95	16
	14	Carausius	286–93	16
Unstratified	1	Radiate	270–90	1
	5	Radiate	260–90	24
	16	House of Constantine	350–60	2
	21	Carausius	286–93	10

Table H. Coins from the Bath House and Officers Quarters (1965)

been capped with bridging tiles, normally 22 in. square, of which only small fragments werefound. About 200 would have been needed to cap all the *pilae* and in turn they would have supported a concrete floor, probably of *opus signinum,* none of which survived.

An examination of the surviving *pilae* in Rooms 1–4, shows that these were not evenly spread across the rooms. In Rooms 1 and 2, two rows of *pilae* on each side of the central channel were closely spaced, whereas those on the outside were more widely spaced. Six complete bridging tiles would have fitted neatly along both rooms (east-west) whereas six more spread across the rooms are not large enough. They cannot individually bridge the central channel and a narrow gap, perhaps 2–5 in. wide, would be left at the centre. It seems certain, therefore, that the central channel had a small corbelled arch along it with one or more additional tiles bridging the gap. The same corbelled arrangements exist in the hypocausts in the Roman Painted House at Dover (Ref. 30), now on view to the public.

(C) *VIA PRINCIPALIS* (Fig. 25)

A single trench (Box 7), dug north-south on the south side of the Bath House, picked up two layers of pebble metalling. In character they certainly matched metalled roads elsewhere inside the fort and by their position it seems certain that they represent part of the major east-west *Via Principalis*. The upper metalling was traced for 8 ft. and found to be about 3 in. in thickness. Beneath this was a mottled soil with pebbles (L. 59), about 4–6 in. thick, which contained a coin (No. 65–17) of Carausius (A.D. 286–93). This in turn sealed the lower metalling, traced for a maximum of 15 ft., which was of a similar thickness to the upper metalling.

(D) THE DRAIN

A substantial stone-capped drain was found running east-west for 30 ft. just outside the apsidal baths of the Bath House. This was not examined in detail and it was only sectioned in one place. There it was about 9 in. wide and 16 in. deep. Its upper sides were of mortared stone and its base flat. It was capped by several very large flat stone blocks, mostly 2–3 ft. in length, only one of which was lifted. The drain appeared to flow eastwards and it seems certain that its main purpose was to take waste water from the three adjacent baths all only 2 ft. to the north. No connecting pipes had survived. The drain probably joined the ditch found 45 ft. to the east in 1969, which seems to have taken the waste water towards the East Gate. The soil deposits nearby (L. 33 and 48), probably representing the progressive build-up of levels outside the Bath House, contained eight coins dating from A.D. 268–360 and a mortarium (No. 203).

(E) THE EARLIER NORTH BUILDING

One small area of pebble foundations was located, at the north-east corner of the Bath House. This was traced for at least 10 ft., running north-south (in Box 12), before its southern end had been removed by the excavation for the hypocaust-system of the Bath House. It was 2 ft. 8 in. wide, about 15 in. deep and consisted of water-rolled pebbles. It seems clear that this formed part of an earlier structure, extending under the adjacent Officers Quarters and relating to the fort-construction period, as found at several other locations inside the fort.

(F) THE POSSIBLE COURTYARD

The large area north of the Bath House and east of the Officers Quarters was briefly examined by small three trenches (Boxes 15, 16 and 20). No structures or features were located, though the area had been extensively disturbed in recent times. If this area contained no Roman structures, then a Courtyard, flanked by the two known large masonry buildings (the Bath House and Officers Quarters), may be implied. If so, large buildings may also have flanked the remaining west and north sides now very largely removed by sea erosion.

No. 11 THE OFFICERS QUARTERS SITE (Fig. 26)

Parts of another substantial Roman masonry building were gradually revealed, also in 1965, in a series of seven trenches (Boxes 8–10, 12–13 and 18–19) immediately north-east of the Bath House. It was set at right-angles to the Bath House and its west wall seemed to line up on the latter's east wall. The space between them was only about 8 ft. Part of the same structure was also located in the cliff-face in 1965–6. The precise shape and overall size of this large building are difficult to determine from the limited area excavated. However, with the southern and eastern limits clearly defined and the northern one suggested by a metalled east-west road found in the cliff-face in 1965, a rectangular structure about 60 x 45 ft. overall seems likely. This could have formed the eastern side of a notional, rectangular courtyard, with the Bath House on its south side and other possible buildings on the other two sides, now largely in the sea. The principal room seems to have been at the centre of the east side where it contained a wide, shallow apse. At least five rooms (**Rooms A–E**) were identified in outline, three with hypocausts and a sixth room can be conjectured (**Room F**). These are listed with the estimated internal dimensions below. Other rooms, or sub-divisions, could have existed and this building remains substantially unexcavated.

	East-West	North-South	Pilae
Room A	20 ft.	18 ft. (into apse) with hypocaust	120
Room B	13 ft.	16 ft. with hypocaust	96
Room C	18 ft.	16 ft. with concrete floor	–
Room D	18 ft.	18 ft.	–
Room E	13 ft.	16 ft. (?) with hypocaust	96
Room F	18 ft.	16 ft. (?) destroyed by sea erosion	–

Room A

This appears to have been the largest room in the building and to have occupied the centre of its east side. Uniquely, in this building it had a wide, shallow apse nearly the full width of the room. Details of all four walls and part of its internal arrangements were found in two trenches (Boxes 8 and 19).

Its west wall, some 2 ft. 2 in. wide, had been heavily robbed, but traces of two courses of sandstone blocks bonded in a pale green mortar over a foundation of small pebbles survived. The north-east and south-east corners of the room were also located, with each being marked by a rectangular respond about 26 x 9 in, The space between the responds was about 17 ft. and this suggests the presence of a high arch across the opening into the apse. It is possible that this opening was sub-divided as most of its length was not excavated. The apse itself was about 18 ft. internally in north-south length, but only about 5–6 ft. in east-west width. Its curving wall was 2 ft. 4 in. thick and it had been built of sandstone blocks set in a pale green mortar with white specks, though it had been substantially robbed.

The room had contained a substantial hypocaust which extended into the apse. This had been built on a base of pebbles, some 4 in. thick, which in turn rested on a layer of white mortar. Traces of 12 lines of *pilae,* all running east-west, were detected and four of these lay within the apse. Several were simply imprints in the floor, but others consisted of a single *tegula,* some with a single square tile (mostly 7½ in. sq.) on top. This was also the method employed in the adjacent Bath House.

The surviving traces of the hypocaust could not be examined in detail, owing to the limited nature of the trenching. In Box 8, however, the imprints of the *pilae* suggest a symmetrical arrangement in the main part of the room excluding the apsidal element. Here eight bases were located and these were in two matching groups of four. A single base flanked the side walls and after a space of 10–12 in. there was a group of three bases, closely spaced. This left a space 14 in. wide between the two groups, which marked the centre of the room. It seems likely that this

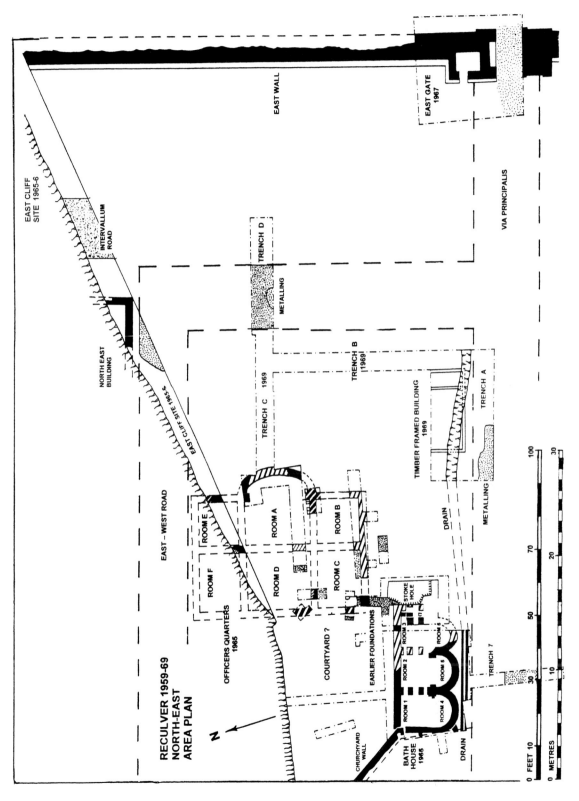

Fig. 26. Reculver 1964–9. Plan of North–East Area.

central channel marks the line of the main flue and suggests an opening in the south wall linking it with a similar arrangement in Room B. The rubble layer over the robbed hypocaust produced six coins (Coin Nos. 3, 4, 6, 7, 13, 14), dating from A.D. 222–395 (see Table H.). Allowing for an even spread of *pilae* across the room, with centres at about 1 ft. 7 in., some ten rows can be fitted between the north and south walls. If correct, then 120 *pilae* could have been contained in Room A. Eight fragments of wall-plaster painted green, pink, red and white were found in the debris and may indicate how Room A was decorated.

Room B

This was revealed in two trenches (Boxes 9 and 19), where parts of the lines of all four walls were found. All had been robbed out, but the room appears to be about 16 ft. by 13 ft. 3 in. The robber-trenches were 26–29 in. wide, they contained traces of pale green mortar and evidence of foundation pebbles. The mortared floor supported a pillared hypocaust, running north-south, of which traces of seven *pilae* survived. Originally there had been a total of eight across the room, of which six survived only as mortared pads and only one intact. All were based on large *tegulae* (11 x 15 in.) with the one surviving supporting a smaller *pila* tile ($7\frac{1}{2}$ x $7\frac{1}{2}$ in.). As in Room A the hypocaust system had a central channel, here 18 in. wide, with three closely spaced *pilae* on each side. The central channel almost certainly connected with that in Room A by means of an arched opening in the north wall dividing the two rooms. It is not clear from which end the hypocaust system was fed and the stoke-hole could have been on either the north or south sides of the building. Allowing for an even spread of *pilae*, with centres about 1 ft. 3 in., twelve north-south rows seem to be indicated. If so, then a total of 96 *pilae* seems likely for this room. A large amount of crumbled *opus signinum* was found on the floor and small amounts of painted wall-plaster came from the robber-trenches. The plaster included 19 fragments of red, white, black and brown, including possible panels (No. 473).

Room C

This was picked up in three trenches (Boxes 9, 12 and 13) when parts of all four walls were located. These had been partly robbed, but where one survived on the south side it was 2 ft. 2 in. wide and built of sandstone blocks set in yellow clay. The floor was made of hard white mortar and pebbles, about 3 in. thick. Where the wall joined the floor on the north side there was a moulding, or fillet, of *opus signinum* about 5 in. wide. In parts the floor was sealed by a layer of orange clay and plaster up to 6 in. in thickness (L.67). In addition, a coin (Coin No. 65–22) of Septimius Severus (A.D. 193–211) was found just above the floor.

Room D

This was revealed in two small trenches (Boxes 13 and 18) and also at the end of a longer trench (Box 8). The west wall had been almost totally destroyed by a World War II pit and only a few sandstone blocks set in clay survived. Traces of what appeared to be a pebble foundation were also noted. The south wall had also been substantially destroyed by another military pit, but again the remnant left was built of sandstone blocks set in clay.

The east wall had also been robbed, but what survived was about 2 ft. 2 in. wide and consisted of sandstone blocks over small beach pebbles, the latter serving as a foundation. The mortar here was pale green in colour. Another foundation of small pebbles, about 3 in. thick and at least 2 ft. 1 in. wide, was found at the west end of Box 8 and was sealed by a thick layer of clay. This seems to represent another earlier foundation on a north-south axis.

Room E

This room was only seen on the cliff-face early in 1965 (p. 66) when only two large wall-stubs were found, the rest of the room having been destroyed by sea erosion. It seems certain that this formed part of the larger building found later in 1965 and that it contained traces of a hypocaust. If so, it seems likely it matched Room B and thus could have contained another 96 *pilae*. Another 19 fragments of wall-plaster in white, red, yellow, maroon and pink were also found, some again suggesting bands or panels (No. 474).

Room F

This room had been totally destroyed by sea erosion and its outline is conjectural. It has been reconstructed on the assumption that the overall building was rectangular and that Room F largely matched Room C.

It is difficult to be certain about the precise form and function of this large building, but it had three heated rooms along its east side and was clearly a high status building. Room A, at the centre of the east side, was clearly the principal room with its wide apse. This resembles an extended dining room familiar on some non-military sites. The building's position adjacent to the small internal Bath House may also be significant. Taken with the hypocausts in three rooms, these factors tend to suggest this had a major domestic function. If so, it can be tentatively identified as the Officers Quarters, or just possibly the Commandant's House.

It should be noted that the walls in the three heated eastern rooms (Rooms A, B and E) were constructed of sandstone blocks set in a pale green mortar. The three western rooms (Rooms C, D and F) seem to have sandstone block walls bonded in clay. This distinction could indicate different periods of construction, but it might also reflect the difference between heated and unheated rooms. The critical wall-junctions were mostly not examined and it is even possible that the superstructure of the three western rooms was timber-framed. The heated rooms at least, are likely to have been taken up to their full height in masonry.

It is estimated that the three heated rooms may have contained a total of about 310 *pilae,* thus incorporating some 3,000–4,000 individual tiles. The *pilae* may have been capped by large bridging tiles, but the narrow spacing of the *pilae* suggests that it is more likely that the floor was supported on corbelled tiled arches. The site of a large stoke-hole, which must have served the extensive hypocaust, is not known but is more likely to have been on the (missing) north side.

No attempt was made to fully excavate this important building, with the work confined just to establish the overall form and layout. Whilst about a quarter of this building has been destroyed by sea-erosion and the remaining walls severely robbed, enough evidence should still remain for a complete examination of its structural detail, internal stratification and also what lies buried beneath it.

THE EARLIER NORTH BUILDING

The south wall of Room C crossed an earlier foundation of flint pebbles, 2 ft. 8 in. wide and running on a north-south axis. These were 5 in. deep and set in clay with a single large sandstone block resting on them. The foundation must represent part of the earlier structure which was also cut by the stoke-hole of the Bath House several feet to the south. In all, it was traced for about 12 ft., but is likely to have extended to both north and south. A short length of an east-west foundation, forming an integral part of the same underlying structure, was found running westwards and is likely to represent an internal wall and thus at least two rooms. Another small patch of flint pebbles was found under Room D and is likely to relate to this earlier foundation. If so, a single building (Period I) at least 40 x 20 ft. and pre-dating both the Bath House and the Officers Quarters (both Period II) seems to be implied, though it is unclear if this was ever completed.

No. 12 THE EAST CLIFF SITE (Figs. 26, 31 and Plates XXVII–XXVIII)

The only area of the Roman fort not protected from the effects of sea erosion lay on the north-east side where a section 180 ft. in length rested on a low cliff no more than 20 ft. above the beach. The writer began recording here in 1952 and noted several important structures and features, duly published in 1958 (Ref. 2). When the Reculver Excavation Group began its excavation on the site it gave first priority to this cliff-section, which it recorded 100 ft. from the east wall of the fort in 1957. The results were published in 1959 (Ref. 3). The writer pressed the Ministry of Public Building and Works to protect the exposed cliff and the Group carried out more rescue excavations in March, 1965 and again in March and August, 1966. This work cut back the cliff to a vertical face and straight line 180 ft. in length, but with widths varying from 2 ft. to 13 ft. This section cut the fort wall at an angle of about 65 degrees and thus the drawn section is oblique. This allowed another look at the fort wall, the Rampart Bank, parts of two masonry buildings, two internal roads, three ovens and pre-Roman ditches cut into the natural Thanet Beds. These are described below (A–G). The new sea wall was built in 1967–68, but ironically the storms of 1995 destroyed much of this. From 1999 another sea wall was constructed here and the writer advised, this time for the Canterbury City Council. The cliff sections produced 21 coins (Table I) and small-finds in bronze (Nos. 351, 370, 375), bone (Nos. 231, 236, 239, 288, 346) and glass (No. 399).

(A) THE EAST WALL OF THE FORT

A broken length of the east wall, some 13 ft. in length, survived at the end of the cliff adjacent to the main sea wall rebuilt in 1953–4 to protect the marshland to the east. Only a width of about 7 ft. was left, standing a maximum of eight courses high, including the internal bottom offset some 15–18 in. in width. A second section of wall, about 8 ft. in length, was then part way down the cliff and has since been destroyed. The fort wall was constructed, as elsewhere on the site, of neat courses of rolled flints and Ragstone set in an ample hard white mortar containing small pebbles. No external facing survived on either section.

A continuous layer of corresponding white mortar (L.32), 1–4 in. in thickness, was traced from the back of the fort wall westwards for a distance of 36 ft. and resting directly on the pre-fort soils. This must represent the mortar-mixing layer left by the builders of the fort. Its level was raised over a low mound of soil (S.25, L.10) extending for about 20 ft. from the fort wall and this is likely to represent the soil upcast from the foundation-trench of the wall itself. A single decorated samian sherd (No. 219), a Form 37 of Antonine date, was found in the soil (L.12) beneath the mortar-mixing floor.

(B) THE RAMPART BANK

As noted elsewhere within the fort, the east wall was found to be backed by a very substantial Bank of dumped soils, mostly clays (L.5–7, 27, 29 and 47). This sealed the mortar-mixing layer. It was traced for about 40 ft. from the fort wall, with a levelling extension reaching to a point at about 51 ft. The section cut in 1965 was oblique to the fort wall and the total effective width was only about 40ft. In detail, the rampart consisted of 15–20 layers of dumped soils, the largest being of sterile orange clay at its base. The other layers were slightly inclined over this and consisted of clays, loams and some bands of mussel shells. Some of the upper layers may have been deposited some years after the original bank was formed. Its surviving maximum depth was about 5 ft, but it is likely to have been much higher nearer the fort wall. The Bank contained a coin (No. 66–8) of Marcus Aurelius (A.D. 150–60), samian Forms 30, 31 and 37(3), mortars (Nos. 185 and 195) of late-second or early-third century date, a stamped tile (No. 449), a complete ivory scabbard-chape

(No. 352) and a glass handle (No. 398). A small pit (Pit 5) found in 1957, cut into the tail of the Bank and contained a samian bowl (No. 210) Form 37 of Cinnamus (A.D. 155–75).

Of special interest were two large ovens and two dog skeletons contained within the Bank. A section of a large oven (Oven I), perhaps originally 6 ft. in diameter, was found within the Rampart Bank some 12 ft. from the fort wall, but not reaching the drawn section in 1966. It had a possible opening on its east side and its base consisted of a layer of sandstone blocks and sand. On these there had been a tiled floor set in clay, of which only fragments of about six tiles survived. The remnant of a low wall, built of sandstone blocks in clay survived about 14 in. high only on the south-west side. The floor and wall had been baked hard. The rest of the oven had been destroyed by an army-trench in 1941 and by sea erosion since. Much of the floor of Oven I had been removed and the whole structure then buried by a dump of clay (1966, L.29) forming part of the upper rampart. From this it seems clear that it must have served the builders of the fort during its construction. Into the upper part of the finished Rampart a second oven (Oven II) had been built effectively above the lower one and separated from it by a layer of clay at least 2 ft. thick. Its base consisted of sandstone blocks and pebbles and had an overall length of about 12 ft. It was from the floor of this oven that two tiles, stamped with the letters C IB (No.445), were rescued from the cliff-face in 1960. Much of Oven II had also been destroyed by army-trenches dug in 1941. A thick layer of carbonised wood (L.28) in the Rampart section clearly extended below Oven II yet appeared too high to be the rake-back from Oven I.

In the clay between Ovens I and II was the skeleton of a medium-sized dog (Dog 1), again partly destroyed by the army-trenches. The skeleton of a larger dog (Dog 2) was found on its side within the rampart about 22 ft. from the fort wall and this had been buried whilst the final layers of the Rampart were being laid. The dumped soils over the Rampart Bank and the general late-Roman deposits contained an important group of material. This included about 90 more sherds of samian ware (Nos. 208, 209, 224), of Forms 18(3), Curle 23 (2), 31(10), 32(4), 33(3), 3)/37(3), 3710), 36, 38(2), 43, 45(11), 54, Ludowici (17) and mortaria, though some matching is possible. The plain mortaria included (Nos. 186, 189 and 197), again of late-second or early-third century date and also three coins (Coin Nos. 66–4, 5, 9) all of late-third century date and several small-finds (Nos. 239, 351, 370, 399). A coin of ELAGABALUS (A.D. 219–22) was also found on the Rampart Bank in 1957 (Coin No. 1957–2)

(C) THE *INTERVALLUM* ROAD

A broad layer of small pebbles (L.44), clearly representing a prepared metalled surface, was located in the oblique section 45–65 ft. from the fort wall. Its actual width was about 18 ft. and it lay just 40 ft. from the fort wall. It was 2–8 in. thick and it lay directly on the pre-fort soils and also covered the levelling tail of the Rampart Bank. It lay about 6 ft. below existing ground-level, it had not been resurfaced and there can be little doubt that it represents the *Intervallum* Road as noted elsewhere inside the fort. It was sealed by general occupation soils, which included an illegible coin (No. 65–7) of late-Roman date and ultimately by a high-level oven (Oven III) of probable post-Roman date. A single sherd of samian ware, a Ludowici Sb of early – mid 3rd century date, was found in association with the metalling.

(D) THE NORTH EAST BUILDING

The south-east corner of a substantial masonry building just survived within the narrow strip of cliff excavated, the remainder having been destroyed by erosion. This corner was positioned about 77 ft. along the datum from the fort wall, but just failed to touch the drawn section. It actually lay about 70 ft. from the fort wall and parallel to it. Only 7 ft. of its east wall and 12 ft. of its south wall remained. These were built of large sandstone blocks set in clay, of which three courses survived to a height of about 1 ft. 8 in. The bottom course was constructed with blocks set at 45 degrees with the larger stones used as facing and smaller ones as the core. The walls were mostly 2 ft. 2 in. in thickness. A space of about 12 ft. separated this building from the west edge of the *Intervallum* Road. A coin (No. 1957–1) of Commodus (A.D. 180–93) was found in the foundation-trench and a coin (No. 65–4) of Claudius II (A.D. 268–70) was found on the clay floor of this building. The general soils above the floor produced three more coins (Nos. 65–3, 5 and 6), a barbarous radiate (A.D. 270–90), one of Theodora (A.D. 337–40) and one illegible (3–4 centuries).

(E) THE INTERNAL EAST-WEST ROAD

Only about 2 ft. from the North-East Building was another area of pebble metalling (1965, L.29) that was traced in section from 82 ft. to 102 ft. from the inside of the fort wall. Another small patch, at 114–120 ft., is likely to have been connected. Both were generally only 1–2 in. thick and both rested on the pre-fort soils. This metalling, framed between the North-East building and the Officers Quarters, is considered to be part of an internal road running east-west with a probable width of about 15 ft. This was also sealed by late-Roman soils (L.11 and l2) containing domestic rubbish.

(F) THE OFFICERS QUARTERS

Two similar masonry walls of another building were found projecting from the exposed cliff-face, some 144 ft. and 162 ft. respectively, from the inside face of the fort wall along the oblique section. Less than 5 ft. of each survived and as they were parallel to each other it seems likely that they had been joined by a north wall, now lost to sea erosion. Indeed, later work immediately to the south, strongly suggested that these walls formed part of the Officers Quarters (p. 62) situated between the cliff and the Roman Bath House. If so, then these walls formed part of Room E. Both walls had been built of sandstone blocks held in a creamy white mortar of which a maximum of six courses survived. The foundations had been cut deeply into the underlying soils and included a band of pebbles. The actual walls were 2 ft. 2 in. wide and 13 ft. apart internally. Although partly robbed, the internal area contained traces of a tiled surface, bands of orange clay and charcoal and some wall-plaster. It seems likely that this room had contained an hypocaust. The adjacent metalled road probably flanked the north side of this building. The east wall actually lay about 127 ft. from the inside face of the fort wall.

(G) THE PREHISTORIC DITCHES

As the cliff section was still subject to sea erosion an extra two weeks were later spent in removing the pre-fort soils to expose the underlying natural Thanet Beds. This work revealed that much of the 180 ft. long section was occupied by a series of at least twelve shallow ditches (Ditches 1–12). These were mostly 2–6 ft. wide and 1–3 ft. deep and variously aligned. All had silted progressively and most contained prehistoric pottery. The ditches occupied about 40% of the excavated area. From this evidence it seems clear that this particular area of the overall site was very extensively used in prehistoric times and must represent part of an extensive settlement site.

   The pottery has been provisionally dated and suggests that some of the ditches date from the Late Bronze Age/Early Iron Age and one to the end of the Iron Age. The latter was later seen to be a continuation of the east ditch of the early Roman Fortlet. The pottery from its upper fill again dated to the mid-first century (Nos. 169–73). Of special interest here was the discovery by the writer in 1953 of the base of a small pit (Pit A), exposed by sea erosion and long-since destroyed, cut into the Thanet Beds. It was about 22 in. by 15 in. and lined with a band of green clay. It contained large fragments of two Late Bronze Age/Early Iron Age pottery vessels. This was at a point about 75 ft. from the fort wall. Again, in 1957, at a point about 92 ft. from the fort wall was another shallow pit, about 4 ft. wide and this contained three spinal discs of a large whale and more Late Bronze Age pottery.

Context	Coin Nos.	Emperor	Date	Exc. Code
Floor of East Building	65–4	Claudius II	268–70	65–18
Soil on Road	65–7	Illegible	3–4C	65–20
Upper Soils – East Building	65–3	Theodora	337–40	65–17
	65–5	Barbarous Radiate	270–90	65–16
	65–6	House of Constantine	350–60	65–16
Unstratified & Other Deposits	65–1	Severus Alexander	222–235	65–3
	65–2	Severus Alexander	222–235	65–1
In Rampart Bank	66–8	Marcus Aurelius	150–60	66–8
Soil over Rampart Bank	66–7	Illegible	3–4C	66–30
	66–4	Gordianus III	238–44	66–2
	66–5	Claudius II	268–70	66–2
	66–9	Victorinus	268–70	66–2
				–
Unstratified	66–1	Faustina	150–180	66–1
	66–2	Barbarous Radiate	270–90	66–1
	66–3	Claudius II	268–70	66–1
	66–6	Illegible	3–4C	66–1
	66–10	Vespasian	69–79	66–1
	66–12	Constans	345–8	66–1
	66–11	Token	16C	66–1

Table I. Coins from the East Cliff Area (1965–6 only)

No. 13 THE NORTH-EAST AREA (Figs. 26 – 28 and Plate XXIX)

The little known area of the fort, north-east of the Bath House, was examined in 1969 when a small rectangular area (Trench-A) and three long trenches (Trenches B–D) were excavated. All four trenches were joined physically and provided both a detailed look at a small area and a useful evaluation of a wider zone. A total area of about 1580 sq. ft. was substantially, but not completely, excavated. Parts of two metalled roads, the south end of a timber-framed building, part of the mid-first century Fortlet and several other features were located and are described below (**A–E**). Several minor features, mostly recent small pits, were also revealed, but are not described here as they probably form part of a much wider spread beyond the limits of the excavation.

(A) THE LATE-ROMAN DRAIN

The first feature revealed during the excavation of Trench A was a shallow gully, running the full east-west length of the excavation. Its minimum length was thus 40 ft., its width about 3 ft. 6 in. and its original depth only about 18 in. It was broadly U-shaped in profile and contained no trace of built structural elements. It cut through the earlier Timber Framed Building and also into the upper filling of the mid-first century Fortlet Ditches.

It had gradually silted with green-grey loam, with the lower 8 in. containing a small amount of domestic debris, two coins (Coin Nos. 22 and 31) and pottery (Nos. 100–3). The upper 10 in. of filling produced another 11 coins (Coin Nos. 3, 12, 13, 16, 17, 18, 21, 25–28) and pottery (Nos. 86–99). All the coins date from about A.D. 270–300, but ten are illegible and the others include one each of Claudius II (A.D. 268–70), one barbarous radiate (A.D. 270–90) and one of Allectus (A.D. 293–6). This suggests that the gully was silting up during the latter part of the third century. Such a long gully must have had a specific function within this large fort and indeed it roughly aligns on the large stone-lined drain to the west which was constructed just outside the Bath House. This took the water from the three apsidal baths on the south side of that structure and certainly some continuation of the drain must have existed on the east side. No trace of any other large drain was detected in either Trenches A or B and it seems clear that this gully was the unlined continuation of the Bath House drain. Its fall was certainly eastwards in the direction of the East Gate, the only known gap in the fort wall on this side.

(B) THE TIMBER FRAMED BUILDING (No. 4 on Period I fort plan, Figs. 27 and 28 and Plate XXX)

The southern end of a large timber-framed building was revealed in Trench A and this clearly extended northwards. It did not appear to exist in Trench C, situated some 50 ft. to the north, so it seems likely that its north end lies somewhere between the two trenches. Its main axis was north-south and thus largely parallel to the east wall of the fort. Its full width was about 25 ft. and this was divided by one internal wall, thus creating a large room with a passageway on its east side. The room measured about 20 ft. and the passageway about 5 ft. in width, respectively. Only about 11 ft. of this north-south length lay within Trench A.

In detail, the outline of the building was revealed by four long, narrow gullies mostly 8–13 in. wide and about 10–24 in. deep. On cleaning these revealed a series of circular outlines containing dark soil, which represented decayed posts. Six large ones (10–12 in. in diameter) formed the south wall, mostly spaced at intervals of about 6 ft. Another 20 posts, mostly 3–5 in. in diameter, were found along the east, centre and west sides and these were mostly 3–6 in. in diameter and about 13–19 in. apart (centres). One or two others may have been removed by cut-features of later date.

It seems likely that the posts had been placed into the bottoms of the gullies and soil compacted around them and almost certainly using the same soil that had been removed. The posts are likely to have continued above ground-level to support an horizontal wall-plate, upon which would have rested the walls and floors of the main structure. No masonry fragments, mortar or tiles, were found in association. Timber-framed buildings of this type are known on other Roman military sites, with the nearest example at Richborough. There, similar gullies contain posts (or piles) identified as supports for granaries with raised floors, but in use during the first century A.D.

The date of the construction of this building is difficult to determine, due to an almost total lack of directly associated artefacts. So far it is the only known building of its type inside the fort, though others could have existed or been missed by the narrow evaluation trenches. It lay over the mid-first century ditches, which had completely silted by the time the timber-framed building was constructed. It was clearly cut through by the late-Roman drain in the third century and it seems that it was never replaced by a masonry building. A single sherd of late-second century samian from one of the post-sockets suggests that it could date from the fort-construction period. Its unusual character at Reculver could suggest a temporary building, but it resembles the early granaries at Richborough and could have provided for the cohort employed in building the fort.

The underlying natural Thanet Beds here were again capped by the pre-fort soils (L. 6 and L.75), generally 6–12 in. in thickness. These mostly cover the various isolated prehistoric features scattered about the site and here also equated with the silt filling of the mid-first century ditches. In Trench C the surface of this layer produced a coin (Coin No. 47) of Severus Alexander (A.D. 222–35) which may have related to the early occupation of the fort.

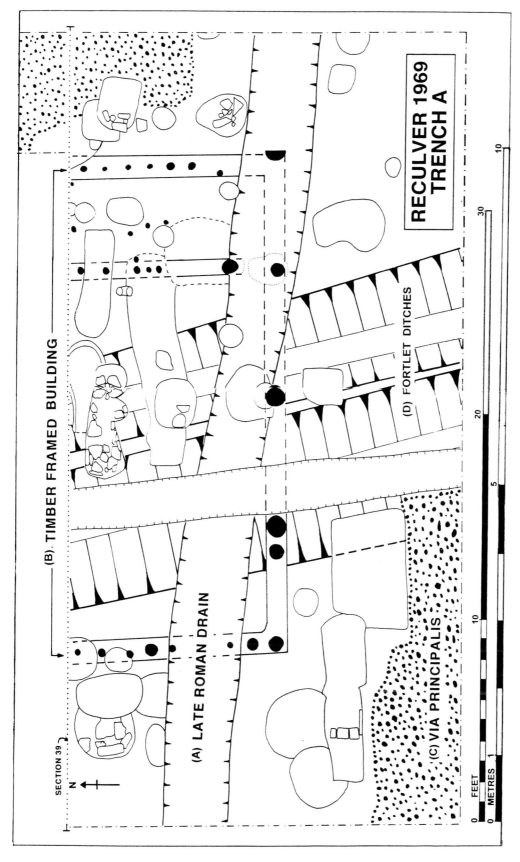

Fig. 27. *Reculver 1969. Plan of Trench A showing Timber Framed Building.*

The main soils in the four trenches, mostly black loams containing numerous fragments of tile, pottery and building materials, represent the extensive Roman occupation of the fort. These can be divided into upper and lower zones, together mostly up to 20 in. in thickness on the west side of this area and up to a maximum of 30 in. at its downhill, eastern edge. The lower black loam produced six coins (Nos. 69–2, 4, 6, 8–10) of late-third and early-fourth century date. The upper black loam contained 17 coins (Nos. 69–5, 19, 29, 32–35, 39, 42–45, 49–53) of late-third to late-fourth century date. The unstratified deposits and minor features contained another 11 coins (Nos. 69– 7, 11, 14, 23, 24, 30, 36, 37, 46, 48, 55) mostly of late-third and fourth century date (see Table J) and mortaria (TS 28 and 31). The pottery from this area included only about 25 sherds of samian ware (Nos. 215, 216 and Stamp No.16), including Forms 18, 31(2), 32, 33(2), 37(2), 38, 45 (2) and Ludowici forms (6), mostly of Antonine – lst half 3rd century date.

(C) THE *VIA PRINCIPALIS*

In the south-west corner of Trench A was a localised area of pebble metalling about 16 ft. in east-west length and at least 5 ft. in width. This lay at a depth of about 2 ft. 4 in. from the present surface, but was not examined in detail. It was cut by various later pits. The metalling closely resembles the several roads found inside the Roman fort and it seems likely that this was an isolated patch which has survived. From its position along the central east-west axis of the fort it seems very likely that this represents the north edge of the *Via Principalis*. Significantly, perhaps, the Late Roman Drain runs roughly parallel to this metalling and at about 8 ft. from its surviving northern edge.

(D) THE MID-FIRST CENTURY FORTLET

One reason for opening up Trench A, an area previously occupied by the old Coastguard Cottages, was to locate the continuation of a pair of parallel ditches found just to the south in 1968. These had also been traced earlier across the east and south areas of the fort. Trench A duly located the ditches, which were also just visible in Trench C about 50 ft. further north. The two ditches occupied a combined width of about 12 ft. and seem to be the earliest feature on this part of the site. They are described below (p. 192). Their filling of brown loam was later cut by the beam-slots of the Timber Framed Building and later still by the Late Roman Drain serving the Bath House.

(E) THE METALLED AREA (Fig. 26)

A broad band of compact pebbles, 19 ft. 4 in. wide and on a north-south axis, was found at the centre of Trench D. This covered the full width of the trench here 7 ft. and clearly extended beyond on both sides. The pebbles had a maximum thickness of 1 ft. 4 in. and were in two distinct layers, the upper set in black loam and the lower in yellow-brown loam (L.60 and L.76).

The southern part of this metalling had subsided into a very large, steep sided pit that was 14 ft. wide, but splayed wider at the top to about 17 ft. 6 in. This pit was not examined in detail, but it was filled with yellow sandy loam with some sandstone blocks (L.77) and was at least 4 ft. deep. No attempt was made to reach the bottom and it gave the appearance of being very much deeper than this. A late-Roman pit (L.73), about 6 ft. 4 in. wide, appeared to cut the metalling, but it is possible that this reflects a major slump at the centre of the underlying pit.

Metalling of this type at Reculver mostly reflects linear roads and on the strength of this single trench it may tentatively be identified as the *Intervallum* Road running on the east side of the fort. Its position, however, at about 60–80 ft. from the inside of the fort wall seems largely appropriate, it is equally possible that this area of metalling was simply put down to consolidate the top of the very large pit which exactly underlies it. The large pit is unusual at Reculver and it may represent some sort of small quarry, or even a large collapsed well. It was clearly filled in before the metalling was laid over it.

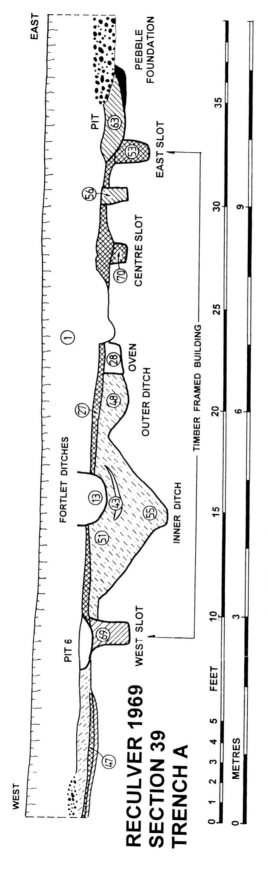

Fig. 28. *Reculver 1969. Section 39 across Timber Framed Building.*

Context	Coin Nos. 1969	Emperor	Date	Exc. Code
Late Roman Drain				
	3	Illegible	3–4C	10
	12, 17, 21, 25, 26, 27, 28	Illegible	3–4C	8
	13	Claudius II	268–70	8
	16	Allectus	293–6	8
	18	Barbarous Radiate	270–90	8
	22, 31	Illegible	3–4C	12
Lower Black Loam				
	4	Claudius II	268–70	5
	6	Constantine I	335–7	5
	8	House of Constantine	310–7	5
	9	Constantinopolis	330–45	5
	2,10	Illegible	3–4C	5
Upper Black Loam				
	29, 32	Barbarous Radiate	270–90	33
	35	Constantine I	320–4	33
	45	Constantius II	355–61	33
	34	Valentinian I	364–75	33
	39, 43	Valens	364–78	33
	5, 19, 33, 42, 44	Illegible	3–4C	33
	51	Claudius II	268–70	68
	52	Victorinus	268–70	68
	53	Allectus	293–6	68
	49	Radiate	260–90	68
	50	Magnentius Maximus	387–8	68
Primary Occupation	47	Severus Alexander	222–35	6
Unstratified or Unrelated				
	37	Marcus Aurelius	160–5	21
	11	Claudius II	268–70	2
	30	Claudius II	268–70	31
	14	Radiate	260–90	2
	23	Radiate	260–90	34
	36	Radiate	260–90	40
	7	Barbarous Radiate	270–90	9
	48	Urbs Roma	330–45	6
	55	Urbs Roma	330–45	1
	46	House of Constantine	350–60	33
	24	Gratian	367–75	2

Table J. Coins from the North East Area (1969)

No. 14 THE EAST AREA (Figs. 29 – 33 and Plates XXXI–XXXV)

In September, 1961 the programme of excavation inside the Roman fort was concentrated on a wide area between the central Headquarters discovered in 1960 and the east wall of the fort. Here a pattern of four evaluation trenches was dug through dense undergrowth and bushes which earlier had formed part of an extensive allotment. Two east-west trenches (Trenches A and B), each roughly 90 ft. in length and 50 ft. apart, were dug between the *Via Quintana* found in 1959 and the central east-west axis of the fort indicated by the position of the East Gate. Each trench was 4 ft. wide and their eastern ends were about 40 ft. from the estimated internal face of the east wall of the fort. In addition, a long north-south trench (Trench C–D), interrupted near its centre, joined the two east-west trenches at a point roughly 85 ft. from the inside face of the fort wall.

These trenches showed a considerable variation in the depth of the soils across the site. Predictably, as in 1959, 1960 and later, the downhill east side revealed soils to a depth of about 6 ft., the greater part well stratified. The soils diminished uphill, westwards, so that at a point roughly 140 ft. from the fort wall most horizontal deposits had been removed. Here undisturbed natural soil was mostly only covered by the normal shallow topsoil. A somewhat similar pattern existed on the north-south axis. At the north, uphill, end of the site the stratified deposits had a depth of 2–3 ft., whereas the south-west area had also been reduced to plough-depth.

The four long trenches revealed the presence of a pair of substantial masonry buildings, almost certainly a matching pair of Roman barracks (East Barrack Nos. 1 and 2), running north-south. The western one of these overlay the foundations of another major Roman building (Earlier East Building) and both partly overlay the fully silted ditches of the mid-first century Fortlet (see p. 98). The three major buildings discovered here, together with other adjacent features, are described below (**A–F**).

In August, 1962 Trenches A and B were both extended westwards so that they had a total length of 132 ft. 7 in. and 129 ft. 2 in. respectively. With Trench C being 70 ft. 6 in. in length and Trench D 89 ft. 6 in. in length, the four trenches totalled about 420 ft. These trenches were supplemented by a series of large and small trenches (Boxes A–T) in 1962 which had to fit around large standing bushes. Then in 1968 a large area-excavation (Fig. 30) was made across the north ends of all three buildings. These revealed substantial detail (Plate XXXV), 38 minor features (Table L) and 12 post-holes (Table K). The dating evidence was generally good and this is discussed after the description of the two main structures.

(A) EAST BARRACK NO. 1

This building was clearly laid out on a north-south axis, with its east wall about 70–80 ft. from the inside face of the fort wall, but not parallel to it. Its north end was about 6 ft. from the *Via Principalis,* whilst its south end was about 8 ft. from the *Via Quintana.* Its length was about 133 ft. 8 in. and the total width was 24 ft.

Three masonry cross-walls were found inside the building and these indicate the presence at one time of at least four rooms (Rooms A–D). The internal lengths of each are given below:

North wall	2 ft. 2 in.
Room A	29 ft. 9 in.
Internal wall	1 ft. 9 in.
Room B	21 ft. 6 in.
Internal wall	1 ft. 10 in.
Room C	46 ft. 6 in.
Internal wall	2 ft. 1 in.
Room D	26 ft. 0 in.
South wall	2 ft. 1 in.
Total	**133 ft. 8 in.** (Internal 123 ft. 3 in)

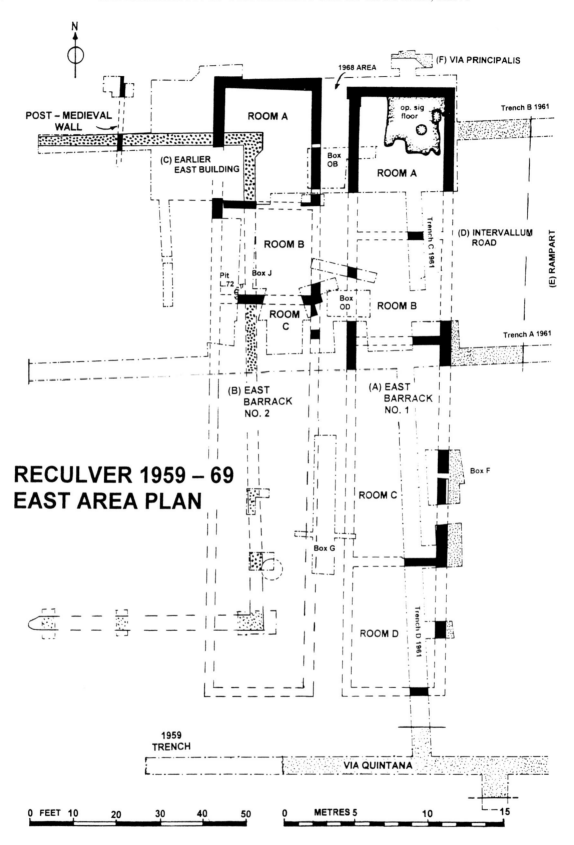

Fig. 29.   *Reculver 1961–9. Plan of East Area showing East Barracks 1 and 2.*

Other internal walls could have existed, possibly even wooden partitions of which no trace survived. All the walls were built of roughly shaped sandstone blocks set in yellow clay, of which one or two courses survived. Unusually, one wall (Wall 10) contained three large fragments of *opus signinum* and one large flat block which could have been a treader in a doorway. The external walls were all 26 in. wide, whilst the internal walls were smaller at 21–25 in. Where it was possible to examine these walls, the external ones were constructed over a foundation of worn beach pebbles laid in a sandy loam. The internal width of the rooms varied from 19 ft. 4 in. to about 20 ft.

The floors were generally constructed of trodden clay, or loam. However, in Room A, a large area of *opus signinum,* about 12 ft. sq., and varying in thickness 2–6 in., was laid, but only reached the north wall. This suggests a later insertion, just possibly laid down where the original floor may have been worn away. Of special interest here was a circular pit (F25), cut roughly centrally through the *opus signinum* floor, some 2 ft. 6 in diameter and 6 in. deep (Plate XXXII). This was bowl-shaped in profile and its base and sides had been scorched orange by intense heat. It had been packed with loam and very small fragments of painted wall-plaster (Group C). On this had been placed a complete hypocaust bridging-tile, 22 in. square and $2\frac{1}{2}$ in. thick, itself packed around with large fragments of a single roof *tegula*. Together these formed a solid base level with the floor surface. This base had been severely burned and is likely to have been constructed to support a small brazier, or even a hearth. The heat from this had cracked the bridging-tile and also scorched the undisturbed soil beneath it.

A substantial area (L.33 in Trench C, L.54 in Trench B and L.20 in 1968 area) of collapsed clay wall, mixed with small fragments of painted wall-plaster, was found over much of the *opus signinum* floor in Room A. This was mostly 4–6 in. in thickness. It sealed a thin band of charcoal and silt which contained domestic rubbish and several coins (see below). A similar layer (L.65) also sealed the clay floor at the south end of Room A. Another much thicker layer, up to 10 in. deep (L.67), extended from above Wall 10 southwards along the clay floor of Room B. The south wall of Room B (Wall 11) had been rendered with plaster, of which barely 4 in. in height survived *in situ*. This was painted red and a thin band of it had fallen onto the adjacent clay floor where it extended for about 1 ft. 11 in. Colours here included black, white, red, blue and green.

Room C was not examined in detail, but Room D also contained an extensive layer of fallen clay wall (L.40), starting at its south wall (Wall 13). The same layer was also found outside the building almost reaching the north edge of the *Via Quintana*. Of special interest was that the clay floor at the south end of Room D had been severely burnt and that the fallen wall upon it consisted of burnt daub and included several iron nails and a fragment of a bronze pipe (Nos. 391, 422). From this evidence it appears that the south end of this building had burnt down and that the walls of the rest of the building had collapsed, largely internally. The buried floors had never been cleared, nor the walls re-used. Two coins, one (Coin No. 61–103) of Gallienus (A.D. 260–8) and another (Coin No. 61–83) of Claudius II (A.D. 268–70) were found on the clay floor. Another, (Coin No. 61–102) of Allectus (A.D. 293–6), was found in the actual fallen clay wall. Two possible ovens, not fully examined, were located at the south end of Room A and a possible furnace, or large oven, at the extreme end of Room C. The latter certainly appeared to be later in date than the Roman building, but is substantially undated.

An infant burial (No. 2) was located in the north-west corner of Room A during the 1968 excavation. This lay in an oval cut, on an east-west axis, above the projecting foundation pebbles. Presumably it had been deposited during the construction of the building, or during its occupation. A second infant burial (No. 1) was found marginally above the surviving masonry of the north wall of Room A and must have been deposited after its walls had collapsed. A third infant burial (not shown) was found in 1962 (Box C) in East Barrack No. 1, buried inside its main east wall, at its junction with the wall dividing walls B and C. It occupied a cavity about 1 ft. 5 in. x 8 in. in the centre of the wall, where a large facing block seemed to have been moved aside to accommodate it. This unusual arrangement appeared to be a deliberate ritual deposit, though there

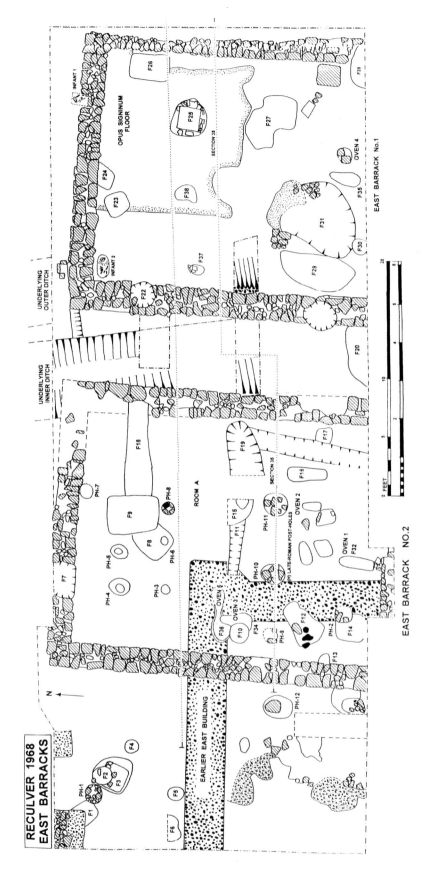

Fig. 30. *Reculver 1968. Plan of East Barracks 1 and 2.*

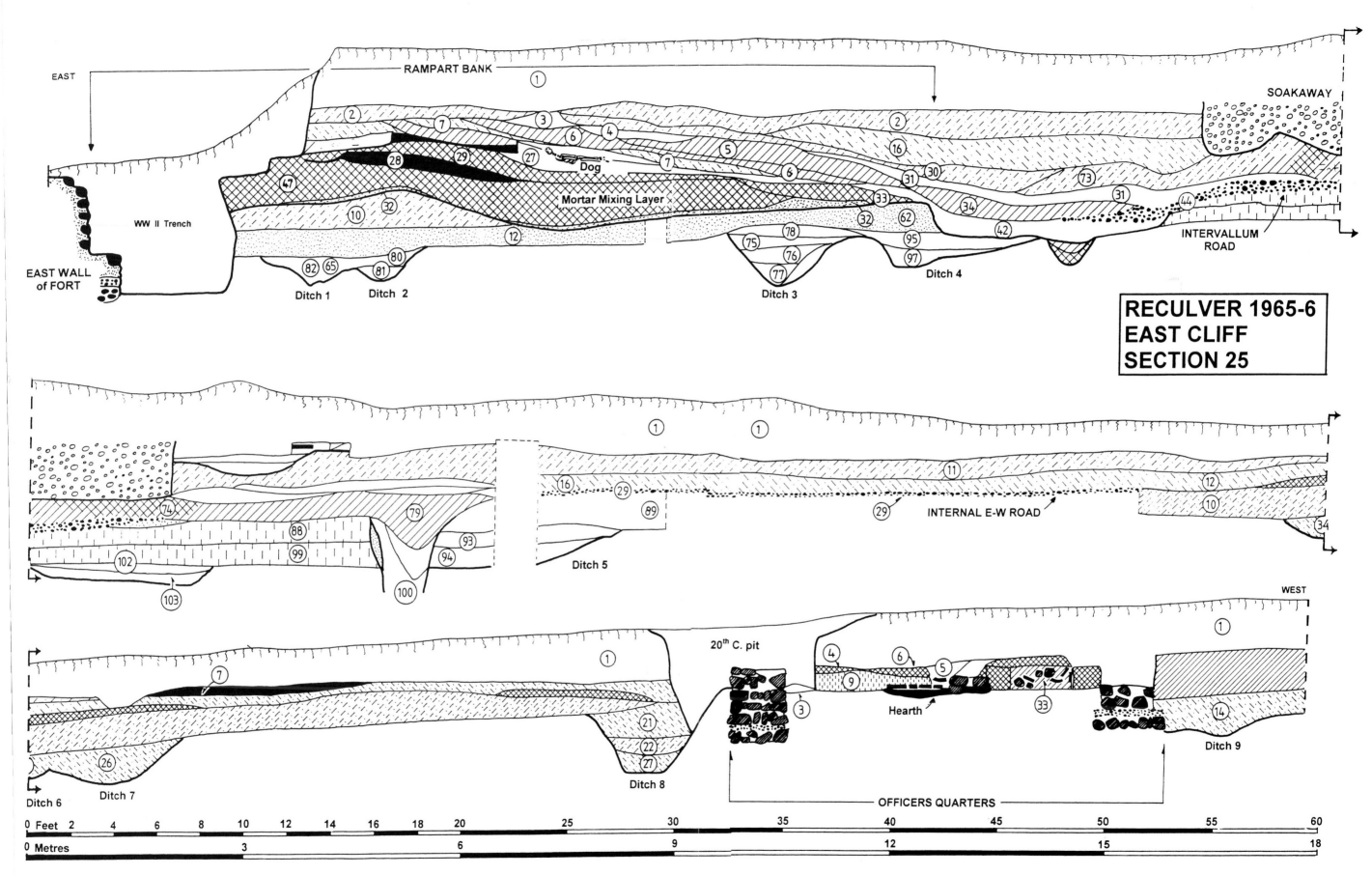

Fig. 31. *Reculver 1965–6. Section 25 along East Cliff.*

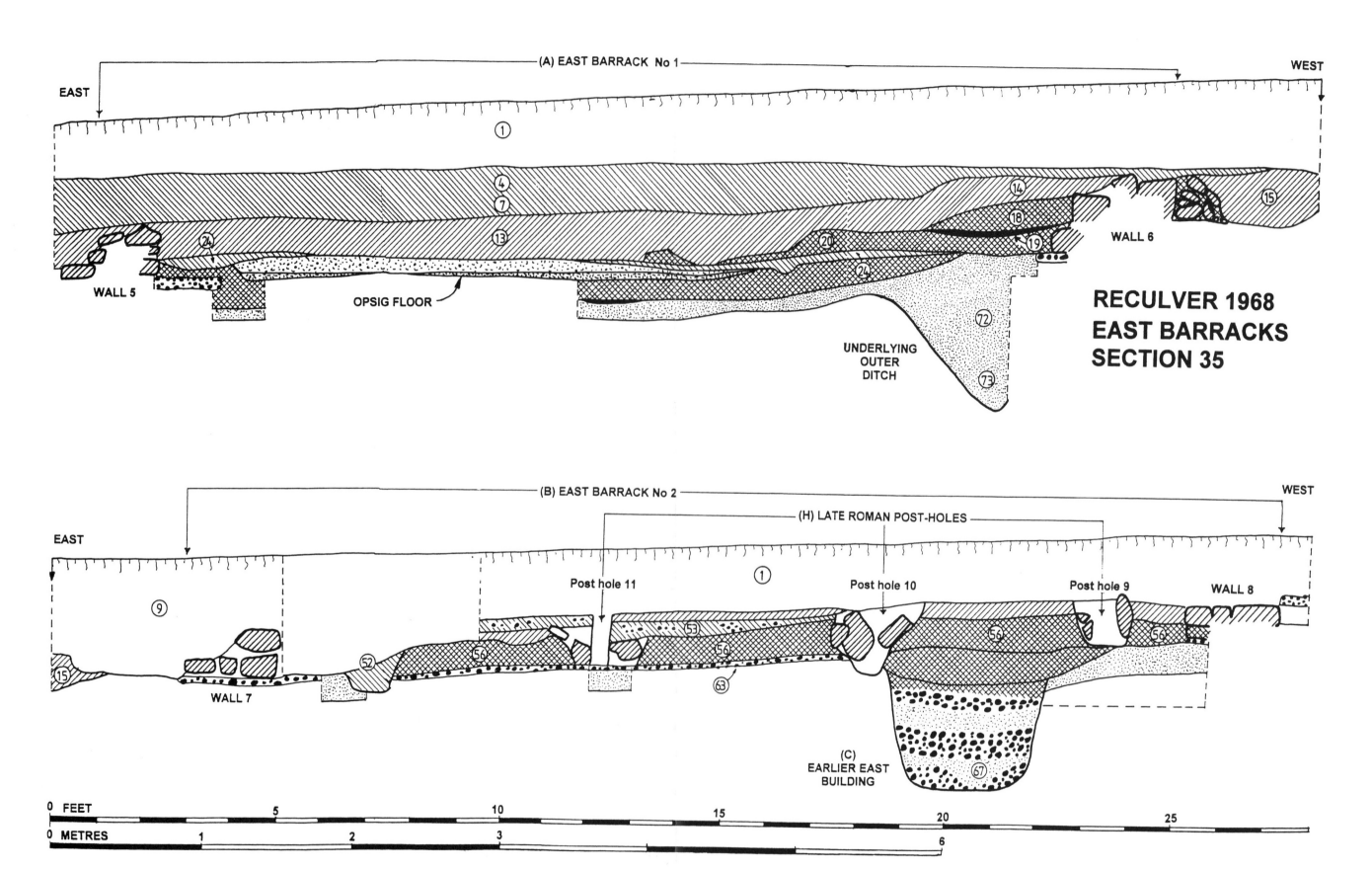

EAST

WEST

① ④ ⑦ ⑬ ②⑭ ⑳ ⑭ ⑱ ⑲ ②④ ⑮ ⑲

WALL 5

WALL 6

OPSIG FLOOR

②④

⑦②

UNDERLYING OUTER DITCH

⑦③

**RECULVER 1968
EAST BARRACKS
SECTION 35**

(B) EAST BARRACK No 2

WEST

(H) LATE ROMAN POST-HOLES

EAST

① Post hole 11 Post hole 10 Post hole 9

WALL 8

⑨

⑮

WALL 7

㊼

⑤⑥

⑤③

⑤⑥

⑤⑥

⑤⑥

㊿

⑥③

(C)
EARLIER EAST
BUILDING

⑥⑦

0 FEET 5 10 15 20 25

0 METRES 1 2 3 6

Fig. 32.   *Reculver 1968. Section 35 across East Barracks and Earlier East Building.*

is a small chance that it was an intrusive feature inserted after the superstructure had been removed.

The external, east side of this building was cut by both Trenches A and B in 1961 and marginally by Boxes F, H and S in 1962. The two main trenches showed raised formations outside the building, each about 9 ft. wide, the former consisting of rubble and the latter of an *opus signinum* mass (L.28) over pebble. In both cases these raised formations, about 6–10 in. in depth, overlay the west ends of the *Intervallum* Road (see below). In Trench A the rubble formation was itself sealed by a much wider pebble layer (L.6), some 16 ft. wide, which seemed to replicate the *Intervallum* Road buried well below. In the three boxes dug in 1962 only the surface of metalling was examined. Clearly, some form of extensive and raised platform extends along much of the east side of this building, significantly higher than internal floor-levels. This could be the base of an external veranda and two coins were found in association with it (Coin Nos. 62–31, 33), both barbarous radiates of A.D. 270–90.

(B) EAST BARRACK NO. 2

This building appears to have been very similar to Barrack No.1, with which it clearly formed one of a pair. It, too, had a main north-south axis and was separated from the other by a space about 6 ft. in width. Its own overall width was 24 ft. 6 in. and its length at least 65 ft. as surviving. Its southern half appears to have been substantially removed, where it lay within the area reduced by later cultivation and erosion (and largely inaccessible at that time). It, too, probably had an original length of about 134 ft., though its north end was about 2 ft. beyond the corresponding north end of East Barrack No.1.

Its walls, too, were mostly built of local sandstone bonded with clay. The external walls were 2 ft. 2 in. wide and the two internal walls were each about 1 ft. 8 in. in width. The latter indicate a minimum of three internal rooms, the internal lengths of which are given below:

North Wall	2 ft. 2 in.
Room A	25 ft.
Internal wall	1 ft. 8 in
Room B	19 ft.
Internal wall	1 ft. 8in.
Room C	15 ft. min.
Total (Min)	**64 ft. 6 in**

THE DATING EVIDENCE FOR THE EAST BARRACKS

The dating evidence across these two large buildings is generally good. The 1961 trenches produced 111 coins, the 1962 trench extensions and boxes another 51 and the large 1968 open area-excavation another 137 coins. Of these 299 coins, over 150 were unstratified, or from unrelated deposits and just over 120 came from key contexts. By far the great majority came from the north end of East Barrack (No. 1) where the stratification was deeper than elsewhere.

Here, the localised *opus signinum* floor in Room A was sealed by a thin band of black loam (L.24), generally 1–3 in. deep containing a small amount of domestic rubbish. This layer contained 28 coins. Its west side was sealed by a dump of orange clay and wall-plaster (L.20), about 7 ft. wide and about 4–6 in. deep. This seems to represent a small section of collapsed, or dumped, wall that created a modest platform in part of Room A. This layer contained a single coin and a lead steel-yard weight (No. 383). It was in turn sealed by a thin 1–3 in. band of black charcoal (L.19), perhaps the rake-back from a nearby domestic oven, which tailed back onto the floor and effectively became part of the layer sealing it. This contained another ten coins, several domestic

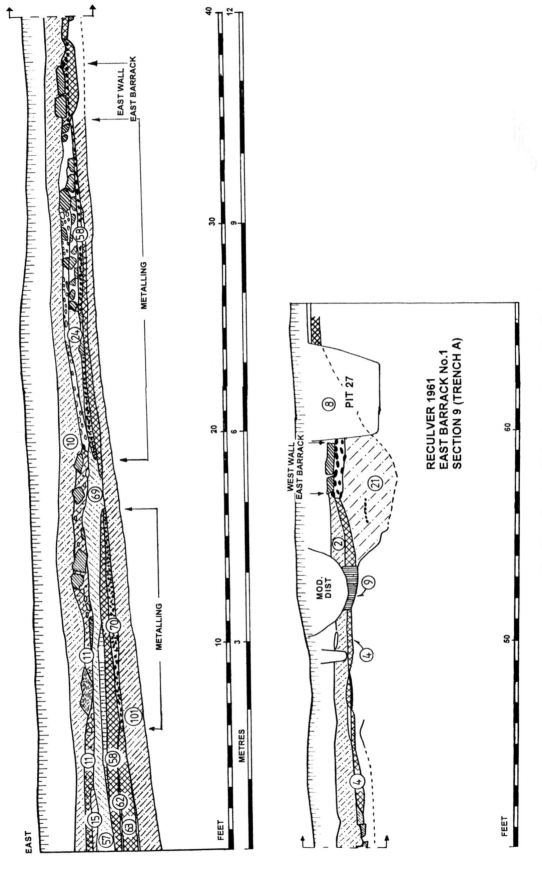

Fig. 33. *Reculver 1961. Section 9 across East Barrack 1.*

objects (Nos. 326,334,371,373,407) and part of a stamped C IB tile (No. 447). It seems likely that these three deposits (L.19, 20 and 24), all represent closely related events and indeed all 41 coins cover the same date range and are listed below:

Denarius ?	Early-third century	1
Philip I	A.D. 244–9	1
Valerian I	253–60	1
Gallienus	260–8	4
Valens	264–78	1
Victorinus	268–70	3
Claudius II	268–70	7
Tetricus I and II	270–73	5
Barbarous Radiates	270–90	9
Corroded		9
		41

Taken as a group, it seems clear that these coins could not have been lost before A.D. 270. Allowing for a short period of circulation and noting the significant absence of coins certainly dating after Tetricus, a date for their loss of about A.D. 275 seems highly likely. Marginally later dates are possible. These soil deposits containing the coins were never cleared from the building and must represent its final use. The scatter of small pits and ovens nearby probably relates to the same final phase of use and another four coins from some of these cover the same span of time. The same primary deposits also produced coarse pottery (Nos.118, 124–35,145–9, 159–60 and a bone handle (No. 367), largely of corresponding date.

These final occupation deposits within the building were soon completely sealed by a deposit of grey-black loam (L.13 and 14), generally 8–12 in. deep, which contained more domestic rubbish, another 39 coins and a bronze mount (No. 376). It is similar in composition to the soils covering the *Via Quintana* excavated in 1959. Whilst late-third century coins are just in the majority, 13 of the coins are of the first half of the 4th century. This layer seems to have largely filled Room A to the top of the surviving walls, by which time it seems certain that the building was no longer in use. The loam had no tip lines in it and seems to have been deposited progressively and in total represents a large volume of soil. The coins are listed below:

Denarius	1	Early third century	
Gallienus	1	A.D. 268–70	
Victorinus	1	268–70	
Quintilian	1	270	
Claudius II	5	268–70	
Tetricus I	2	270–73	
Barbarous Radiates	10	270–90	
Allectus	1	293–6	
Constantine I	2	310–24	
Constantine II	2	330–45	
House of Constantine	7	335–60	
Constans	1	345–48	
Urbs Roma		330–45	
Corroded	4		
	39		

The stratification strongly suggests that with the deposition of Layers 13 and 14, the East Barrack No. 1 was effectively buried and invisible. The same layers also produced coarse pottery (Nos. 150–4) of largely corresponding date. This area was then sealed by a layer of black loam (L. 7) mostly 4–6 in. in depth. This seems to represent the final Roman deposit. It also seems likely, though not conclusive, that the post-hole structure to the west (PH 1–12) related to this final occupation deposit. Certainly its post-holes had been cut through the soil filling of the East Barrack No. 2 from a higher level sometime after its final use. Another 31 coins were found in this deposit and these are listed below. In contrast to the underlying deposits, the majority of the coins dated from the 4th century, with the latest being one of Gratian (A.D. 378–83). More coarse pottery (Nos. 104–17, 119–123,136–40, 150–8) was also recovered from these late Roman deposits.

Gallienus	1	A.D.	260–68
Claudius II	1		268–70
Tetricus I & II	3		270–73
Barbarous Radiates	2		270–90
Carausius	1		286–93
Constantine I	4		310–35
Constantine II	1		320–30
Helena	1		337–40
Urbs Roma	3		330–45
House of Constantine	1		335–45
Constans	1		345–48
Constantius II	2		335–50
Valens	3		364–78
Gratian	1		378–83
Corroded	6		
	31		

The whole area was found to be buried and sealed by a deep layer of fine black loam which represented the soil disturbed by the deep digging of extensive allotment-gardens here in the early-20th century. This contained many more coins, all regarded as unstratified and these are listed below.

Emperor	Date	Nos.	Emperor	Date	Nos.
Trajan	A.D 98–117	1	Barbarous Radiates	270–90	31
Commodus	180–92	1	Constantius I	300–05	1
Elagabalus	218–22	1	Crispus	317–20	1
Severus Alexander	222–35	1	Constantine I	320–35	7
Gordian III	238–44	1	Constantine II	335–45	4
Philip I	244–9	1	Urbs Roma	330–45	5
Gallienus	260–8	3	Constantinopolis	330–45	5
Claudius II	268–70	10	Populus Romanus	330–40	1
Aurelian	268–73	1	Helena	337–41	1
Postumus	260–8	1	Theodora	337–40	1
Victorinus	268–70	5	Constans	337–50	3
Tetricus I	270–3	11	Constantius II	335–45	4
Tetricus II	270–3	4	House of Constantine	330–60	7
Carausius	286–93	5	Magnentius	350–3	1
Allectus	293–6	4	Valentinian I	364–75	1
Tacitus	276	1	House of Valentinian	364–78	2
Diocletian	284–94	2	Illegible	3–4 C	22
Maximian I	317	1	Others	–	8
Maximian I Herc.	297–305	3			
Radiates	260–90	4		**Total**	**161**

(C) THE EARLIER EAST BUILDING (No. 3 on Period I plan and Plate XXXV)

The 1961 and 1962 excavations gradually detected the pebble foundations of a substantial building, largely concealed underneath the East Barrack No. 2. The 1968 area-excavation examined this in greater detail, showing it to be the north-east corner and produced the first full cross-section (Fig. 32, Section 35).

In plan, only three sides of this building lay within the excavated areas. It is possible that traces of its fourth side yet survive in the reduced area to the west. The north side was traced for a minimum of 52 ft., partially beneath the East Barrack No. 2 and the layer of possible metalling along its west side. The east side was traced for about 110 ft., largely beneath the floors and walls of the same Barrack, which with two corners seems to represent its full length. The north and east walls joined at right-angles beneath Room 1 of the barrack, where there was also a small external buttress about 1 ft. 9 in. in width. The south side was traced for a distance of about 55 ft. in a series of small test-pits where it seemed to expire, though just possibly the deepest course of foundation could yet survive.

The three sides located consisted entirely of worn beach pebbles, set in layers in a wide foundation-trench, with no trace of masonry above, or related floors. Either these had been totally removed, or else the building was never taken beyond the foundation stage. No internal divisions were noted, but these could exist beyond the limits of the excavation.

In detail, the foundation-trench generally had steep to vertical sides, was mostly 3 ft. 4 in. wide at the top and at the intact northern end was still about 2 ft. deep. Here it consisted of three layers of large beach pebbles alternating with layers of soil. The soil closely matched the undisturbed natural Thanet Sand here and it seems clear that this was simply the replacement of soil removed when the trenches were dug. The layers of pebble were 4–10 in. thick and the separating layers mostly about 3 in. A pit cut by the east foundation (1962 Box J L.72) contained samian vessels dated A.D. 65–80 (Nos. 214, 222) including a base (Form 29) stamped Martialis (Stamp No. 5, No 227) of A.D. 50–65. The upper packing of the foundation-trench contained a samian base (Form 33) of Antonine date (Stamp No.14).

(D) THE *INTERVALLUM ROAD* (Fig. 29)

The presence of an *Intervallum* Road at the tail of the Rampart Bank elsewhere inside the Roman fort, suggested that one should also exist on the east side of the fort. Accordingly, Trenches A and B were laid out to overlap such a feature and both trenches produced metalling which appears to represent this road. In Trench B a substantial mass of gravel (L.31), from 2–12 in. in thickness, at a point about 54–73 ft. (hence 15 ft. wide) from the inside face of the fort wall, seems to represent this road. In Trench A, however, just 50 ft. further to the south two much thinner bands of gravel (L.70 and L.14) at 46–56 ft. (hence 10 ft. wide) and 59–75 ft. (hence 16 ft. wide), from the inside face of the fort wall, respectively, seem to represent this road too. Presumably this variation could be reconciled in the unexcavated zone between the trenches. Either way the metalling in both trenches now terminates at the east wall of the East Barrack No. 1, though there is a suggestion in one place that the foundations of this wall cut them. All three areas of metalling lay directly on the pre-fort soils and should, therefore, relate to the fort construction period. A coin (Coin No. 61–92) of Aelius (A.D. 136–8) was found in these primary soils, which also produced a brooch (No. 321), two more scabbard-chapes (Nos. 354, 357), a stamped samian base (Form 37) of late-second century date (Stamp No. 15) and coarse pottery. The deposits above the metalling layers included dumped clays (S. 9, L.58), loams with domestic rubbish (L.15, 57, 69) and rubble (L.16).

(E) THE RAMPART BANK

The 1959 trench had revealed the presence of a substantial Rampart Bank, tailing back about 50 ft. from the inside face of the east wall of the fort. It was for this reason that Trenches A and B were started about 40 ft. from the same fort wall so that they might overlap the tail of the bank if this existed in the same form here.

Only a slight trace of the possible tail of the bank was found in both trenches. This took the form of tapering layers of dumped soils (L.42 in Trench B and L.63 in Trench A), which in Trench A sealed a clear section of the mortar-mixing floor associated with the construction of the fort wall. The layers generally expired about 46–50 ft. from the fort wall and this is about right for the tail of the Bank, though this may require confirmation.

(F) THE *VIA PRINCIPALIS*

The extreme north end of Trench C located the edge of a thin band of metalling, at a point about 6 ft. from the outside north wall of the East Barrack No.1. This lay directly on the pre-fort soils and is likely to represent the outside, south edge of the *Via Principalis* leading from the adjacent East Gate. The continuation of this metalling lay beneath the tarmac path and thus outside the limits of excavation.

(G) THE *VIA QUINTANA* (Fig. 29)

Trench D was extended southwards to reach the long trench dug in 1959, which fortuitously ran up the centre of the hitherto unknown *Via Quintana*. As planned, this new trench picked up the north edge of the *Via Quintana* where another 7 ft. of the road was revealed, tapering away to

P.H. No.	Shape	Size Inches	Depth Inches	Sides	Base	Exc. Box	Fill	Notes
1	Circ	20	N.Exc.	–	–	J30	Stone-packed	Over med. Recent ?
2	Circ	16	10	Vert	Flat	K31	Br. loam and Stone-packed	Above Period I foundations
3	Circ	10	3	Vert	Flat	K31	Br. Loam	
4	Oval	21 x 17	7	Steep	Flat	J31	Black loam	Central Post 9in. diam.
5	Oval	18 x 13	7	Steep	Flat	J31	Black loam with daub	Central Post 8 x 6 in.
6	Circ	8	10	Vert	Flat	K31	Black loam	Cut by Pit 8
7	Oval	16 x 13	9	Vert	Flat	J31	Br. loam, tile	By North Wall
8	Circ	12	6?	Vert	Flat	K31	Br. loam and stone	Central Post-Hole 5 x 4 in
9	Oval	12 x 15	12	Steep	Flat	K31	Loam, stones	1961 Section
10	Oval	24 x 20	16	Steep	Flat	K31	Loam and stones	1961 Section Central Post 8 in.
11	Circ	24	14	Steep	Flat	K31	–	1961 Section. Central Post 8 in
12	Oval	30 x 20	16	Vert	Cupped	K31	Bl. loam and single stone	1961 Section. Cuts single stone

Table K. Post-Holes at north end of East Barrack No. 2 (1961 and 1968)

F.No.	Shape	Size	Depth	Sides	Base	Box	Fill	Notes
1	Rect.	22"x24"	–	–	Flat	J30	L45	Pit above Roman road
2	Circ.	18"	19"	Steep	Round	J30	–	Pit over medieval shaft
3	Circ.	26"	8ft min.	Vert.	Unseen	J30	L36	Med. shaft. Cuts Roman Rd
4	Circ.	14"	–	Steep	Round	J30	–	Pit in top of Roman road
5	Oval	14"x18"	12"	Steep	Round	K30	–	Pit dug through lower road
6	Irreg.	28"	13"	Steep	Round	K30	–	Pit under lower road
7	Oval	39"x20"	64"min.	Vert.	Not seen	J31	L37	Medieval pit. Cuts north wall of West Building
8	Sub-rect.	36"x30"	16"	Sloping	Flat	J30	L22	Pit cuts through floor. Appears to be over medieval shaft
9	Rect.	54"x40"	20"min	Vert.	Unseen	J31	L38	Med. shaft. Cuts Roman deposit
10	Circ	19"	–	–	Flat	K31	–	Pit cuts floor over oven
11	Oval	16"x11"	–	–	–	K31	L55	Gully dug into floor
12	Irreg.	48"x33"	13"	–	–	K31	L47	Pit dug through floor. Did not reach PI footings
13	Irreg.	12"x12"	3"	–	–	K31	–	Small depression. Cuts floor
14	Square	28"x28"	13"	–	Flat	K31	L39	Pit cuts floor
15	Circ?	27"	14"	–	–	K31	–	Pit sealed by med. Pit
16	Oblong	40"x14"	5"	–	Flat	K32	L54	Slot cut into floor
17	Sub-rect.	16"x16"	–	–	–	K32	–	Pit in floor. Cut by med. gully
18	Oblong	8'x20–30"	10"	Steep	Round	J32	–	Gully beneath floor and wall.
19	Oval	54"x36"	11"	Steep	Flat	K32	L57	Pit cuts floor and gully (L52)
20	Irreg.	60"x22"min.	11"min.	Sloping	Not seen	K32	L30 L.48	Pit between walls of Barrack Coin 68–40 Claudius II 268–70
21	Oval	36"x30"	8"	–	Flat	K32	L31	Pit cuts wall of Barracks
22	Oval	30"x24"	18"	–	–	J32	L8	Pit cuts wall of Barracks
23	Rect.	24"x24"	11"	–	Flat	J33	–	Pit cuts *op. sig.* floor Coarse pottery Nos. 141–144
24	Sub-rect.	24"min.x21"	10"	–	Flat	J33	–	Pit cuts wall and *op.sig.* floor
25	Circ.	30"	6"	–	Flat	K33	L76	Pit cuts *op. sig.* floor. Sq. tile

F.No.	Shape	Size	Depth	Sides	Base	Box	Fill	Notes
26	Rect	40"x26"	24"	Vert.	Flat	J33		Pit cuts *op. sig.* floor
27	Irreg.	63"x42"	–	Sloping	–	K33	L69	Pit cuts floor, sealed by clay
28	Circ.	44"x14"	–	–	–	K33	L68	Pit cuts floor and wall of Barracks. Coins 68–129, 134, 135 (AD 330–50)
29	Irreg.	78"x36"	–		–	K32	–	Not exc. (sandstone blocks)
30	Circ.	15"	11"	Steep	Cup	K33	–	
31	Circ.	78"	8"	Sloping	Flat	K33	L74	Burnt area in floor
32	Oblong	36"x11"	–	Vert.	Flat	K31	L58	Oven 1 cuts into floor Samian stamp 2 (No. 229)
33	Oblong	20"x9"	–	–	–	K31	–	Oven 2, not excavated
34	Keyhole	33"x20"max.	–	–	–	K31	–	Oven 3, not exc. Over PI foundations
35	Oval	31"x15"max	–	–	–	K33	–	Oven 4, not excavated
36	Keyhole	4'6"x18"min	6"min.	Sloping	Round	TR–B	L115	Oven 5 clay lining
37	Oval	16"x10"	3"	–	–	TR–B	L59	Pit contains tiles and Coins 61–80, 81) Carausius (AD 286–93) and Gallienius (AD 260–8)
38	Oval	42"x24"	–	–	–	TR–B+ TR–C	L75	Pit cuts *op. sig.* floor. Coin Nos. 61–91, Tetricus II (AD 270–3)

Table L. Details of features at north end of East Barracks (Nos.1 and 2), 1961 and 1968.

nothing at a point about 7 ft. from the external south wall of the East Barrack No. 1. A single coin (No. 62–73) of Tetricus I (A.D. 270–3) was found in the road and another (No. 62–75) of Constantius II (A.D. 350–5) in the soil above the road.

(H) LATE-ROMAN POST-HOLES (Table K)

It seems clear from the deposits in Trench A–D that the collapsed or burnt walls of both East Barracks 1 and 2 were never cleared away, or the walls rebuilt. The site was steadily buried under a loamy soil containing domestic rubbish and a light scatter of building debris. These layers also contained Roman coins, mostly of early-4th century date.

No trace of new masonry or new floors above the barracks was obviously revealed in the trenches, though a number of intrusive features could relate to a later phase of light timber buildings. Indeed the 1968 area-excavation revealed a line of four large post-holes (P.H. 9–12), running east-west across the north end of East Barrack No. 2 and cutting through the soil sealing it. These were generally 15–30 in. in diameter, lightly packed with tile and stone. They occupy a line about 17 ft. 3 in. in length and are spaced at intervals of between 5 ft. 3in. and 6 ft. This line could represent a wall of a building, or equally a boundary. Either way, it cannot be earlier than A.D. 300 and the total absence of material of post-Roman date in association with it largely suggests that the posts date from the fourth century A.D. In addition, another 38 features were found at the north end of the barracks, mostly pits and ovens and these are listed (Table L).

The excavations across most of the East Barracks, largely revealed only marginally stratified soil deposits, due in part to the shallow depths and the recent deep allotment digging. Apart from the coins they also produced a large collection of pottery and small-finds, 25 of the latter being illustrated. These include objects of bronze such as a brooch (No. 315), rings (Nos. 325, 340), a bracelet (No. 338), a spoon (No. 372), a key (No. 377) and a buckle (No. 396). Bone objects include pins (Nos. 233, 241), a small harpoon (No. 359) and two handles (Nos. 360, 364). Other objects include a jet pin (No. 397), a jet bead (No. 402), spindle whorls (Nos. 409,414) and a figurine (No. 455). Of the pottery, only some of the samian ware (Nos. 211, 213, 220, 225, 226) and mortaria (Nos. 187, 190, 194, 198, 200, 201, 204 and TS24) are illustrated. Excluding the 1st century and pit material, about 120 samian sherds were recovered. These include Forms 18/31(2), Curle 21(3), 30, 31(12), 33(6), 36(2), 37(11), 38(5), 43, 45(10), Dech. 72, Walters 79, Ludiwici (16) and mortaria(9), though some sherds could be matching. The great majority is Antonine – 1st half 3rd century.

―――――――――

No. 15 THE WEST AREA (Figs. 34 and 35 and Plates XXXVI–XXXVIII)

As part of the programme to investigate the internal buildings of the fort, an area-excavation was carried out in 1966 on the west side of the main Coastguard Station and this was largely under the supervision of Gerald Cramp. This had to be confined to the area of what had been the Coastguard lawn, as tarmac drives and maintained gardens occupied the rest of the area. In detail, an area about 48 x 32 ft. was excavated, running southwards from the sea eroded north face and at a point about 45–95 ft. from the estimated inside face of the west wall of the fort. The work was carried out in August (Boxes A5–Z9) and extended in October when additional smaller trenches (Box Z10) were excavated on the north-east side. The excavations revealed parts of two large Roman masonry buildings (A and B) and other features (C and D). These are described below. The main area was covered by a 10ft. grid, which with baulks of 2ft. on the gridlines, created boxes 8ft. sq. The boxes were largely excavated, but the baulks were mostly left intact.

The area contained a somewhat complex series of deposits, both large and small, some of which expired beneath the soil baulks that were not removed. Some of the lower deposits may represent levelling layers put down to offset the slope of the hill on this side. Others seem to represent occupation deposits relating to Building A, but many were truncated by the ovens, other features and post-Roman cuts. The confusion of these deposits makes interpretation very difficult, but seven coins were found within the structure and include one each of Hadrian (A.D. 117–38), Claudius II (A.D. 268–70) and a radiate (A.D. 260–90) together with four illegible (3–4 centuries). What appear to be fort-construction layers contained two coins, one each of Septimius Severus (A.D. 193–211) and Herennia Etruscilla (A.D.250–3), the latter probably intrusive. The unstratified and unrelated deposits contained another 28 coins (Table O), of which eight are dated before A.D. 202, ten are 3rd century and three are 4th century, six are illegible and four are post-Roman. Significantly, perhaps, this site produced a disproportionately high number of early coins and this could reflect a specialised use of this area in the fort-construction Period.

(A) THE WEST BUILDING

The greater part of the area excavated was occupied by the northern section of a large building, laid out on a north-south axis and situated about 65–90 ft. inside the estimated west wall of the fort. Its east and west walls were traced for a minimum of about 32 ft. and its overall width was 25 ft. Its foundations consisted of worn beach pebbles, mostly 2ft. wide, and on these sat a sandstone block wall, bonded in clay. Strangely, the wall above this was 2ft. 3 in. wide and offset westwards by a clear 6 in. This only survived in detail on the east side and it either represents a minor realignment of the wall or, just possibly, a rebuild. The north wall largely survived only as foundations it having been substantially robbed. It was not clear if the building had extended further to the north, as any evidence had been removed by erosion or later pits.

A small section of a beach pebble foundation was found on the east side of the building and this appeared to extend eastwards. It lay at the very edge of the excavation and could not be examined in detail. A short section of a similar east-west foundation, 2 ft. 2 in. wide, was found in Box Z10 and this could originally have joined the north-east corner of the West Building. If so, then these two smaller foundations would have been about 20 ft. apart. Several possibilities arise from this, but the evidence is insufficient to draw certain conclusions.

Internally, the building does not seem to have been subdivided, but it contained traces of ten ovens (see Table N), mostly at the southern end of the excavation. The largest (Oven 1) was at the north end where four *tegulae* tiles laid flat served as a base and allowed hot air into a narrow flue just 8 in. wide. The flue was built of sandstone blocks set in yellow clay and all the exposed surfaces were burnt hard. The north end of the flue lay under a soil-baulk that was not removed and the complete form of the oven is thus not known. It contained two coins, one of Caracalla (A.D. 201–6) and one illegible. The other ovens mostly consisted of ovoid holes cut into the underlying soils, sometimes with burnt faces and at least one (Oven 4) with a base of large tile fragments. Oven 8 contained a coin of Commodus (A.D. 180–92).

Various small pits and gullies were also located, some clearly associated with the building and others of medieval, or much later, date (see Table M). The base for the Coastguard flagpole, which appears on many photographs of Reculver, was found in Box A7. Nearby, large pits filled with sand or concrete, probably mark where the flagpole stays were anchored. The north-east corner of the Roman building was partly cut by a rectangular pit (F20) some 3 ft. 4 in. x 2 ft. 8 in., dug in Roman times to a depth of about 3 ft. 4 in. It contained sandy loams, several sandstone blocks, a large piece of angle-iron and a coin of Tetricus I (A.D. 270–3). Another Pit, F25, contained a coin of Commodus (A.D. 180–92). A shallow gully (F28) in Box Z8 was detected with difficulty as it has been backfilled with subsoil. It ran north-south under Oven I and contained two iron water-pipe collars (No. 435). There can be little doubt that this gully must have contained wooden water-pipes to which the iron collars provided vital connectors. This was the only such evidence of a water-pipe from inside the fort, but it is possible that others had existed and not been seen due to the backfilling with subsoil. It seems likely that this pipe-line related to the fort construction period.

Of special interest, however, were the skeletons of three human infants found within the building and clearly buried in Roman times. These were found incidentally in the only two critical cuts made through the walls of the building and statistically, at least, it seems likely that others may exist in the much longer lengths of walls not examined. Infant 1 (in Box B9) was laid out supine, head south, alongside the lower section of the east wall of the building and completely sealed by the upper wall which had anyway been realigned westwards. It lay in an ill-defined cut into the underlying soils, effectively alongside the foundation pebbles, but covered by the soil already removed. The skeleton measured 19 in. x 8 in. in the ground and appears to represent a newly born baby.

Feature	Type	Period	Box Nos.	Deposit	Notes
1	Pit	20th Century	A5	–	WW II
2	Pit	Roman?	A5	–	Below Medieval
3	Pit	Medieval	A5	42, 56, 79	
4	Pit	20th Century	Z6	–	
5	Area of	Roman	Z7	–	West of Roman Wall
6		Roman	A6	–	West of Roman Wall
7, 8 , 9	Pit	20th Century	Z7 + A7	–	WW II
10	Gully	Roman?	A7	89, 90	Over Feature 26
11	Gully	Pre-Historic?	A7	109	Not fully examined
12	Gully	Medieval	B7	15	Coin 66–9
13	Pit	Roman	B7	32	
14	Pit	Roman?	Y8	–	Largely Eroded
15	Pit	20th Century	Y8	–	Cuts Roman North Wall
16	Pit	20th Century	Z8	–	Cuts Oven 1
17	Gully	20th Century	A8	–	
18	Pit	20th Century	A8	–	
19	Pit	Roman	B8	152	Tetine
20	Pit	Roman	Y9	51, 57, 58, 94	Coin 66–22, samian stamp No.
21	Pit	Roman	Z9	97	Under Roman East Wall
22	Pit	Roman	A9	–	
23	Pit	20th Century	A9	–	Cuts Roman East Wall
24	Gully	Roman	B9	22	Coins 66–44 and 66–45
25	Pit	Roman	B9	76	Coin 66–34
26	Pit	Roman	A7 + A8	64	Under Feature 10
27	Pit	Roman?	B7	83	Cut by Gully Feature 12
28	Broken Tile	Roman	Z8	–	
29	Pipe Trench	Roman	Z8	–	2 Water-pipe rings

Table M. Features in the West Building (1966).

Infants 2 and 3 (Plate XXXVIII) were both found at the internal north-east corner of the building and both had been buried east-west with the head at the east end. The head of Infant 2 was 4 in. from the inner face of the north wall and 6 in. from the inner face of the east wall. It occupied an area of at least 12 x 8 in. with its legs bent and apart. Infant 3 was 8 in. beneath Infant 2 and its head and shoulders were under the upper section of the east wall. In a crouched position it occupied an area of only 13 x 5 in. and its ill-defined grave had been cut through the pre-fort soils so that the body rested on the natural Thanet Sand below. It seems unlikely that these two infants were buried at the same time, to judge by the positions and it seems Infant 3 was buried first. Both were probably newly born, or still-born.

In addition, a total of ten ovens of varying sizes were framed by the main walls of the West Building (see table below). These were clearly not exactly contemporary for Oven 6 was earlier than two of the others which in turn were replaced by Oven 4. Three of the ovens (Oven 1, 2 and 4) lay in a rough line down the centre of the building and about 10 ft. apart. All were accessed from the north end and had small flues leading to wider chambers. The stratigraphy relating to all the ovens was confused and it is possible that the earlier ones pre-dated the building. What may be significant is that three coins (Nos. 66–5, 34 and 39) of Commodus (A.D. 180–92) were found

Oven	Site Nos.	Deposit	Box Nos.	Notes
1	x	43, 36	Z8	Samian F.43, Coin 66–13, Caracalla (A.D. 201–6)
2	x	–	A8	
3	x	–	A8	
4	1	71, 84	B8	
5	Upper 4	156	B8	
6	Lower 7	–	B8	
7	2	124	B8	(Under Oven 6)
8	6	92,118	B8	Coin 66–39, Commodus (A.D. 180–92)
9	3	119	B8	
10	Burnt Area	–	A9	

Table N. Ovens inside West Building (1966).

within a very localised area at the south-east corner of the excavation. One came from Oven 8, another from Pit F25 and the third from a gully (F.24).

(B) THE EARLIER WEST BUILDING (not on plan)

The later trenches (Box Z10) at the north-east corner on this particular site revealed part of a large building that must have been unrelated to the main West Building. Only a single north-south wall of this second building was found, of which only a length of 16 ft. was uncovered. This mostly took the form of a massive beach pebble foundation 3 ft. 4 in. wide, consisting of two layers of pebbles 3–5 in. thick separated by a thin band of soil and having a total depth of 10 in. A section of the actual wall of the building, some 8 ft. 6 in. in length, had survived one or two courses high. This consisted of sandstone blocks set in a white mortar, containing some chalk specks, 2 ft. 9 in. wide and placed centrally on the wider pebble foundation.

This very large wall clearly extended in both directions, but no trace of a matching north-south wall was found in the area-excavation to the west. From this it seems likely that the rest of the building lay to the east, under (what was then) the Coastguard Station and its attached cottages built at the end of the 19th century. The wall found lay about 11 ft. 6 in. east of the West Building and thus about 102–104 ft. from the estimated west wall of the fort. It also seemed to cut a smaller east-west pebble foundation just 2 ft. 2 in. wide. The exact relationship with this remains unclear. In addition, it is possible that Pit F25 and also Oven 8 could relate to this early structure, even though on plan both sit inside the later West Building. Each contained a coin of Commodus (A.D. 180–92).

From the character of this mortared wall and its large foundation it is likely (though not conclusive) that this building formed part of the original Period I fort-construction layout. If so, it is likely that it occupied much of the space available on the west side of the *principia*. With its west wall located a maximum width of about 120 ft. is available for this building, allowing for say 20 ft. separating it from the *principia*. A major building here, in the central division of the fort, is likely though it is still possible that it was one of two or even three built to fill the available space.

(C) THE *INTERVALLUM* ROAD

An extensive area of pebble metalling was found along the entire west side of the West Building, hence over a north-south length of at least 30 ft. Its west edge overlapped the tail of the Rampart

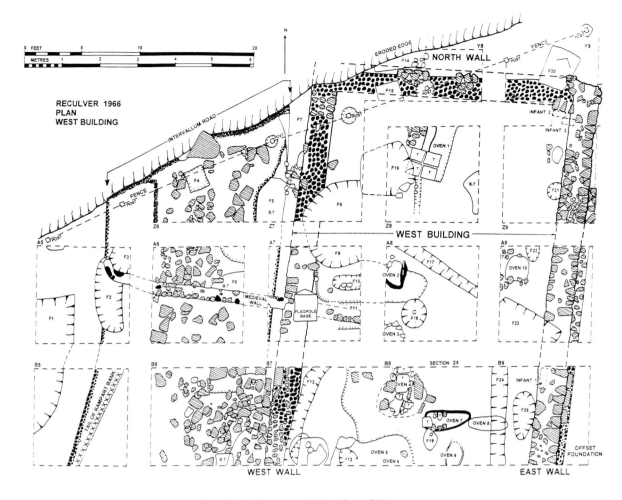

Fig. 34. *Reculver 1966. Plan of West Area.*

Bank and its width was about 15 ft. There can be little doubt that this metalling represents a laid road and from its position estimated to be 50–65 ft. from the fort wall, it would largely coincide with the *Intervallum* Road here. It was generally 2–5 in. in thickness and mostly rested on the pre-fort soils. The Road contained three coins (Nos. 66–27,28 and 31), one of Claudius II (A.D. 268–70), one of Carausius (A.D. 286–93) and one illegible (3–4 centuries).

Its surface was covered by a thin band of soil upon which was a wide spread of sandstone blocks and fragments of Roman roof tile. These appeared partly laid and in places created a flattish surface. Clearly, the underlying road was no longer in use at this stage and the stones may represent a replacement surface, or the base of some form of external veranda on the west side of the building.

(D) THE RAMPART BANK

A tapering layer of orange clay was located on the west side of the excavated area and this lay on top of both the deep pre-fort soils and some construction soils. It was traced for at least 7 ft. and it is clear that it extended westwards, probably right up to the fort wall where its thickness would have greatly increased. From its position, character and the fact that its tapering edge was partly

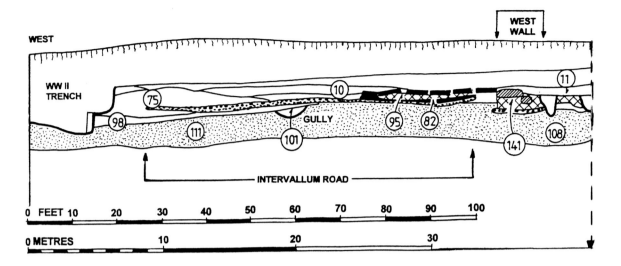

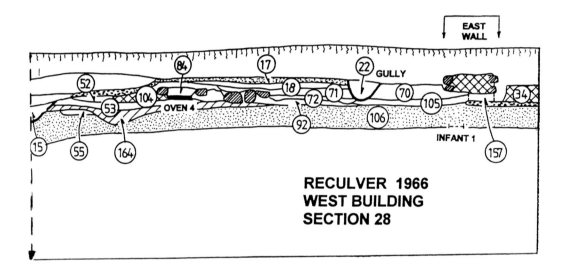

Fig. 35.   *Reculver 1966. Section 28 across West Building.*

sealed by the *Intervallum* Road, there seems little doubt that this layer formed the tail of the Rampart Bank, as noted elsewhere inside the fort. It extended to a point no more than 50 ft. from the estimated position of the fort wall.

The West Site also produced domestic rubbish including pottery and small-finds. The former included mortaria (No. 188, 193, TS18 and TS32) all of 3rd and 4th century date and mostly found in post-Roman deposits. The samian ware (Nos. 230 and Stamp 10) included at least 60 sherds from Forms 30, 31(8), 33, 37(8), 36(7), 43, 45(5) and Ludowici forms(4). Most are Antonine – lst half of 3rd century. The small-finds included objects of bronze (Nos. 299, 318, 319, 332, 335, 379, 394, 405, 413), bone (Nos. 236,290,346,353) and glass (No. 400). The bronze objects include two brooches, a needle and a ring, whilst the bone objects include another scabbard-chape.

Context	Coin Nos.	Emperor	Date	Site Code
Primary soils	46	Herennia Etruscilla	250–3	Under L92
	47	Septimius Severus	193–211	163
In the Intervallum Road	27	Illegible	3–4C	78
	28	Carausius	286–93	78
	31	Claudius II	268–70	100
Oven 1	13	Caracalla	201–6	36
	15	Illegible	3–4C	36
Oven 8	39	Commodus	180–92	118
Pit F20	22	Tetricus I	270–3	58
Pit F25	34	Commodus	180–92	76
Inside Building	20	Claudius II	268–70	53
	42	Illegible	3–4C	53
	32	Radiate	260–90	85
	33	Illegible	3–4C	85
	38	Hadrian	117–38	85
	36, 37	Illegible	3–4C	72
Gully F12	9	Hadrian	117–38	15
Gully F24	44	Commodus	180–92	22
	45	Octacilia Severa	244–9	22
Unstratified and Unrelated Deposits	1	Illegible	3–4C	1
	2	Barbarous Radiate	270–90	1
	3, 4	Carausius	286–93	1
	5	Commodus	180–92	1
	6	Charles I or II	17C	1
	7	Marcus Aurelius	161–80	1
	8	Antoninus Pius	138–61	13
	10	Elagabalus	218–22	1
	11, 12, 29, 40	Illegible	3–4C	1
	14	Illegible	–	1
	16	Edward I– III	13–14C	18
	17	Illegible	17C	20
	18	Urbs Roma	330–40	41
	19	Gallienus	260–8	18
	21	Urbs Roma	330–5	62
	23	Edward I – III	13–14C	–
	24	Constantine I	310–17	50
	25	Herennia Etruscilla	250–3	31
	30	Radiate	260–90	–
	35	Claudius II	268–70	–
	41	Barbarous Radiate	270–90	–
	43	Faustina II	160–80	1
	48	Claudius II	268–70	1
	49	Geta	200–2	1

Table O. Coins from the West Building (1966).

NO. 16 THE NORTH-WEST BUILDING (under church) – (Fig. 72)

In 1969, a selective programme of excavation was carried out inside the ruins of St. Mary's church. This revealed important new information on the church, but it also revealed a short length of a wall of a Roman building not previously known (in Trenches 3 and 4).

In detail, the wall ran on a roughly east-west axis under the *opus signinum* floor in the north aisle of the church, where it had been cut by at least one grave and a small circular pit. It was traced for 11 ft., but it clearly extended beyond in both directions. It was constructed of sandstone blocks set in yellow clay, of which only one course survived (6 in. high). It appeared to rest on a shallow foundation of small pebbles and white mortar, just 2 in. deep. It was generally 2 ft. 1in. wide, though its width could have increased to 2 ft. 6in. if adjacent sandstone blocks represented an offset. Part of the south face was intact, but the north face had been damaged, mainly by a later grave. Its top lay 2 ft. 1in. below present ground-level.

The limited extent of the excavation here makes interpretation difficult. The wall appears typical of many Roman walls found elsewhere inside the fort and all regarded as relating to Period II. Even so, it is likely that this wall formed one side of a substantial masonry building situated on the north side of the *Via Principalis* and about 45 ft. from it. It also lay just west of the conjectured *Via Praetoria* and as such may be the only Roman building to have survived erosion in the north-west quarter of the fort. The overall size and shape of this building cannot be determined, but it is likely that it was a barrack, one of several inside the fort. It lay only 25 ft. from the cliff edge, but no trace of it appeared when part of this was exposed by the sea in about 1990.

NO. 17 THE CORN-DRYING OVEN (S.E. OF THE FORT) – (Fig. 36 and Plates XXXIX–XL)

Regular patrols of the area surrounding the Roman fort occasionally produced useful evidence of the extramural structures, or settlement. One such event occurred in October, 1963 when workmen were found digging the foundation-trenches of a new toilet block on the Council caravan site. This was at a point about 200 ft. diagonally south-east of the corner of the Roman fort in an area little explored (Fig. 5). It was immediately clear that an unknown Roman structure had been revealed and the story how this was saved from destruction, fully excavated and reburied was told in 2002 (Ref. 31). A small area to its west was excavated in September, 1964 when a large stoke-hole was located and partially excavated.

The structure took the form of a main chamber some 16 x 15 ft. overall, connected via a short furnace-tunnel 10 ft. long, to the large stoke-hole at least 9 ft. wide on its west side. The structure had been built about 3 ft. into the ground and constructed of flint, tile and sandstone blocks set in a dense orange clay. The stoke-hole seemed to have been unlined, though it was not fully examined. Three possible post-holes were found near its south-west edge and may represent the supports for a canopy over the actual stoke-hole.

In detail, the north, east and south walls of the main chamber were about 2 ft. 4 in. thick and survived to a height of about 3 ft. 4 in. Of these, the north and south walls both contained hollow flue-channels, each about 24 x 12 ins., running along their lengths. Both walls had seven smaller lateral flues, linking the main flue-channel with the central chamber, though of varying sizes. Of these, the central flue in each wall was the largest, at about 9 x 6 in. whilst the remaining flues

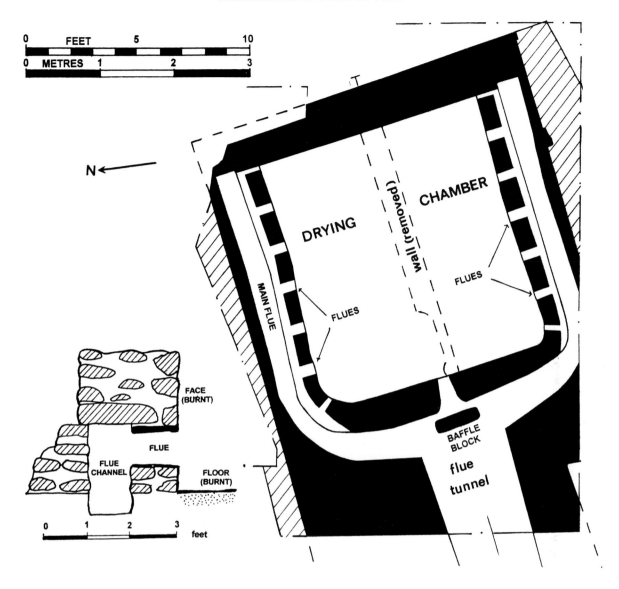

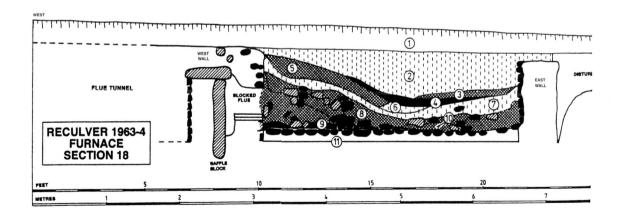

Fig. 36. *Reculver 1963–4. Plan and Section 18 of Corn Drying Oven.*

diminished in size towards the corners where the smallest was about 8 x 4 in. All 14 smaller flues had been constructed with six large fragments of Roman tile laid horizontally on each side, with a Roman brick as a capstone. The main flue-channels inside the walls were capped with large sandstone blocks.

The west wall of the structure was much more substantial for it not only contained an internal flue-channel, linking with the main flue-channels inside the north and south walls, but it also incorporated the furnace-tunnel. In all it was about 11 ft. in length and this included about 12 in. for the internal flue and about 10 ft. for the furnace-tunnel. It contained a single, lateral flue, about 13 x 8 in., again linked with the main internal chamber and thus produced a total of 15 lateral flues in all. In addition, a very large sandstone block, about 30 x 24 in. and 5 in. thick, had been placed on end to create a vertical heat baffle, or deflector, at the east end of the furnace-tunnel. The tunnel was constructed with large fragments of Roman brick placed on edge.

Most of the structure showed clear signs of severe heat. The stoke-hole was largely unburnt and presumably the fuel was stored here and the stoking operation controlled from this position. The west end of the furnace-tunnel, was severely burned and most of the bricks here were badly damaged by the intense heat. Clearly, this was where the fire had been laid and stoked. The heat from the fire had then passed along the furnace-tunnel, deflected left and right by the centrally placed baffle and then passed along the hollow flue-channels inside the lateral walls and then into the main chamber through the 15 smaller flues. The whole process was devised to generate hot air for the main chamber, which was to some extent insulated, being largely underground. A line of flints, some 12 in. wide, across the centre of the chamber marked the position of a central wall, later removed. Its imprint showed clearly on the face of the east wall and it seems likely that originally it divided the chamber into two equal parts, each about 11 x 5 ft.

An examination of the internal walls of the main chamber showed that substantial modifications had been carried out. Two of the smaller flues had been blocked off, the larger one in the west wall and the one closest to it in the south wall, thus leaving just 13 still open. The blocking consisted of clay and tile fragments. The central wall had also been removed and the actual main chamber had been used as the furnace. This scorched the floor and baked all the internal wall surfaces very hard and left a thin black layer of charcoal over the whole area. It also baked hard the clay covering of the two blocked flues.

An east-west section (Section 18) across the internal chamber revealed a thick layer of charcoal (L.9) over the burnt floor. This was sealed by a deep deposit of orange clay, flints and sandstone blocks (L.8) which seems to represent the collapse of part of the superstructure. This was in turn covered by layers, (L.6 and L.7) of grey-black loamy silts, over which there was more clay (L.5). Above this was another layer of black charcoal (L.4), perhaps dumped here from an adjacent area. A band of yellow clay (L.3) lay on this and the remaining void was filled by a deep layer, some 2 ft. thick at its centre, of grey-black loam (L.2) representing a progressive silting. Near its top was a sherd of medieval pottery. It seems likely that the filling of this structure gradually silted over a long period of time and may still have shown as a slight hollow in the 13th century or later. No artefacts were recovered from the central chamber.

The precise function of this elaborate structure is not clear. It appears to be unique and cleverly engineered. Its aim was to conduct hot air into the main chamber, presumably as a drying function and Professor Sir Ian Richmond suggested (per. com.) that it was a corn-drying oven. If so, the central wall may have supported lateral racks fixed into the side walls. No trace of any such fixings was found and it seems likely that these would have been higher up at ground-level and certainly above the tops of the small flues. Presumably corn, or even other food-stuffs, such as fish, could have been dried here in the same way as the more normal Roman corn-dryers operated.

The superstructure seems to have been destroyed and the main-chamber and stoke-hole filled with soil and some stone debris. The excavation produced almost no artefacts. On balance, it is highly likely that this structure was constructed by the military garrison sometime in the 3rd century and eventually abandoned. It is possible that similar structures could survive in this area, but none appeared along the line of the adjacent access road when this was totally replaced in 1994–5 (Ref. 32). The whole line, some 500 yards long, was closely monitored by the K.A.R.U. and the only substantial structure revealed was a possible Roman road running north-west of the corn-drying oven. Several minor ditches and features were, however, located. Finally, both this road and the oven lay beyond the outer defensive ditch of the fort.

No. 18 THE EXTRAMURAL SETTLEMENT (Figs. 4 and 5 and Plates XLVI–XLVIII)

It seems clear that significant Roman structures and features existed on both the west and north sides of the Roman fort. There can be little doubt that most of these formed part of an extensive civil settlement, or *vicus*, outside the fort. Only those on the west side were recorded in detail, entirely by the writer, mainly from 1952–58, but also up until 2004. Here, the evidence took the form of 12 well-shafts, four pits, a hearth, a cremation burial, evidence of a metalled road leading from the west gate of the fort and a collection of unstratified artefacts. All of these were soon published (Refs. 1 and 2).

The wells (Table P, lettered A–M) had mostly been about 14–20 ft. deep when dug in Roman times, but as the sea eroded the cliff only the bottoms, between one and seven feet deep, remained for investigation. Even then, the excavations had to be fitted in between the tides and the shafts quickly back-filled for safety. Most traces of these were removed by beach-surface erosion in a matter of months. The wells were discovered over a distance of about 700 ft. and it seems likely that they flanked either side of the road into the fort. No masonry, or deep ditches, were revealed here though a few minor features such as post-holes could have existed, but were undetected due to the continuous erosion.

Well	West of Fort (ft)	MHWM (ft)	From Cliff (ft)	Shape	Size	Depth and Notes
A	580	-40	70	Rect	4. x 3 ft.	? Black fill + Clay lining
B	630	-40	70	"	4 x 3 ft.	? " " " "
C	740	–	–	"	3 x 3 ft.	10 in.
D	810	-15	45	"	5 x 5 ft.	2ft. 2in. Black fill and Samian
E	840	+2	24	"	4 x 3½ ft.	3½ ft. Samian
F	880	+16	?	"	5 x 4½ ft.	5 ft. Black fill and Samian
G	470	–	On face	Circ	3 ft.	1 ft. 1 in. Samian
H	520	–	17	Rect	4 x 3½ in.	4 ft.
J	1000	–	55	"	–	1 ft.
K	1120	–	2	"	5 x 3½ in.	7 ft. 4 in. Pottery vessel
L	480	–	18	"	4½. x 3 ft.	2½ ft. Black fill
M	420	–	On face	Circ	3 ft. 9 in.	4 ft. 8 in. Coin & female skeleton
Burial	750	–	"	–	–	2½ ft. Bone in pottery vessel

Table P. Details of Roman Wells found west of the Fort

In detail, ten of the wells were rectangular in plan and ranged in size from 3 ft. (Well C) to 5 ft. (Well D) at beach level. Two circular ones were 3 ft. and 3 ft. 9 in. in diameter, respectively. Six of the wells contained a sticky black (smelly) silt suggesting that they had remained open for many years. Four more were filled with a sandy loam, probably representing collapsed material from the sides of the well. All had been cut down into the hard sandstone layer which underlay the soft sand section of the Thanet Beds and thus effectively tapped the water-table. One pottery vessel, clearly used for drawing water, was found intact at the bottom of Well K. Another complete pottery vessel was found at the bottom of Well M.

Whilst most wells produced some domestic rubbish, two had contained human female skeletons exposed by the sea in the cliff face in the upper section of the well shafts (Ref. 16). Well L, found initially by others, revealed two complete skeletons accompanied by two bracelets and three bronze rings. The rings here have been dated to the second half of the 3rd century. A third skeleton, from Well M, again found by others, had a necklace, two bracelets and a ring. Well M, when later relocated and excavated by the writer, produced a coin of Gordianus III (A.D. 238–44) near its base. It seems clear that these female skeletons do not represent orthodox burials, nor accidents and it is likely that the three women were victims and that their bodies complete with jewellery, were thrown into these two abandoned wells and never recovered. It is to be regretted that these important discoveries were neither properly excavated, nor even recorded by those who made the discoveries. It is just possible that more skeletons remain to be found nearby in other abandoned wells inside the line of the 1957 sea-wall.

The pottery recovered from the wells was mainly of late-2nd and early-3rd century date, as was much of the unstratified material. Samian ware predominated and both stamped and decorated vessels were found in addition to about 100 coins. In addition, several small-finds were recovered from this area including a bronze brooch (No. 317), a possible bone stylus (No. 248) from Well D and an iron buckle (No. 427) from Well M. In general the finds dated from A.D. 170–360. This agrees well with the evidence from inside the fort. Of special interest, for wider studies, is the information gained on the rate of coastal erosion here. When Well K was excavated by the writer in 1957 it was only 2 ft. from the cliff face, 7 ft. 4 in. deep and located on a ledge about 3 ft. high. When relocated by the writer in 2001 it was 28 ft. from the cliff face and just 6 in. deep, even though latterly it had been substantially protected by a steel frame holding back quantities of large stones. By 2001 the sea had destroyed the steel frame, removed the stone and cut back the cliff and ledge and also lowered the beach surface. Hence, in 44 years the cliff had retreated 26 ft. and the beach surface dropped by about 4 ft. in spite of the partial protection.

There can be little doubt that these finds relate to an extramural settlement on the west side of the fort. The original concrete sea-wall has protected the first 430 ft. west of the fort and prevented erosion and chance discoveries. It is thus not known what had existed in that zone, but clearly the fort's defensive ditches would have occupied the first 80 ft, now partly covered by the King Ethelbert Inn. The discoveries were mostly made at a distance of 430–1120 ft. west of the fort and this suggests the extent of the civil settlement. It is not known how far this extended northwards in the area destroyed by the sea, nor if it extended inland. It is unlikely to have extended inland more than 200 ft. for the low-lying marshland there is likely to mark the limit.

It is also clear that substantial structures and wells had existed north of the fort and these, too, must have formed part of the extramural settlement. Battely (who died in 1708) reports brick substructures and mosaic flooring and it seems likely that these represent a substantial masonry building, with a *hypocaust,* north of the fort. The most likely structure would have been an external Bath House (Period I) relating to the fort and whilst mosaic flooring is unusual, this could be a reference to plain red tessellation. In the same general area were cisterns, 10–12 ft. deep and broad, lined with oak stakes and planks and bottomed with puddled clay. There can be little doubt that these were constructed as water-storage cisterns, almost certainly for collecting rain-water, or for tapping the water-table. It seems highly likely that evidence of minor structures and even timber-buildings was entirely missed. The objects recovered from this area seem to have a wider date-range, but significantly include coins of Tiberius and Nero as being fresh and unworn and also six British coins. The coins are likely to relate to the mid-1st century Fortlet found beneath the central area of the later stone fort and were clearly not part of the latter's extramural settlement.

On the east side little is known, but again the fort's ditches occupied the first 80 ft. Beyond, only the corn-drying oven found accidentally in 1963 (p. 92) and a metalled road (Ref. 32) excavated in 1994, are known. Minor trial-holes in this general area showed undisturbed natural soils at a shallow depth, but small ditches, minor features or an isolated larger structure could still exist here. It is not known how the east side has been affected by erosion, though clearly some 3 ft. of soil has been reduced close to the fort wall.

Little is known of the area to the south of the fort, now entirely covered by the council caravan site. Again the first 80 ft. from the fort wall was occupied by the defensive ditches and random test-holes produced no features beyond. Again it is not known how much of this area has been reduced by ploughing and minor features and isolated structures could still survive, if deeply cut.

CHAPTER V

THE MID-FIRST CENTURY FORTLET
(FIGS. 37–39 AND PLATES XLI–XLIV)

In all, some ten or more sections of ditch containing mid-first century pottery were found during the extensive evaluation-trenching programme. Collectively, these appear to form three sides of a broadly rectangular area (Fig. 37) sealed beneath the stone-fort's construction levels and internal buildings. These seem to represent a Roman fort, or Fortlet, of the Conquest period (see Discussion p. 192).

The south side was picked up by Trenches A and B below the rear division of the fort in 1963. Here the excavation located a pair of similar ditches in each trench (Section 15) running on an east-west axis largely parallel to and about 35–40 ft. inside the south wall of the later fort. The trenches were 50 ft. apart and clearly the ditches extend for at least 60 ft. on this south side. The inner ditch was 6 ft. wide and 4 ft. deep, whilst the smaller outer ditch was about 4 ft. wide and 2 ft. deep, though both probably reduced by weathering (Fig. 39A). The combined profile was 15 ft. in width and both ditches had silted with an even dark brown loam (L.64). Both produced occasional sherds of mid-1st century pottery, including a samian Form 15/17 of pre-Flavian date. Just outside the lip of the inner ditch in each trench was a shallow gully, mostly 2 by 1ft. also silted. Its function is not clear, but a palisade trench is the most likely possibility. By projection, to meet the presumed east and west ditches, the overall length of the south side can be calculated as about 210 ft.

What appears to be the eastern side of the enclosure was picked up on eight sites. In most cases the same broad profile was detected and the same silt and scattered potsherds recovered, though not the flanking gully beyond the inner lip. The ditch was traced for over 270 ft., on a broadly north-south line to a point where it was cut by the eroded cliff. If it connected with the south ditch, as seems likely, then a roughly right-angled corner is produced by projection and a minimum length of 340 ft. is indicated. One problem is that two different alignments appear to be represented on the east side!

In detail, the 1959 trench along the *Via Quintana* and also Trench A in 1961, clearly picked up the ditches on the east side, but the profiles were unclear. It was, however, in 1963 that a small excavation was undertaken near the middle of the east side (Box OB) to examine the ditches in detail (Fig. 39B). A broad W-profile, some 14 ft. wide was revealed (Section 17B) and more mid-1st century sherds recovered. Close examination, however, revealed that at this point the inner ditch had been dug deeper by about 3 ft. The sides were found to have remained hard, whilst the bottom was barely 12 ins. wide. The lower section of the inner ditch seems to have been backfilled with mottled soils which contrasted with the normal even fill elsewhere. Another trench was cut nearby in 1964 (Box OD) and this mostly examined the inner ditch which was again deeper (Fig. 38, Section 20). Significantly, too, the upper ditch fill had been cut through by a narrow channel which seems to represent a partial re-cut of the ditch. This had silted with a dense mud-silt (L.5–6) which again produced mid-first century pottery (Nos. 161–8).

Clearly, there was some significant variation of the ditches at this point. In addition, the east ditches also appear to realign here swinging perhaps 25 degrees to the west. Additionally, two circular stone-packed post-holes were found on the central berm and, if directly associated, suggests something structural. Perhaps the most likely explanation is that this formed part of a

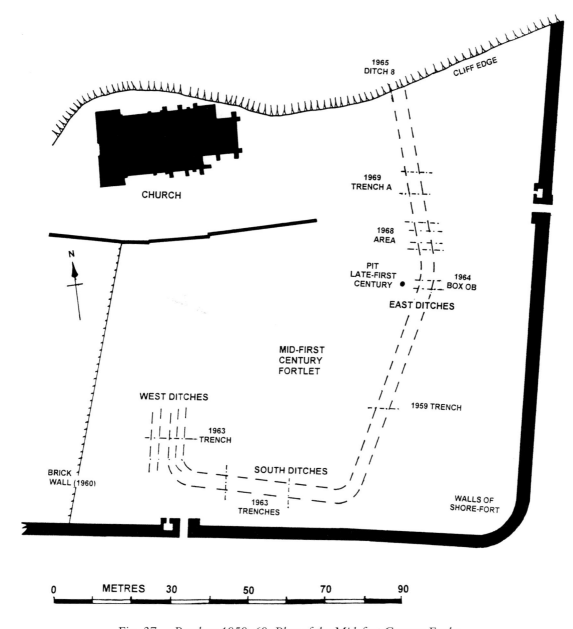

Fig. 37.   *Reculver 1959–69. Plan of the Mid-first Century Fortlet.*

wooden bridge over the ditch. If so, this might also suggest that here was an important point on the east side of the enclosure. It might also explain the realignment and the extra depth of the original ditch and its later re-cutting. At the very least this point contains significant variations, but only future work may resolve the matter. Even so, the overlying Roman masonry will present a continuing problem. The upper filling of the ditches hereabouts produced a samian Form 18 of early-Flavian date. In another trench (1962 Box G) both ditches were located and produced a human femur (L.79) and a dog's skull in the silt filling of the lower sections of the ditches. The femur is likely to have come from a disturbed adult burial, though none is known inside the excavated area.

The main area of investigation was in 1968 when the two ditches were found with difficulty running beneath the East Barracks (p. 73). Here, both the larger inner and the smaller outer ditch

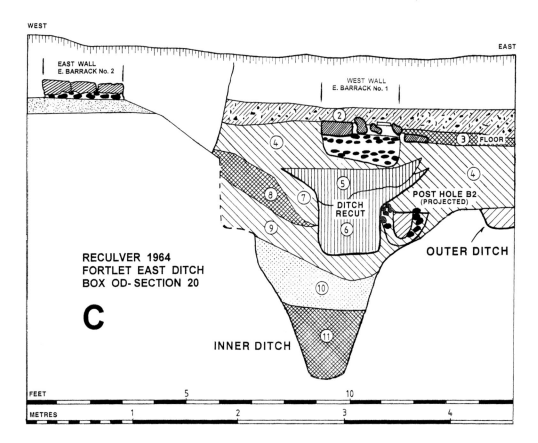

Fig. 38.   *Reculver 1964. Section 20 across East Ditches of Fortlet (C).*

were located and the overall width estimated as 15 ft. A length of 28 ft. was certainly detected and the ditches clearly extended to both north and south. Again, small mid-1st century potsherds were recovered, including a samian Form 27 of early-Flavian date.

With the demolition of the old Coast Guard Station at about the end of 1968, it was possible to examine the continuation of the mid-first century ditches on the north side of the main east-west footpath through the fort. Here, in 1969, it was possible to open up an area some 40 x 20ft. (Area A). Both ditches (Fig. 28), again with a largely W-profile, continued on the new alignment and their consolidated filling had been overbuilt by a large Timber Framed Building (p. 68) which was not removed during the excavation. In addition, the ditches had been cut through by the late-Roman ditch draining the Bath House towards the East Gate. The same ditches were located in Trench C, some 50 ft. to the north. In Area A the inner ditch was about 8 ft. wide, 3 ft. deep and had a flat base just 9 ins. wide. The smaller outer ditch was about 4 ft. wide and about 2 ft. deep, hence some 12 ft. in overall width. Finally, the continuation of the east ditches was found on the exposed East Cliff (Ditch 8) in 1966 (p. 66), where again part of the broad profile was revealed. Here the ditches were cut by Room E of the Officers Quarters and produced a few more sherds of mid-1st century pottery (Nos.169–73) from the small area available.

As regards what appears to be the west side of the fortlet, this was only seen in one trench in 1963 (Trench C). There two north-south ditches were found, the east one about 12 ft. wide and 3 ft. deep (Fig. D) and the western one about 8 ft. wide and 4 ft. deep. They were some 12 ft. apart and the profiles differed. It is not clear from this single section exactly how these two ditches related to each other, nor their exact alignments. Provisionally they are here regarded as jointly

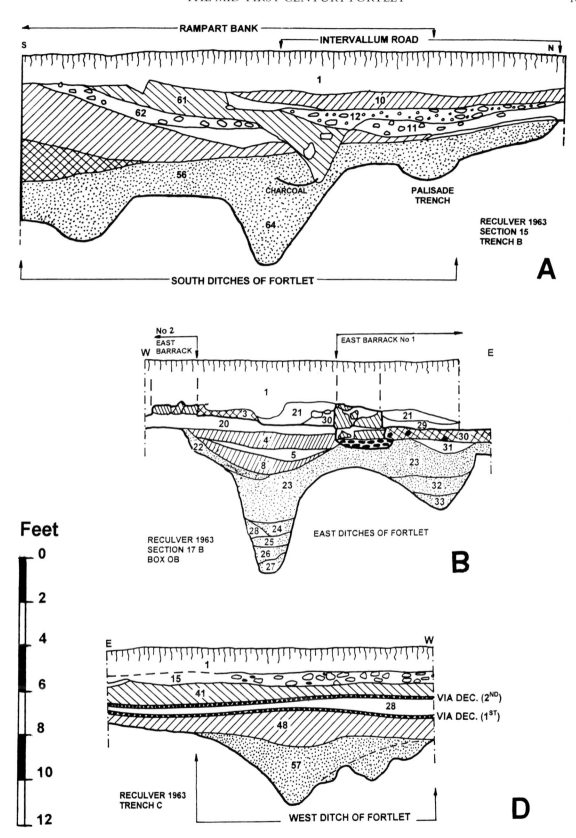

Fig. 39. *Reculver 1963. Sections of South (A), East (B) and West (D) Ditches of Fortlet.*

forming the west side of the fortlet, but their continuation northwards may have been largely reduced by the extensive soil reduction in that area. A single sherd of samian ware, a Form 18 of Flavian date, was found at the top of the filling of the western ditch. As the two ditches were revealed only part way through the excavation an extra trench (Box JH) was opened to the immediate south. This picked up the inner ditch again, but here it was turning to the south-east where it seems likely that it would eventually have linked up with the inner ditch found on the south side in Trenches A and B (also in 1963). If so, a roughly rounded corner is achieved, though other possibilities exist. The ditch in Box JH also continued southwards just possibly to link with the outer ditch in Trenches A and B. Only more work could have resolved the matter. In all, only some 15 ft. of the west ditch was revealed. Two sherds of samian ware, a Form 18 and a Ritterling 12 of pre-Flavian date, came from the upper filling of the ditches in Box JH.

Apart from a light scatter of mid-1st century potsherds, one special find here was the head of an ox (Plate XLIV). This was found in an upright position, only about 10ins. above the bottom of the ditch in Box JH, where it had been discarded. Its frontal above the eyes had been smashed in, or pole-axed, leaving a ragged hole about 2 ins. wide. It seems likely that the skull was the discarded remnant of an animal slaughtered for its meat, perhaps by the occupants of the Fortlet.

One other feature of 1st century date was found on the South Gatehouse excavation in 1964 (p. 32). There, a short length of gully or ditch, about 6 ft. long and running in a north-east by south-west direction, extended beneath the unexcavated section. It contained coarse potsherds, a fragment of a samian Form 18 of Flavian date and a stamped samian base (Stamp No.11) of Vitalis (A.D.65–90). Its relationship to the Fortlet ditches, some 50–60ft. to the north, is difficult to gauge. The overall plan of the Fortlet and its wider implications are discussed below (p. 192).

CHAPTER VI

THE EXCAVATED OBJECTS

(1) THE COINS

by RICHARD REECE

This report is written solely on the coin evidence – the excavator will redress the balance by suggesting a more complete picture in his discussion. I feel sure that it is better for the reader to have two interpretations which differ in detail rather one in which all variation has been suppressed.

The full coin list gives details of all the coins found in the recent past. Some of the 121 coins described as 3rd–4th C may yield more information on cleaning, but there is no reason why they should alter the balance now established. In other words, since the majority of identifiable coins belong to the radiate period (260 to 296) it is a fair guess that the majority of corroded coins are similar. The identification of the medieval coins is very provisional and the site would clearly benefit from a full survey by a medieval specialist.

Two coins stand out as remarkable finds in England. The Provincia Dacia of Aemilian is probably the only British example of such a coin, but they are better known on the Danube and in the Balkans. The coin of Trajan Decius showing the portrait of Vespasian is described by Roman Imperial Coinage as rare and that means that not only do few turn up, but even the great collections do not see them very often. The arrival of these two coins of the period 250 to 253 at Reculver means that some unusual mechanism of import is at work. By far the simplest explanation is in terms of the movement of people, most of whom brought purses with them. To suggest a troop movement from the Danube is going too far too fast, but this is the sort of thing that must account for these coins. Neither coin can have had a long life. The Aemilian is a middle sized bronze coin, a Dupondius, an As, or their equivalent. Any of these coins that survived till the 270's were probably converted to Barbarous Radiates by the 280's. The Trajan Decius is a base silver radiate. This type of coin must have one of the shortest lives of any Roman coin. Issued in the 250's they were in the middle of the slide in silver content which, in the next ten years had decreased to almost zero. Middling silver like this would have been preferentially extracted from circulation quickly in the 260's and 270's because each one could provide the silver for four or five of the very basest coins. These two coins therefore came into Britain after 250 and would have been removed from general circulation inside the empire by 280.

The other coins in the list form a group which looks unusual because of the number of coins of the early third century — normally a time of scarcity of new coin in most of Britain — and the enormous peak of radiate coins compared with the trickle of fourth century issues. That is, the number of radiate coins would not be surprising if the lists went on to show two or three times that number of coins in the fourth century, but this is not the case. Now that we have started to talk about numbers we can more easily see what is happening in diagrams than in words.

The first diagram (fig Q) is constructed from table 1 and is no more than a visual representation of Reculver against a British background. The necessary figures are assembled in table 1 and start with the actual number of coins from Reculver (column 2) divided up into the usual periods of about 20 years (column 1) which in the early empire are imperial reigns, and in the later empire periods related to the different issues of coins. In column 3 the coins are expressed as coins per thousand. As the total of identifiable or datable coins is 641 column 3 is roughly twice column 2. Column 4 gives the average value in each period of coins per thousand from a range of sites in

Britain (Reece 1995). Column 5 doubles the values of column 4 and column 6 gives the coins from Reculver as a percentage of twice the British average. This may seem to introduce an extra complication, but I hope that the reason will become clear when the figures are reduced to a diagram.

1	2	3	4	5	6
to 43	0	0	8	16	0
43–54	0	0	18	36	0
54–69	1	2	8	16	10
69–96	2	3	33	66	5
96–117	2	3	9	38	8
117–138	8	12	16	32	40
138–161	9	14	17	34	40
161–180	13	20	11	22	93
180–192	9	14	4	8	172
193–222	21	33	13	26	127
222–238	18	28	6	12	230
238–260	18	28	7	14	194
260–275	205	320	146	292	110
275–296	164	256	135	270	95
296–317	16	25	18	36	71
317–330	25	39	42	84	47
330–348	71	111	246	492	23
348–364	34	53	87	174	31
364–378	17	30	105	210	14
378–388	3	5	4	8	54
388–402	3	5	57	114	4

On fig Q the 100% line represents twice the British average; the average is at 50%. By definition the values from all the sites used to form the average lie around that average – from zero to up to twice the average. So on the diagram 'normality' lies between 0 and 100%. There are five values at Reculver which lie above 'normality'; they start from 180 to 193, go to a peak in 222 to 238, and then return to normality in the early fourth century. These periods of unusual coin loss cover the period from 180 to 260 and this makes the peculiarity even more surprising since this is the time of least coin loss in Britain.

When Septimius Severus brought an army to Britain in the early years of the third century he established some new bases and restored others. The new bases – for example Carpow in Scotland – were allowed to fall into disuse after the campaigns and their coin lists show a clear peak of coins for the period 193 to 222 (Bateson and Holmes 1997, 529). The establishment of an imperial base at York must have had a remarkable effect on the economy of that city so we might expect this to show clearly on the diagram of coins from York when they are published. This period is heavily under the influence of the historical (written) sources so that 'the events' are restricted to the campaigns of a single emperor. But this picture is beginning to be questioned by some workers in Scotland who see a rather more diffused picture accumulating from the material sources. Thus there seems to be a start to events earlier than the attested campaigns of Severus and some material aspects continue after the withdrawal under his son Caracalla.

Set against the historical background Reculver has oddities that might assist the building of a new picture. The first signs of firm occupation, in the coin list at least, are during the reign of Marcus Aurelius (161 to 180). There is nothing unusual about a good number of coins of this emperor but at Reculver they go above average for the first time in the sequence. If the rest of the

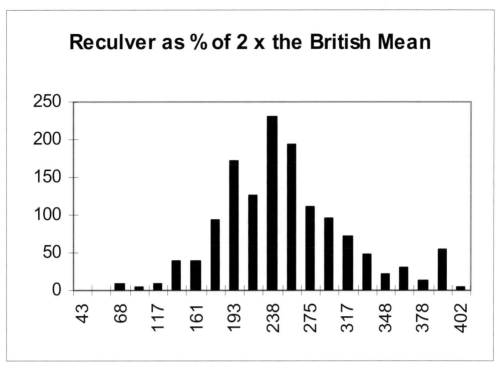

Fig. Q. *The coins from Reculver plotted as a percentage of twice the average of coin finds from British sites. The numbers on the horizontal axis of the diagram give the date at which the period closed. Thus 180 stands for the period from 161 to 180.*

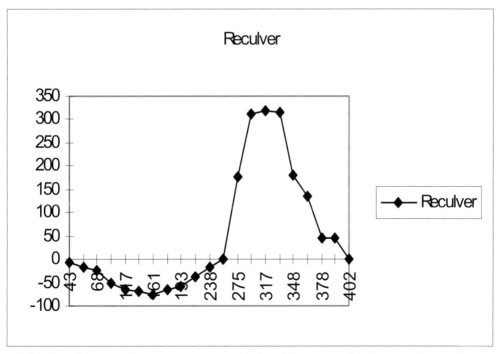

Fig. R. *Coinage at Reculver seen against the British average value shown as the zero line.*

material record from the excavations agrees this might suggest a foundation in the 160s or 170s. This idea is encouraged by the remarkable loss of coins of Commodus (180 to 192) which is far above the British average, and even above the 'normal' range which stops around 100%.

An important point must be made here about absolute and relative numbers of coins. There are in fact 9 coins of Commodus compared with 13 of Marcus Aurelius – is this enough evidence on which to make emphatic claims? The point at issue is not the number 8, which are less than the 14 at Reculver's neighbour, Richborough. Richborough moves from 37 coins of M Aurelius down to 14 coins of Commodus, and most other sites in Britain follow this downward movement. Reculver is odd because the move downwards is much less than most other British sites. While the reliability of any coin sample can be questioned this is to miss the point. The numbers are small, the site has not been totally excavated, and other factors can be brought into play. But these factors provide roughly the same problems on almost every other site in Britain. Despite these factors on almost every site a pattern emerges of a substantial drop in coins found from Marcus Aurelius to Commodus; Reculver, with exactly the same factors at work, bucks this fairly general trend.

The very high peak in the period 222 to 238, which is four times the British average, rests on only 16 coins, yet this is one of the highest actual numbers of such coins from a British excavation. The period when historical sources insist on activity in Britain, from 193 to 222, is in fact a lower period at Reculver where coin loss is within the limits of British normality.

All this might support the idea that events are on the move in Britain during the reign of Commodus; provisions are being made, bases built, and, if Scottish coin hoards are so interpreted, Barbarians are being tranquillised by injections of denarii. Then, after a period of preparation, the emperor in person takes the field – perhaps hoping for a moment of glory. There is clearly a strong reflection of the Claudian conquest here, with the hard work being done by an advance force, but the emperor appearing for the final march. During the final build-up and the imperial campaigns Reculver, far from the fray, takes a support role, but the hoped for moment of glory did not materialise and Caledonia was left to its own devices. The emperor died at York, his son gave up the campaigns, and Britain left written history for some time. But Reculver did not share in the general depression (if such in fact existed).

After the historical and material withdrawal from Caledonia Reculver is so much re-invigorated that it hits its highest coin loss; relative among periods at Reculver, almost absolute among other sites for that period. The next period, 238 to 260 saw the import of two very unusual coins, and at least some of the peak of coins struck in 222 to 238 might well have come into Britain during this period. All this suggests an unusually strong coin supply and use at the already flourishing Reculver from the Severan withdrawal (c.212) to at least 260.

By 296 coin loss at Reculver had returned to the normal British pattern which continued throughout the 4th century. Up to 330 Reculver is at the average value, but it falls below for the normally prolific period 330 to 348, recovers a little for 348 to 364, and is then unusually low for 364 to 378. The bump in the diagram for 378 to 388 is caused by only 3 coins in a very variable, but usually scarce period. This gives 6 coins per thousand instead of the expected 5 and is not a suitable foundation on which to build further historical fantasy. More important is the absence of silver coin in the second half of the fourth century. While these coins are not common finds (about 1 coin in every thousand) their presence can sometimes suggest a link to the military establishment. It seems unlikely, as judged from the coins, that Reculver is fully garrisoned in the later fourth century and it can certainly not be described, from the coin finds at least, as flourishing.

Since we have compared Reculver with an average formed from 140 British sites, and tried to interpret the results as applied to Reculver, we ought to see whether there are other similar sites in the sample. The method used is that outlined in Britannia (Reece 1995) which produces the diagram in fig R.

The important point in interpreting fig R is to see the horizontal line labelled 0 as the British background. At times Reculver moves above this background, at other times, below; it is the movement that matters. Thus Reculver starts weakly compared with the British average and so moves downwards. It does not add on coins, period by period, as much as the average site. About

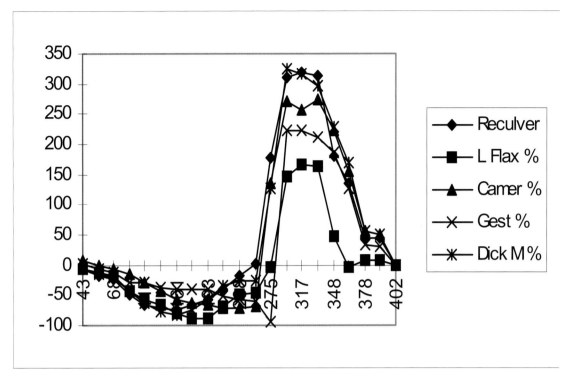

Fig. S. *Reculver compared with its closest numerical relatives in Britain. L Flax; Lincoln Flaxengate; Camer; Camerton; Gest, Gestingthorpe; Dick M, Dickets Mead.*

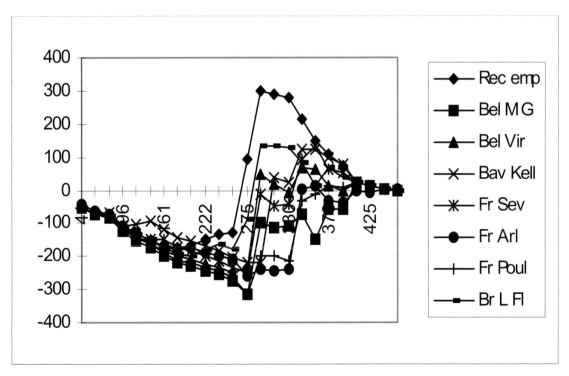

Fig. T. *Reculver compared with other similar sites throughout the empire. Bel, sites in Begium; Bav, sites in Bavaria; Fr, sites in France. Reculver and Lincoln Flaxengate (Br L Fl) as before.*

161 the downward slide stops and Reculver adds on coins more quickly than the average site. This trend accelerates so that Reculver is adding on far more coins in the periods 260 to 275 and 275 to 296 than most sites in Britain. There are then two periods of absolute 'averageness' where Reculver adds on coins at exactly the same rate as the average site – the diagram stays level from 296 to 317 and 317 to 330. After that a precipitous decline sets in with Reculver never again adding on coins at the same rate as the average British site.

To show how Reculver compares with other individual places first in Britain and then beyond more diagrams are needed. The same method (Reece 1995) has been used as in Fig Y. If Reculver had been used in the 140 sites which provided both the background and the discussion, with diagrams, in Britannia 1995 it would have appeared in fig 16 with seven other sites – the Flaxengate site at Lincoln, Lord Verulam's site collection from the area of Verulamium, the Wollaston House excavations at Dorchester (Dorset), the rural settlement of Camerton in Somerset, the Gestingthorpe Roman Villa in Essex, the small town at Kenchester in Herefordshire, and the villa at Dickets Mead in Hertfordshire. Details of publications can be found in Roman Coins from 140 sites in Britain (Reece 1991). Only four of the comparisons are shown on fig S to avoid confusion. Those left out cluster around Flaxengate.

There is one link between some of the sites (Verulam, Gestingthorpe and Dickets Mead), that of clear decline after the early fourth century, but otherwise they are a rather disparate collection. On most of the sites the great rise in coinage of 260 to 275 and 275 to 296 is obvious simply because the expected volume of fourth century coinage, which should balance the diagram and even out the peak, is absent. Comparison with the other diagrams in Britannia 1995 will show that the change in direction of the Reculver diagram after 161 is very unusual; but this is swamped in these diagrams by the much more common feature of many third century coins and far fewer coins of the fourth century.

The Flaxengate site at Lincoln in the lower, rather than the upper town, may have some similarities with Reculver, but that depends on whether the concentration of similarly unusual early third century coinage there is due to unusual supply or simply rubbish disposal. In the fascicule of Lincoln reports devoted to coins (Mann and Reece 1983) I suggested that the unusual presence of those coins could be due to the lower town being used as a rubbish dump in the third century and being little used thereafter. On the other hand, those coins could not have been deposited if they had not been distributed to Lincoln from the producing authority. The issue and distribution of coinage in the early third century is clearly a subject which would repay further study, especially in relation to coin finds in Britain. At present it seems safe to say that such coinage is found particularly in the East of Britain, from Kent to Carpow, and is much less visible in the West. This leads on to a comparison between Reculver and sites throughout the empire.

The method used to produce Fig T is exactly the same as that used to produce the earlier diagrams except that the sites used to prepare the background consists of 108 sites from around the empire rather than 140 sites all in Britain. Full details of the sites and the method have not yet been published, but an extended discussion may be found in Reece 2003.

The results of this comparison are fairly clear. The sites which show ups and downs in their diagrams similar to those at Reculver are indeed near at hand, geographically. They belong in Belgium and in France rather than the Rhein, the Danube, the East or the Mediterranean region. The only British site to fall into the group is one we have already encountered; sites in the West of Britain fall into completely different groups even when judged against coins throughout the empire. The message is that Reculver is more closely related by its pattern of coin loss to sites in modern Belgium and France than to sites in the west of Britain.

There is still one further point which needs to be investigated. British sites, in general, are known for their low proportion of early coins and their high proportion of coins of the fourth century – features found more on individual sites abroad than in regional patterns. These differences may be hiding quite strong similarities between the period 43 to 260 at Reculver and sites abroad and in the same way strong links in the period 260 to 450 may hidden by major differences in early coins. Reculver judged against an empire wide background can be seen for the earlier period in fig U and for the later period in fig V.

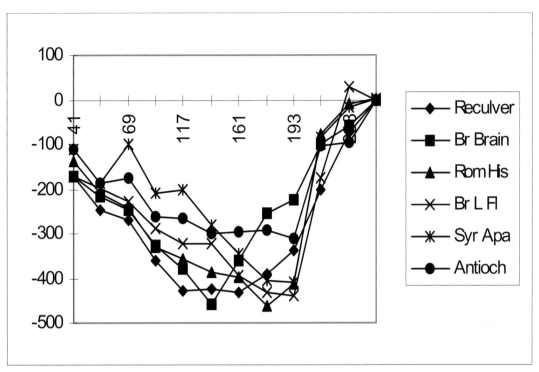

Fig. U.   *Reculver compared with other similar sites around the empire, up to AD 260. Br Brain, Braintree; Rom Hist, Histria in Romania; Br L Fl, Lincoln Flaxengate; Syr Apa; Apamaea in Syria; Antioch on the Orontes.*

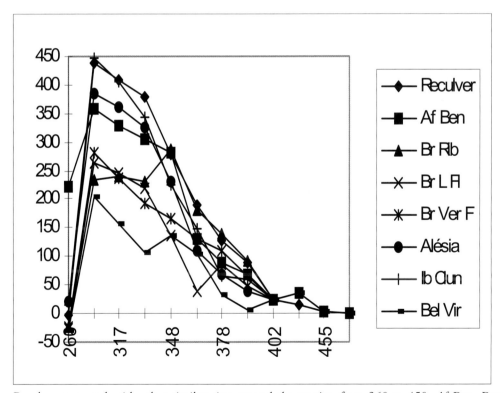

Fig. V.   *Reculver compared with other similar sites around the empire, from 260 to 450. Af Ben, Benghazi in Africa; in Britain – Rib, Ribchester, L Fl, Lincoln Flaxengate, Ver F, Frere's Verulamium; Alésia in France; Clunia in Spain; Bel Vir, Vireux in Belgium.*

Fig U. shows that there are several other sites round the empire that have fewer coins than average of the first century but which recover in the second century.

In Britain the absence of fourth century complications allows Braintree in Essex to come into the picture, otherwise the closest sites to Reculver are exotic with the Levant and the Black Sea represented. The differences between these similar sites are the moment at which they begin to recover from their early dearth of coins, and the steps by which they do it. Braintree represents several other sites that recover from about 138 – during the reign of Antoninus Pius while Antioch, Apamaea, Histria and Flaxengate only recover under Septimius Severus (193 to 222). Reculver is almost in a class of its own in that it recovers in several equal stage after 161. This agrees with what we have already seen from other diagrams, but makes more forcibly the point that such behaviour is extremely difficult to parallel in detail.

Fig V gives rather less detail because it consist mainly of sites which seem to run down in the fourth century. We suspected that from British comparisons; empire wide comparisons make the point more strongly. Thus the great activity in the Oppidum of Alésia is before the third century, and fourth century activity is on a much smaller scale. At Benghazi a new wall is built through the early town in the late third century thus strongly cutting the occupation down in scale. Emporium/Rosas in Catalonia would make the point even more strongly, but it has been removed from the diagram because it would reduce the scale of all the other sites. There a thriving early city is confined in a very small late enclave. For the third time the late activity at Reculver is seen to be slight, from the coin evidence. But in this case it is not a matter of being overshadowed by a bulk of early coins. The point is that the promise shown by coins of the late third century is not maintained. Working purely from the coin evidence it looks as if an important centre of operations of the period 160 to 275 is reduced to a supporting role thereafter.

Coin references

Up to A.D. 330 all references are to RIC except for the coin of Aemilian where a reference is given to Pick (1910). After 330 references are either to HK (330 to 348) or CK (348 to 402). These are respectively part I (HK) and part II (CK) of Carson, Hill and Kent 1960.

Bibliography

Bateson D and N Holmes 1997 Roman and Medieval coins found in Scotland, 1988–95, in Proceedings of the Society of Antiquaries of Scotland 127, 527–61.

Carson RAG, PV Hill, and JPC Kent 1960 Late Roman Bronze Coinage, London

Mann J and R Reece 1983 Roman coins from Lincoln 1970–1979, Archaeology of Lincoln vol. VI–2, CBA, London.

Pick B 1910 Die antiken Münzen Nord-Greichenlands: Vol I part 2. Dacien und Moesien, Berlin.

Reece R 1991 Roman coins from 140 sites in Britain, Cotswold Studies IV, Cirencester

Reece R. 1995 Site-finds in Roman Britain, Britannia 26, 179–206.

Reece R 2003 Comparing the coin finds from St-Bertrand-de-Comminges and Toulouse, Journal of Roman Archaeology 16, 611–23.

RIC edd. H. Mattingly, EA Sydenham, CHV Sutherland, RAG Carson, JPC Kent, and AM Burnett, Roman Imperial Coinage vols I to X, London 1923–94.

Reculver — full coin list

1	Nero	Dupondius as 378
1	Vespasian	As, copy as 497
1	Trajan	Sestertius reverse illegible
4	Hadrian	290, as 587, as 631, 970
1	Aelius	(Hadrian) 1063
4	Antoninus Pius	as 656, as 868, Sestertius illegible (2)
7	Marcus Aurelius	(Ant Pius) 1240, (MA) as 795, as 804, 1237, Sestertius reverse Victory, Sestertius reverse illegible, (Commodus) 658

2	Faustina II	Sestertius reverse illegible, As reverse illegible
6	Commodus	as 297, 323.a., as 324, as 355, 550, Sestertius corroded
1	Crispina	669
1	1st–2ndC	Sestertius otherwise illegible
1	2nd C	Sestertius halved
2	1st–3rd C	Corroded and illegible bronzes (2)
2	Septimius Severus	264 but no wheel under seat, as 689
2	Julia Domna	Denarius (1 corroded, 1 uncertain)
1	Geta	23
1	Caracalla	144.b.
2	Elagabalus	88, as 88
6	Severus Alexander	32, 64, 67, 160, 221, 250
3	Severus Alexander	296, denarii corroded (2)
3	Julia Mamaea	341 in copper, 343, Denarius illegible
1	Maximinus I	Sestertius reverse corroded
6	Early 3rd C	Corroded denarii (6)
2	Gordian III	as 143 but legend of RIC 1, 300.b.
2	Philip I	37A, Radiate uncertain
2	Otacilia Severa	Radiate: Otacilia Severa Aug / Rev Gordian III 245, Radiate corroded
1	Trajan Decius	80 (Restored Vespasian)
2	Herennia Etruscilla	(Trajan D) 59.b., as 66
1	Aemilian	Provincia Dacia, Pick 18, 58, AN VIII
1	Valerian I	15
1	Valerian II	3
1	Saloninus ?	as 24?
1	Salonina	(sole reign) 20
21	Gallienus	157, 163, 164, 176, as 176, 178, 179, 180, as 180, 181, 207, 236 (2), 238, 243, 252, 256, 283, reverse illegbile (3)
62	Claudius II	as 10–12, 15, as 15 (2), as 32, 54, 61, 62 (2), 66 (2), 71, as 72, 75, 80, 87, 91, as 91, as 98, copy as 98, 99, as 100, 102, 103, 104, 109, 146, 261(17), 266 (11), copy of 266 (3), uncertain (4)
1	Claudius II or Aurelian	Reverse illegible
1	Quintilian	33
4	Postumus	74, as 75, as 80?, reverse illegible
17	Victorinus	65, 71, 78 (2), copy of 78, copy of 112, 114 (3), 118 (6), reverse Pax, reverse illegible
45	Tetricus I	52, 56 (2), 68, 76, 79 (2), 87 (6), copy of 90, 100 (3), as 100 (5), 102, 112, 118, 121 (4), as 121, 132, 136, reverse Spes, reverse uncertain (12)
23	Tetricus II	As 223, 224, as 248, 254 (3), copy as 254, 260 (5), 270 (3), as 270 (2), 272 (3), copy as 272, 280?, reverse illegible
21	Carausius	98, 101, 155 (2), 475, 880, as 880 (6), 893 unmarked, as 893 unmarked (3), 982 unmarked, 983 unmarked (2), reverse Pax with vertical sceptre, reverse legend illegible / Victory placing shield on small column to r.
1	Diocletian/Carausius	20
1	Maximian/Carausius	40
9	Allectus	33, 35, 55 (6), 79, 128 (4), corroded
1	Tacitus	illegible
1	Carinus	212
1	Diocletian ?	as RIC 5 no 49
1	Maximian I Herc	RIC 5, no 399

37	Radiate	Reverse Laetitia, ? reverse Salus, reverse standing figure, corroded and uncertain (34)
106	Barbarous Radiates	Reverses from Altar (2), Comes (2), Fides (2), Fortuna (4), Hilaritas, Invictus (3), Laetitia, Liberalitas, Moneta, Pax (14), Sacrificial Implements (4), Salus (9), Soli, Spes (6), Spes Publica, Victoria, Virtus (6)
4	Maximian I Herc	RIC 6 London 6.b. (2), 26.b.; 7 Rome 110
1	Constantius I	RIC 6 Trier 555
3	Crispus	RIC 7 Lyon 74, copy as Lyon 138–9, Arles 241
26	Constantine I	RIC 6 London 121.a., 129, 202; Lyon 307: RIC 7 London 10, 263, 267, 289, 293, 294; Trier 101–2, 132, 213, 306, 341, 342, 368, 435; Lyon 5 (2); as Arles 23; Siscia 159 HK 60, 87, 180, 186
9	Constantine II	RIC 7 London 216, 296 (3), Trier 505 HK very good copy of 49, 68, copy of 181 416
13	Urbs Roma	HK as 51 (2), copies as 51 (7), 58, 65, copy of 68, 85, 70, 76 (2), 184, copy as 184 (2), 546, Hybrid Obv as 185 / Rev as 184
6	Constantinopolis	HK as 52 (2), copies as 52 (8), as 52 but odd mintmark, 59, 66, 71
1	Populus Romanus	HK 1067
2	Helena	HK as 112 (2)
2	Theodora	HK 113, as 113
12	Constans	HK as 138, copy of 138, as 140, 140.a., 145, 150, 160, 251, 261, 267, 454: CK 35
10	Constantius II	RIC 8 as Arles 253: HK copy as 50, copy of 64, as 89 (2), 94, 189, 455: CK 32, 253
40	House of Constantine	RIC 7 copy as Trier 355; as Arles 228: HK copy as 48, as 87 (4), copy as 87 (6), small copies as 87 (2), as 88 (2), copy as 137, 965 CK copies as 25 (15), Illegible (6)
6	Magnentius	CK 5, excellent small copy (AE4) as 5, 7, 66, 238, as 238
5	Valentinian I	CK 311, 346, 724, 1390, 1414–1415
8	Valens	CK as 276, 322, 478, 502, as 528, 713, 1021,1417
2	House of Valentinian	CK as 275 (2)
4	Gratian	CK 529 (2); (378–383) 371, 378
1	Valentinian II	CK as 389
1	Theodosius I	CK 565
1	Magnus Maximus?	CK as 560
1	Honorius	CK as 570
5	3rd C	Corroded and illegible (5)
6	4th C	Corroded and illegible (6)
121	3rd–4th C	Otherwise illegible (121)
1	Coenwulf of Mercia	Brooke plate VI no 3
1	Henry II	Penny
2	Edward I–III?	Pennies (2)
1	Henry VIII	Silver
5	Medieval	Farthing, Seal?, counter (2), copper imitation of penny
3	Charles I	Farthing (3)
2	Charles II	Farthing (2)
3	Counters	Barnard as France 15–22, corroded (2)
1	17th C	Token ?
1	William and Mary	Halfpenny
2	George III	Penny 1797, Halfpenny 1806–7

2	Victoria	Pennies 1861, 1887
1	George V	1920
7	Miscellaneous	Uncertain, corroded and broken(7)

Additional list: Coins from the site stolen from the Herne Bay Museum

1	Septimius Severus	193–211
1	Tacitus	275–276
1	Carausius	286–293
1	Allectus	293–296
1	Diocletian	296–305
1	Constans	330–348
1	Constantius II	348–361
1	Magnentius	350–353

A further 56 coins already published (see Ref. 3) have been included in the calculations. Listed by period of striking they are:

69–96	1	161–180	6	238–260	4	330–348	3
96–117	1	180–192	1	260–275	11	348–364	2
117–138	3	192–222	9	275–296	2	364–378	2
138–161	4	222–238	2	296–317	5	Total	56

(2) THE COARSE POTTERY (Figs. 40–48)

by MIKE BENNETT

Over 20,000 sherds of Roman coarse pottery were recovered from the excavations. The lack of resources has prevented a detailed fabric analysis of this collection, but a number of general points can be made. Some of the key dating groups are included in the Catalogue below (Nos. 1–173) and have been described by Mike Bennett.

Apart from the small amount of coarse pottery of mid-1st and late-1st century date, there seems to be an absence of pottery dating to the first half of the 2nd century. Material of the second half of the 2nd century, 3rd century and 4th century is, however, abundant.

What also emerges is that the range of pottery seems to be somewhat limited. The stratigraphically early groups largely include only cooking pots with outcurved or distinctly flattened rims, small jars of poppy-head beaker profiles and black burnished dishes, with upright or bead rims, with decoration mostly confined to external curvilinear patterns. These types predominate and the problem comes in providing a close date for them! Traditionally, the dishes have been described as Antonine, or late-Antonine. These certainly occur in the Period III deposits in the *Classis Britannica* fort at Dover (A.D. 190–208) where the latest sealed coin was one of Septimius Severus minted in A.D. 202. The evidence at Dover suggests the garrison withdrew in A.D. 208 and never returned. Certainly the collapsed buildings there were being covered with soil in the first half of the third century. On the Dover evidence these distinctive dishes were certainly in circulation at the end of the second century.

Catalogue of Illustrated Coarse Pottery

1959 *Via Quintana* Site. Under Road (REC-59 L.4)

No. 1 Cooking-pot with outcurved rim of grog-tempered ware with grey-brown fabric and surface.

No. 2 Jar with rolled rim of sandy ware with buff-grey fabric and grey-brown surface.

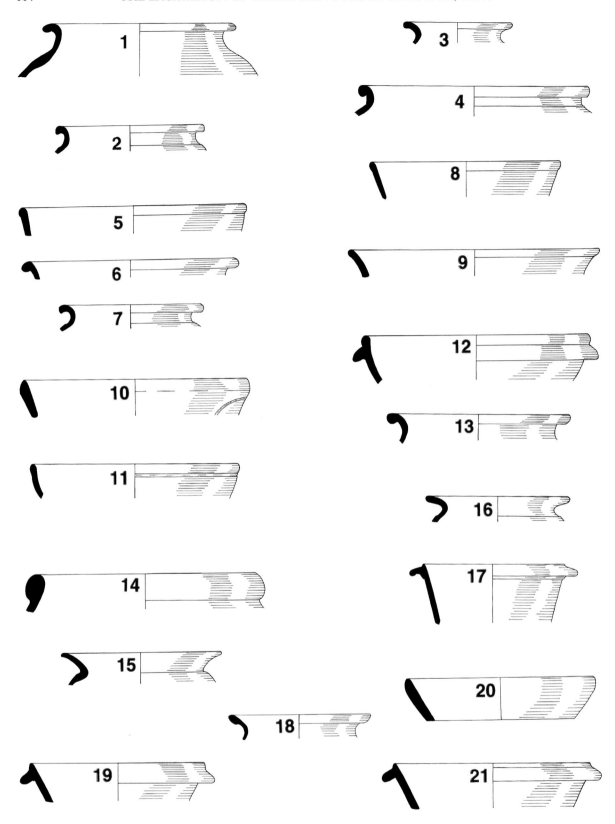

Fig. 40.   *Roman Coarse Pottery (1/4).*

No. 3   Cooking-pot with cavetto rim of sandy ware with grey-black fabric and grey-black burnished surface.

No. 4   Cooking-pot with rolled rim of sandy ware with grey-brown fabric and surface.

No. 5   Dish with upright rim of sandy ware with grey-brown fabric and grey-black burnished surface.

No. 6   Dish with bead rim of sandy ware with grey-brown fabric and burnished black surface.

No. 7   Jar with outcurved rim of sandy ware with grey-brown fabric and surface.

No. 8   Dish with upright rim of sandy ware with grey-brown fabric and grey-black burnished surface.

No. 9   Cooking-pot with cavetto rim of sandy ware with grey-brown fabric and grey-black burnished external surface.

1959   *Via Quintana* **Site. Road (REC-59 L.3)**

No. 10   Dish with upright rim of sandy ware with grey-black fabric and surface, with burnished curvilinear pattern.

No. 11   Dish with upright rim of sandy ware with grey-brown fabric and surface, burnished.

1959   *Via Quintana* **Site. Loam over road (REC-59 L.5)**

No. 12   Dish with down-turned flanged rim of grog-tempered ware with grey-brown fabric and surface.

No. 13   Cooking-pot with outcurved rim of sandy ware with buff-grey fabric and grey-black surface.

No. 14   Dollium with thickened bead rim of sandy ware with grey-brown fabric and surface.

No. 15   Cooking-pot with cavetto rim of sandy ware with grey-brown fabric and grey-black burnished surface.

No. 16   Cooking-pot with cavetto rim of sandy ware with buff-grey fabric and surface.

No. 17   Dish with flanged rim of sandy ware with grey fabric and grey-brown surface.

No. 18   Cooking-pot with outcurved thickened rim of sandy ware with grey-brown fabric and grey-black surface.

No. 19   Dish with down-turned flanged rim in sandy ware with grey-brown fabric and grey-black burnished surface.

No. 20   Dish with upright rim of sandy ware with grey-brown fabric and grey-black burnished surface.

No. 21   Dish with flanged rim of sandy ware with grey-brown fabric and surface.

No. 22   Bottle with outcurved rim of sandy ware with grey-brown fabric and surface.

No. 23   Jar with beaded rim of sandy ware with grey-brown fabric and grey-brown burnished surface.

No. 24   Small bottle of fine ware with buff fabric and brown colour coat surface and applied with lattice decoration.

No. 25   Dish with upright rim of sandy ware with grey-brown fabric and grey-black burnished surface.

No. 26   Jar with outcurved rim of sandy ware with grey-brown fabric and surface.

No. 27   Dish with upright-curved rim of sandy ware with brown fabric and grey-brown surface.

1959   *Via Quintana* **Site. Black loam over L.5 (REC-59 L.2)**

No. 28   Jar with outcurved rolled rim of sandy ware with grey-brown fabric and surface and groove on shoulder.

No. 29   Dish with bead rim of sandy ware with grey-brown fabric and surface.

No. 30   Dish with flanged rim of sandy ware with grey-buff fabric and grey-black burnished surface.

No. 31   Cooking-pot with out-turned rim of sandy ware with grey-buff fabric and surface.

No. 32   Bowl with bead rim of sandy ware with grey-brown fabric and surface with groove below burnished rim.

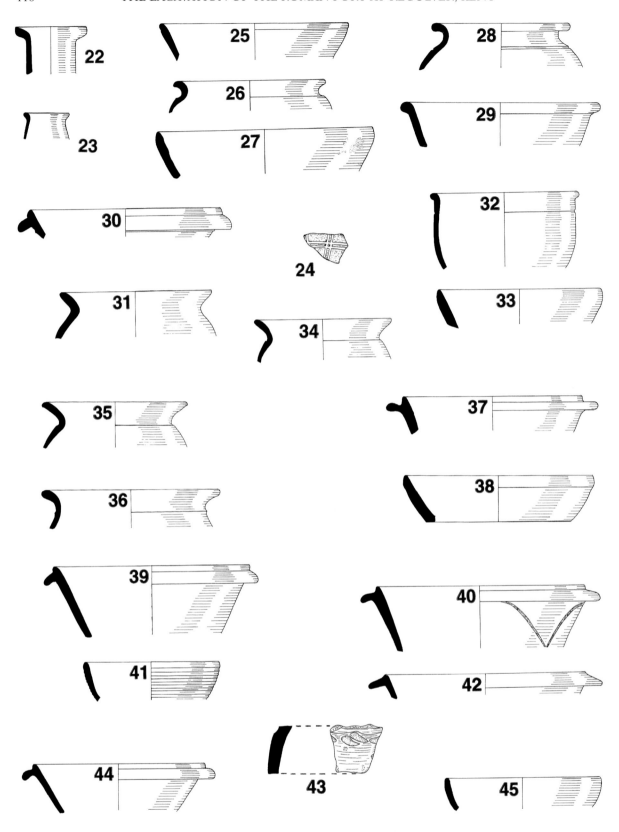

Fig. 41.   *Roman Coarse Pottery (1/4).*

No. 33   Dish with upright rim of sandy ware with grey-brown fabric and grey-brown burnished surface.

No. 34   Jar with cavetto rim of sandy ware with grey-brown fabric and grey-black burnished surface with groove at neck.

No. 35   Jar with everted rim of sandy ware with grey-brown fabric and grey-black burnished surface.

No. 36   Cooking-pot with thickened outcurved rim in sandy ware with grey-brown fabric and surface burnished inside rim.

No. 37   Dish with flanged upright rim of grog-tempered ware with grey-brown fabric and surface.

No. 38   Dish with upright rim of grog-tempered ware with grey-brown fabric and grey-black burnished surface.

No. 39   Dish with flanged rim of sandy ware with grey-brown fabric and surface.

No. 40   Dish with flanged rim of sandy ware with grey-buff fabric and grey-black burnished surface with curvilinear decoration.

No. 41   Dish with upright rim of sandy ware with grey-black fabric and grey-black burnished surface with faint ridges on surface.

No. 42   Bowl with flanged rim of sandy ware with orange-buff fabric and orange-red slip surface.

No. 43   Wall sherd of storage jar of grog-tempered ware with grey-brown fabric and grey-black surface and stick-stabbed decoration.

No. 44   Dish with flanged rim of sandy ware with grey-brown fabric and grey-black surface with burnished rim.

No. 45   Dish with upright curved rim of sandy ware with grey-brown fabric and grey-black surface.

1967   **East Gate Site. Pit in Rampart Bank (REC-67 L.16, 27, 28)**

No. 46   Dish with flanged rim of sandy ware with buff fabric and grey surface and burnished overall.

No. 47   Jar with outcurved rim of sandy ware with buff fabric and grey burnished surface.

No. 48   Dish with flanged rim of sandy ware with buff fabric and grey-black surface, burnished overall.

No. 49   Dish with flanged rim of sandy ware with grey-buff fabric and grey surface and lightly burnished.

No. 50   Dish with flanged rim of sandy ware with grey fabric and surface, burnished overall.

No. 51   Jar with outcurved rim of sandy ware with grey-buff fabric and grey surface, burnished externally.

No. 52   Dish with upright rim of sandy ware with grey-black fabric and surface, burnished overall.

1960   **Central Area. Primary Layer in Sacellum (REC-60 L.21)**

No. 53   Cooking Layer 21 pot with outcurved rim of grog-tempered ware with grey fabric and grey-black burnished surface.

No. 54   Dish with flanged rim of sandy ware with grey fabric and grey-black burnished surface.

No. 55   Dish with flanged rim of sandy ware with grey-black fabric and surface.

No. 56   Cooking-pot with outcurved rim of grog-tempered ware with grey-brown fabric and grey-black surface.

No. 57   Cooking-pot with out-turned rim of sandy ware with grey-brown fabric and grey-brown burnished surface.

No. 58   Cooking-pot with outcurved thickened rim of sandy with grey-buff fabric and grey-black surface and rilling on shoulder.

No. 59   Cooking-pot with outcurved rim of grog-tempered ware with grey-buff fabric and grey-buff burnished surface.

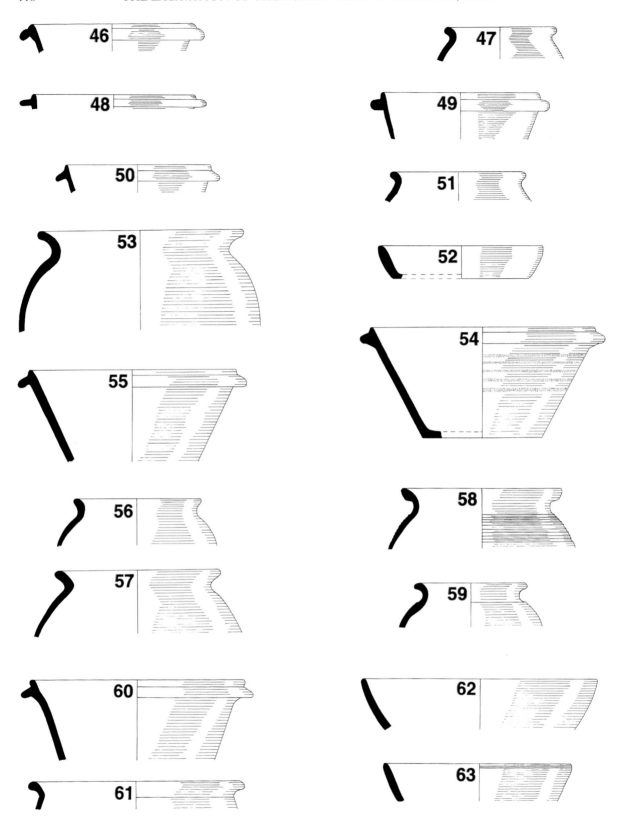

Fig. 42.   *Roman Coarse Pottery (1/4).*

No. 60   Dish with flanged rim of sandy ware with grey-brown fabric and grey-buff surface.

No. 61   Jar with outcurved rim of sandy ware with grey fabric and grey burnished surface.

No. 62   Dish with upright curved rim of sandy ware with grey-brown fabric and grey-black burnished surface.

No. 63   Dish with upright rim of sandy ware with grey-brown fabric and grey-black burnished surface.

No. 64   Dish with flanged bead rim of sandy ware with grey-black fabric and grey-black burnished surface and lattice pattern.

No. 65   Dish with upright rim of sandy ware with grey-black fabric and grey-black burnished surface and curvilinear pattern.

No. 66   Dish with flanged rim of sandy ware with grey-black fabric and grey-black burnished surface.

No. 67   Dish with flanged rim of sandy ware with grey fabric and grey-black burnished surface.

No. 68   Dish with upright thickened rim of sandy ware with grey-brown fabric and grey-black surface.

No. 69   Bottle with flanged rim of fine ware with pale orange fabric and red-orange burnished surface with both handles missing.

1963   Water Cistern east of *principia* (REC-63 F. L.5 and L.9)

No. 70   Jar (lower half) of fine sandy ware with dark grey fabric and grey-black surface and burnished at base.

No. 71   Bottle with tapered spout in fine sandy ware with grey fabric and grey-black surface, burnished externally.

No. 72   Jar with outcurved rim of sandy ware with grey fabric and grey-black surface, burnished externally.

1963   South Area. Soil between roads (REC-63 L.10)

No. 73   Wall sherd of beaker of fine ware with grey-pink fabric and grey-black surface and white en-barbotine pattern and faint rouletted band.

No. 74   Dish with upright rim of sandy ware with grey fabric and grey-black burnished surface.

No. 75   Dish with flanged rim of sandy ware with grey-buff fabric and grey-black surface and burnished with curvilinear pattern.

1963   South Area. (REC-63 L.28)

No. 76   Dish with outcurved bead rim of sandy ware with buff fabric and grey surface burnished.

No. 77   Dish with flanged rim of sandy ware with grey fabric and grey-black surface burnished.

No. 78   Cooking-pot with outcurved rim of sandy ware with grey fabric and grey-black surface and burnished externally.

No. 79   Cooking-pot with outcurved rim of sandy ware with grey-buff fabric and grey-black surface, burnished.

No. 80   Cooking-pot with rolled rim of sandy ware with grey-buff fabric and grey surface, burnished.

No. 81   Wall sherd of jar of fine ware with grey fabric and surface and cordon on shoulder and lattice pattern.

No. 82   Dish with flanged rim of sandy ware with grey fabric and surface and burnished on rim.

No. 83   Dish with flanged rim of sandy ware with grey fabric and surface and lightly burnished.

No. 84   Dish with upright rim of sandy ware with grey fabric and grey-black surface and burnished overall with curvilinear decoration.

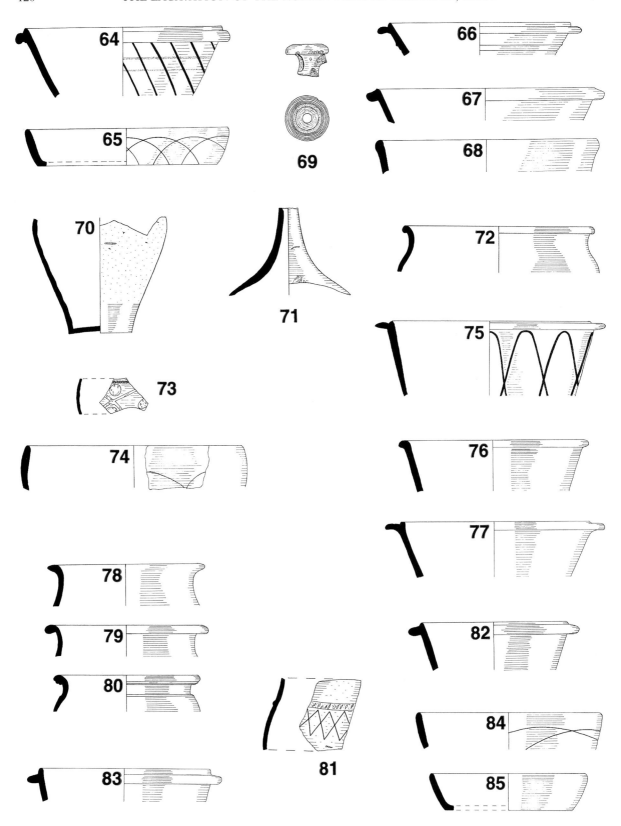

Fig. 43.   *Roman Coarse Pottery (1/4).*

No. 85   Dish with upright rim of sandy ware with grey fabric and grey-buff surface and lightly burnished.

1969   **North East Area. Upper Fill of Late-Roman Drain (REC-69 L.8 and L.10)**

No. 86   Cooking-pot with outcurved rim of sandy ware with grey-buff fabric and surface.

No. 87   Dish with upright rim of sandy ware with grey-cream fabric and grey surface, burnished overall.

No. 88   Dish with upright rim of sandy ware with grey-buff fabric and grey surface, burnished overall.

No. 89   Dish with upright rim of sandy ware with grey fabric and grey-buff surface, burnished overall.

No. 90   Bowl with bead rim of sandy ware with buff fabric and grey surface and burnished lines on exterior.

No. 91   Cooking-pot with outcurved rim of sandy ware with grey fabric and grey-buff surface and burnished cordons under rim.

No. 92   Cooking-pot with outcurved rim of fine sandy ware with grey fabric and surface and burnished curvilinear pattern.

No. 93   Cooking-pot with cavetto rim of sandy ware with grey fabric and grey-black surface, burnished externally.

No. 94   Dish with flanged rim of sandy ware with grey-buff fabric and grey surface, burnished externally.

No. 95   Dish with upright rim of sandy ware with light grey fabric and grey-black surface, burnished overall.

No. 96   Dish with flanged rim of sandy ware with grey fabric and grey-brown surface, burnished overall.

No. 97   Dish with flanged rim of sandy ware with grey-buff fabric and grey surface, burnished overall.

No. 98   Dish with flanged rim of sandy ware with light grey fabric and grey surface, burnished overall.

No. 99   Cooking-pot with everted rim of grog-tempered ware with grey fabric and grey-black burnished surface.

1969   **North East Area. Primary Fill of Late-Roman Drain (REC-69 L.12)**

No. 100   Cooking-pot with cavetto rim of sandy ware with grey-buff fabric and grey-black surface, burnished externally.

No. 101   Dish with rolled bead rim of sandy ware with light grey fabric and grey surface, burnished overall.

No. 102   Dish with upright rim of sandy ware with buff fabric and pink-brown slip surface.

No. 103   Dish with upright rim of sandy ware with grey fabric and grey-black surface, burnished overall.

1968   **East Barracks. Late-Roman general deposits (REC-68 L.7 R-XG)**

No. 104   Dish with upright rim of grog-tempered ware with grey-brown fabric and grey-black surface.

No. 105   Jar with flattened outcurved rim of grog-tempered ware with grey-black fabric a burnished surface.

No. 106   Base of bottle of fine ware with orange-red fabric and orange surface and impressed dimple decoration.

No. 107   Dish with flanged down-turned rim of sandy ware with grey-buff fabric and buff burnished surface and grooves under flange.

No. 108   Beaker with bead rim of fine ware with pink fabric and metallic brown slip surface.

No. 109   Bowl with outcurved rim of fine ware with cream-buff fabric and orange-brown slip surface.

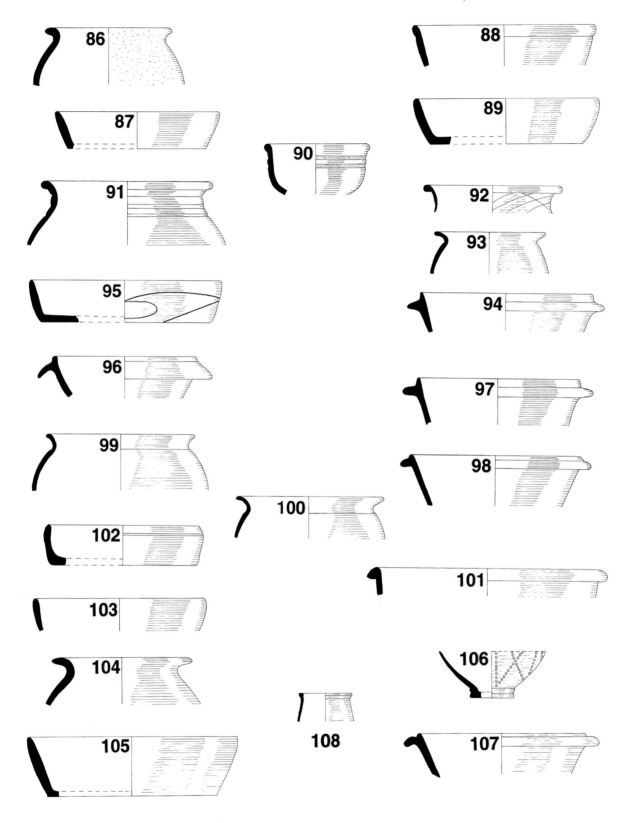

Fig. 44.   *Roman Coarse Pottery (1/4).*

No. 110   Dish with flanged rim of sandy ware with grey-brown fabric and grey-black burnished surface.
No. 111   Jar with outcurved rim of sandy ware with grey-brown fabric and grey-black surface.
No. 112   Dish with upright curved rim of grog-tempered ware with grey-black fabric and grey-black burnished surface.
No. 113   Jar with outcurved rim of grog-tempered ware with grey-brown fabric and grey-buff burnished surface and unburnished band below rim.
No. 114   Dish with flanged rim of grog-tempered ware with grey-brown fabric and grey-black surface and burnished flange.
No. 115   Dish with upright rim of grog-tempered ware with grey-brown fabric and black burnished surface.
No. 116   Bottle with bead rim of fine ware with grey-buff interior and grey-brown slip.
No. 117   Jar with outcurved flattened rim of sandy ware with grey-black fabric and surface.

1968   East Barracks. Primary deposit (REC-68 L.19 R-XS)
No. 118   Beaker with upright bead rim of fine ware with red-brown fabric and grey-brown slip surface.

1968   East Barracks. (REC-68 L.16 R-XP)
No. 119   Cooking-pot with outcurved rim of sandy ware with red-brown fabric and grey-black burnished surface.
No. 120   Jar with double-beaded rim of sandy ware with grey-brown fabric and grey-black burnished surface with groove on neck.
No. 121   Dish with upright rim of sandy ware with grey-brown fabric and grey-black surface.
No. 122   Dish with flanged rim of fine ware with buff fabric and orange burnished surface.
No. 123   Mortarium bowl with flanged rim of fine ware with white fabric and brown-white surface with painted triangles on rim.

1968   East Barracks. Primary deposit (REC-68 L.24 R-XX)
No. 124   Dish with upright rim of sandy ware with grey-black fabric and grey-black burnished surface and curvilinear decoration.
No. 125   Dish with upright rim of grog-tempered ware with grey-brown fabric and grey-black burnished surface and curvilinear decoration.
No. 126   Dish with flanged rim of grog-tempered ware with grey-black fabric and grey-black burnished surface and burnished line.
No. 127   Jar with outcurved rim of sandy ware with grey-buff fabric and grey-black burnished surface.
No. 128   Jar with outcurved rim of sandy ware with grey-brown fabric and black surface and burnished rim.
No. 129   Beaker with beaded rim of fine ware with buff fabric and metallic blue-black slip surface.
No. 130   Dish with flanged rim of grog-tempered ware with grey-black fabric and grey-blue burnished rim on surface and burnished curvilinear pattern.
No. 131   Cooking-pot with outcurved rolled rim of sandy ware with grey fabric and grey-brown burnished surface.
No. 132   Jar with outcurved rim of sandy ware with grey-brown fabric and grey surface.
No. 133   Dish with upright rim of sandy ware with grey-black fabric and grey-black burnished surface.
No. 134   Beaker with beaded rim of fine ware with grey-buff fabric and metallic blue-black slip surface with groove under rim.
No. 135   Dish with upright rim of sandy ware with grey-black fabric and grey-black burnished surface.

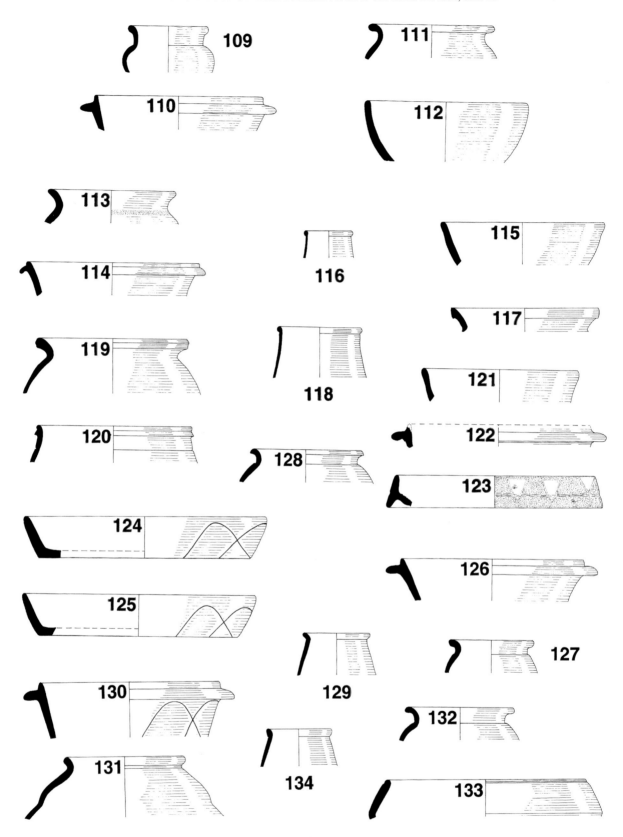

Fig. 45.   *Roman Coarse Pottery (1/4).*

1968   **East Barracks. Late-Roman general soil deposit (REC-68 L.7 R-XG)**

No. 136   Dish with bead rim of sandy ware with grey-brown fabric and grey-black burnished surface.

No. 137   Dish with flanged rim of sandy ware with grey-brown fabric and grey-black burnished surface.

No. 138   Jar with outcurved rim of sandy ware with grey-brown fabric and grey-black burnished surface.

No. 139   Dish with upright rim of sandy ware with grey-buff fabric and light grey surface.

No. 140   Bowl with bead rim of fine ware with grey-buff fabric and orange-buff slip surface with rouletting below rim.

1968   **East Barracks. Pit 23 in J33 (REC-68 L.6 R-XF)**

No. 141   Dish with flanged rim of sandy ware with grey-brown fabric and grey-brown surface with burnished rim.

No. 142   Jar with outcurved rim of grog-tempered ware with grey-black fabric and grey-black surface.

No. 143   Dish with upright curved rim of sandy ware with grey-black fabric and burnished surface.

No. 144   Jar with outcurved rim of grog-tempered ware with grey-brown fabric and grey-black burnished surface.

1968   **East Barracks. Primary deposit (REC-68 L.20 R-XT)**

No. 145   Dish with heavy bead rim of sandy ware with grey-brown fabric and grey-black surface with burnished lines on body.

No. 146   Bowl with upright rim of fine ware with buff-cream fabric and brown slip surface with rouletted pattern.

No. 147   Jar with cavetto rim of sandy ware with grey-brown fabric and grey-black surface burnished inside rim.

No. 148   Jar with outcurved rim of sandy ware with grey-buff fabric and grey-black burnished surface.

No. 149   Dish with upright rim of sandy ware with grey-black fabric and grey-black burnished surface.

1968   **East Barracks. Soil sealing primary deposits (REC-68 L.14 R-XN)**

No. 150   Dish with flanged rim of grog-tempered ware with grey-brown fabric and grey-buff surface.

No. 151   Jar with out-turned rim of grog-tempered ware with grey-brown fabric and surface.

No. 152   Dish with flanged rim of sandy ware with grey-buff interior and grey-black burnished surface.

No. 153   Dish with upright rim of sandy ware with grey-brown fabric and grey-black burnished surface.

No. 154   Jar with thickened outcurved rim of sandy ware with grey-brown fabric and surface.

1968   **East Barracks. Late-Roman general soil deposit (REC-68 L.12 R-XL)**

No. 155   Cooking-pot with cavetto rim of sandy ware with grey-buff fabric and buff-brown burnished surface.

No. 156   Jar with rolled rim of sandy ware with buff fabric and light grey surface.

No. 157   Dish with flanged rim of sandy ware with grey fabric and grey burnished surface.

No. 158   Dish with upright rim of sandy ware with grey-brown fabric and grey surface with burnished rim.

1968   **East Barracks. Final levelling of Fortlet Ditches (REC-68 L.21 R-XU)**

No. 159   Dish with bead rim of sandy ware with grey fabric and grey-black burnished surface.

No. 160   Jar with outcurved rim of sandy ware with grey-buff fabric and surface.

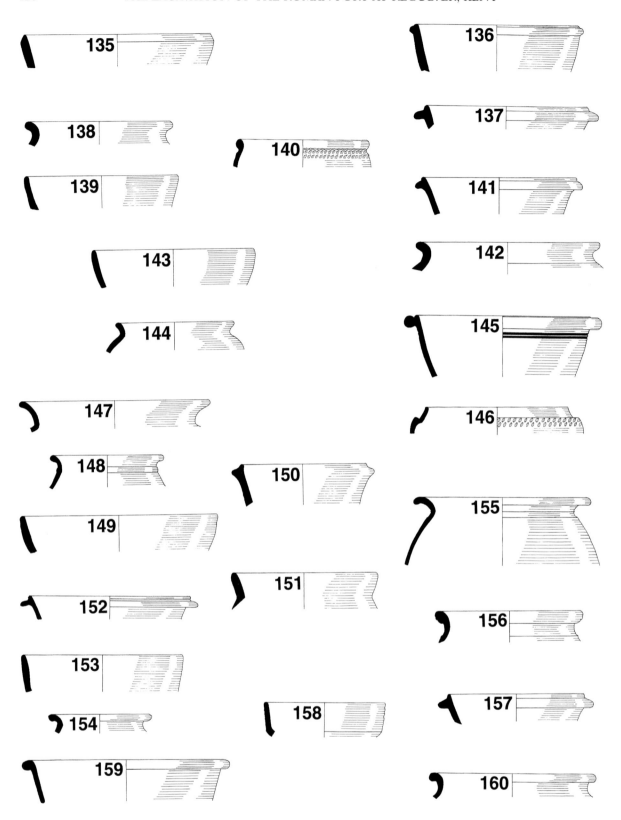

Fig. 46.   *Roman Coarse Pottery (1/4).*

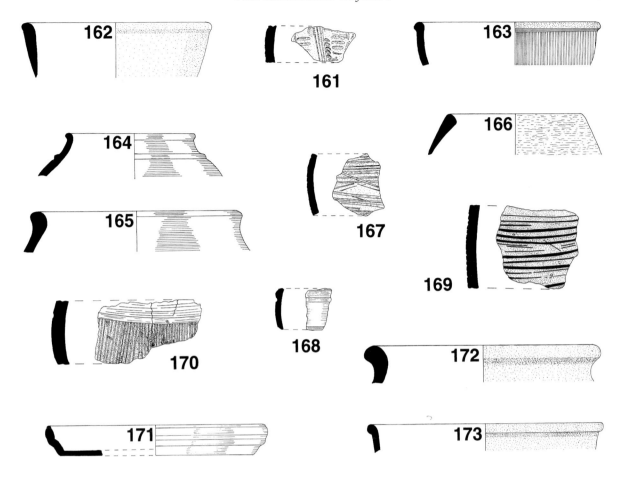

Fig. 47. *Coarse Pottery (1/4).*

1964   Fortlet ditches. Box OD (REC-64 L.4, L.5 and L.6 R-DV R-DU R-DW)

No. 161   Cooking-pot of grog-tempered ware with grey fabric and light brown surface with cross-combed decoration.

No. 162   Cooking-pot with upright and thickened rim of grog-tempered ware with grey fabric and buff-black surface and vertical combing.

No. 163   Cooking-pot with upright bead rim of sandy ware with grey-buff fabric and buff surface and horizontal grooves and vertical combing.

No. 164   Cooking-pot with outcurved rim of grog-tempered ware with grey fabric and brown surface and cordon on neck.

No. 165   Storage jar with outcurved thickened rim of sandy ware with grey fabric and brown surface.

No. 166   Cooking-pot with bead rim of sandy ware with buff fabric and grey-buff surface and burnished externally.

No. 167   Wall sherd of cooking-pot of grog-tempered ware with grey-buff fabric and brown-buff surface and vertical combing.

No. 168   Wall sherd of cooking-pot of grog-tempered ware with grey fabric and grey-brown surface and bold cordon on shoulder.

1965   East Cliff Site. Ditch 8 (REC-65 L.21 R-GR)

No. 169   Storage jar (rim missing) of grog-tempered ware with grey-buff fabric, grey-black surface and combed decoration.

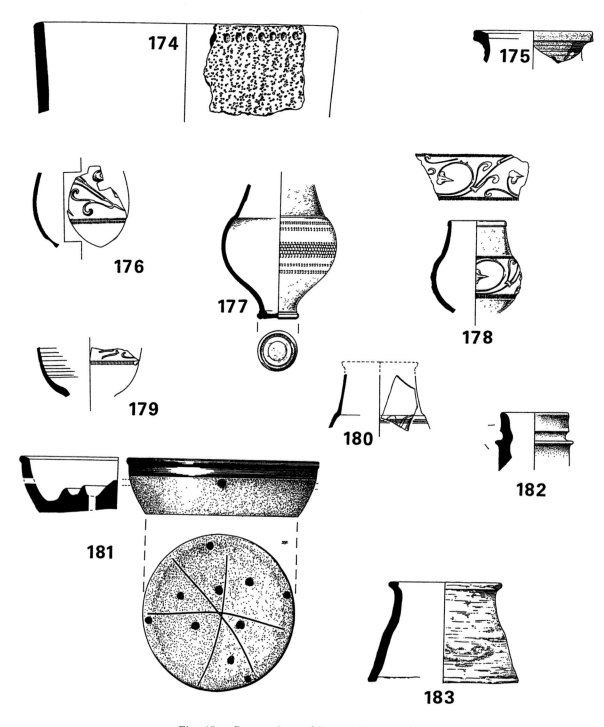

Fig. 48.   *Bronze Age and Roman Pottery (1/4).*

No. 170   Storage jar (rim missing) of grog-tempered ware with grey-buff fabric, buff-black surface and cordon and combing on shoulder.

No. 171   Dish with upright rim of sandy ware with light grey fabric and grey-buff surface. Copy of a Gallo-Belgic cordoned vessel. fabric

No. 172   Storage jar with rolled rim of sandy ware with orange-buff fabric and buff-cream surface.

No. 173   Dish with bead rim of calcite-gritted ware with black fabric and grey-black surface.

Other Pottery (Fig. 48)

No. 174   Large bucket urn with upright rim of calcite-gritted ware of grey-black fabric and buff-brown surface. Finger-tip decoration below rim. Bronze Age (REC-66 L.27).

No. 175   Jug with outcurved rim of fine ware, cream fabric and buff surface, with patch of yellow glaze. Probably 14th century. (REC-65 L.18).

No. 176   Beaker (rim missing) of fine Rhenish ware of pale red fabric and black metallic slip. Enbarbotine foiliate decoration. Late 2nd – early 3rd century (REC-59-KF640).

No. 177   Beaker (rim missing) of fine ware with brown surface. Bands of rouletting on body.

No. 178   Beaker with beaded upright rim of fine ware with black-brown surface. Enbarbotine foliate decoration.

No. 179   Beaker (rim missing) of fine Rhenish ware, pink fabric and grey-black metallic slip (REC-61- ?).

No. 180   Beaker (rim missing) of fine ware, with grey fabric and grey-black metallic slip. Similar to No. 176(REC-66-L.36 LH).

No. 181   Cheese-press dish (complete) with thickened rim of grey-black fabric and black surface. Its inside displays three concentric rings for pressing food-stuffs and also ten perforations in base to facilitate straining. Crude cross pattern on base (REC-68 L.58 R-ZF).

No. 182   Water-pipe spigot in hard sandy red fabric and orange-buff surface. Rebate below rim (REC-60–400).

No. 183   Jug with outcurved rim of coarse ware with red-brown surface.

(3) THE MORTARIA (Figs. 49–50).

By Kay Hartley

This definitive study by Kay Hartley is under three main headings; (A) Type Series (TS1–TS32); (B) Fabrics (Fabric 1–14) and (C) Bibliography. Where the vessel selected for the Type Series is illustrated, it is prefixed by its illustration number (e.g. No.184) and identified by the year (e.g. 1959), site, context and its site code (e.g. REC-59 L.20). Those not illustrated are prefixed Not. Ill.

(A) TYPE SERIES (= TS)

No. 184 TS1. 1959 Via Quintana. Base of Rampart Bank (REC-59-77 L.20) joins **R-59-55; R-59-94** joining **R-59-203**, from the same vessel. 135+80+60+25gms. Diam. 280mm. 15%, 10%, 9% TS11, Fabric 1, probably Canterbury, with Colchester as the alternative possibility. A form and spout typical of these potteries *c.* A.D. 170–210. Symonds and Wade 1999, 185, fig. 4.15, no. 284 is a slightly earlier version of this form with broader rim-section; TS1 is generally similar to Hull 1963, fig. 63, no. 9, but with a less deep version of the spout which may be marginally later in date than the large one. Slightly burnt.

No. 185 TS2. 1966 East Cliff Site. Top of Rampart Bank (REC-66 L.6/7 R-LY)
160gms Diam. 270mm 14% Fabric 4, possibly self-coloured, east- or mid-Kent. TS 2 (type specimen). Mortarium with collared rim and two grooves at the bottom of the collar. This is similar in rim-form to mortaria made at Colchester and Canterbury in Fabric 1 in the late second to early third century. Many such mortaria are too late to be stamped, but a mortarium of Call[es] from Springhead is generally similar in form. *c.* A.D. 170–230. Some burning.

No. 186 TS3. 1966 East Cliff Site. On Rampart Bank (REC-66 L.31 R-LC)
130gms. Diam. 270mm. 11% Fabric 3, East or Mid-Kent. TS3, (type specimen), with near invisible bead, convex collar and small neat spout (for comments on basic form of spout see TS4). It is highly unusual, if not unique, for mortaria of this type to be stamped. The stamp is impressed horizontally along the collar to the left of the spout and would have been matched by an identical stamp on the other side of the spout. It is complete and reads CALLEC. All of his stamps end in EC (FE ligatured) or FEC which are common abbreviated forms of FECIT. His name begins in CALL, but this is also an abbreviated form. The end of his name cannot be restored with certainty, but Calles is noted in Spain as a name (Holder 1896). His mortaria have now been noted from Brentford; Charne, Otford; Canterbury (2); Reculver (2) and Springhead. The distribution points to a workshop in Kent. All of his recorded mortaria have some kind of collared or wall-sided rim. Various types of wall-sided or hammerhead forms were made occasionally, even as early as A.D. 140, but they are essentially rare among stamped mortaria. There is no instance of any other potter with more than two recorded mortaria, who consistently used these forms to the exclusion of flanged forms. This consistent use points to a date within the period A.D. 160–190. The use of collared rims went on into the third century, but the practice of stamping was dying out in Britain during the Antonine period. A date later than the end of the second century is unlikely for his work and a date later than the early third century virtually impossible. There are, incidentally, collared mortaria with herringbone stamps and a mortarium from East Malling, Kent, stamped [...]FEC retrograde which could be from same workshop.

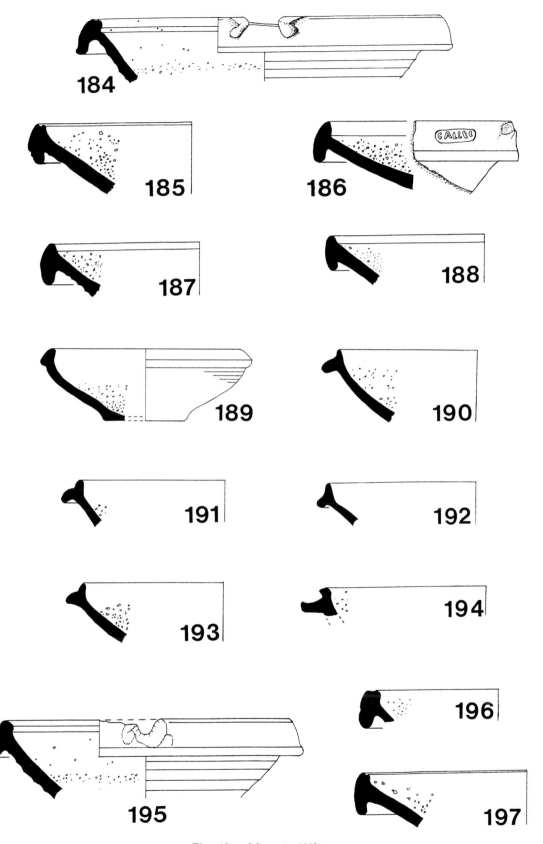

Fig. 49. *Mortaria (1/3).*

Other mortaria:

1966 (R-LZ L-31) joins bodysherd R-LB. These are from TS3 or from another identical mortarium, the only difference being a slightly thinner core.
60gms +70gms. Diam. 270. 10% Fabric 3. TS3. Well-worn.
(R-AK) 45gms. Diam. 270mm. 8% Fabric 4. TS3. Similar to R-LC in type, date and source, but differing in fabric.

No. 187   TS4. 1962 East Barracks Site, pit in Box G (REC-62 L.100 R-AB)
105gms. Diam. 270mm. 8% Fabric 4, East or Mid-Kent. TS4 (type specimen). Another mortarium with slightly convex collar type, between hammerhead and Gillam 272 in form. The type is generally similar to forms widely current in the Rhineland. It was imported into Britain on quite a large scale from the mid-second century into the third century and possibly later (see TS16-17). Generally similar mortaria were made in Britain at Colchester and in Kent, but rarely outside these areas. This example is close to TS3, but lacks any bead definition and has a different type of spout formed by breaking the bead and turning it out over the flange. This kind of spout began to be made at a later date than the TS3 spout. TS4 has a neatly corrugated exterior, a feature rare in British mortaria but common in those of similar type made in the Rhineland. TS3 and TS4 are presumably imitations of these imports. The optimum date for TS4 is late second to early third century, probably not later than A.D. 250 at the latest. Heavily worn in the bottom.

No. 188   TS5. 1966 West Site, primary layer (REC-66 L.79 R-PM)
70gms. Diam. 270mm. 7% TS 5 (type specimen), Fabric 4, possibly self-coloured, East or Mid-Kent. Mortarium with unusual, stubby, collar rim. Probably third century, perhaps first half. Some burning.

No. 189   TS6. 1962 East Cliff Site, on Rampart Bank (REC-62 L.31 R-LC)
300gms (R-LC). Diam. 240mm 41% Fabric 4, East- or Mid-Kent. TS6 (type specimen). Small mortarium of segmental form with unusual, stubby rim; not earlier than the third century.

No. 190   TS7. 1962 East Barracks Site, Trench B (REC-62 L.59 R-AY)
joining R-BX 85gms. Diam. 270mm. 9.5% Fabric 5, east or mid-Kent. TS7 (type specimen). Three joining sherds from a small segmental bowl-shaped mortarium with near horizontal flange, approximating to Fulford type 81.3 (1975); closer parallels are noted from Poundbury (Sparey Green 1987, fig. 85, nos.2 and 9). Fourth century
Other vessels:
1961 (R-1457) 25gms. Diam. 240mm 12% Fabric 5, TS7, East or Mid-Kent; with bead-turned spout. Fourth century.

**No. 191   TS8. 1960 Central Area, General Occupation Deposit (REC-60 L.14
R405)** joins **R406** 45gms. Diam. 250mm. 14% TS8 (type specimen), Fabric 5, probably self-coloured; East or Mid-Kent. Two joining sherds from a mortarium shaped like a segmental bowl with high bead and neat, small, rounded, but downcurved flange. The rim-profile can be generally similar to Oxford type M22.7 (Young 1977); it can be matched at Brancaster (Hartley in Hinchliffe 1985, Type 194.1 in oxidised and reduced fabrics, M8 and M9). In the New Forest potteries the form is covered by Fulford 81. Fourth century.
Other vessels:
1966 (R-LB L-30) 30gms. Diam. 240mm. 10% Fabric 5, heavily burnt throughout. Ts8 with half of the spout, formed by breaking the bead and turning it out over the flange.

Fourth century.
1966 (R-LB L-30) 25gms. Diam. 240mm. 10% Fabric 5. TS8 with straighter flange, something between TS7 and TS8. Fourth century.

No. 192   TS9. 1963 South Area, Trench A **(REC-63 L.55 R-CO)** (25gms) **joins 1962 (R-Q L.14)** (15gms) 260mm. 9.5% Fabric 5, East or Mid-Kent. TS9 (type specimen), with high bead and straight, diagonally downpointed flange probably intended to be covered by Fulford 81. An identical mortarium has been noted from Canterbury (CXXII JI Pit 2/2, unpublished). Fourth century.
Other vessels:
1961 (L-1131) ????30gms. 280mm. 9% TS-9, but with longer flange; bead-broken and turned-out spout. Fabric 5, East or Mid-Kent. Burnt. Fourth century.

No. 193   TS10. 1966 West Site, Unstratified (REC-66 L.1 R-NA)
35gms. Diam. 240mm. 7% TS10 (type specimen) Fabric 5, possibly self-coloured, East or Mid-Kent. Small mortarium with high bead and stubby triangular flange; a typical late form (Fulford 81.4; see also Sparey Green 1987, fig. 85, no.10). Fourth century.

No. 194   TS11. 1961 East Barracks Area, Trench A (REC-61- 256 L.6)
30 gms. 290mm. 4% Fabric 5, possibly self-coloured, East or Mid-Kent. TS 11 (type specimen), with high, wide flat bead with central groove and a wide horizontal to near horizontal flange ending in an upward pointing knob. The spout was formed by turning out the bead over the flange. This unusual rim-profile can be closely paralleled only in forms favoured by potters working in the Lower Nene valley in the fourth century (Great Casterton (Corder 1951, fig. 9, no. 29 in a destruction deposit of *c.* A.D. 375), Verulamium (Frere 1984, fig. 109, no. 2631 in deposit dated A.D. 375–400), and from Burgh Castle (Johnson 1983, fig. 44, no. 237). Fourth century.
Other vessels:
1966 (R-KP L16) 25gms. Ts11. Fabric 5, perhaps self-coloured, East or Mid-Kent. Fourth century.
1969 (RR-L L12) 45gms. Fabric 5, East or Mid-Kent. The flange does not survive but the surviving profile indicates that it is TS11. Fourth century.
Comments:
TS-1 in Fabric 1 and TS 12–14 in Fabric 2 are in the cream to buff and creamy brown fabrics commonly associated with known potteries in Canterbury and Colchester. TS2–11 fall into two or three, oxidised fabric groups: i. TS3 in Fabric 3, ii TS2 and TS4–6 in Fabric 4, and iii TS7–11 in Fabric 5. Fabrics 3 and 4 are probably variants of one fabric type and Fabric 5 is a much finer version. The mortaria in these fabrics are not all of the same date, but it may be that the clays used were from the same geological beds. The distribution, notably of the mortaria of Call(es), whose stamps provide easy traceability, point to these clays lying in Mid- or East Kent. These fabrics and trituration grits are covered within Fabrics 2A–E in Hartley in Bennett and Frere et al. 1982, 152 and have been recorded mostly, if not solely, in East and Mid-Kent. The mortaria in Fabrics 3–5 appear to fall into two groups dating, A.D. 160/170–250 and fourth century. The mortaria in the cream to creamy brown Fabrics 1–2 fit in the earlier of these two periods.

Nos. 7–10 are small segmental bowl-shaped mortaria closely similar in form to fine ware mortaria made in the New Forest potteries (Fulford 1975, fig. 22 nos. 81.3–4 and p.70, Type 81). Fulford dates these New Forest equivalents to the second half of the fourth century, but this small but notable cluster at Reculver suggests that the New Forest prototypes were being produced earlier in the fourth century because there was little activity at Reculver after A.D. 360 (B. Philp pers. comm.).

These forms have some general similarity to form M22 at Oxford and similar mortaria made in the Much Hadham potteries, but the Reculver examples follow the New Forest profile tradition very closely. Such mortaria in Fabric 5 are not common, one example is known from Canterbury (see TS9), but their identification as a group will make recognition easier in the future. There is no question of them being New Forest ware (M. Lyne pers. comm.) so they must come from a small workshop operating in East or Mid-Kent in the second half of the fourth century. Since their forms very clearly follow New Forest types rather than the much commoner Oxford ones these mortaria could well be the work of a migrant potter from the New Forest potteries. It is worth noting that they are prominent in this collection, absent in nearby Ickham and virtually, if not entirely, absent in the large quantity of mortaria from Richborough. Further work on their distribution in Kent will help to pinpoint the location of the workshop.

No. 195 **TS12. 1957 East Cliff Site, Pit 5 (REC-57- 68 L.68) :1954 pit 5; RUB/4/2 or 14/2** is from the same vessel 370gms and 205gms Diam. 255mm. 38% and 20% TS12 (type specimen) Fabric 2, Canterbury or Colchester. Mortarium with wide bead and undulating collar, the exterior deeply corrugated and spout formed by breaking the bead and turning it out over the flange.

No. 196 **TS13. 1964 South Gate Site (REC-64 L.18 R-EK)** two joining sherds 155gms. Diam. 220mm. 29% TS13 (type specimen), similar to TS12, with straight collar and a spout of the type shown on Hull 1963, fig. 64, no. 2). Fabric 2, Canterbury or Colchester.

No. 197 **TS14. 1966 East Cliff Site, Upper Loam (REC-66 L.16 R-KP)**
60gms. Diam 290mm. 7% TS14 (type specimen), with the type of collar very commonly used in the Rhineland, but this example in Fabric 2, attributable to Canterbury or Colchester.
Other vessels:
1963 (R-CZ L-54) 65gms. Diam. 290mm. 9% TS15. Fabric 2, Canterbury or Colchester.

The Rhineland prototypes, (among them TS16–17), of Types 12–14, never appear in Britain before the mid-second century; it is not known when they ceased to be made or imported, but A.D. 250/300 are possible dates. The numbers found in Britain of these types in Fabrics 1–2 are limited and this is probably because production here ended early, before or *c.* A.D. 250 and because the workshops involved were supplying relatively local markets. The use of a related form by a stamping potter (TS3, Call(es)) supports its early use and the late second to early third century is the optimum date for production at Canterbury and Colchester because it follows onto the industries established and flourishing in the Antonine period. Production must have been much reduced in the late second century after the loss of their markets in Scotland and north-eastern England. Production in both areas continued into the third century, but these workshops were now serving relatively local regions. There is no evidence to indicate more than minimal mortarium production at Colchester and possibly none at Canterbury after *c.* A.D. 250. Generally similar mortaria were made in similar fabric in northern France, but the potters there appear to have continued to use their technique of internal concentric scoring in conjunction with these forms (personal examination of mortaria at Noyon (Oise)). There is no evidence to show that such mortaria were being imported into Britain in more than the most minimal numbers (Hartley in prep. a, and Hartley 1998, 205–206).

Not Ill. **TS15. 1959 Via Quintana Site, Under Road (REC-59- 152 L.4)**
40gms Diam. 270mm. 6% TS15 (type specimen), a typical example of form Gillam 255; for a close parallel see Philp 1981, fig. 54, no. 383. Fabric 6, Import from the Oise/Somme area of northern France (Hartley 1998, 203–206).

Other vessels:
1965 (R-GI L-11) 50gms. Diam. 260mm. 8%. TS15, slight variant on the type. Fabric 6, import from the Oise/Somme area. Burnt.

No. 198   TS16. 1963 East Barracks Site, Box OK (REC-63 R-CA) joins R-61–1002 and R-61–1671

260+90+125gms. Diam. 360mm. 15% TS16 (type specimen). Fabric 7, Rhineland (Tomber and Dore 1998, 78, (RHL WH)). Three joining sherds giving the complete profile of a mortarium with curved, vertical rim or collar, turned under at the bottom. This example is typical of one group of such imports, in that the interior is covered with evenly distributed, finely fragmented, quartz trituration grit which frequently extends below the bead which was folded down over it. The deeply corrugated exterior is also characteristic of many of this type. imported from Lower Germany; they are all probably from the same workshop, but its precise whereabouts is unknown. The rim-form falls technically into Gillam form 272, but see Holbrook and Bidwell 1991, fig. 84, no. C56 for a close parallel, pp. 204 and 207 for further comments. A.D. 140–250+. Worn smooth in the bottom; two of the sherds have been heavily burnt after fracture and the rimsherd is also burnt.
Other vessels:
1964 (R-ES L-???) 135gms. Diam. 320mm. 10% TS16, Fabric 7, Rhineland.
(R-NA L-1) 85gms. Diam. 370mm. 6%. TS16, Fabric 7, Rhineland.

No. 199   TS17. 1967 Via Quintana Site, Primary Soil (REC-67 L.107 WG-50)

115gms. Diam. 270mm 11% TS17 (type specimen), Fabric 7, Rhineland. Similar to Holbrook and Bidwell 1991, fig. 84, C56. Worn.

Not Ill.   TS18. 1966 West Site (REC-66 L.30 R-LB)

55gms. Diam. 290mm 10% TS18 (type specimen), Fabric 8, Mancetter-Hartshill. A four-reeded hammerhead with pronounced re-entrant angle at the top of the body. Personal examination of mortaria from Carpow (Dore) and Cramond (Holmes 2003, 50–51) in Scotland and of mortaria from kilns at Hartshill and Mancetter (unpublished) show that four-reeded mortaria were first made in these potteries in the very late second century, but were almost certainly commonest in the first half of third century. They continued to be made on a smaller scale into the fourth century. The re-entrant angle is not an early feature and is most commonly found in mortaria made at Cantley, Doncaster (Buckland, in prep) by potters likely to have come from the Warwickshire potteries. The date is probably within the period A.D. 250–350. **BP–find parallel**

No. 200   TS19. 1961 East Barracks Site, Occupation Soil (REC-61–1468 L.52)

60gms. Diam. 250mm. 10% TS19 (type specimen), Fabric 8, Mancetter-Hartshill potteries, Warwickshire. A mortarium with thin, smooth rim between a hammerhead and a wall-side, decorated with plain band and attached, solid triangles of red-brown paint placed at intervals (2 adjoining on sherd). The thin walls and hard fabric combined with this rim-profile point to a date in the fourth century. Generally similar forms were found at Segontium (Casey et al.1993, fig. 17.31).

Not Ill.   TS20. 1959 Via Quintana Site, Lower Occupation Soil

(REC-59–302 L.5) 55gms Diam. 290mm. 9% TS20 in Fabric 9, made in potteries in the Castor-Stibbington area of the lower Nene valley. Four-reeded, near hammerhead type with strong, upright bead; distal end of flange inturned (cf Perrin 1999, fig. 78, M25, for a close parallel). This is the only sherd from these potteries with a full rim-section which could be usefully drawn. It does not represent the others in detail, but the reeding and

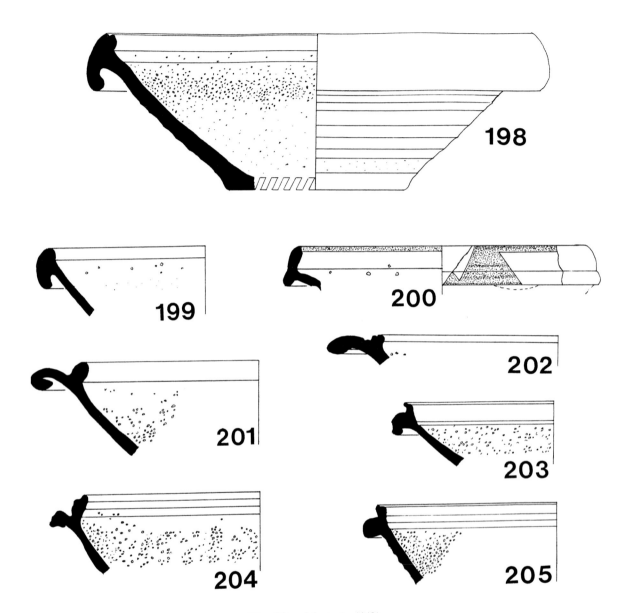

Fig. 50.   *Mortaria (1/3).*

distal swelling where the end of the flange is inturned, is common to all of the 8–10 vessels present.

Other vessels:

R-DA i 65gms. Two joining sherds with incomplete rim-section from a reeded hammerhead. Fabric 9, Lower Nene valley. A.D. 220–400. Burnt.

R-DA ii 30gms. Incomplete rim-section from a second reeded hammerhead. Fabric 9, Lower Nene valley. A.D. 220–400. Burnt.

REC/59/486 30gms. Incomplete rim-section from a third reeded hammerhead. Fabric 9, Lower Nene valley. A.D. 220–400.

REC/61/67 45gms. Diam. 390mm. 7% Flange fragment from a reeded hammerhead; generally similar to Mackreth 1996, fig. 115, M71. Fabric 9, Lower Nene valley. A.D. 230–400.

R-AW 15gms. Flange fragment from a reeded hammerhead. Fabric 9, Lower Nene valley. A.D. 220–400. Burnt.

R-CZ 20gms. Bead and spout fragment, incomplete rim-section. Fabric 9, Lower Nene valley. A.D. 220–400.

R-KP 60gms. Incomplete rim-section from a reeded hammerhead. Fabric 9, Lower Nene valley. A.D. 220–400.

REC/59/303 20gms. Diam. 370mm. 4% Flange and thumb-impressed spout fragment from a reeded hammerhead generally similar to Perrin 1999, fig. 78, M38. Fabric 9, Lower Nene valley. c. A.D. 250–400.

REC/59/301 25gms. Diam. 320mm. 6% Reeded hammerhead generally similar to Mackreth 1996, fig. 114, M19. Fabric 9, Lower Nene valley. A.D. 230–400.

No. 201 TS21. 1963 East Barracks Site, Well Shaft (REC-63 Box OB R-BX)

230gms. Diam. 380mm. 9% TS21 (type specimen) in Fabric 10, made in the Oxford potteries. This mortarium is identical to Young type M17.3 (Young 1977, fig.21); dated to A.D. 240–300.

Other vessels:

R-DN 40gms. Diam. 220mm. 12% Fabric 10, Oxford. Identical to Young type M17.3 (*ibid.*) with bead cut and turned out over flange to form spout. A.D. 240–300.

R-V (2 sherds; burnt) 185gms join R-BQ 20gms Diam. 310mm. 19% Fabric 10, Oxford. Identical to Young type M17.3 (*ibid.*); A.D. 240–300.

R 61–1750–1755 (6 sherds) 130gms. Diam. 260mm. 17% Fabric 10, Oxford. Generally similar to Young type M17.3 (*ibid.*); A.D. 240–300.

R 61–1092 30gms. Diam. 260mm. 9% Flange fragment. Fabric 10, Oxford. Young M17.3 (*ibid.*); A.D. 240–300.

R-60–415 15gms. Diam.230mm. 9% Flange fragment. Fabric 10, Oxford. Young M17.3 (*ibid.*); A.D. 240–300.

R-60–565 10gms. Diam. 250mm. 6% Flange fragment. Fabric 10, Oxford. Young M17.3 (*ibid.*); A.D. 240–300.

R-61–1095 5gms. Diam 250mm. 5% Flange fragment. Fabric 10, Oxford. Young M17.3 (*ibid.*); A.D. 240–300.

R-63 East caravan site unstrats. 280gms. Diam. 300mm. 27% Fabric 10, Oxford. Young M17.3 (*ibid.*), bead turned out over flange to form spout. A.D. 240–300.

R-DA 55gms.Diam. 290mm. 9% Fabric 10, Oxford. similar to Young M17.2, spout as above (*ibid.*); A.D. 240–300.

R-59–240 joining REC-59–284 40gms. Diam. 270mm. 8% Fabric 10, Oxford. Young M17.2 (*ibid.*); A.D. 240–300.

R-59–240 60gms. Diam. 260mm. 14% Fabric 10, Oxford. Young M17.8 (*ibid.*); A.D. 240–300.

R-NC L-330gms. Incomplete rim-section. Fabric 10, Oxford. Probably Young M17 (*ibid.*); A.D. 240–300.

No. 202   TS22. 1964 South Gate Site, Upper Occupation Soil (REC-64 L.85 R-FQ)
120gms. Diam. 410mm.10% TS22 (type specimen) in Fabric 10, made in the Oxford potteries. Young type M18, which is similar to M17, but closed in under the flange (*ibid*). A.D. 240–300.
Other vessels:
R-LB 140gms Diam. 320mm. 8% Young type M18, (*ibid*). Burnt. A.D. 240–300.
R-IK 110gms. Diam. 330mm. 10% Young type M18, (*ibid*). A.D. 240–300.
R-61–439 40gms. Diam. 260mm. 8% Young type M18, (*ibid*). A.D. 240–300.
R-RJ on label, RR-J on pot (L10) 85gms. Diam. 280mm. 9% Young type M18, (*ibid*). Burnt or overfired. A.D. 240–300.
R-EE 158 L12/14 1964 70gms. Diam. 320mm. 5% Young type M18, (*ibid*). A.D. 240–300.
R-61–285 50gms. Diam. 250mm. 5% Young type M18, (*ibid*). Burnt. A.D. 240–300.
R-59–257 45gms. Diam. 330mm. 6% Flange fragment. Young type M18, (*ibid*). A.D. 240–300.
R-NC 10gms. 4% Flange fragment. Probably Young type M18, (*ibid*). A.D. 240–300.

Fragmentary rim sherds in Fabric 10, Oxford potteries. Likely to be M17 or M18, but cannot be typed with certainty. A.D. 240–300/400.
R-61–1756 25gms.
R/M 50gms.
R/NA 25gms. Burnt.
R/DA 20gms.
R-61–1032 5gms.
R-59–371 35gms. Burnt.

No. 203   TS23. 1965 Bath House Site, Soil Outside Apse (REC-65 L.48 R-IS)
150gms. Diam. 270mm. 24% Fabric 10, Oxford potteries. Between Young form M22.8 and M22.11. A.D. 240–400.
Other vessels:
R-60–57 L-2 25gms. Diam 240mm. 5% Fabric 10, Oxford potteries. Young M22.8. A.D. 240–400.

Not Ill.   TS24. 1962 East Barracks Site, Trench B (REC-62 L.57 R-BR)
45gms. Diam. 250mm. 9% Fabric 10, Oxford potteries. Atkinson 1941, fig. 5, no. 74 A.D. 240–400. Slight burning on R-BR.
Other vessels:
R-60–210 35gms. Diam. 250mm. 7% Fabric 10 Oxford potteries. Atkinson 1941, fig. 5, no. 74, Young M22 A.D. 240–400.
R-NE L-5 1966 75gms. Diam. 240mm. 18% Fabric 10, Oxford potteries. Atkinson 1941, fig. 5, no. 74, Young M22 A.D. 240–400.

Not Ill.   TS25. 1960 Central Area, Sacellum (REC-60–280 L.20)
55gms. Diam. 250mm. 12% Fabric 10, Oxford potteries Young type M22 (cf Atkinson 1941, fig. 5, no 76 for a fairly close parallel). A.D. 240–400.
Other vessels:
(R-JT L-77) 1965 105gms. 320mm. 12% Fabric 10, Oxford potteries. Young type 22.3 A.D. 240–400. Slightly singed.

No. 204   TS26. 1961 East Barracks Site, Upper Occupation Soil
(REC-61–1464 L.52) 155gms. Diam. 350mm. 14% Fabric 10, Oxford potteries. Generally similar to Young type M22.8. A.D. 240–400; typologically one would expect this to be fourth century rather than earlier. Burnt.

No. 205   TS27. 1962 East Barracks Area, Trench B (REC-62 L.2 R-M)
115gms. Diam. 250mm. 10% Fabric 10, Oxford potteries. Similar to Young type M22.14; Atkinson 1941, fig. 5, No.79 is a closer parallel). A.D. 240–400.

Not Ill.   TS28. 1969 North East Area, Occupation Soil (REC-69 L.68 RR-BP)
25gms. Diam. 260mm. 5% Fabric 10, Oxford potteries. Young M22.4. A.D. 240–400.

Not Ill.   TS29. 1962 East Barracks Site, Box B (REC-62 L.4 R-F)
45gms. Diam. 270mm. 12%, Fabric 11, Oxford potteries. Young M22.10. A.D. 240–400.

Not Ill.   TS30. 1960 Central Area, Sacellum (REC-60–273 L.20)
30gms. Diam. 260mm. 6% Fabric 10, Oxford potteries. Young form M22 with angular flange reminiscent of the angular flanged C100 forms in Fabric 12. A.D. 240–400.
Other vessels:
(R-NA L1) 1966 25gms. Diam. *c.* 250mm. 6% Fabric 10, Oxford potteries. Young M22, close to TS30. A.D. 240–400.
(R-NA L1) 1966 35gms. Diam. 250mm. 8% Fabric 10, Oxford potteries. Young M22, close to TS30. A.D. 240–400. Burnt.

Not Ill.   TS31. 1969 North East Area, Trench B (REC-69 L.3 RR-C)
40gms. Diam. 290mm. 6% Fabric 12, Oxford potteries, Young form C100.2. Fourth-century.
Other vessels:
R-61–1130 10gms. 4% Fragmentary. Fabric 12, Oxford potteries, Young C100. Fourth-century.

Not Ill. TS32. 1966 West Site, Medieval Deposit (REC-66 L.3 R-NC)
50gms. Diam. ?230mm. 9% Fabric 12, Oxford potteries. Young form C97 with lion's head spout. A.D. 240–400.
Other vessels:
(RR-E L5) 10gms. 5% Fragmentary Fabric 12, Oxford potteries. Young form C97. A.D. 240–400.

(B) FABRICS

Fabric 1 Probably Canterbury, with Colchester as an alternative possibility **(TS–1)**
Self-coloured, fine-textured, pale brown fabric. Inclusions: fairly frequent, tiny but ill-sorted, quartz with some orange-brown material, probably flint and occasional black material; very rare larger quartz and flint. Trituration grit: flint with some quartz. These potteries also produced mainly cream fabrics and the virtually brown ones are mostly, late second-century or early third-century.
Bodysherd:
R-61–431 10gms. A harder and finer textured version of Fabric 1.

Fabric 2 Canterbury or Colchester **(TS.12, 13 and 14)**
Self-coloured, fairly fine-textured, fabric; colour varies through cream, yellowish-cream to creamy brown, occasionally with pink core; texture moderate to hard; surface can be powdery. Inclusions: frequent, minute, fragmented quartz, black and red-brown material well-mixed throughout the fabric; sometimes with sporadic larger inclusions of the same materials. Trituration grit: flint and quartz. The clay used is similar to that used at Colchester, some other parts of East Anglia and parts of northern France (Fabric 6) as well as in Canterbury in the second to early third century. In fact, the iron free clays in Colchester/Canterbury can only be distinguished from those used in northern France by rigorous analysis (Hartley and Tomber in prep. section III, Scientific Analysis),

so that distinction by macroscopic examination depends on the forms used and any unusual characteristics of manufacture. The mortaria in Fabric 2 all lack characteristics present in the mortaria known to have been made in northern France. The workshop known to have existed at Canterbury in the Antonine period (Kirkman 1940) was using similar clay and there are late second-century to early third century mortaria found at Canterbury and elsewhere in Kent which are likely to have been made locally. These suggest that the industry continued into the third century. The Reculver mortaria in Fabric 2 probably all belong to the third century though a late second-century date cannot be ruled out. The alternative source is Colchester which would have been very accessible. The industry there had passed its peak and was no longer sending mortaria to the north, but rim-profiles like TS12–14 were being made there and Kent could have been a nearby and very useful market (Hull 1963, Figs. 89 and 99). Only excavation of further kilns in Kent will show whether these mortaria in Fabric 2 are local rather than from Colchester. On present evidence Colchester seems more likely.

Bodysherds:

> (R-HI L-122) 120gms. Well-worn. Probably Fabric 2 rather than 6.

Fabric 3 East- or mid-Kent **(TS-3)**
Hard, orange-brown fabric with thick, well-defined, purplish brown core (Munsell 5YR 6/3) and cream slip. Inclusions: fairly frequent, ill-sorted, tiny to small, red-brown, quartz, black (?slag), and some voids. Trituration grit: abundant, tiny to medium-sized, flint, white, transparent and pinkish quartz, red-brown sandstone and a little black (?slag).

Other sherds:

> R-LC 10gms. a base sherd in Fabric 3, probably belongs to TS3.
> R-DA 5gms. bead and collar fragment of type made by Call(es). Fabric 3. Probably A.D. 160–220.
> RR-I bodysherd;

Fabric 4 Mid- or East Kent (Fabrics 3 and 4 merge into each other) **(TS-2, 4, 5 and 6)**
Very hard fabric, red-brown in colour with very thick core which may be purplish, grey or dense black and which can extend almost to the surface. Inclusions: a matrix of moderate to frequent, (barely visible at x20 magnification), black, quartz, grey and red-brown material with some sporadic larger grits of similar rock. There are sometimes voids where inclusions have either burnt out during firing or fallen out. The fabric has a cream slip. Trituration grit: mostly white flint with some quartz including rare pinkish quartz, a little red-brown rock (possibly haematite), and opaque black material.

Bodysherds:

> R-TD 1966 10gms.
> R-V 35gms.
> R-59–133 10gms. 25gms. body/base sherd;

Fabric 5 East- or Mid-Kent (The sherds in this fabric are fourth century) **(TS-7–11)**
Very hard, fine-textured, orange-brown fabric with brownish-grey to dark grey core. Inclusions: rare, opaque red-brown and black material. Trituration grit: quartz, flint with a little red-brown sandstone and quartz sandstone. A cream slip may have been normal, but TS8 is self-coloured.

Bodysherds:

> R-V 10gms. Flake from a rim with long flange, just possibly TS9. Fabric 5 with black core, east or mid-Kent. Fourth century.
> R-FL 1964 L68 150gms. Fabric 5 bodybase sherd worn and burnt.

Fabric 6 Northern France, probably the Oise/Somme region **(TS-15)**
Impossible to distinguish from Fabric 2 in macroscopic examination (see above), but from northern France, where clays of the same type are available. There is good evidence for Gillam 255 mortaria being made at workshops in the Oise/Somme area (Hartley 1998, 203–206), which

provided imports to Britain in the first and second centuries; there is no evidence to support these forms being made in Britain.

Fabric 7 Rhineland (unknown site in Rhine, Meuse or Mosel valleys) **(TS-16 and 17)**
Self-coloured, hard, fairly fine-textured, cream to off-white fabric. Inclusions: fairly frequent to frequent, tiny, mostly quartz with some red-brown material. Trituration grit: tiny fragmented quartz. All four mortaria in this fabric have similar characteristics. (Tomber and Dore 1998, 78, (RHL WH))
Bodysherds:
> R-TJ L-1 145gms. Body/base sherd. Fabric 6, Rhineland. Heavily worn, burnt.

Fabric 8 Mancetter-Hartshill potteries, Warwickshire **(TS-18 and 19)**
Hard, very fine-textured, well-fired, creamy white fabric; self-coloured or with self-coloured slip. Inclusions: moderate, very tiny, transparent quartz with occasional orange-brown material. Trituration grit: hard, red-brown and black material, believed to be re-fired pottery and tile. (This fabric description applies only to the three sherds present which represent one variant of the fabrics; hardness and fineness are particularly characteristic of some of the third and fourth-century mortaria from this pottery.)
Bodysherd:
> 70gms. later than A.D. 130. Fabric 8, Mancetter-Hartshill.

Fabric 9 Lower Nene valley, Castor/Stibbington area **(TS-20)**
Hard, off-white fabric, occasionally with greyish core; buff slip often fired to an ochre colour. Inclusions: moderate to fairly frequent, mostly barely visible, quartz, red-brown and slag with a few sporadic medium-sized red-brown, ?slag fragments. Trituration grits: dense, black slag.
Bodysherds:
> (R-AK) 10gms. Fabric 9. A.D. 220–400.

Fabric 10 Oxford (Young 1977); Tomber & Dore 1998,174–175) **(TS-21–28 and 30)**
Self-coloured, fairly fine-textured, cream/off-white fabric. Inclusions: few sporadic quartz and some orange-brown, but more visible at x20 magnification. Trituration grit: abundant, transparent, and translucent, pinkish and brownish quartz.
Bodysherds:
> RR-E 2 sherds 45gms.
> R-NC L-3 45gms.
> R-V 15gms.
> R-61–257 15gms. Burnt
> RR-AG 20gms. 2 sherds.
> R-59–2516 60gms. Burnt.
> R-59–2514 50gms base/bodysherd.
> R-59–172 50gms. 2 sherds.
> R-59–233 15gms.
> R-60–115 120gms 3 joining sherds from base and side. Burnt.
> R-60–212 25gms.
> R-61–1093 100gms. 2 sherds from two different bases, both burnt.
> R-61–1713 15gms.
> R-EX L-42 25gms. Body/base sherd.
> R-CR L-41 10gms.
> R-TN L-5 1966 25gms.
> R-HP L-6 1965 25gms.
> R-TA L-1 1966 10gms. Burnt.
> R-KU L-22 1966 15gms.
> RR-O L-15 1969 20gms. Body/base sherd.

RR-T L-20 1969 10gms.
R-U 30gms. 3 sherds. Burnt.
R-AR 10gms.
R-Z 20gms. Body/base sherd.
R-61–821 35gms.
R-61–1094 joining REC/61/819 85gms. Burnt.
R-61–820 35gms.
R-61–258 40gms. Body/base sherd.
R-61–622 15gms.
R-61–823 5gms.
R-61–1065 10gms.
R-61–824 5gms.

Fabric 11 Oxford potteries A.D. 240–400 **(TS-29)**
Fine-textured, micaceous, red-brown fabric, sometimes with brownish-grey core. Inclusions: very rare quartz, black and red-brown material. Trituration grit: as Fabric 10. Fabric 11 is essentially the same as Fabric 12 except for having a white/buff slip.
Bodysherds:
RR-AG 15gms.
R-M 50gms. Fabric 5 Body/base sherd:

Fabric 12 Oxford potteries AD240–400 **(TS-31 and 32)**
The body fabric and the trituration grit are exactly as Fabric 11, but the slip is red-brown and can at its best be samian-like.
Bodysherds:
R-59–451 25gms. Heavily burnt.
RR-BP L-68 10gms.
RR-AG 15gms. 2 sherds. R-IM L-42 10gms. Burnt.
R-ND L-4 10gms. Bodysherd.

Fabric 13 variant of Fabric 12, Oxford
Fine-textured, pale orange-brown fabric, fired to cream near the surfaces. Inclusions: barely visible at less than x20; frequent, minute quartz, some red-brown. Trituration grit: exactly as Fabrics 10–12. Red slip, similar to the red slip produced in the Oxford potteries; surface very smooth.
Bodysherd:
RR-BP L-68 10gms. Worn. Only sherd in Fabric 13.

Fabric 14 Unknown source
Probably intended to be buff but the only sherd is heavily burnt throughout; texture slightly granular. Inclusions: frequent, ill-sorted, mostly quartz, but includes some black, ?slag and rare red-brown material. The trituration grit on the single sherd is worn almost away, but it included pinkish quartz, quartz sandstone and possibly flint.
Untyped vessel (not illus.) R-PR L-82 1966 90gms. Fabric 14. Flanged mortarium with incomplete rim-profile, some similarity to Fulford 1975, fig. 25, no.103, but the trituration grit is inappropriate for the New Forest potteries. Heavily worn and burnt. Probably A.D. 240–400.

(C) BIBLIOGRAPHY

Atkinson, R.J.C., 'A Romano-British Potters' Field at Cowley, Oxon' *Oxoniensia VI,* 1941, 9–21.
Bennett, Paul, Frere, S. S., and Stow, Sally, 1982 *Excavations at Canterbury Castle, The Archaeology of Canterbury 1.* Kent Archaeological Soc. Hartley, K 'The mortaria' 150–158.
Joanna Bird (ed.), *Form and Fabric: studies in Rome's material past in honour of B. R. Hartley.* Oxbow Mon. 80, 199–217. Oxford, 1998.

Casey, P.J., Davies, J.L., and Evans, J., 1993, *Excavations at Segontium (Caernarfon) Roman Fort, 1975–1979*. CBA Rept. 90.

Corder, P, ed. 1951 *The Roman town and villa at Great Casterton, Rutland*. University of Nottingham

Dore, J. and Wilkes, J.J., 1999 'Excavations directed by JD Leach and JJ Wilkes on the site of a Roman fortress at Carpow, Perthshire, 1964–79, *Proc. Soc. Antiq. Scot 129*, 481–575, Scotland. Dore, J, 'Roman pottery' 537–52.

Frere, Sheppard 1984, *Verulamium Excavations, Volume III*. Monograph No. 1. Oxford University Comm. Arch. Oxford, 1984, 280–293.

Fulford, M G, 1975 *New Forest Roman Pottery: Manufacture and Distribution with a Corpus of the Pottery Types*. British Archaeol Rep B17, Hampshire.

Gillam J.P., 1970 *Types of Roman Coarse Pottery Vessels in Northern Britain*. 3rd. edn. Newcastle upon Tyne, 1970.

Hartley, Katharine F., and Tomber, Roberta in prep *A mortarium bibliography with reference to Roman Britain*.

Hartley 1998: in Joanna Bird (ed.) 1998, 199–217.

Hinchliffe, John with Sparey Green, Christopher 1985, *Excavations at Brancaster 1974 and 1977*. East Ang. Arch Rept. 2.

Neil Holbrook and Paul T. Bidwell, *Roman Finds from Exeter*. Exeter Arch. Reps. no. 4. Exeter, 1991.

Holmes, Nicholas, 2003, *Excavation on Roman sites at Cramond*, Edinburgh, 1875–1978. Soc. of Ant of Scot Monograph 23.

M.R. Hull, *The Roman Potters' Kilns of Colchester*. Reps. Res. Comm. Antiq. London, no.XXI. Oxford, 1963.

Holder, Alfred, 1896, *Alt-Celtischer Sprachschatz*. Leipzig.

Johnson, Stephen 1983, *Burgh Castle, Excavations by Charles Green 1958–61*. East Ang. Arch. no. 20.

Kirkman, J.S., 'Canterbury kiln site. The pottery.' *Arch Cant LIII* (1940), 118–133. (This is the pottery report for Webster, Graham 1940: 'A Roman pottery kiln at ibid., 109–116.)

Mackreth, D.F., *Orton Hall Farm: A Roman and Early Anglo-Saxon Farmstead*. East Anglian Archaeology Report no. 76.

Perrin, J.R. 1999, *Roman Pottery from Excavations at and near to the Roman Small Town of Durobrivae, Water Newton, Cambridgeshire, 1956–58*. Journal of Roman Pottery Studies vol. 8.

Philp, Brian 1981, *The Excavation of the Roman Forts of the Classis Britannica at Dover 1970–1977*. Kent Monog Ser.3

Sparey Green, C. 1987, *Excavations at Poundbury. Volume I: The Settlements*. Dorset N.H. and Arch. Soc. Monog. 7

Symonds, Robin P and Wade S., 1999: *Roman Pottery from excavations in Colchester, 1971–86* (eds. P. Bidwell and A. Croom). Colchester Arch Trust K.F.Hartley, 'The stamped mortaria 195–211. Tomber, Roberta and Dore, John, *The National Roman Fabric Collection*. Museum of London Archaeology Service, 1998. Young, Christopher J., The Roman Pottery Industry of the Oxford Region, (BAR 43, 1977).

(4) THE SAMIAN WARE (Fig. 51)

Summary by Joanna Bird

The earliest piece of samian identified from the site is a shallow dish decorated with an applied scroll and dated to the Tiberian-Claudian period. Other 1st century samian, however, is later, with no vessels that can be dated before the Neronian period and most of it is of Neronian or Neronian-Flavian date. It includes two decorated bowls of form Dr 29 and the base of a third stamped by Martialis 1, one Dr 30 and at least five examples of Dr 37; none of the decorated ware can be attributed to a specific potter. The 1st century plain forms include a bowl of form Ritterling 12, but consist mainly of Dr 18 and Dr 15/17, one with a stamp of Vitalis ii. All these wares are South Gaulish and probably all from La Graufesenque. More unusually, there are also two South Gaulish bowls of early-2nd century date, both of Form 37, one probably in the style of Attillus of Montans and one by Natalis-Marinus of Banassac.

Central Gaulish products of 2nd century date apparently all originate at Lezoux; despite the presence of early-2nd century South Gaulish bowls, there are no wares from the contemporary potteries at Les Martres-de-Veyre. Apart from a bowl of Hadrianic or early-Antonine date which has stylistic links with such potters as X-5 and X-6, the decorated ware – some fourteen bowls – is mainly of Antonine date, including single examples of Dr 30 by Doeccus and perhaps Paternus II or Banvus, two examples of Dr 37 by Doeccus and Cinnamus group, and single Dr 37 bowls by Iullinus and perhaps Divixtus and Paternus II; one bowl of mid-to late Antonine date carries an unidentified mould-stamp. The plain wares include two Hadrianic to mid-Antonine stamps, of Paullus iv and Sollemnis i, later Antonine forms such as Dr 31R and Dr 45 are well represented and there are contemporary stamps of Carussa, Maternus iv and Saturninus ii.

The East Gaulish wares come from Trier, Rheinzabern and the Argonne, and date from the later-2nd century to the mid-3rd; there are also Argonne wares of later-3rd to 4th century date, including one roller-stamped example of form Chenet 320. Antonine Argonne wares include a Dr 37 in the style of Tribunus, a Dr 45 mortarium with lion-head spout and incised forms. The Trier wares include five decorated Dr 37 bowls, with single bowls attributed to Afer, Afer-Marinus and probably Criciro, a plain-ware stamp of Materninus ii, and Ludowici SMb/c and Dr 43 with barbotine decoration. There is also a high proportion of Trier mortarium sherds, many of them heavily worn, though they do not necessarily represent a large number of individual vessels. The eleven decorated Rheinzabern bowls include three or four by Julius II-Julianus I and single vessels attributed to Cerialis IV, Cerialis VI or Primitivus I and Atto I or Firmus II, there are also four Rheinzabern plain-ware stamps, of Cucio, Domitianus, Julianus iii and an unidentified potter. Among the plain forms are jars or large beakers of form Dr 54, late versions of Ludowici Sb with the rounded profile of Sh and unstamped examples of Dr 33.

CATALOGUE OF SAMIAN WARE

The catalogue is arranged by year, then by layer number and site code . The catalogue includes imported Argonne, marbled and 'a l'eponge' wares. The following abbreviations are used:

SG = South Gaul (La Graufesenque unless stated otherwise)
CG = Central Gaul (Lezoux unless stated otherwise)
EG = East Gaul
EGR = East Gaul, Rheinzabern
EGT = East Gaul, Trier

1957 Beach and Cliff Areas

L-1	F	(3 sherds) Dr 37, style of Tribunus: see R-LA (= F Pit) Antonine
		Dr 31, CG, Antonine
		Two SG sherds, second half 1st century
L-14	70	Ludowici Sb, EGR, first half 3rd century
		Dish sherd, EGR
L-16	F	Dr 45, Argonne, late 2nd to 4th century
Pit	F	Dr 37, Rheinzabern. The ovolo (Ricken & Fischer 1963, type E26) and medallion (K18) were both used by Atto (B F Atto) and Firmus II. First half 3rd century (No.221).
		Dr 37 (= 1 F) Antonine?
		CG sherd
		EGR sherd

1959 Via Quintana Area

L-2	426	Mortarium, EGT, late 2nd to first half 3rd century; worn
	457	Argonne Mortarium, late 2nd to 4th century
L-4	125	Mortarium, EGT, late 2nd to first half 3rd century, very worn
	128	EGR mortarium, late 2nd to mid-3rd century

	130	Curle 23, CG, Antonine
	131	CG sherd
	129	Dr 33, CG, Antonine
L-5	308	Ludowici Sb, EGR, early to mid-3rd century
	322	Dr 31, CG, Antonine
	315	Dr 36, EGR, first half 3rd century
	316	EGT sherd
	317	EGT sherd
	318	Dr 43, EGR, first half 3rd century
	320	EGR sherd
	321	Ludowici Sb, EGR, late 2nd to first half 3rd century
	294	Dr 37, Lezoux. Beaded panels including a figure of Vulcan, probably one regularly used by Cinnamus group (e.g. Stanfield & Simpson, pl. 159, 25) *c.* A.D. 145–75
L-11	250	Sherd, large jar probably EGR, early to mid-3rd century
L-12	198	CG sherd
L-13	177	EGR footring sherd

1960 Central Area

L-3	250	Ludowici Sb/Sh, EGT, early to mid-3rd century
L-5/6	364	Dr 18/31, CG, Hadrianic-early Antonine
	365	Chenet 320, Argonne, 4th century
	370	Dr 18, SG, pre or early-Flavian
L-7	102	Curle 23, CG, Antonine; scorched. Graffito on rim, possibly reading]IAF
L-8	04	(Two sherds) Dr 18, SG, Flavian
L-10	21	EGR sherd
L-12	159	Curle 23, CG, Antonine
L-1		Dr 30 in the style of Doeccus of Lezoux. The triton and borders are on Stanfield & Simpson 1958, pl. 149, 35, the shell on pl. 150, 39. *c.* A.D. 165–200 Dechelette 72 copy decorated with pairs of incised diagonals and verticals. Sandy pink fabric with worn red colour-coat; probably south-east England. (No. 218) Dr 38, EGR, first half 3rd century.ss
L-13	63	(Two joining sherds) Dr 37, South Gaul. Basal band of upright cordate leaves with a row of rosettes in small rings between their tips; the motif above is not identifiable. Flavian.
	64	Mortarium, Argonne, late 2nd to 4th century,
	69	Dr 36, SG, Flavian
	70	Flange fragment, EGT
	71	Argonne sherd
L-14	02	Ludowici Sb, EGR, early to mid-3rd century
L-5/6	402	Mortarium, EGT, late 2nd to first half 3rd century; heavily worn
L-14	404	EGR sherd
	403	Mortarium, EGT, late 2nd to first half 3rd century
	417	Dr 33, EGR, first half 3rd century
	421	Mortarium, EGT, late 2nd to first half 3rd century
	511	Dr 27, SG, Flavian; burnt
		Ludowici, Sb, EGR, early to mid-3rd century
		EGR sherd
		Chenet 320, Argonne, 4th century
		Chenet 320, Argonne, 4th century
		Flagon sherd with a thin marbled orange-red slip on the exterior

		Imported from Germany (Lower Rhineland Marbled Ware), mid-3rd to 4th century (cf Bird & Williams 1983)
L-15	27	Dr 45, EGT, late 2nd to early 3rd century
L-20	276	Joins 546? 271
	277	Dr 30, Lezoux. Beaded panel containing an arcade on a corded column; the column may be Rogers 1974, type P76, used by Paternus II and Banvus. Mid-late Antonine
	279	Dr 45, EGT, late 2nd to early 3rd century
	281	Dr 31R. CG, mid-late Antonine
	282	Dr 36, SG, Flavian
L-21	01	Dr 37R, coarse rouletting; probably Argonne, and 3rd century
	KF03	Dr 33, Saturninus. A.D. 160–200. See BMD Report No.9 (No.228).

1961 East Barracks Area

L-1	58	Dr 33, Pavlim, A.D 135–70. See BMD Report No.8 (No.225)
L-10	800	EGR sherd, late 2nd to mid-3rd century; probably same as 805
	802	Curle 21, CG, mid-late Antonine
	805	Curle 21, probably, EGR, late 2nd to mid-3rd century
	807	Dr 37, CG, tip of decoration at base; Hadrianic-Antonine
	809	Dr 31/Ludowici Sa, probably EG but lightly burnt all over; late 2nd to first half 3rd century
L-12	R-E	Dr 37, Rheinzabern. The ovolo is not identifiable; the rosette is Ricken & Fischer 1963, type 037. Early to mid-3rd century; swallowtail for repair (No. 211).
	R-E	Dr 37, EGR, early to mid-3rd century; burnt material adhering
	R-E	Dr 33, EGR, early to mid-3rd century
	R-E	Dr 38, EGR, early to mid-3rd century
	R-E	Dr 43, EGT, late 2nd to early-3rd century
	R-E	Walters 79, CG, mid to late-Antonine
	R-E	Ludowici Sb/Sh, groove on interior, EGR, early to mid-3rd century
	R-E	CG sherd. Hadrianic-Antonine
L-14	566	Dr 45, EGT, first half 3rd century
L-15	1000	Round-bodied jar or large beaker, no slip on interior, EGR, late 2nd to first half 3rd century
L-18	1741	Burnt sherd, probably CG and Antonine
L-20	1055	Dr 38, EGR, late 2nd to first half 3rd century
L-29	1116	Dr 31R/Ludowici Sb, EGR, late 2nd to first half 3rd century
L-31	149	Dr 37, EGR, second quarter 3rd century
L-37	1719	SG sherd
L-42	133	Dr 45, EGT, late 2nd to early 3rd century
L-44	233	Chenet 320, Argonne, 4th century
L-45	1354	Dr 30 or Dr 37, EGT, late 2nd to early 3rd century
L-48	217	(Two joining sherds) Mortarium, EGT, late 2nd to first half 3rd century
	218	(Two joining sherds) Dr 45, Argonne, late 2nd to 4th century
L-56,57	1623	Ludowici Sb, EGT, early to mid-3rd century
	1628	Sherd, flanged bowl in a l'eponge' ware from western France (Fulford 1977, 45–47), 4th century; burnt.
L-58	R-D	Rounded dish foot, EGT, early to mid 3rd century
	R-D	(Seven sherds, six joining). Flanged bowl in a l'eponge' ware from western France (Fullford 1977, 45–47), 4th century; burnt and abraded. Probably = 1628 in L-56, L-57
L-65	110	EGT mortarium, first half 3rd century

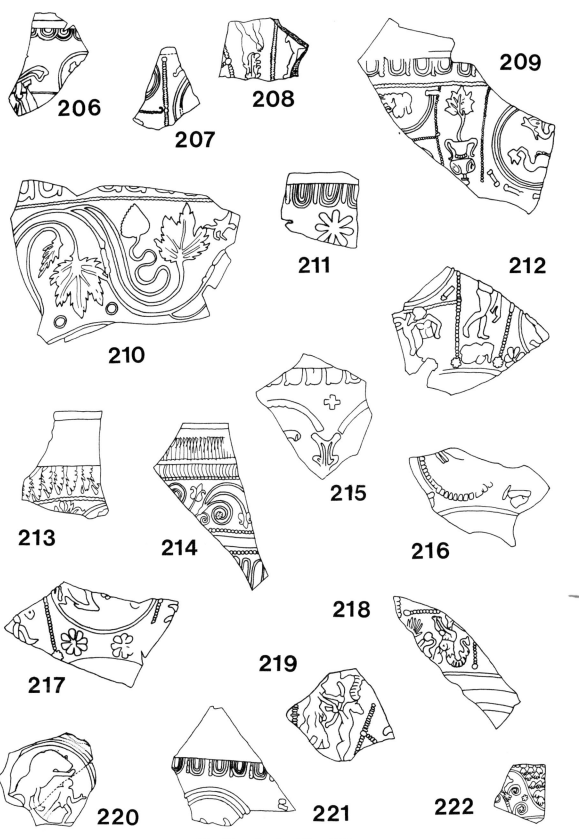

Fig. 51. *Samian Ware (1/2).*

	113	Dr 31R, CG, mid to late Antonine
L-77	1517	Dr 31R, mid-to late-Antonine, See BMD Report No.13.
L-100	61	Eight fragments, one pot, EGT
	126	Dr 45, EGT, Late 2nd to early 3rd century; swallowtail hole for repair
	161	EGR sherd

KF61   (Fourteen joining sherds) Dr 37, Lezoux; the fragmentary mould-stamp M cannot be identified. The decoration and the coarse modelling of the details such as the beads and the large rosettes indicate a mid-to late Antonine date. There are links with such potters as Advocisus, who used the figure of Apollo (Bird 1986, no. 2.24) and the seated group of Demeter and Kore (Rogers 1999, pl. 1, 3) Censorinus, whose style includes a similar large rosette (Stanfield & Simpson 1958, pl. 102, 18) and Atilianus and Paternus II, who both used the Demeter group (Rogers 1999, fig. 7, 1, and pl. 77, 11). The other figure is Oswald 1936–37, type 638. Late 2nd century. See BMD Report No. 15. (No. 217).

L-70,	116	1702 Ludowici Tg, mid-late Antonine
L-118	1720	Dr 37, South Gaul. The detail is blurred, but the decoration probably includes a shallow panel of wavy-lines and arrowheads above a triple medallion. Flavian
L-119	535	CG sherd, Hadrianic-Antonine
	984	Dr 37, Montans. The pair of internal grooves, the pale fabric and brownish slip are all characteristic of Montans ware. The row of grass-tufts used as an ovolo is on a bowl from Long Lane, Southwark, assigned to Attillus or an associated potter; below is a scroll with foliage motifs. *c.* A.D. 110–40 (No.213).
	55	Dr 33, Hadrianic-Antonine
L-33	56	Dr 38, EGR, late 2nd to first half of 3rd century; abraded
	60	(Eight joining sherds) Dr 45, EGT, early to mid-3rd century
	66	Ludowici Sb, EGT, early to mid-3rd century
	373	EGT sherd
	410–414	(Five sherds) Dr 18/31, CG, Hadrianic to early Antonine
	1029	(Two joining sherds) Dr 18R, SG, Flavian –Trajanic
	1087	Dr 31R, rouletted fabric; EGT, later 2nd to early 3rd century

1962 East Barracks Area

L-2	R-M	Dr 18/31 or 18/31R, CG, probably Hadrianic
L-3	62	Dr 45, EGT, first half 3rd century
L-9	213	Dr 37, Central Gaul. Running stag and pinnate leaf; the leaf suggests Paternus II (e.g. Rogers 1999, pl. 78, 23). Mid to late Antonine; burnt
	R-W	Ludowici Sb, EGR, first half 3rd century
		Dr 45, late 2nd to first half of 3rd century
L-12	R-X	SG sherd
L-13	R-AR	CG sherd
L-29	R-BS	Ludowici Sb, EGR, first half 3rd century
L-31	R-BT	Round-bodied jar, EGT, first half 3rd century
L-33	R-N	Mortarium, CG, late 2nd century; little wear on grits
		CG sherd, probably Dr 31, Antonine
L-34	R-BK	Mortarium, EGR, late 2nd to early 3rd century
L-35	R-AJ	Ludowici Sb, EGR, first half 3rd century
		EGT sherd
L-40	R-O	(Two joining sherds) Dr 38, EGR, second quarter 3rd century

		Dr 37 foot, very massive, EGT, second quarter 3rd century; little wear on underside
L-45	R-BQ	Shallow plain wall decorated with an applied double scroll, probably from a small platter copying *Conspectus* form 6.2 (Ettlinger et al. 1990). SG, Tiberian-Claudian (Three sherds, two joining) Dr 45, CG, late 2nd century Bowl or dish, EGR, late 2nd to first half 3rd century
L-47	R-BB	Ludowici Sb, EGR, early to mid-3rd century
L-48	204	Ludowici Sb, stamped Domitianus. late 2nd century. See BMD Report No. 3 (No.226)
L-49	R-AU	EGR dish sherd, late 2nd to first half 3rd century Dr 30, South Gaul. There is no complete impression of the ovolo but the shape of the lower end suggests type QQ, recorded for Lupus ii (Dannell, Dickinson & Vernhet 1998), *c.* A.D. 50–65
L-52	206	(Two joining sherds) Dr 37 in the style of Doeccus of Lezoux. Medallion containing a small naked figure (Stanfield & Simpson 1958, pl. 149, 27) and a boar; the bear is on a bowl in Doeccus' style from Silchester (Reading Museum 81.798). *c.* A.D. 165–200. (No. 220).
L-52	R-AM	(Two sherds) Ludowici Sb, EGR, first half of 3rd century Curle 21, EGR, first half 3rd century
L-53	R-AP	Ludowici Sb, EGR, first half 3rd century EGT sherd
L-54	R-BP	Dr 36, heavy rim, no barbotine; EGT, early to mid-3rd century
L-55	R-BC	Argonne bowl sherd, late 3rd to 4th century
L-56	R-BH	(Three joining sherds) Dr 38, EGT, early to mid-3rd century
L-58	R-AV	Dr 18R, SG, Flavian-Trajanic Dr 31, CG, Antonine; worn under foot
L-61	R-AQ	Dr 15/17 or 18, SG, pre- or early Flavian
	217	Argonne Sherd, later 2nd or early 4th century
L-63	218	Dr 15/17 or 18, SG, pre- or early Flavian (=219)
	219	(Two sherds) Dr 15/17 or 18, SG, Pre- or early Flavian (=218)
L-?	228	Mortarium, Argonne, late 2nd to 4th century; worn
L-67	R-AW	(Two sherds) Dechelette 72, incised foliage motifs; CG. Antonine
	205	Dr 29, South Gaul. Upper zone scroll with lyre-shaped buds, lower zone gadroons *c.* A.D. 50–70 (No. 214)
L-72	208	DR 15/17, SG, pre- or early Flavian
	202	Dr 29, SG, stamped Martialis, c. A.D. 50–65. See BMD Report No. 5. (No.227)
	203	Dr 29, SG. Lower zone scroll winding over an arrangement of two double spirals with (probably) a trifid leaf on top; the upper spaces are filled with arrowheads *c.* A.D. 60–80 (No.222)
L-78	–	EGT bowl sherd
L-80	R-AK	Dr 31, CG, Antonine Ludowici Sb, EGR, first half 3rd century Mortarium, EGR, late 2nd to first half 3rd century EGR sherd
L-101	R-Y	Dr. 33, CG, Mid-to late-Antonine. Uncertain stamp. See BMD Report No. l4.
L-34	R-P	Dr 36, CG, Hadrianic-Antonine
L-35	R-V	Dr 37, South Gaul. Double-bordered ovolo, probably with a ring tongue terminal. *c.* A.D.70–85
–	R-Z	Dr 31, CG, Antonine; burnt Dr 45, EGT, late 2nd to first half 3rd century

1963 SOUTH AREA

L-4	R-DM	Ludowici Sb, EGR, early to mid-3rd century
L-9	R-BX	Dr 45, CG, late 2nd century
L-10	R-DJ	Ludowici Sb/Sh, grooved interior, EGT, early to mid-3rd century
L-11	R-DP	Dr 15/17R or 18R, SG, pre- or early Flavian SG footring sherd
L-12	R-DQ	closed form sherd, CG, Hadrianic – Antonine
L-13	R-DB	Dr 15/17 or 18, SG, pre- or early Flavian (=R-DA)
		Dr 27, SG, pre- or early Flavian
L-15	R-DE	Dr 37, South Gaul. Medallion with cupid (Hermet 1934, type 36) in a panel with corner tendrils. *c.* A.D. 75–90
		Dr 18, SG, Neronian-Flavian
		Closed form, CG, Hadrianic - Antonine
L-16	R-BV	CG sherd, (Box OB)
L-25	R-DF	EGR sherd
		Burnt Samian sherd
L-26	R-DG	Closed form, CG, Hadrianic – Antonine,
		Dr 31R, CG, mid- to late Antonine,
		Dr 33, EGR, late 2nd to first half 3rd century
L-27	R-DC	Ludowici Sb, EGR, first half 3rd century
L28	R-DA	(Two joining sherds) Dr 15/17 or 18, SG, pre- or early Flavian (=R-DB)
		Ludowici Sb, EGR, first half 3rd century
		Closed form, EGR, incised decoration; late 2nd to first half 3rd century
		Mortarium, EGT, late 2nd to first half 3rd century
		EGT sherd
L-41	R-CR	Dr 38, EGR, first half 3rd century
L-44	R-CV	Dr 43 or Curle 21, EGR, late 2nd to first half of 3rd century
L-45	R-DR	Dr 31R, CG, mid- to late Antonine
L-48	R-CH	Dr 18, SG, pre-Flavian
L-52	R-DN	Dr 45, EG (probably Argonne), late 2nd to 4th century
L-54	R-CZ	Dr 37, Trier, with an ovolu used by Afer, Dubitatus and Paternianus (Gard 1937, type R19; Folzer 1913, type 954). Second quarter of 3rd century
		Dr 37, EG, late 2nd to first half 3rd century
L-55	R-CO	Ludowici Sb, EGR, late 2nd to first half 3rd century
		(Two sherds) Mortarium, EGT, late 2nd to first half 3rd century
L-56	R-CD	Dr 15/17, SG, pre-Flavian
L-74	R-CF	Ritterling 12, SG, pre-Flavian
		Dr 18 or 18R, SG, pre- or early Flavian
L-22		Dr 37, Central Gaul. The abraded details include a beaded vase (Rogers 1974, type T32) and a tripod (cf Q9). The vase suggests links with such potters as X-5 and X-6. Hadrianic-early Antonine
L-19		Dr 18R, SG, Flavian

1964 South Gatehouse

L-9	R-EJ	Dish. cf Ludowici Ty EG, first half 3rd century; burnt
		Dr 45, EGT, late 2nd to early 3rd century
		Dr 45, Argonne, late 2nd to early 3rd century
L-10/14	R-EE	Dr 33, EGR, later 2nd to early 3rd century
		Ludowici Sb, EGR, first half of 3rd century
		Closed form, EGT, first half of 3rd century
		Burnt sherd, probably Argonne

L-19   R-EL   Mortarium base, EGT, late 2nd to early 3rd century
                CG sherd
L-21   R-EN   Dr 31R, CG, mid to late Antonine
L-26   R-EP   Walters 79, EG, late 2nd to early 3rd century
L-33   R-ER   Dr 31R, CG, mid to late Antonine
L-47   R-FB   CG sherd, burnt
L-50   R-FD   EGR sherd
L-65   R-FI   Ludowici Tg, CG, Mid – to late Antonine
                Dr 18/31, CG, Hadrianic-Antonine
                Dr 32/Ludowici Th, EG, early to mid 3rd century (= R-FJ)
                EG sherd
L-66   R-FJ   (Four joining sherds) Dr 32/Ludowici Th, EG, early to mid 3rd century,
                burnt (= R-FI)
L-68   R-FL   Curle 21, EG, early to mid 3rd century; round hole for repair
L-87   R-FP   (Two joining sherds) Mortarium, Trier, first half 3rd century
L-91   R-FT   EGR sherd
L-108   R-FY   Ludowici Sb, EGR, first half 3rd century. swallowtail cut for repair
                Mortarium, Argonne, late 2nd to 4th century
L-121   R-HH   Dr 18, SG, pre- or early Flavian
L-122   R-HI   Dr 18 or 18R, SG, Flavian
L-123   R-HJ   Dr 18, stamped by Vitalis, SG, A.D.65–90. See DMB Report No.11.

1965 Bath House Site

L-3   R-HM   (Two joining sherds), Dr 36, CG, Antonine
L-5   R-HO   Dr 31R, CG, mid- to late Antonine
L-7   R-HQ   Dr 31R, CG, mid- to late Antonine
                Chenet 320, Argonne, 4th century
L-12   R-GJ   Sherd, large dish/platter, EGT, late 2nd to first half 3rd century
L-13   R-HT   Chenet 320, Argonne. Six rows of the roller-stamped pattern survive,
                squares of alternately facing diagonals sometimes grouped in pairs. 4th
                century
L-16   R-HV   Dr 27, SG, Flavian
L-19   R-HX   Dr 45, Argonne, late 2nd to 4th century
L-23   R-GT   Dr 43, barbotine leaf on flange; EGT, early to mid-3rd century
L-24   R-GU   (Two sherds) Dr 45, CG, later 2nd century; overfired, unworn (= R-KN,
                R-KV, R-LV, R-MG and R-MA)
L-28   R-GY   Dr 37 in the style of Afer of Trier. The ovolo and figure of Venus leaning
                on a column are on a bowl in his style from London (Bird 1986, no. 2.82);
                this bowl also has a small medallion with unidentified motif. Second
                quarter of 3rd century. The mould had a crack, and there is a swallowtail
                hole for a repair (No. 206)
                Dr 31R, CG, mid- to late Antonine
L-61   R-JE   Ludowici Sb/Sh, EGR, early to mid 3rd century

1965 East Cliff Site

L-9   R-GG   (Two sherds) Mortarium, EGT, late 2nd to early 3rd century (= R-1)
L-16   R-GM   Dr 18, SG, Flavian
L-46   R-IQ   Dr 45, EGR, first half 3rd century
L-48   R-IS   Dr 31R, CG, mid- to late Antonine

1966 East Cliff Site

L-1   R-KC   Dr 31R, CG, mid- to late Antonine
                      Dr 31R, CG, mid- to late Antonine
                      Dr 45, CG, later 2nd century

L-2   R-KD   Dr 37, EG, top of ovolo; early to mid-3rd century, burnt
                      (Six sherds) Dr 37 in the style of Iullinis of Lezoux. The ovolo and beaded
                      border are on Stanfield & Simpson 1958, pl. 126, 13, the leaf, festoon and
                      corded border on pl. 126, 18, the vase, festoon, small medallion and
                      astralgalus on pl. 126, 11, the mask on pl. 126, 17, and the large medallion
                      on pl, 125, 8. The lower of the two dolphins is probably the one on Rogers
                      1999, pl. 57, 14, c. A.D. 160–90 (= sherds in R-LC and 313, 1967 KF46).
                      The sherd from R-KD is burnt. (No.209).
                      Ludowici Sb, EGR, early to mid 3rd century
                      Dr 31R, CG, mid- to late Antonine
                      Mortarium, EGT, late 2nd to early 3rd century; burnt (= R-LT)
                      CG sherd, Antonine

L-3   R-KE   Ludowici Sb/Sh, grooved interior, EGR, early to mid 3rd century
                      Ludowici Sb, EGR, late 2nd to first half 3rd century

L-4   R-SW   Dr 37, Rheinzabern. The ovolo (Ricken & Fischer 1963, type E11) and
                      stag (T83) were both used by Cerialis VI and Primitivus I. Early to mid-3rd
                      century
                      Dr 31, CG, Antonine
                      (Two sherds) Dr 38, CG, Hadrianic-Antonine
                      Dr 38, CG, Antonine
                      Dr 33, CG, Antonine
                      Mortarium, CG, later 2nd century

L-6   R-KI   Dr 31R, CG, mid to late-Antonine
                      Dr 32, EGR, first half 3rd century (= R-KJ)
                      Dr 30 or 37, EGT, later 2nd to early-3rd century
                      EGR dish sherd
                      EGR sherd

L-7   R-KJ   Ludowici Sb, EGR, first half 3rd century
                      (Three joining sherds) Dr 32, EGR, first half 3rd century (= R-KI)

L-14   R-KN   Dr 45, CG, later-2nd century; overfired. unworn (= R-GU, R-KV, R-LV,
                      R-MG and R-MA)

L-16   R-KP   Ludowici Sb/Sh, EG, stamped by Iulianus, A.D. 200–60. See BMD Report
                      No.4. (No.224)
                      Ludowici Sb/Sh, grooved interior, EGR, early to mid-3rd century
                      Dr 31/Ludowici Sa, Argonne, later-2nd to early-3rd century
                      Dr 38, EGT, first half 3rd century
                      Dr 45, later-2nd to mid-3rd century; burnt
                      Mortarium, CG, later-2nd century
                      Mortarium, CG, later-2nd century
                      Mortarium, EGT, later-2nd to first half 3rd century
                      Three sherds, EGT
                      Small beaker, probably Argonne, late-2nd to 4th century

L-19   R-KS   Dr 30 or 37, EGT, later-2nd to first half 3rd century
                      Ludowici Sb, EGR, first half 3rd century
                      CG sherd
                      EGR sherd

L-22   R-KU   EGR sherd

L-24   R-KV   (Five sherds) Dr 45, with hatching beside lion mask; CG, later-2nd century
                      Overfired, unworn (= R-GU, R-KN, R-LV, R-MG and R-MA)

		Dr 18, SG, Flavian
		(Two joining sherds) Dr 54, EGR, late-2nd to first half 3rd century
L-25	R-KW	(Two joining sherds) Dr 45, Argonne late-2nd to 4th century; very worn
L-26	R-KX	Curle 23, CG, Antonine
		Curle 23, CG, Antonine
		CG sherd, Antonine
L-27	R-KY	Dr 31R, CG, mid-late Antonine
L-29	R-LA	Dr 37, CG. Panels with beaded borders; the caryatid, Oswald 1936–37, type 1207A, was regularly used by Divixtus (Stanfield & Simpson 1958, pl. 115,1). Antonine Dr 37 in the style of Tribunus of Lavoye. For the lattice of wavy lines, cf Chenet & Gaudron 1955, fig. 57, R, a stamped mould; the trifid, rosette and what is probably this ovolo are also recorded for him (Oswald 1945, fig. 6, xxv, xxxv and xliii). Antonine (= R-LR and 1957 1, 123) (No.208)
		Dr 37, CG, with part of double medallion; Antonine
		Dr 30 or 37, CG, Antonine
		Dr 31, CG, Antonine
		Dr 31R, CG, mid to late Antonine
		CG sherd -30
L-30	R-LB	Dr 37 in the style of Julius II-Julianus I of Rheinzabern. The acanthus is Ricken & Fisher, 1963, type P111, the beadrow 0256 and the gladiator M227. Second quarter of the 3rd century
		Dr 37, EGR, early to mid-3rd century
		Dr 32, EGR, early to mid-3rd century
		Dish, EGR, early to mid-3rd century
		Dr 31, CG, Antonine
		Ludowici Sb, EGR, early to mid-3rd century
		Ludowici Sb, EGT, early to mid-3rd century
		Dr 31/Ludowici Sa, Sb, burnt
		(Six sherds) Dr 43, EG, late- 2nd to early-3rd century; burnt (= R-LC)
		Dr 45, CG, later 2nd century
		(Four sherds) Dr 45, Argonne, later- 2nd to 4th century
		Mortarium, Argonne, later- 2nd to 4th century
		Three sherds, CG
		Two sherds, EGT
L-31	R-LC	(Four sherds) Dr 37, style of lullinus; see R-KD
		Dr 37, Rheinzabern. Part of leaf at base. Late-2nd to first half 3rd century
		(Eight sherds) Dr 45 with approximately half of the fine lion-head spout; the upper wall is at least 63 mm deep. Argonne, late-2nd to early-3rd century
		Dr 33, unstamped, EGR, early to mid-3rd century
		Dr 32, EGR, early to mid-3rd century
		Ludowici Sb/Sh, grooved interior, EGR, early to mid-3rd century
		Ludowici Sa/Sb, EGT, late-2nd to early-3rd century
		Ludowici Sa/Sb, EGR, late-2nd to first half 3rd century
		Beaker, Ludowici V series; solid pedestal with offset at top, grooved foot; EGR, late-2nd to first half of 3rd century; scorched
		(Three sherds) Dr 43, EG, late-2nd to early-3rd century (= R-LB)
		Dr 45, EGT, first half 3rd century
		EGT, mortarium sherd, late-2nd to first half 3rd century
		EGR sherd
L-34	R-LF	CG bowl/dish sherds, Antonine
L-35	R-LG	Dr 31R, CG, mid to late-Antonine
		Dr 36, EGR, late-2nd to early-3rd century

                   Dish foot, CG, Antonine; burnt

L-36   R-LH   Dr.33, CG, Stamped by Maternus, A.D. 160–80. (No.223). See BD Report No. 7

L-38   R-LJ   Dr 45, Argonne, late-2nd to early-3rd century (= R-LC)

L-39   R-LK   (Nine joining sherds) Dr 37 in the style of Cinnamus of Lezoux. The ovolo, border, vine leaf and frilled leaf are on Stansfield & Simpson 1958, pl. 161, 53, the bird and narrow leaf on pl. 162, 61. *c.* A.D. 155–175. (No.210).

L-42   R-LN   Dr 37 in the style of Julius II – Julianus I of Rheinzabern. Hare Ricken & Fischer 1963, type T154a, in medallion K7 with stand 0161. Second quarter of the 3rd century

L-44   R-LP   Ludowici Sb, EGR, early to mid-3rd century

L-46   R-LR   Dr 37, style of Tribunus; see R-LA

L-48   R-LT   Mortarium, EGT, late-2nd to early-3rd century (= R-KD)

L-49   R-LU   Dr 31R, CG, mid-to late Antonine

L-50   R-LV   Dr 45, CG, later-2nd century; overfired, unworn (= R-GU, R-KN, R-KV, R-MG and R-MA)

L-60   R-MA   Dr 45, with incisions and round lion-mask, CG, late-2nd century; overfired (R-GU, R-KN, R-KV, R-LV and R-MG)
                   Dr 18, SG, pre-Flavian

L-73   R-MF   Dr 37, EGR, fragment of double medallion or festoon; early to mid-3rd century

L-74   R-MG   Dr 37, EGR, part of double medallion or festoon; early to mid-3rd century (= R-MF) (Two sherds) Dr 30 or 37, EGR, late-2nd to first half 3rd century Ludowici Sa/Sb, EGR, late 2nd to first half of 3rd century
                   Dr 45, CG, late-2nd century, overfired, unworn (= R-GU, R-KN, R-KV and R-LV) Mortarium, EGR, late-2nd to first half 3rd century

L-85   R-MO   Ludowici Sb/Sh, groove on interior, EGR, early to mid-3rd century

L-87   R-MQ   Ludowici Sb/Sh, EGR, early to mid-3rd century

L-12   Dr 37, Central Gaul. Beaded panels, including a Diana and hind (Oswald 1936–37. type 106) and a possible cornucopia. Antonine (No. 219).

1966 West Site

L-1   R-NA   Dr 37, Trier. The ovolo is probably one used by Criciro (cf Bird 1986, no. 2.71)
                   Early to mid-3rd century
                   Dr 18, SG, Flavian
                   Dr 15/17 or 18, SG, pre or early-Flavian
                   Ludowici Sb, EGR, late-2nd to first half 3rd century
                   Flanged bowl, 'a l'eponge' ware from western France, 4th century; cf. Fulford 1977, 45–47 (joins R-RL)

L-2   R-NB   Ludowici Tg, CG, mid to late-Antonine
                   Dr 31R, CG, mid to late-Antonine
                   Dr 31R, CG, mid to late-Antonine

L-3   R-NC   Dr 31R, CG, mid to late-Antonine; worn
                   Dr 31, CG, Antonine; graffito]KLA under base
                   Dr 30 or 37, EGR, early to mid-3rd century

L-4   R-ND   Closed form, no slip on interior; Argonne, probably later-3rd to 4th century

L-9   R-NH   Dish, probably Dr 36, CG, Antonine

L-18   R-NP   (Two joining sherds) Dr 30 or 37, EGR, early to mid-3rd century
                   EGR sherd

L-19   RNQ   Dr 37, Rheinzabern. Plain single medallion. Early to mid-3rd century

Dr 37, Trier. Rosette between medallions or festoons. First half of 3rd century

Dr 43 with edge of spout, CG, late 2nd century.

L-20	R-NR	EGR sherd
L-30	R-NX	Dr 36, CG, Antonine
L-35	R-OC	Mortarium, EGT, first half 3rd century
L-45	R-OK	Mortarium, Argonne, late 2nd to 4th century
		Dr 37, CG, Antonine
L-47	R-OM	Dr 36, EGR, late 2nd to early 3rd century
L-48	R-ON	(Three sherds, two joining) Dr 18, SG, pre or early-Flavian
L-58	R-OV	Dr 33, CG, Stamped by Sollemnis, A.D. 130–150.(No. 230). See BMD Report No.10.
L-60	R-OW	Dr 37, EGT, early to mid-3rd century; burnt
L-62	R-OY	Dr 37, South Gaul. Double-bordered ovolo with rosette or trident tongue tip. Flavian
L-68	R-PE	(Two joining sherds) Dr 38, EGR, early to mid-3rd century
		Dr 45, CG, later-2nd century
		Dr 45, later-2nd to mid-third century; burnt
L-72	R-PG	Dr 45, EGT, early to mid-3rd century
		Dr 45, CG, later-2nd century
L-73	R-PH	Dr 31R, CG, mid-late Antonine
L-77	R-PK	Beaker decorated overall with tall narrow facets; probably Argonne and late-2nd to early-3rd century
L-78	R-PL	Dr 36, CG, Hadrianic-Antonine
		Large closed form, Argonne, later-2nd to 4th century
L-82	R-PR	Dr 30, CG, with top of abraded ovolo; Hadrianic-Antonine
		Dr 45, EGT, early to mid-3rd century
L-88	R-MR	(Two sherds) Dr 27, SG, pre or early-Flavian
L-94	R-QB	Dr 36 probably, CG, Hadrianic-Antonine
L-98	R-QF	(Five sherds) Dr 37 in the style of Doeccus of Lezoux. The ovolo borders, festoons and sea-horse are on Stanfield & Simpson 1958, pl. 149, 32. *c.* A.D. 165–200; burnt
		(Three sherds) Dr 37 in the style of Cerialis IV of Rheinzabern. The ovolo is Ricken & Fischer 1963, type E3, the tripod 011; the other motif may be the arcade, KB133.
		First half 3rd century
L-101	R-QI	Dr 37, burnt and not identifiable
L-109	R-QQ	Dish (Dr 32 etc.), EGT, late 2nd to early-3rd century
L-112	R-QT	Dr 31R, CG probably, mid to late-Antonine; burnt
		Dr 36, EGR, late-2nd to early-3rd century
L-116	R-QX	Sherd, possibly Ludowici SMb/c, decorated with barbotine wavy lines, EGT, early to mid-3rd century
L-121	R-RB	Dechelette, 72/Dr 54, Argonne, edge of incised decoration; later-2nd to early-3rd century
L-125	R-RF	Dr 33, CG, Antonine
L-131	R-RL	Flanged bowl, 'a l'eponge' ware from western France; marbled on the upper surface but predominantly dark red underneath. 4th century; cf Fulford 1977, 45–47 (joins R-NA)
		Dr 37, Rheinzabern. Blurred ovolo. First half 3rd century.
L-134	R-RO	Ludowici Sb, EGT, late-2nd to mid-3rd century
		Mortarium, CG, late-2nd century; worn
L-139	R-RT	Dr 36, SG, early to mid-Flavian
L-140	R-RU	(Three joining sherds) Dr 31,CG, Antonine

L-146   R-SA   Ludowici Sa/Sb, EGR, late-2nd to first half 3rd century
L-148   R-SC   Dr 31, CG, Antonine
               Mortarium sherd, EGR, late-2nd to first half 3rd century
L-151   R-SF   Dr 36, EGR, early to mid-3rd century
L-154   R-SI   EGT sherd
L-168   R-TD   Mortarium, CG, late-2nd century
L-1   R-ST   Dr 31, or 3lR, CG, Stamped by Carussa , A.D.160–190. See BMD Report
               No.1.

1967 East Gatehouse Site

L-1   R-TJ   Dr 36, CG, Antonine
               Dr 31, CG, Antonine; possible hole for repair
L-7   R-TP   Dr 31, EGT, later-2nd to first half 3rd century
               Dr 31, Argonne, later-2nd to early-3rd century
               (Two sherds) Mortarium, EGT, first half 3rd century; worn
L-10   R-TS   CG sherd, Antonine
L-13   R-TV   Dr 37, CG, Antonine
L-18   R-UA   Dr 37, Rheinzabern. The ovolo (Ricken & Fischer 1963, type E45 was
               used by several potters, especially Julius II-Julianus I. Early to mid-3rd
               century
               Dr 45, EGT, first half 3rd century
               (Six joining sherds) Ludowici Sb, EGR, first half 3rd century
L-20   R-UC   Dr 32 probably, EGR, first half 3rd century
               Mortarium, EGT, late-2nd to first half 3rd century
               EGT sherd
L-24   R-UG   Dr 37, Banassac. The ovolo is Hofmann 1988, fig. 18,E, attributed to
               Natalis and to Marinus, and the figure is his type 49 (= Hermet 1934, type
               98); the arrangement of small overlapping arcades is unusual. Mees
               suggests a date range before A.D. 120 to at least 140 for bowls with this
               ovolo (1995, 111). Possibly graffito]X on rim
               band (= R-UH)
               Two CG sherds, Antonine
L-25   R-UH   Dr 37, Banassac: see R-UG
L-35   R-UR   Dr 30, CG, Antonine
L-39   R-UV   Dr 33, EGT, late-2nd to early-3rd century
L-41   R-UX   Dr 31R, CG, mid-late Antonine

1967 Via Quintana

L-101   R-WA   Dr 32, EGR, early to mid-3rd century
               Dr 37, CG, Hadrianic-early Antonine
               Dr 45, EGR, late-2nd to early-3rd century
               Mortarium, EGT, late-2nd to first half 3rd century; very worn
               Mortarium, EGR, late-2nd to first half 3rd century; worn
L-102   R-WB   Ludowici Sb, EGR, early to mid-3rd century
               EGT sherd
L-103   R-WC   Chenet 324, Argonne, late-3rd to 4th century
L-104   R-WD   (Three joining sherds) Dr 33, unstamped, EGR; early-mid 3rd century
               Ludowici Sb, EGR, first half 3rd century; scorched
               Dr 37, CG, Antonine
               Walters 79 probably, mid to late-Antonine or later; burnt
               Round-bodied closed form. EGT, early to mid-3rd century

EG mortarium sherd, worn
EG sherd

L-105　R-WE　Dr 54, EGR, early to mid-3rd century
Ludowici Sb, EGR, early to mid-3rd century
Dr 38, EGR, early to mid-3rd century
Dr 18/31, CG, Hadrianic to early-Antonine
Dr 37 or Chenet 320, Argonne, later-2nd to 4th century
Argonne sherd

L-106　R-WF　Dr 37 or Chenet 320, Argonne, later-2nd to 4th century
Dr 30 or 37, CG, Antonine

L-107　R-WG　Curle 15 or 23, CG, Antonine
Dr 45, EGR, early to mid-3rd century

L-109　R-WI　Dr 31, CG, Antonine. Uncertain stamp. See BMD Report No.12.
EGT sherd

L-110　R-WJ　Dr 33, SG, Flavian

L-111　R-WK　Ludowic Sb/Sh, EGR, early to mid-3rd century
Dr 32R, early to mid-3rd century

L-112　R-WL　Dr 31, CG, Antonine
Ludowici Sb, EGR, first half 3rd century
EG sherd

L-113　R-WM　(Two joining sherds) Dr 45, Argonne, late-2nd to 4th century
Curle 15 or 23, CG, Antonine
Walters 79 or Ludowici Tg, CG, mid to late-Antonine

L-117　R-WQ　Ludowici Sb/Sh, EGR, early to mid-3rd century
Dr 18, SG, Flavian

KF46　Dr 37, style of lullinus; see R-KD

1968 East Barracks Site

KF24　Mortarium base, EGT, early to mid-3rd century; heavily worn; burnt

L-1　R-XA　CG sherd, mid to late-Antonine
Dr 31, CG, Antonine
Mortarium, EGT, late-2nd to early-3rd century (= R-GG)
Dr 33, CG, Antonine
Dr 45, EGR, late-2nd to early-3rd century
Closed form, EGR, first half 3rd century

L-7　R-XG　Dr 31, CG, Antonine
Dr 31R, CG, mid to late-Antonine
Dr 31R, CG, mid to late-Antonine
Dr 45, EGT, late-2nd to early-3rd century

L-9　R-XI　CG sherd, Antonine

L-10　R-XJ　Dr 38, CG, Antonine
Ludowici Sb, EG, early to mid-3rd century; burnt
Ludowici Sb, EGR, first half 3rd century
Mortarium, EGR, first half 3rd century
Mortarium, EG, burnt

L-11　R-XK　Small bowl, EGR, early to mid-3rd century

L-12　R-XL　Mortarium, EGR, first half 3rd century

L-13　R-XM　Ritterling 13 (inkwell), SG, Flavian (= R-XN)
Ludowici Sb, EGT, first half 3rd century
Dr 33, EGR, late-2nd to first half 3rd century
Two EGT sherds

L-14　R-XN　Ritterling 13 (inkwell), SG, Flavian (= R-XM)

L-17 R-XQ Bowl/dish, SG, Flavian
L-18 K32   Dish, EGR, first half 3rd century
L-21 R-XU Dr 27, SG, pre or early-Flavian
L-28 R-YB EGR sherd
L-33 R-YG Decorated fragment, possibly with part of a figure; SG, Flavian
             Dr 45, EGR, first half 3rd century, scorched
L-36 R-YJ Dr 29, SG, pre or early-Flavian
             Dr 45, CG, late-2nd century; burnt
L-39 R-YM Mortarium, EGT, late-2nd to first half 3rd century
L-40 R-YN Dr 38, EGT, first half 3rd century
L-41 R-YO Dr 15/17R or 18R, SG, pre or early-Flavian; burnt
L-49 R-YW Ludowici Sb, EGR, early to mid-3rd century
L-53 R-ZA EGR sherd
L-58 R-ZF Dish or Bowl, EGT, late 2nd or 1st half third century. Stamped by Cucio.
             See BMD Report No.2. (No.229)

1969 North East Area

L-6   RR-F Dr 18, SG, pre or early-Flavian
             Ludowici Sb, EGR, first half 3rd century
L-7   RR-G Dr 38, CG, Antonine; worn
L-8   RR-H Dr 37, in the style of Julius II-Julianus I of Rheinzabern. The ovolo is
             Ricken & Fischer 1963, type, E17, the stand O161, the cross 053 and the
             arcade KB73. Second quarter of the 3rd century. (No.215)
             CG sherd, Antonine
L-10 RR-J Ludowici Sb/Sh, grooved interior EGR; early to mid-3rd century
L-13 RR-M (Three sherds) Mortarium, EGT, late-2nd to first half 3rd century
L-15 RR-O Ludowici Sb, EGR, first half 3rd century
L-20 RR-T Argonne sherd, very worn inside
L-21 RR-U (Two sherds) Ludowici Sb, EGR, first half 3rd century
L-24 RR-X EGR sherd
L-33 RR-AG Ludowici Sb, EGT, late-2nd to early-3rd century
             CG sherd
             EGT sherd
L-37 RR-AK Dr 32, EGT, early to mid-3rd century
L-39 RR-AM Argonne base, late-2nd to 4th century
L-50 RR-AX (Two joining sherds) Dr 33, CG, Antonine
             (Two joining sherds) Dr 33, EGT, later-2nd to early-3rd century
L-53 RR-BA Mortarium, Argonne, late-2nd to 4th century
L-60 RR-BH (Two joining sherds) Dr 45, EGT, late-2nd to first half 3rd century
             Ludowici Sb, EGR, early to mid-3rd century
L-65 RR-BM Dr 31, EGR, late 2nd century or first half 3rd century. Stamped C]. See
             BMD Report No. 16.
L-68 RR-BP Dr 31, CG, Antonine
             Dr 45, EGR, first half 3rd century
L-73 RR-BU Ludowici Sb/Sh, grooved fabric, EGR, early to mid-3rd century
L-75 RR-BW (Two joining sherds) Dr 37 in the style of Afer-Marinus of Trier. The
             medallion (Gard 1937, type K39) and bird (T132) are both recorded for
             them; the dolphin is Folzer 1913, type 692. Second quarter of 3rd century
             (No. 216)

1969 Church Area

L-100 RR-CA CG sherd, Antonine

L-101   RR-CB Dr 37, Central Gaul. Beaded panels, including an incomplete figure with
         a spear or staff. Hadrianic-Antonine
L-103   RR-CD Dr 30 or 37, EG, late-2nd to first half 3rd century
L-110   RR-CK Ludowici Sb, EGR, early to mid-3rd century

Samian Bibliography

Bird, J., 1986 Samian wares, in L. Miller, J. Schofield & M. Rhodes, *The Roman quay at St. Magnus House, London, Excavations at New Fresh Wharf. Lower Thames Street, London, 1974–78* (ed. T. Dyson). London Middlesex Archaeol. Soc. Special Paper, **8**, 139–185.

Bird, J., & Williams, D., 1983 German marbled flagons in Roman Britain, *Britannia*, **14**, 247–252.

Chenet, G., & Gaudron, G., 1955 *La ceramique sigillee d'Argonne des Ile et IIIe et IIIe siecles,* Gallia Supplement, **6** (Paris).

Dannell, G., Dickinson, B., & Vernhet, A., 1998 Ovolos on Dragendorff form 30 from the collections of F. Hermet and D. Rey, in *Form and fabric. Studies in Rome's material past in honour of B.R. Hartley* (ed. J. Bird), Oxbow Monograph, **80**, 69–109 (Oxford).

Ettlinger. E., Hedinger, B., Hoffmann, B., Kenrick, P.M., Pucci, G., Roth-Rubi, K., Schneider, G., von Schnurbein, S., Wells, C.M., & Zabehlicky-Scheffenegger, S., 1990 *Conspectus formarum terrae sigillatae italico modo confectae,* Materialen zur romisch-germanischen Keramik, **10** (Bonn).

Folzer, E., 1913 *Die Bilderschusseln der ostgallischen Sigillata-Manufakturen,* Romische Keramik in Trier, **1** (Bonn).

Fulford, M., 1977 Pottery and Britain's foreign trade in the later Roman period, in *Pottery and early commerce. Characterization and trade in Roman and later ceramics* (ed. D.P.S. Peacock), 35–84 (London).

Gard, L., 1937 *Reliefsigillata des 3. und 4. Jahrhunderts aus den Werkstatten von Trier* (unpublished thesis, Univ. Tubingen).

Hermet, F., 1934 *La Graufesenque (Condatomago)* (Paris).

Hoffmann. B., 1988 *L'atelier de Banassac.* Revue Archaeologique SITES Hors-serie, **33** (Gonfaron).

Mees, A.W., 1995 *Modelsignierte Dekorationen auf sudgallischer Terra Sigillata,* Forschungen und Berichte zur Vor-und Fruhgeschichte in Baden-Wurttemberg, **54** (Stuttgart).

Oswald, F., 1936–37 *Index of figure-types on terra sigillata ('samian ware'),* Annals Archaeol. Anthropol., **23.1–4, 24.1–4** (Liverpool).

Oswald, F., 1945 Decorated ware from Lavoye, *J. Roman Stud., ***35**, 49–57.

Ricken, H., & Fischer, C. (ed.), 1963 *Die Bilderschusseln der romischen Topfer von Rheinzabern. Textband mit Typenbildern zu Katalog VI der Ausgrabungen von Wilhelm Ludowici in Rheinzabern 1901–1914,* Materialen zur romisch-germanischen Keramik, **7** (Bonn).

Rogers, G.B., 1974 *Poteries sigillees de la Gaule Centrale, I – les motifs non figures,* Gallia Supplement, **28** (Paris).

Rogers, G.B., 1999 *Poteries sigillees de la Gaule Centrale II – les potiers, 2 vols.,* Cahiers du Centre Archeologique de Lezoux, **1**/Revue Archaeologique SITES Hors-serie, **40** (Lezoux).

Stanfield, J.A., & Simpson, G., 1958 *Central Gaulish potters* (London).

Young, C.J., 1977 *The Roman pottery industry of the Oxford region,* Brit. Archaeol. Rep., **43** (Oxford).

(5) THE SAMIAN POTTERS' STAMPS (Fig. 52)

by BRENDA DICKINSON

Each entry gives: excavation number, potter (i, ii etc., where homonyms are involved) die form, reading published example (if any), pottery of origin, discussion, date.
Superscript a and b indicate:

(a)   A stamp attested at the pottery in question.
(b)   Not attested at the pottery, but other stamps of the same potter used there.
Litigatured letters are underlined.

1   (1966 REC-66 L.1 R-ST). Unstratified west of fort. Carussa 3a, 31 or 31R C.ARVSSA (Dickinson 1986, 188, 3.28) Lezoux. *c.* A.D. 160–190.
2   (1968 REC-68 L.58 R-ZF) East Barracks Site, F32. Cucio la, Dish or bowl CVCIOI... Rheinzabern. Late 2nd Century or first half of the 3rd Century (No. 229).
3   (1962 REC 62–204 L.48). East Barracks Site, Trench B. Domitianus 4a, Lud. Sb DOMITIANVS Rheinzabern. Late 2nd Century (No. 226).
4   (1968 REC-66 L.16 R-KP). East Cliff Site. Iulianus iii 4i, Lud. Sb/Sh IVLIANVS Rheinzabern. *c.* A.D. 200–260 (No. 224).
5   (1962 REC-62–202 L.72). East Barracks Site, pit under wall. Martialis i 9a, 29 [MARTIAL] ISFEC La Graufesenque. *c.* A.D. 50–65 (No.227).
6   (1966 REC-66 L.16). East Cliff Site. Materninus ii 3b, Lud. Sb MATER.....S Trier. *c.* A.D. 180–260.
7   (1966 L.36 R-LH). East Cliff Site. Maternus iv 1a, 33 [MA]TERN[I] (Dickinson 1996, Fig. 142, 52) Lezoux. *c.* A.D. 160–180 (No. 223).
8   (1961 REC-61 L.58). East Barracks Site, unstratified. Paullus iv 5a, 33 PAVLIM (Walke 1965, Taf. 43, 287–8, where the stoke between A and V is not shown) Lezoux. *c.* A.D. 135–170 (Fig. 225).
9   (1960 REC-60-KF 03 L.21). Central Area, primary layer in Sacellum. Saturninus ii 1b, 33 SATVRNINOF (Dickinson 1986, 195, 3.185) Lezoux. *c.* A.D. 160–200 (No. 228).
10   (1966 REC-66 L.58 R-OV). West Site, F.20. Sollemnis i 3a, 33 SOLLEMMNI.M Lezoux. *c.* A.D. 130–150 (No. 230).
11   (1964 REC-64 L.123 R-HJ). South Gate Site, pre-fort ditch. Vitalis ii 8h, or 8h', 18 OF. VITA (Polak 2000, pl.25, V69) La Graufesenque. *c.* A.D. 65–90.
12   (1967 REC-67 L.109 R-WI). Via Quintana Site. CA[on form 31, Central Gaulish. Antonine.
13   (1961 REC-61 1517 L.67). East Barracks, Trench C.]M on form 31R, Central Gaulish. Mid-to late-Antonine.
14   (1962 REC-62 L.101 R-Y). East Barracks Site, Box J. Foundation-trench. V[on form 33, Central Gaulish. Mid-to late-Antonine.
15   (1961 REC-61 L.61). Trench D, Metalling on primary soils. M[on form 37, A mould-stamp in the decoration, Central Gaulish late 2nd Century (No. 217).
16   (1969 REC-69 L.65 RR-BM). Trench A, Pit.]. C .[on form 31 (Sa). East Gaulish (Rheinzabern), Late 2nd Century or first half of the 3rd Century.

Bibliography

Dickinson, B.M., 1986 Potters' stamps and signatures on Samian, in L. Miller, J. Scofield & M. Rhodes, *The Roman Quay at St Magnus House, London*. London and Middlesex Archaeological Society Special Paper No.8, 186–98. London.

Dickinson, B.M., 1996 Samian Potters' stamps, in R.P.J. Jackson & T.W. Potter, Excavations at Stonea, Cambridgeshire 1980–85, 421–27, London.

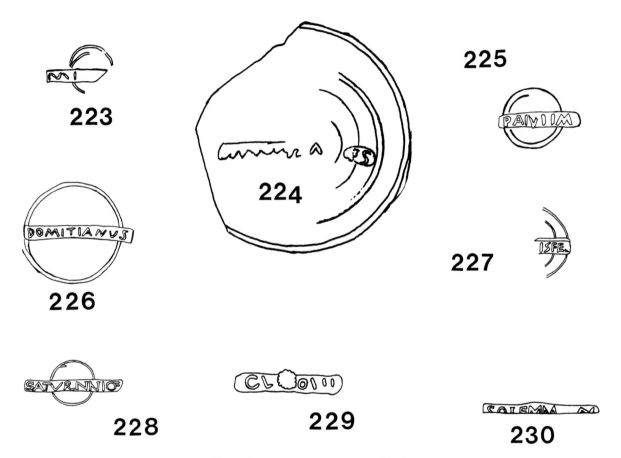

Fig. 52.   *Samian Ware Stamps (1/1).*

Polak, M., 2000 South Gaulish Terra Sigillata with potters' stamps from Vechten, Rei Cretariae Romanae Fautorum Acta Supplementum 9, Nijmegen.

Walke, N., 1965 Das Romische Donaukastell Straubing-Sorviodurum, Limesforschungen 3, Berlin.

═══════════════

(6) THE SMALL FINDS (Nos. 231–461)

By Maurice Chenery

Over 240 small-finds from the Roman fort are illustrated and described here. These include a wide range of objects in bronze, iron, bone, pottery or other materials. Of special interest are fragments of three inscriptions (Nos. 441–444), five stamped tiles (Nos. 445–9) and seven scabbard chapes (Nos. 352–8). Parallels have mostly been drawn from the very comprehensive volume of small-finds from Roman Colchester (Ref. 87), here prefixed with the letters Col. Other parallels have been drawn with finds from the nearby Roman fort at Richborough, identified by the volume number (I–V). The copper-alloy objects are still described as bronze. Each object has been uniquely identified and the site codes mostly listed by year, layer, KF (Key Find) or SF (Small Find) register number and often the deposit-code.

No. 231	Bone pin. Complete, head carved with seven rings, each with diagonal cuts (REC-66 L.3 KF6).
No. 232	Bone pin. Complete, with thickened shaft and large rectangular notched head (REC-63 L.28 KF48).
No. 233	Bone pin. Point missing, with cone-shaped head decorated with incised lines (REC-61 L.12 SF36).
No. 234	Bone pin. Point missing, with cuboid faceted head. (REC-68 L-77 R-ZY).
No. 235	Bone pin. Complete, with thickened shaft and flattened head (REC-63 L.28 KF57).
No. 236	Bone pin. Complete, with large head decorated with incised grooves (REC-66 L.72 R-PG).
No. 237	Bone pin. Complete, with small conical pointed head (REC-60 L.12 KF12).
No. 238	Bone pin. Complete, with long shaft and slightly faceted head (REC-64 L.89).
No. 239	Bone pin. Complete, with head decorated with four encircling grooves (REC-66 L.42 KF131 R-LN).
No. 240	Bone pin. Complete, similar to No. 237 (REC-64 L.12 KF4).
No. 241	Bone pin. Shaft broken, with head decorated with three pronounced rings (REC-61 L.12. SF39).
Nos. 242–7	Six bone pins. Various head shapes, largely similar to above.
No. 248	Large bone object, perhaps a stylus. Complete, crudely carved with large faceted head (REC-57-Well D).
Nos. 249–87	Thirty nine bone pins. Mostly complete, various head shapes, largely similar to above.
No. 288	Bone needle. Damaged, large, rounded head and eye missing (REC-66 L.1 R-NA).
No. 289	Bone needle. Complete, fine with even taper and elongated eye (REC-57-Pit).
No. 290	Bone needle. Complete, large, crudely carved with token head (REC-66 L.131).
No. 291	Bone needle. Point missing, with curved shaft and irregular eye (REC-60 L.10 SF2).
Nos. 292–5	Four bone pins. All damaged, similar to above.

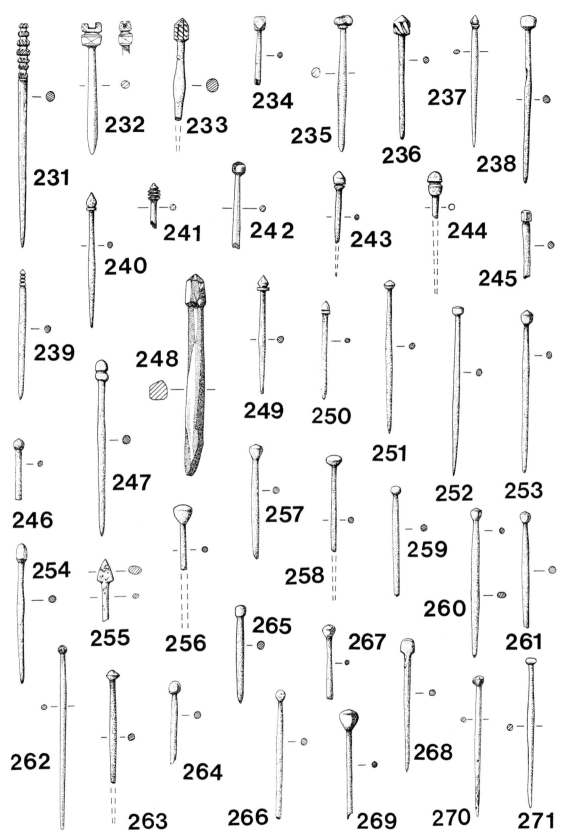

Fig. 53.   *Bone Pins (1/2).*

No. 296   Bronze needle. Point missing, finely cast, rectangular section, elongated eye (REC-60 L.7 SF07).

No. 297   Bronze pin. Complete, with conical head and decorated with fine grooves (REC-61 L.15 SF30).

No. 298   Bronze hook. Complete, thickened shaft bent over at top to form eye (REC-69 L.68 RR-BP).

No. 299   Bronze needle. Complete, small slender shaft and minute eye (REC-66 L.109 R-QQ).

No. 300   Bronze pin. Complete, small with bent shaft and faceted head (REC-61 L.1 SF21).

No. 301   Bronze terminal. Incomplete, consisting of large head and shaft enclosed by separate coiled bronze strip (REC-60-L.1 SF19).

No. 302   Bronze pin. Complete, with globular head decorated with multiple radiating lines (REC-60 L. 10 SF17).

No. 303   Bronze bracelet with tapered terminal and broken at one end. Bent, decorated on outer edge with a pattern of alternating chevrons. Length 246mm (REC-60 L.14 SF16).

No. 304   Bracelet of twisted bronze, with linking eyelet and hooked terminals. Diam. 48mm. Probably for a child (REC-60 L.21 SF24).

No. 305   Circular bracelet of twisted bronze around an iron core. Hook and eye terminals. Diam. 50mm (REC-64 L.42 R-EX).

No. 306   Fragment of flat bronze bracelet. Simple decoration of fine notches along both sides (REC-59 L.2 SF19).

No. 307   Fragment of flat bronze bracelet with simple notched decoration on both sides. Similar to No. 306 (REC-59 L.2 SF19).

No. 308   Similar to Nos. 306–7. (REC-60 L.12).

No. 309   Bone bracelet. About half complete and oval in section. Diam. 60mm. (REC-61 L.60).

No. 310   Complete bronze bracelet. Plain bronze wire with terminals resembling serpent heads. Diam. 75mm (REC-59 L.7 SF4).

No. 311   Fragment of thick bronze bracelet. Square section and undecorated (REC-59 L.5 SF25).

No. 312   Broken bronze bracelet constructed with five wire strands. See Col.1633 (REC-60 L.14 SF8).

No. 313   Complete bronze bracelet with enlarged terminals. Oval, plain and heavily corroded (REC-64 L.20 KF9).

No. 314   Crossbow-type bronze brooch, with broken spring and pin missing. A third century type. See Richborough IV, Nos 54–6. Length 67mm (REC-61 L.8 SF18).

No. 315   Crossbow-type bronze brooch, with pin missing. A third century type. Length 54mm. (REC-62 L.7 KF70).

No. 316   Bronze brooch with large spring. Pin and catch plate missing. See Col.56 (REC-64 L.1).

No. 317   Crossbow-type bronze brooch, twisted and damaged with pin and terminals missing. Length 53mm (REC-57 L.1) from Beach area.

No. 318   Inlaid bronze brooch of Aucissa type, with pin missing. Three panels with inlaid enamel decoration, with rows of small crosses in either circular or rectangular frames. Three pointed claw-like terminals at each end (REC-66 L.50 KF140).

No. 319   Large bronze brooch of trumpet-type. Solid catchplate and end perforation for suspension. See Richborough IV, Nos. 40–1(REC-66 L.51 KF136).

No. 320   Bronze disc brooch with pin missing. Badly corroded, but with traces of yellow inlay. Diam. 33mm. See Col.80 (REC-64 L.21 KF10).

No. 321   Small bronze crossbow-type brooch, with cross-bars missing, but pin complete. A third century type. Length 65mm (REC-61 L.77 SF20).

No. 322   Bronze finger-ring. Plain, diam.18mm., width 2mm. (REC-66 L.72 KF58).

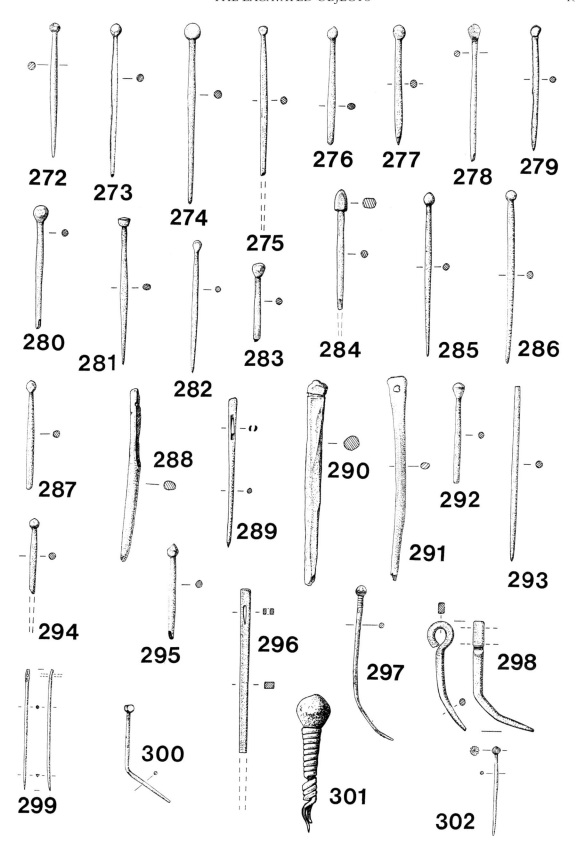

Fig. 54. *Bone and Bronze Pins and Needles (1/2), except Nos. 296,298 and 301 (1/1).*

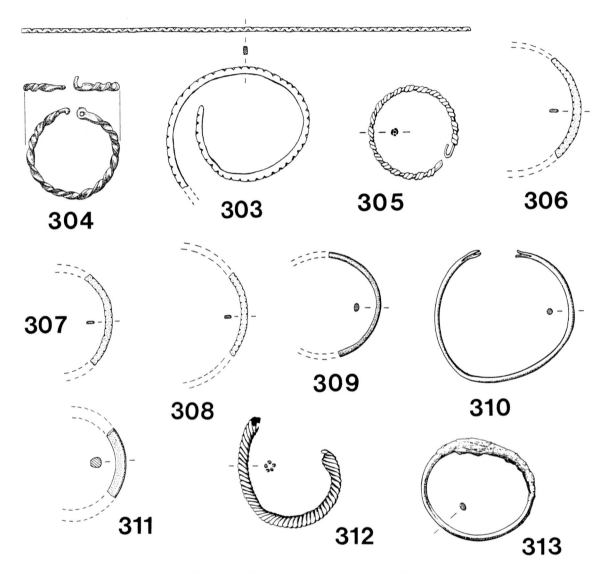

Fig. 55. *Bronze and Bone Bracelets (1/2).*

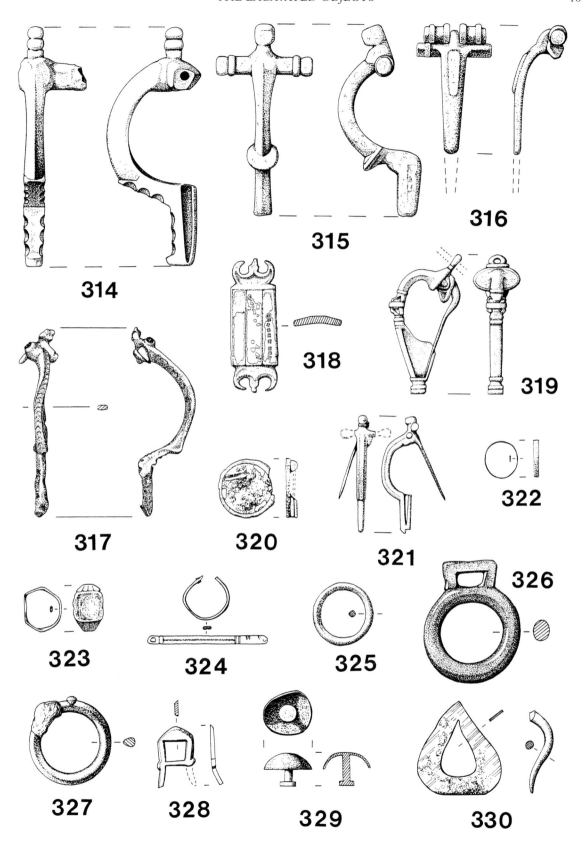

Fig. 56. *Bronze Brooches, Rings and Fittings (1/2), except Nos. 314–7 and 320 (1/1).*

No. 323   Bronze finger-ring, with flat bezel, but intaglio missing. (REC-66 L.72 KF58).

No. 324   Bronze finger-ring. Terminals with hole and 'lug' for fastening and decorated with faint grooves and notches (REC-69 L.54 RR-BB).

No. 325   Bronze circular ring, diam. 35mm. Plain. (REC-61 L.12 SF40).

No. 326   Large bronze terret, with internal diam. 37mm. The loop is slightly oval and 11mm. in thickness. The rectangular projection is for a strap fixing. See Col.2543 (REC-68 L.19 KF51).

No. 327   Circular bronze ring, diam. 48mm. Plain, corroded (REC-63 L.4 R-BV).

No. 328   Broken bronze buckle. Probably post-Roman (REC-63 L.104 KF10 R-DJ).

No. 329   Large circular bronze stud, diam. 28mm. Domed head with circular shaft 17mm. long (REC-64 L.52 KF19).

No. 330   Flat bronze mount, or fastening. Pin on back (REC-62 L.7 KF79).

No. 331   Double-headed bronze stud, diam. 12mm. See Col.4031 (REC-61 L.54 SF19).

No. 332   Circular, plain bronze button, diam. 9mm. and small eyelet on back. Probably post-Roman (REC-62 L.12 KF78).

No. 333   Small bronze nail, length 38mm. Square section and flat head. See col.3081 (REC-62 L.15 KF77).

No. 334   Bronze double-headed stud, diam. 10mm. Similar to No. 331 (REC-68 L.19 R-XS).

No. 335   Bronze mount with attachment loop and semi-circular notches in rim. See Col.4205 and Richborough V, No. 140 (Rec-66 L.142 R-RW).

No. 336   Bronze mount with attached rivets (REC-61 L.1 SF32).

No. 337   Incomplete bone bracelet, width 5mm. decorated with tapered cuts along both sides. Terminals decorated with a broad cross bordered by three parallel cuts. Both terminals have a small hole for fastening, one with bronze staining (REC-68 L.7 R-XG).

No. 338   Bronze bracelet, D-section, diam. 58mm. (REC-61 L.43 SF60).

No. 339   Broken bone bracelet, with plain square section (REC-59 L.2 SF18).

No. 340   Fragment of bone ring, diam. 23mm. Rectangular section. Crudely fashioned and undecorated (REC-62 L.7 KF84).

No. 341   Circular bone ring, diam. 19mm. Shamfered external edge with sub-rectangular central hole about 7mm. Plain, crudely fashioned (REC-59 L.5 KF28).

No. 342   Fragmentary bone comb. Flat plate, width 10mm., supporting three teeth held by an iron rivet (REC-60 L.10 SF3).

No. 343   Similar to No. 342. Six broad teeth and eight fine teeth on opposite sides. See Richborough IV No. 216. (REC-60 L.10 SF3).

No. 344   Fragment of bone comb, with end-plate pierced by three holes and possible scratched 'graffiti'. Nine teeth survive (REC-62 L.1).

No. 345   Circular flat bone disc, or gaming counter, diam.26mm. and thickness of 5mm. Slightly domed upper surface with a shallow pierced central hole (REC-60 L.14 SF05).

No. 346   Thin circular bone counter, diam. 22mm. and thickness 2mm. Plain, with concave upper surface (REC-66 L.82 R-PR).

No. 347   Circular bone counter, diam. 28mm. thickness 6mm. Plain with convex upper surface (REC-68 L.75 R-ZW).

No. 348   Bone toggle, cut from animal leg bone. Narrow slot, width 2mm. cut halfway. Length 18mm, diam. 24mm. max. (REC-64 L.19).

No. 349   Bronze finger-ring with diamond-shaped bezel and possible stone (REC-62 L.1 KF80) unstratified.

No. 350   Cast bronze horse-figure, with incised mane and legs partly broken. Length 34mm., height 22mm. (REC-63 L.1 KF6).

No. 351   Plain circular, bronze bead, diam. 18mm. and perforation 8mm. (REC-66 L.31 R-LC).

No. 352   Complete ivory scabbard chape, with linear ridges, end notches and two decorative

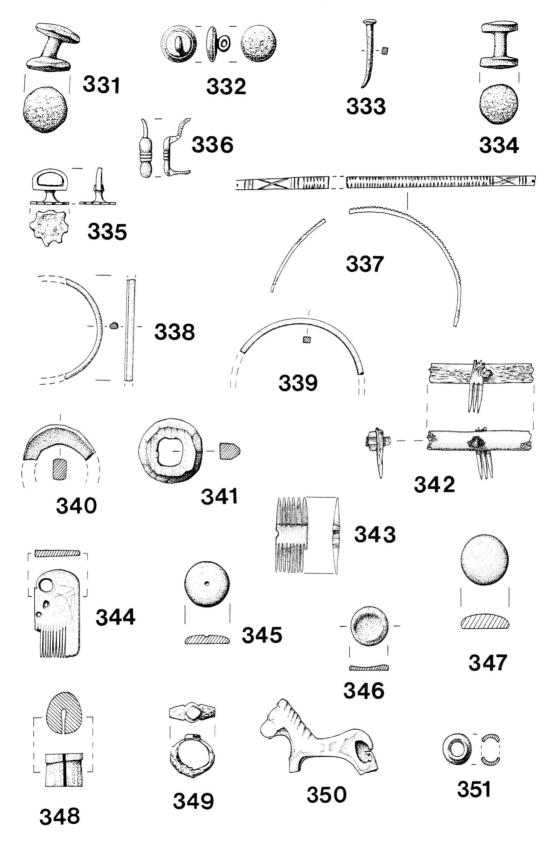

Fig. 57. *Bronze, Bone and Glass objects (1/2), except Nos. 331–2, 334, 340–1 & 350 (1/1).*

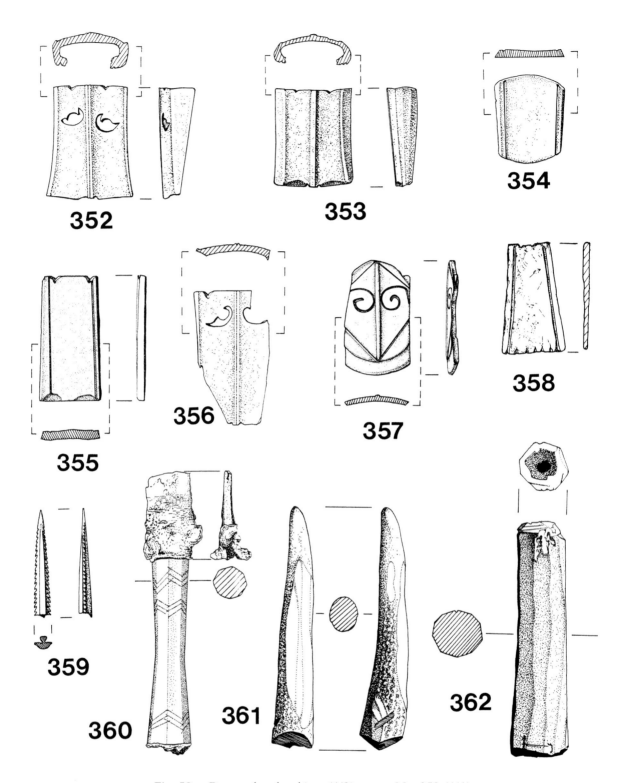

Fig. 58.   *Bone and antler objects (1/2), except No. 359 (1/1).*

pelta-shaped cut-outs. See Col.4242. Length 60mm., width 48mm. (REC-66 L.7 R-KJ).

No. 353   Complete bone scabbard chape, with linear ridges and end notches. Length 50mm., width 44mm. (REC-66 L.87 KF144).

No. 354   Complete bone scabbard chape with linear ridges and end notches. Length 65mm. width 34mm. (REC-61 L.62 SF68).

No. 356   Damaged ivory scabbard chape, with central rib and two pelta-shaped cut-outs, notched at both ends. Length 70mm. width 40mm min. (REC-67 L.10 R-TS). Similar to Richborough III No. 22

No. 357   Damaged bone scabbard chape. Bold central rib dividing two panels with matching incised decoration. Length 61mm., width 36mm. (REC-61 L.58 SF16). See Richborough V, No. 228.

No. 358   Tapered bone scabbard chape with side ridges and notched ends (REC-64 L.5 R-DV).

No. 359   Broken bone fish-harpoon. Double-sided barbs and fine point, length 28mm. Nineteen barbs survive (REC-62 L.7 KF76).

No. 360   Octagonal bone knife-handle with incised chevron decoration. A badly corroded iron mass at one end represents a broken blade. Length of handle 100mm. See Col.2932 (REC-62 L.16 KF17).

No. 361   Tool or handle cut from antler. Cut marks along one side. Length 128mm. (REC-68 L.34 R-YH)

No. 362   Crudely carved bone handle, length 120mm., roughly octagonal in section. Drilled hole through length for retaining dowel of fixed blade (REC-68 L.69 R-ZQ).

No. 363   Simple bone handle cut from animal leg bone. Length 100mm. Three incised decorative Patterns on surface. See Col.2929–30 (REC-63 L.2).

No. 364   Crudely carved bone handle. Length 148mm. (REC-62 L.54 KF100).

No. 365   Part of a circular bone handle. Length 70mm. Central section decorated with 17 ring and dot designs and three incised lines (REC-63 L.1).

No. 366   Section of No. 365 above.

No. 367   Crudely cut bone handle, oval in section. Length 75mm. (REC-61 L.33 SF29).

No. 368   Damaged bronze tweezers, undecorated. Length 65mm. See Col.1877 (REC-69 L.48 RR-AV).

No. 369   Bronze tweezers, blades cast together, with broken suspension loop. Length 50mm. min. (REC-69 L.60 RR-BH).

No. 370   Small bronze knife-blade, with tang. Length 75mm. (REC-66 L.30 R-LB).

No. 371   Bowl of bronze spoon, oval. Length 44mm. and width 26mm. (REC-68 L.19 KF50).

No. 372   Circular bronze spoon, handle missing. Diam. 27mm. See Col.2018 (REC-62 L.34 KF68).

No. 373   Rectangular handle with bronze sheet covering iron ferrule and suspension loop at end. Length 70mm. width 18mm. (REC-68 L.19 KF52).

No. 374   Finely cast bronze handle of tool, or weapon. Pommel decorated with ring and bead mouldings and the shaft is hollow. Hexagonal in section. Length 90mm. min. (REC-64 L.19 R-EL)

No. 375   Circular bronze object, cast in one piece. Diam. 15–22mm. Possibly a stopper for a water pipe (REC-66 L.31 R-LC).

No. 376   Circular bronze object, or mount, with central hole and arm fixed to one side. Diam.28mm. (REC-68 L.13 R-XM).

No. 377   Bronze slide key cast in one section, with suspension loop and decorated catch. See Col.4153, Richborough IV No. 218 and Richborough V Nos. 196–203 (REC-62 L.26 KF46).

No. 378   Complete bronze stylus, circular in section, with tapered eraser. Length 100mm. (REC-57 L.1).

No. 379   Flat decorated bronze mount, or handle. Length 64mm. (REC-66 L.33 R-OA).

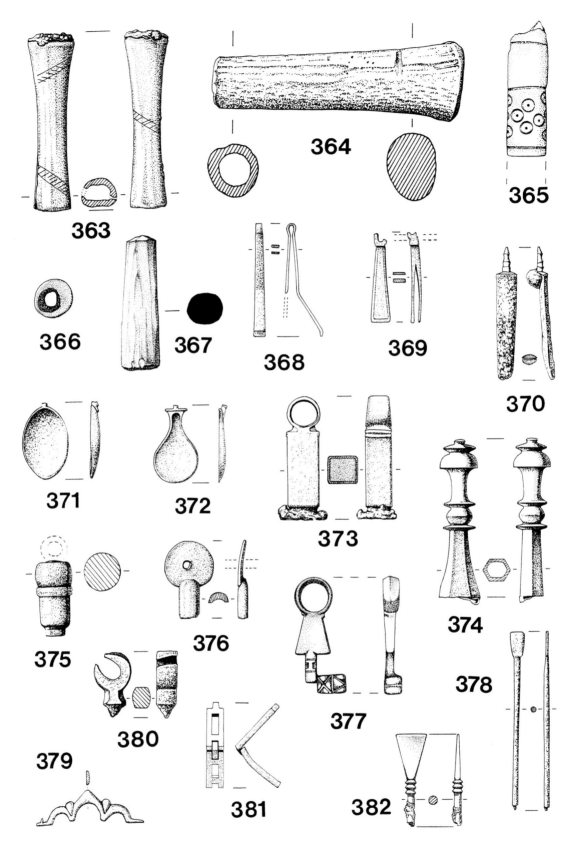

Fig. 59.   *Bone and Bronze objects (1/2).*

No. 380   Open-ended, 'spanner-shaped' bronze fitting or terminal. Length 38mm. (REC-63 L.34 KF11).

No. 381   Two rectangular bronze links, with connecting hinge and rectangular cut-outs. Each link is 35mm. long and 11mm. wide (REC-L.68).

No. 382   Broken bronze stylus with short section of shaft and complete eraser, the latter 5–18mm. in width (REC-63 L.33 KF36).

No. 383   Lead-filled steelyard-weight, cased in bronze sheeting, with suspension loop at top attached to a bronze ring. Weight 120g. (REC-68 L.20 KF126). Very similar to Richborough I, No. 21.

No. 384   Ten fragments of flat bronze strips, straight or curved, with rivet holes for attachment. Possible mounts or fittings for a box, or furniture. (REC-60 L.21).

No. 385   Fragment of a large bronze casting, curved and with six external linear grooves. Just possibly from a votive object or statue (REC-64 L.88).

No. 386   L-shaped sheet bronze corner-plate, with rectangular arms each with two rivet holes and rectangular cut. Outside corner has a single rivet hole. Probable box fitting (REC-60 L.21 SF25)

No. 387 (a)   Bronze fitting, with hooked top and flat shank. Length 34mm. (REC-60 L.21).

(b)   Flat bronze fitting, or mount, with end pierced by rivet hole. Length 43mm. (REC-60 L.21).

No. 388   Bronze fitting, U-shaped in section, decorated on top with faint bands and pierced by three pairs of rivet holes. Length 50mm. min. (REC-60 L.21).

No. 389 (a)   Two linking pieces of bronze, a flat sheet clamped within a rolled strip (REC-60 L.21).

(b)   Small bronze rod, square section. Length 39mm. min. (REC-60 L.21).

(c)   Folded bronze strip with ends pinched together (REC-60 L.21).

No. 390   Bronze strip, possibly part of a bracelet, with ring and dot decoration. Length 41mm. min. (REC-59 SF21 L.1).

No. 391   Bronze tubular pipe, slightly bent. Length 160mm. Diam. 15–20mm. (REC-61 L.48).

No. 392   Sheet bronze fitting, or mount. Decorated with horizontal wave and line motifs and projecting shield-like panels on one edge, the latter with possible plant and animal motifs. Length 75mm. min. (REC-60 L.5/6 SF28).

No. 393   Bronze fitting. Decorated with wave-like pattern bordered by fine dots. Length 22mm. min. (REC-63 L.39 KF53).

No. 394   Fine bronze sheet, decorated with an intricate pattern of leaves and tendrils, with a single hole pierced through the panel. Length 85mm. min. (REC-66 KF122 L.1).

No. 395   Blue glass bead, lozenge-shaped with bevelled sides, with cord hole through long axis. Length 17mm. width 11mm. See Col.1426 (REC-65 L.42 R-IM).

No. 396   Bronze buckle, ovoid in shape, with rectangular tongue. The loop has decorative mouldings on one side. Length 32mm. (REC-62 L.34 KF73).

No. 397   Jet pin with broken shaft and faceted head (REC-61 L.43 SF34).

No. 398   Complete glass handle, part of a fine white vessel, possibly one of a pair. (REC-66 L.29 R-LA).

No. 399   Glass strap-handle. Length 62mm. width 52mm. Tapering towards body (REC-66 L.31 R-LC).

No. 400   Neck of pale green glass bottle. Diam. 51mm. Post-roman (REC-66 L.132 R-RM).

No. 401   Flat pale green glass bead. Rectangular with chamfers on long sides and two suspension holes through long axis. Length 17mm. width 11mm. (REC-69 L.30 RR-AD).

No. 402   Rectangular jet bead, with three ribs and two suspension holes through short axis. Length 18mm. width 12mm. (REC-61 L.65 SF64).

No. 403   Glass ringstone with intaglio of Jupiter seated. See specialist report p. 182 (REC-62 L.48 KF23).

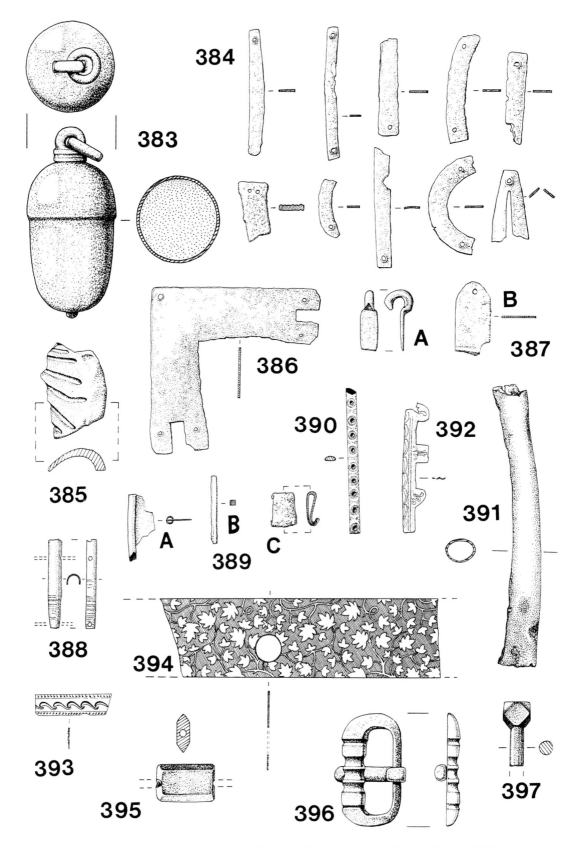

Fig. 60. *Bronze, Glass and Jet objects (1/2), except Nos. 390 and 393–7 (1/1).*

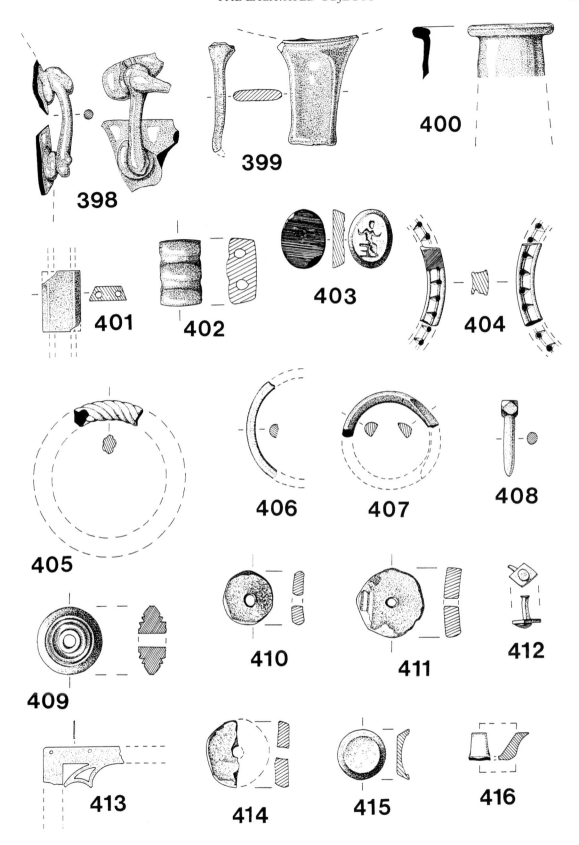

Fig. 61. *Glass, Bronze, Shale and Pottery objects (1/2), except Nos. 398 & 401–4 (1/1).*

No. 404   Fragment of shale bracelet, with teardrop-shaped motifs on both sides (REC-63 KF49 L.28 R-CJ).

No. 405   Fragment of shale bracelet, decorated with continuous spiral (REC-66 L.140 R-RU).

No. 406   Fragment of shale bracelet, semi-circular in section (REC-67 L.114 R-WN).

No. 407   Fragment of shale bracelet, semi-circular in section and partly flattened on outer surface (REC-68 L.19 R-XS).

No. 408   Complete shale pin with square faceted head. Short, stout shaft. Length 44mm. (REC L.1).

No. 409   Shale spindle whorl, biconical in section, grooves lathe-turned. Diam. 39mm. (REC-61 L.47 SF51).

No. 410   Pottery spindle whorl with central perforation. Diam. 31mm. (REC-61 L.1 SF58).

No. 411   Pottery spindle whorl with central perforation. Diam. 39mm. (REC-64 L.31 R-EQ).

No. 412   Bronze rivet, turned over through fragment of plate. Length 19mm. (REC-61 L.1 SF23).

No. 413   Bronze fitting, or mount, cut from thin sheet. Open-work decoration in angle and three rivet holes. Length 48mm. min. (REC-66 L.111 R-QS).

No. 414   Pottery spindle whorl (broken), with central perforation. Diam. 40mm. (REC-61 L.19 SF27).

No. 415   Circular, cast bronze dish-shaped object, deeply counter-sunk face and chamfer. Diam. 28mm. (REC-61 L.1 SF24).

No. 416   Cast bronze object, slightly tapered, but broadly rectangular in section. (REC-61 L.2 SF65).

Nos. 417–9   Six iron arrow-head blades, flat, leaf-shaped, some with ferrules (REC-60 L.21). From the *Sacellum* of the headquarters. Another group of iron arrowheads was recovered from the Headquarters building at Housesteads during the excavations in 1898.

No. 420   Iron arrow-head blade, triangular in shape, with two barbs and point missing. Part of the wooden arrow-shaft remains in the ferrule (REC-65 L.15 R-HU), pit with medieval pottery.

No. 421   Leaf-shaped iron arrow-head with three edges and extant ferrule (REC L.1).

No. 422   Iron spike of ferrule with broken point, diam. 23mm. max. (REC-61 L.48 SF63).

No. 423   Iron split-pin, rectangular in section, length 55mm. See Col.4066 and Richborough V, No. 279. (REC-60 L.14).

No. 424   Large clench nail, with square section and domed head. Length 210mm. (REC-60 L.5–6).

No. 425   Flat-headed iron nail, with square section and point missing. Length 84mm. (REC-61 L.38).

No. 426   Iron object, or tool, shoehorn-shaped with hooked end. Length 104mm. (REC-60 L.13).

No. 427   Iron buckle loop. Heavily corroded, tongue missing. (REC-57 WELL M SF18).

No. 428   Square-headed iron nail, with square shaft and point missing. Length 64mm. (REC-61 L.61).

No. 429   Iron stylus with short point and eraser blade slightly damaged.(REC-63 L.27 KF55).

No. 430   Ring-headed iron pin with broken shaft and square section (REC-60 L.14).

No. 431   Iron fitting, or hook with shaft terminating in a squared, counter-sunk head (REC-60 L.14).

No. 432   Iron tool or hinge, larger section splayed and linked to a possible hinge or loop (REC-60 L.13 SF20).

No. 433   Heavily corroded iron key with simple loop for suspension. Length 60mm. (REC-60 L.13).

No. 434   T-shaped iron object, with short rod, circular shaft and suspension loop. Length 65mm. (REC-61 L.1 SF56).

No. 435   A pair of iron water-pipe collars. Diam. 72mm. width 22mm. (REC-66 KF150).

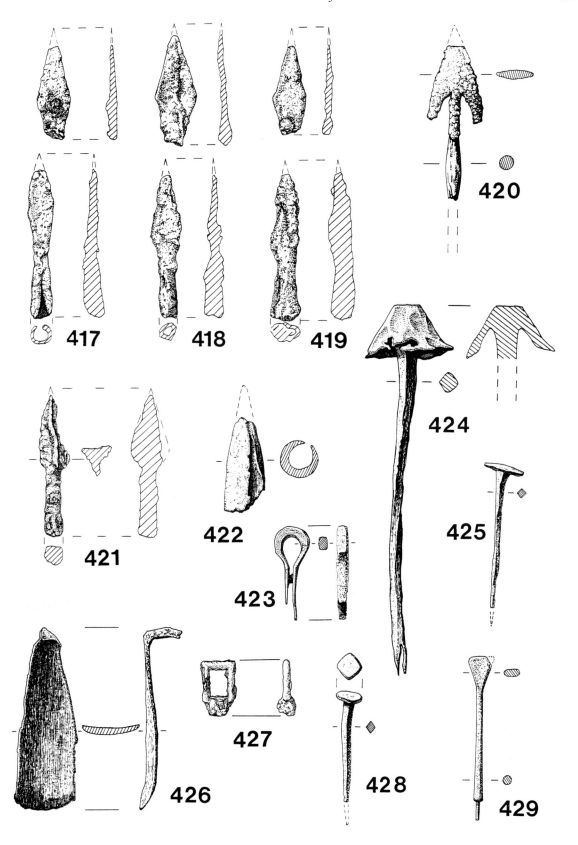

Fig. 62. *Iron Arrowheads, Nails and other objects (1/2).*

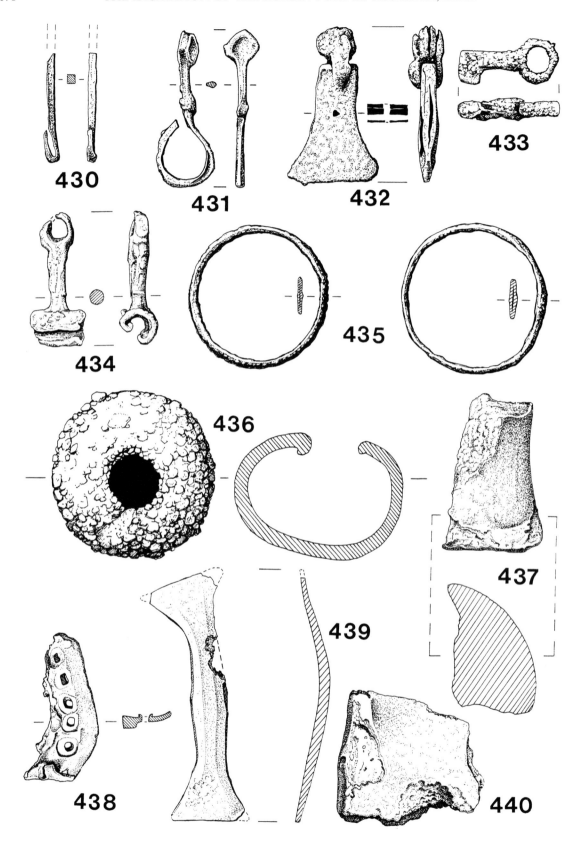

Fig. 63. *Iron, Lead and Baked clay objects (1/2).*

No. 436   Corroded iron ball, hollow, diam. 100mm., aperture 30mm. on one side (REC-66 L.18 KF132) in association with a medieval coin.

No. 437   Fragment of a baked clay object, probably the lower part of a loom weight. Late Bronze Age (REC-63 L.69 KF63).

No. 438   Lead strip, with five perforations for rivets (REC-60 L.3 SF33).

No. 439   Lead clamp with splayed ends for securing stone blocks together (REC-60 L.3 SF30).

No. 440   Fragment of a baked clay object, part of No. 437.

No. 441   Fragment of a large stone inscription, top left corner. Large seriffed letter T[. Good quality lettering. Grey sandstone from the Oldhaven Beds, thickness 40mm. min. (REC-65 L.1). Found in 1965 on the East Gatehouse site, unstratified.

No. 442   Fragment of a stone inscription. Letter]R[, above]R?IA[. Poor quality lettering. Pink-brown sandstone from the Oldhaven Beds, thickness 48mm. (REC-59 L.5 KF65). From *Via Quintana* site.

No. 443   Fragment of a stone inscription. Seriffed letter]V[. Good quality lettering. Grey sandstone from the Oldhaven Beds, thickness 55mm. (REC-60 L.21) From *Sacellum*.

No. 444   Fragment of stone inscription (matching No. 443). Letters]LN[on top line, letters]NCI?[on second line and]E[on third line (REC-60 L.21). From *Sacellum*.

No. 445   Complete tile with stamped letters C IB, stamp outline 140 x 40mm. (REC-60 from Oven II).

No. 446   Fragment of tile with stamped letter]C[, stamp outline 63 min. x 30mm, thickness 13mm. (REC-61 L.1 SF1).

No. 447   Fragment of tile with stamped letters]IB, stamp outline 100 x 30mm. min., thickness 18mm. (REC-68 L.43 KF127) on burnt floor.

No. 448   Fragment of tile with letter C[, stamp outline 40 x 25mm. min., thickness 21mm. (REC-59 L.5 KF59 Pit).

No. 449   Fragment of combed tile stamped with letter C[, stamp outline 50 x 23mm. min., thickness 14–18mm. (REC-66 L.7 R-KJ).

No. 450   Shale object with small perforation, possible pendant, length 33mm. (REC-59 L.1 SF22)

No. 451   Pottery counter cut from base of a samian vessel. Diam. 30mm. (REC-63 L.26 KF45 R-DG).

No. 452   Bronze water pipe, twisted and in two parts (REC-62-F) from cistern east of *principia*.

No. 453   Two fragments of a small clay lamp, with broken handle and wick-hole (REC-59 L.16 SF6).

No. 454   Pottery face-mask of female with parted, combed hair. Buff fabric with faint traces of external brown slip (REC-57 L.1). From beach west of fort.

No. 455   Fragment of pipe-clay figurine, showing basket-work. Possible Dea Nutrix (REC-62–223 L.45).

No. 456   Flint scraper with secondary working, grey and patch of cortex. (REC-64 L.31) Late Neolithic.

No. 457   Fragment of a pipe-clay figurine, showing feet? Possible Pseudo-Venus (REC-59 L.5).

No. 458   Complete flint handaxe with tranchet flake at tip, grey-black and patch of cortex at butt. Tip damaged through use. Size 148 x 50 x 30mm. (REC-60 L.9 SF4). A Mesolithic type.

No. 459–61   Three stone tesserae. No. 459 from a red tile with black core, no mortar, 28 x 20 x 14mm. No. 460–1 from grey Lias? stone with traces of mortar on four sides, 21 x 18 x 14mm. and 18 x 14 x 14mm. (REC-62 L.80 R-AK Well 17).

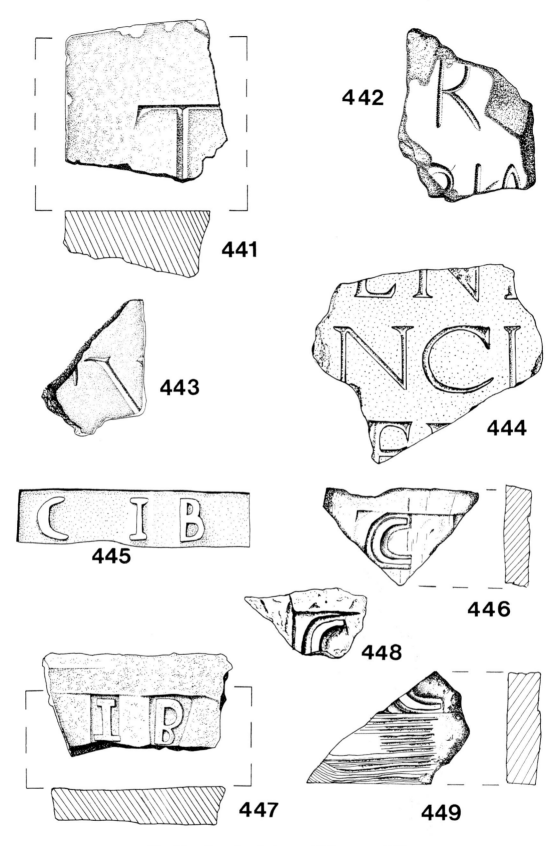

Fig. 64.   *Stone Inscriptions and Tile-stamps (1/2).*

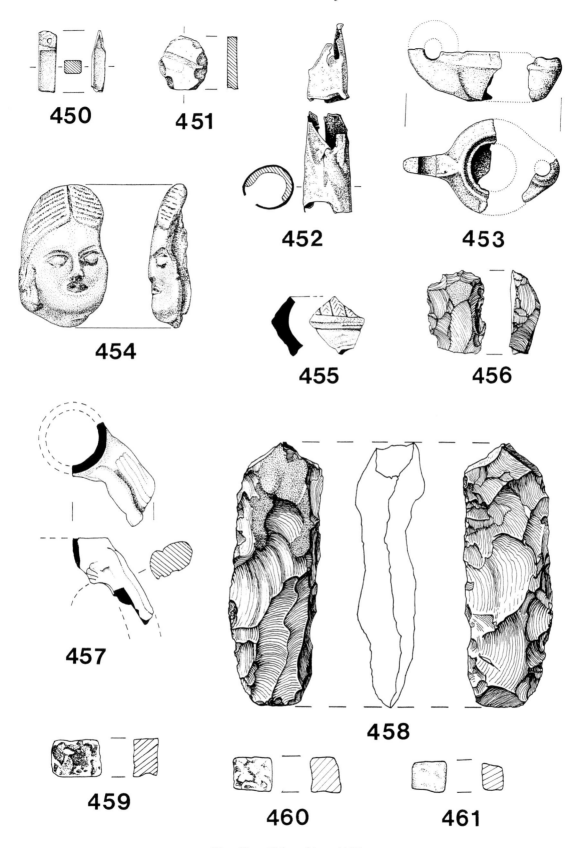

450

451

452

453

454

455

456

457

458

459

460

461

Fig. 65.   *Other objects (1/2).*

(7) THE INTAGLIO (1962 KF 23 L48 No. 403)

by MARTIN HENIG

Glass ringstone with blue upper face on a dark ground, imitating the variety of onyx known as nicolo. It is oval in shape with sides which bevel outwards (shape F2, see Henig 1978, 35, fig. 1). Lower face 16 mm. x 12 mm.; upper face 14 mm. by 10 mm.; thickness 3 mm.

The surface is rather abraded; nevertheless the intaglio device, which is moulded not cut, yields a reasonably clear impression, depicting Jupiter, enthroned to the left, holding his sceptre upright in his left hand and a thunderbolt (*fulmen*) in his outstretched right hand. An eagle is depicted in front of him. There is a ground line.

The original gem which formed the master from whose impression the piece was cast was cut in the first or second century. The general form of the seated god, based ultimately on the famous statue of Zeus at Olympia by the great sculptor of the fifth century B.C., Pheidias (from which the type of the Roman Jupiter Capitolinus was later to be derived), is common on gems and there are a number from Britain though these happen to hold other attributes, eagle, victory or patera (Henig 1978, nos. 1, 4–8). However, other intaglios found elsewhere, for instance a chalcedony and a red jasper in Hanover (Zazoff 1975, nos. 1362, 1363) and a chalcedony in the Getty Museum, Malibu (Spier 1992, no. 263) show him with a thunderbolt.

Jupiter is naturally depicted on nicolo-glass copies (Henig 1978, nos. 2 and 10) including one from Canterbury (Henig 1995, 1003 no. 207) though none of these certainly holds a thunderbolt, as can be seen on two matching glass intaglios, one from Aquileia, now in Vienna (Zwierlein-Diehl 1979, no. 958) and the other in Trier (Krug 1995, 204–5 no.32, Taf. 49).

These follow a different model from the Reculver seal, the figure of Jupiter being more hunched and the thunderbolt larger. However, a most remarkable cache of 19 unset intaglios, found in 1902 during excavations for a hospital at Bonn, included two which were identical in every respect to the Reculver seal (Platz-Horster 1984, 11–16 and 38–9 nos. 11 and 12, Taf. 4); moreover another example is known from Cologne, set in a ring of probable third century date (Platz-Horster 1984, 48–9 no. 32, Taf 8). It is very tempting to see them all as the product of a single workshop probably in the Rhineland although it is possible that they were imported in bulk from elsewhere, perhaps Aquileia, evidently a major centre of gem production (Sena Chiesa 1966).

The newly examined Reculver intaglio is thus of very considerable interest. It not only provides evidence of the personal faith of a member of the third century garrison in Jupiter Optimus Maximus, but also attests a direct link with a known workshop making glass gems on the continent

Henig	1978	M. Henig	A Corpus of Roman Engraved Gemstones from British Sites, BAR 8, 2nd edn. (Oxford)
Henig	1995	M. Henig	'The Roman Finger Rings', pp. 1000–5 in K.Blockley, et al. Excavations in the Marlowe Car Park and surrounding areas (Canterbury).
Krug	1995	A. Krug	'Romische Gemmen im Rheinischen Landesmuseum Trier', Bericht der Romisch-Germanischen Kommission 76, 160–218
Platz-Horster	1984	G. Platz-Horster	Die antiken Gemmen im Rheinischen Landesmuseum, Bonn (Bonn)
Sena Chiesa	1966	G. Sena Chiesa	Geeme del Museo Nationale di Aquileia (Aquileia)
Spier	1992	J. Spier	Ancient gems and finger rings. Catalogue of the collections (The J.Paul Getty Museum, Malibu)
Zazoff	1975	P. Zazoff	Antike Gemmen in Deutschen Sammlungen. IV Hannover, Kestner-Museum (Wiesbaden)

(8) THE PAINTED WALL PLASTER (Figs. 66–8)

Some 1,708 fragments (55.33 kg.) of painted wall-plaster were recovered from the excavations inside the Roman fort from 1959–69. As a collection the fragments are largely unremarkable, particularly when compared with that from the Roman Painted House at nearby Dover (Ref. 30) where brilliant architectural, floral and human forms were found both *in situ* and amongst 22,500 fragments within Rooms 1–6, or nearby. The Reculver plaster does, however, form an important addition to that recovered from Roman military sites where painted plaster has not been found in large quantities. All the plaster is fragmentary and much in poor condition. Some from the Bath House shows clear evidence of two, or even three, layers and this is the only certain evidence of re-plastering at Reculver.

Over 90% of the fragments found came from five main groups (Groups **A–E** below), with the rest mixed with domestic rubbish over a wide area. Only one small area was found *in situ* and that on the south wall of Room B of the East Barrack No.1 (p. 75). There, a short length at floor-level, barely 4 inches high, was painted red and may represent a low-level dado. Small fragments nearby were painted black, white, red, blue and green, all plain. In addition, a small patch of red painted plaster was found on the floor of the South-West Building, where it is likely to have fallen from an adjacent wall.

GROUP A. A total of 392 fragments of painted plaster came from the *sacellum* of the *Principia* excavation in 1960 (p. 46). Here, the primary layer (L.21) contained 280 pieces and the demolition rubble (L.20) which sealed it, another 112 fragments. The plaster from the two layers is similar and can be treated as a single group. The great majority is plain with only about 40 pieces showing dual or multiple coloured designs, mostly linear panels. The mortar generally seems to be similar, mostly a grey-white in colour with small inclusions of chalk and black and brown grits. Two main thicknesses occur, the thinner generally 5–12 mm. and the other 12–30 mm. In detail, the main plain colours were red (209) and white (79), with creamy-yellow (46), green (14) and maroon (5). The remaining 40 fragments (Fig. 66, No. 462) suggest at least four panels, probably orange, green, maroon and white, of unknown size, but containing faint traces of blue and red designs. The panels appear lined with triple borders of black (6 mm.), red (18 mm.) and white (6 mm.), or white (7 mm.), maroon (15 mm.) and white (8 mm.).

GROUP B. A total of about 548 fragments of painted wall plaster was recovered from the area of the Roman Bath House. These were found in about 20 contexts, though these lay within the very extensively robbed building and thus have little stratigraphical value. At least five broad fabric types of plaster can be detected and these could either reflect the varying functions of different rooms, or else redecoration at different times.

TYPE 1. Some 202 fragments were of painted designs on white plaster, laid on thick *opus signinum* renderings. The majority appeared stained and the exact patterns are difficult to determine. Many fragments had a second layer of *opus signinum* applied to them and this also had been painted.

The primary layer of coarse *opus signinum* mostly 15–20 mm. in thickness had been painted with tones of black and orange-yellow, some perhaps faintly curving. The secondary layer of fine *opus signinum*, mostly only 5–7 mm. in thickness, had been painted with zones of white. On to this had been painted at least one double medallion in red, framing a motif or floral device (Fig. 67, Nos. 463–4). Another double medallion appears to be in black on a yellow ground (Nos. 465–6). Another fragment showed a straight red band (15 mm. wide) over white, perhaps part of a rectangular frame (No. 467). Other fragments were painted with mottled black and pale orange, suggesting both curved and linear patterns. Others were painted maroon, pink and mottled blue Nos. 468, 470 and 472). One fragment seems to show part of a column base (No. 471).

Several of the larger fragments exhibited deep cuts on their surfaces, clearly made with a chisel or small pick, mostly 23–35 mm. wide and 5–10 mm. deep. It seems certain that these cuts had been made to provide a keying for a third layer of plaster, though only seven fragments with three

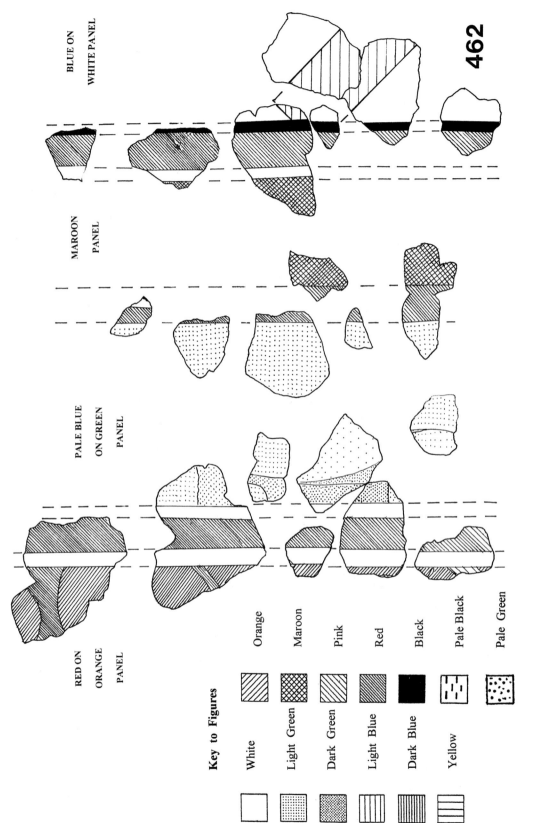

Fig. 66.　*Roman Painted Wall-plaster (Group A) from the sacellum (1/2).*

layers were found. Here, the third layer of white-pink *opus signinum* was 10–20 mm. thick and it had been painted white, red and orange. This included red bands, 20 mm. wide, framing white areas some of which had uncertain pale orange motifs (Fig. 68, No. 469.)

TYPE 2. About 230 fragments were of an off-white mortar with occasional chalk inclusions, mostly 6–10 mm. thick and coated with a 1 mm. white plaster. The colours were mostly plain white, red, pale orange, cream, black and yellow. Decoration was mostly limited to narrow bands such as black (12 mm.) on white; red (9 mm.) on white; maroon (6 mm.) on green; white (7 mm.) on red and pale orange (15 mm.) over white.

TYPE 3. Another 59 fragments were of a thick lumpy white mortar often 25 mm. thick, with a 2 mm. skin of white plaster on its surface. Again areas of red, white, green, maroon, blue are present and include a floor fillet moulding and a possible high-level cornice.

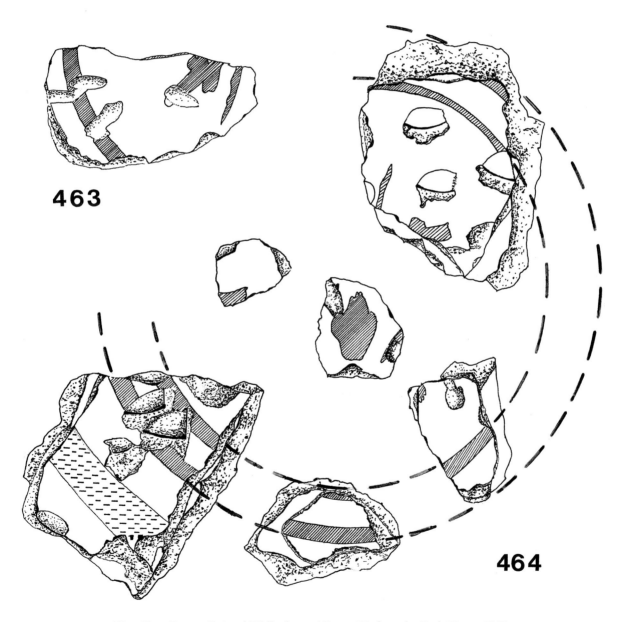

Fig. 67.   *Roman Painted Wall-plaster (Group B) from the Bath House (1/2).*

TYPE 4. Less than ten fragments of a coarse pale buff mortar, generally 10–20 mm. thick and coated with a 10 mm. skin of plaster were also found. These were painted red, white and pink.

TYPE 5. Only four fragments of a distinctive cream mortar containing numerous black grit inclusions, were all painted white.

GROUP C. Another 98 small, fragmentary pieces of painted wall plaster came from the area of Room A in the East Barrack No. 1 in 1968. Of these, 21 came from small pits and 60 mixed in a layer of orange clay that seems to represent wall collapses (L.20) on the west side of the room. Another four fragments came from the primary layer (L.24) on the floor and 16 more from the north-east corner (L.75). The great majority seems to be painted onto a fine cream-grey mortar, mostly 5–10 mm. thick, painted in plain white (57), red (21), blue (2) and green (2). It seems likely that this represents the surviving final plaster from the walls of this room. The other 16 fragments all came from Pit F25, cut through the *opus signinum* floor and into which the large bridging tile had been laid. The plaster from here is marginally a finer grey-white colour and mostly 12–17 mm. thick. Red and white again predominate, but two pieces show a black band of at least 25 mm. wide bordering the white. Several of the white pieces show deliberate flecks of red, maroon and yellow paint over the white, almost certainly to create a marbled effect often used on low-level dados, as at Dover. The distinction between the two groups may be more apparent than significant, but it could suggest that the plaster in Pit 25 came from another room or building.

GROUP D. Another 52 fragments of painted wall-plaster were found in the limited areas excavated inside the building described as the Officers Quarters. Room A produced eight fragments of either green, pink or red, the latter with a white band (9 mm.) across it. Room B produced 19 fragments, mainly red and including one with adjacent bands of white (11 mm.) and black (9 mm.) over it. Another fragment from the same room, on a more gritty mortar, had adjacent bands of brown (24 mm.), white (22 mm.), brown (10 mm.) and yellow-brown (min. 8 mm.)- (Fig. 68, No. 473). Room E, on the cliff edge, produced another 19 fragments, mostly painted white, red, yellow and maroon. In addition, one piece had two bands of yellow (10 mm.) on a white ground (Fig. 68, No. 474), whilst another had a pink border supporting small projections of uncertain form. From this evidence it seems likely that most, or all, of the rooms in this building had been brightly decorated with a range of colours some in linear designs.

GROUP E. Another 386 fragments of painted wall-plaster were found in a layer of loam (L.29) dumped on the tail of the Rampart Bank close to the East Gatehouse, in 1967. Another 156 fragments found nearby were almost certainly from the same deposit, though unstratified. Collectively, all this plaster consists of a cream-white mortar with occasional inclusions of chalk and black grits. It is mainly 8–14mm. in thickness. The predominant colour is white (174), with some red and white (93), some pink and red (50), or black and white (40). Other fragments were painted pink, maroon, black or green. Limited patterns suggest possible floral designs in red, green and black, but no panels. It seems likely that this plaster came from an adjacent building, perhaps even East Barrack No. 1, which contained plaster on a broadly similar fabric. This may have fallen, or been removed, from an internal wall and discarded nearby.

This leaves just 76 fragments from different contexts about the fort with the majority of these coming from Trenches A–D in the north-east area excavated in 1969. Some of these match the plaster from the East Barrack (Group C) or the Bath House (Group B), both adjacent. It seems clear from the plaster recovered that the *Sacellum*, Bath House, Officers Quarters and Rooms A and B of the East Barrack No. 1, were all decorated internally with painted designs. Considering the scale of the post-Roman decay, demolition and stone-robbing, it must be that much more plaster had originally existed. Indeed, every building inside the fort could have been decorated with painted plaster much of which is likely to have decayed and been removed during the time the buildings were occupied. When spread out the plaster recovered may only cover about three square yards and it seems highly likely that much less than 1% of the original plaster has survived and

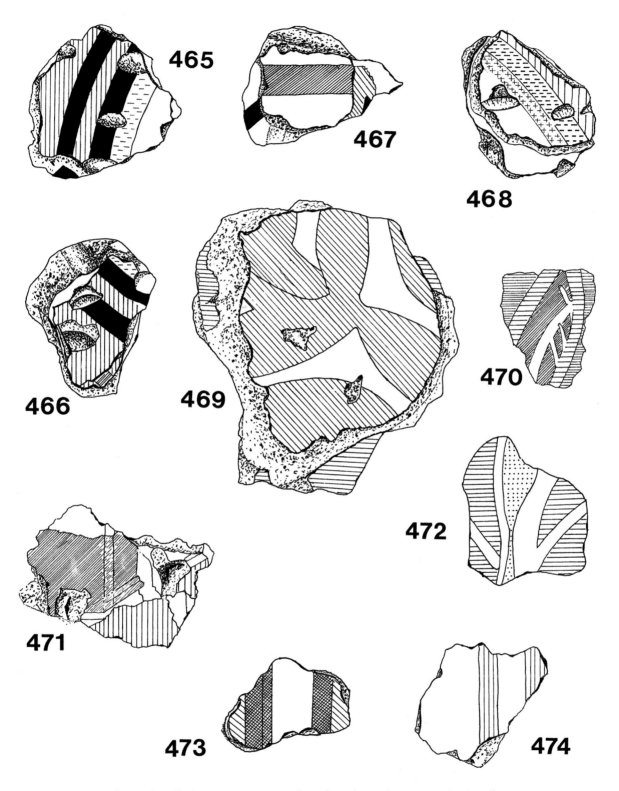

Fig. 68. *Roman Painted Wall-plaster (Groups B and D) from the Bath House (1/2) & Officers Quarters (1/2).*

indeed this may be in proportion to the extent of the heavily robbed internal buildings. Other Shore-forts, where excavated, have also produced small amounts of painted wall-plaster, as at Caister-on-Sea (Ref. 53), Portchester (Ref. 51) and Brancaster (Ref. 56).

Catalogue of the Painted Wall Plaster

From the *sacellum* of the *Principia* (Group A)

No. 462   A fine white plaster just 4mm. thick. Fragments arranged to show parts of four panels. A red design over an orange ground (left), a dark and pale blue design over a green ground and a maroon panel (centre) and a pale blue design over a white ground (right) (REC-60–21).

From the Bath House (Group B – type 1)

No. 463   A coarse primary, cream-pink *opus signinum* 22 mm. thick, rendered over with a fine 5mm. layer of pink opus signinum. This fragment shows part of a double medallion in red over a white field, enclosing a foliate design, also in red. The surface exhibits four clear pick or chisel marks, the keying for an extra layer of plaster, probably never applied. In section, the primary layer of plaster appears white whilst the second rendering, has the illustrated design (R-FX L.104).

No. 464   Six fragments of painted plaster similar to No. 463, showing a double medallion in red with an estimated diameter of about 280mm., again enclosing possible floral motifs. The surface also shows extensive pick or chisel marks for keying in another layer of plaster, probably never applied. In section, all show a primary layer of white plaster, upon which the secondary rendering 5–7 mm. thick has been applied and on which the design has been painted (R-FX L.104).

No. 465–6   Mortar similar to that of Nos. 463–4. Two fragments of plaster of a double medallion in black on a yellow field, enclosing a possible white and pale black design. The primary layer of white paint shows slight traces of red and black lines, but is sealed by the second rendering 6mm. thick upon which the design is painted. The latter also exhibits chisel marks for keying (R-HY and R-FX).

No. 467   Mortar similar to Nos. 463–6. A fragment of plaster with a single broad red band 16mm. wide over a white field. The primary layer of plaster shows bands of black on a yellow and white field. This is sealed by 4 mm. of the secondary rendering on which the design is painted (R-FX L.104).

No. 468   Mortar similar to Nos. 463–7. A fragment of plaster showing an arc in pale black over a yellow field, flanking an off-white strip. The primary layer appears to be painted in white and is covered by a 5–6 mm. secondary rendering on which the design is painted (R-FX L.104).

No. 469   There are three distinct layers of mortar. The primary layer is a coarse pink-cream *opus signinum* 16–18 mm. thick with an off-white stained surface. The second layer is a fine pink *opus signinum* 6–8 mm. thick also with a stained surface. The final layer is a white mortar containing occasional tile chips and painted with propeller-like motif in orange over a white field (R-HS L.11).

No. 470   Plaster similar to Nos. 463–8. A fragment of plaster, perhaps with a floral design in red, light blue and dark blue. This could represent a large bud with leaves (R-JF L.62).

No. 471   Plaster similar to No. 469. A fragment of plaster showing a possible column base in red with adjacent yellow field, perhaps superimposed over a pale green and white design. Two clear pick marks show keying for an intended subsequent layer (R-FX L.104).

No. 472   Mortar similar to Nos. 463–8. A fragment of plaster showing pale blue and green design, possibly floral. These may represent a bud with leaves (R-HX L.19).

From the Officers Quarters (Group D)

No. 473   **Room B**. A grey-white mortar 10–12 mm. thick. A fragment of plaster with painted bands of orange, brown, white, brown and orange. Perhaps part of a rectangular panel (R-IN L.43).

No. 474   **Room E**. Mortar similar to No. 473 and 14–16 mm. thick. A fragment of plaster with two painted yellow bands over a white field. May be part of a panel (R-HD L.33).

---

(9) THE GLASS

A total of about 450 fragments of glass was recovered from the excavations from 1959–69, but due to lack of funding this has not been subjected to a definitive study. Of these, about 270 are regarded as window-glass and the remaining 180 fragments from glass vessels. Of the window glass, about 150 pieces were clearly medieval and the great majority was excavated from inside the medieval church in 1969, or from the nearby Roman Bath House in 1965. Most of this was poor quality glass, that has crystallised, but which still showed traces of painted patterns. It was typically medieval in character and is likely to have come from the church windows sometime before the church was demolished in 1809.

The remaining 120 fragments clearly came from Roman windows inside the fort. The excavation thus produced about 300 fragments of Roman glass, which statistically (on an excavation sample of 4%) could suggest a total collection of 7,000–8,000 pieces for the complete fort! The window glass varied in thickness from 2–5 mm, and was mostly pale green in colour and largely translucent. Over a third was matt on both sides, nearly a third was matt on one side and polished on the other, whilst the remainder was polished on both sides. Only two corner pieces and also 15 fragments with bevelled edges were found and the largest fragment was only 2–3 in. in length. It seems likely that the fragments came from small panel sets in wooden window frames. The fragments came from widely spaced sites within the fort and indicate that some, or all, of the internal buildings had glazed windows.

The vessel glass is more varied, in thickness, colour and form. Bases, rims and side pieces are represented. Most are pale green or white fragments that may be from bottles, bowls, beakers or cups. Decoration is limited, but includes, applied leaves, incised lines and slight corrugations. The fragments mostly came from domestic rubbish deposits about the fort, in which glass vessels were clearly in common use.

---

(10) THE BOX-FLUE TILES (Fig. 69)

Although small fragments of box-flue tiles were found at several points within the fort by far the main collection came from the rubble inside the heavily robbed Bath House where they had clearly been incorporated into the hypocaust system. These included a number of hollow voussoirs. Several other fragments came from the rubble in the ruins of the sacellum of the principia. No detailed analysis has been made of the whole collection and only six are illustrated (Nos. 475–80).

No. 475   Box-flue voussoir, side section tapering from 153–68 mm.in its minimum length of 183 mm. Thickness 20mm. Keyed pattern applied with large four and five toothed combs (R-HY). From the Bath House.

No. 476   Similar to No. 475, but keyed with four toothed comb (R-JU). From the Bath House.

No. 477   Box-flue voussoir, end section 165 x 127 mm. Thickness 20 mm. Keyed with six toothed comb (R-IE). From the Bath House.

No. 478   Similar to No. 477, end section 176 x 115 mm. Keyed with wide four toothed comb (R-HS). From the Bath House.

No. 479   Probable voussoir, showing side broken at each end, but tapering from 145–50 mm. Thickness 16 mm. Keyed with four toothed comb (REC-60 L.2O). From rubble in *sacellum.*

No. 480   Box-flue tile, 157 mm. (min) x 143 mm.(min). Thickness 15 mm. Keyed with fine six toothed comb (REC-61 L.106). From Trench B in East Area.

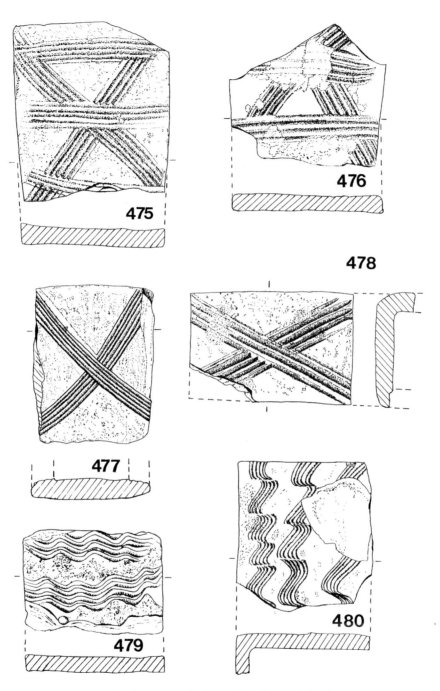

Fig. 69. *Box-flue Tiles from the Fort (1/3).*

CHAPTER VII

DISCUSSION

(1) THE PREHISTORIC FEATURES

One of the earliest discoveries on the site was a small pit containing late-Bronze Age and early-Iron Age pottery. This was exposed by the sea in the East Cliff in 1953 (Pit A) where it clearly underlay Roman deposits inside the fort. Slightly later, in 1957, a larger pit was exposed nearby (p. 66) which also produced late-Bronze Age pottery and three spinal discs of a large whale.

This exposed section of cliff was fully excavated on the East Cliff Site in 1965–6 when twelve ditches were found spread along a distance of about 150 ft. These were variously aligned, about 2–6 ft. wide and generally 1–3 ft. deep. They occupied about 40% of the available area, had progressively silted and mostly contained late-Bronze Age and early-Iron Age potsherds. Only one contained mid-1st century pottery. To judge by the relative positions of the ditches they are unlikely to be of the same precise date, but an extensive phased settlement site seems to be indicated. Another ditch, of similar form, was found 110 ft. to the south-east during the 1967 East Gatehouse excavation and this may indicate that the prehistoric settlement area extends as far as that. Either way, it is certain that prehistoric features, mostly late-Bronze Age and Early-Iron Age, exist under the north-east sector of the fort and may have extended outside its east wall to the area partly cut through by the fort's defensive ditches. The extensive excavations at the nearby Roman fort at Richborough, from 1922–38, also revealed prehistoric cut features over much of the site (Ref. 33).

Elsewhere at Reculver, apart from a possible prehistoric feature (F.11) on the West Site in 1966, no other such feature was certainly located inside the fort. The excavations, however, seldom removed all of the primary Roman deposits and other prehistoric features could exist. In addition, about 92% of the surviving area was untouched by the 1957–69 excavations. Apart from an occasional struck flint flake the only significant stone tool found was a tranchet-axe of mesolithic form (No.458). This appears in pristine condition and is likely to have been a casual loss. It was found in 1960 in the area of the Roman *principia*.

(2) THE MID – FIRST CENTURY FORTLET

The discovery of a series of largely similar ditches, beneath the shore-fort construction levels, produced the outline of three sides of an enclosure. The longest east side, certainly traced for 270 ft., ran on two alignments appearing to join near its centre. By projection southwards to meet the projected line of the south ditches, a total minimum length of 340 ft. is obtained. Similarly, by projection to meet the lines of both of the east and west ditches, the south side appears to have a width of about 210 ft. Only some 15 ft. of the presumed west side was located, but there is a chance that the continuation of this survives further north in the large area not excavated. Any corresponding north ditch has presumably been destroyed by sea-erosion.

It must be stressed, however, that only a small percentage of the ditches traced was excavated and very little indeed of their internal area. Furthermore, as this enclosure was largely centred on the top of the hill it has suffered a considerable degree of ground-reduction through ploughing and erosion. In addition, other parts remain sealed beneath the roads and buildings of the later shore-fort. Even so, the details and dating evidence are sufficient to identify the enclosure as a Roman military defensive earthwork of mid-1st century date. Its area and ditches largely match smaller Roman forts elsewhere, but in view of its limited excavation the term "Fortlet" has been adopted here.

On the available evidence, therefore, a sub-rectangular area about 210 ft. (64m.) in internal width and at least 350 ft. (107m.) in length is indicated. This encloses an area of nearly two acres (0.7 hectares) and seems to be largely centred on the top of the hill. A realignment on the east side could represent a second phase, while the deepening and recut of the east ditch at the point of realignment may be significant. The two packed post-holes found here might just possibly represent the site of a wooden bridge. All the ditches contained an even dark brown loam, strongly suggesting a progressive silting over a long period of time.

The double ditches, mostly revealing a broadly W-profile, are unusual for native domestic enclosures of 1st century A.D. date, when the norm was a single ditch as at Faversham (Ref. 34), Keston (Ref. 35) and Lenham (Ref. 36). The profile is more reminiscent of a Roman military feature and indeed W-profile ditches are known at a number of early Roman military sites (Ref. 37). Furthermore, double defensive ditches of varying forms are a very common feature of such sites across much of the country. Some recorded ditch widths and depths agree well with those at Reculver, where the inner ditch width of 6 ft. and a depth of 4 ft., were revealed. In particular, the Roman forts at Castleshaw, Yorks (6 x 2½ ft), Melandra, Derbys.(8 x 3 ft.) and Red Hill, Shropshire (6½ x 3 ft.) offer good parallels. At nearby Richborough (Ref. 38) the double ditches, dug as part of a major bridge-head fortified base in A.D. 43, were 23 ft. in overall width, whereas those at Reculver were mostly only 15 ft. in overall width. In both cases the inner ditch was the largest, whilst at Richborough a causewayed entrance was also found. Interestingly, the Richborough ditches, traced for over 2,100 ft.(640m.), show a realignment near their northern end.

So, too, does the overall internal area 350 x 210 ft.(107m. min. x 64m.) at Reculver conform with several other early forts, such as the Claudian fort at Nanstallon, Cornwall 318 x 279 ft. (97 x 85m.) and the late-1st century forts at Broomholm, Dumfries 344 x 230 ft.(105 x 70m.), Pentrich, Derbys. 298 x 239 ft.(91 x 73m.) and Red Hill, Shropshire 325 x 230 ft. (99 x 70m.), these being the overall dimensions.

The small amount of pottery from the Reculver ditches, mostly appears to be native wares including combed cooking pots and storage jars of mid-1st century date. A little imported Gallo-Belgic *terra nigra* is present, but the samian ware from the whole site only includes one vessel of Tiberius-Claudius. Several sherds of Flavian samian ware were, however, recovered from the upper silts in the ditches. Of equal significance are coins of Tiberius and Nero, found in about 1700, said to be "fresh and unworn" and six British coins (Ref. 39). These must have been found at least 300 ft. further to the north whilst the sea was eroding the cliffs. These coins, taken with the newly found enclosure, with its W-profile ditches, strongly supports a Roman occupation of the site sometime in the middle decades of the 1st century. Such an occupation at this time must almost certainly have had a military function and a fortified base of the Conquest period is thus highly probable. The enclosure found, with its double ditches, is clearly reminiscent of a small fort, but it is equally possible that a larger area was enclosed on the north side now lost to the sea. If so, a larger additional fortification may also have existed and the ditches found in 1959–69 may even have served as an annex to it.

(3) THE LATER – FIRST CENTURY MATERIAL

Whilst generally there were no features, or structures, sandwiched between the fully silted ditches of the mid-1st century Fortlet and the fort-construction deposits, a limited amount of pottery from the site generally dates from the second half of the 1st century A.D. This takes the form of about 30 samian ware sherds (Forms 15/17, 18, 36 and decorated Forms 29 (3), 37 (5), but strangely only two small groups of coarse pottery. Significantly, whilst about seven sherds came from the upper fill of the Fortlet ditches much of the rest was found in direct association with Antonine and later pottery. A circular pit, about 3 ft. in diameter and 2 ft. deep, was found (in Box J) about 20 ft. west of the east ditches of the mid-1st century Fortlet. This was sealed by the foundations of the Earlier East Building and also by a wall of East Barrack No.2 and it contained a filling of black sticky loam. It produced fragments of four samian vessels, Forms 15/17, 29 (2) and 37, one of which was stamped by Martialis and all dated A.D. 50–80.

The implications of this limited evidence are unclear. It implies a modest use of the site in the second half of the 1st century. This may reflect the latent re-use by the military of the original base, or perhaps the adoption of part of the overall site by a small domestic site. Alternatively, it could be an area on the fringe of a much larger settlement now lost to the sea. If so, the large number of chance finds from the cliffs and foreshore over the past three centuries should have contained much more late-1st century material. On balance, minor use of the overall site in the second half of the 1st century seems indicated.

(4) THE ROMAN FORT – PERIOD I (Fig. 70)

Whatever the implications of the evidence of the later-1st century settlement at Reculver, it seems very clear that the large stone fort was constructed on an open and unoccupied site. On all the three surviving sides the mortar-mixing layer for the fort wall lay directly on the old land-surface which also contained occasional potsherds of prehistoric date. In addition, the construction-levels clearly overlay the fully silted ditches of the mid-1st century Fortlet. The site chosen was a low hill, on the west side of the wide tidal channel, with the fort being placed centrally on its highest point and the ground falling away on at least three sides.

The fort wall enclosed an area about 582 x 560 ft. (177 x 171m.) and thus about 7½ acres (3 hectares). It was 10 ft. wide at the base, reduced by two internal offsets to 8 ft. at a point about 6 ft. above the ground and supported on a foundation of rolled beach pebbles, mostly about 1 ft. in depth. It was mainly constructed of flint and ragstone, held in a hard white pebbly mortar (really a light concrete), but contained no courses of bonding tiles, or evidence of external bastions. The external facing stones were of ashlar blocks of Kentish Ragstone and there is some evidence of two external plinths at the East Gatehouse. The fort wall now survives to a maximum height of about 8 ft. 6 in., but it is likely that originally it reached to a height of 15–25 ft., including a parapet.

The fort's corners were rounded and the only corner examined (in 1958) was found to be supported internally by a buttress some 5 ft. wide, perhaps the base of a stair, or ballistarium platform. The claim, elsewhere, that Reculver had internal corner turrets is not supported by any evidence. Two external ditches, certainly on the east and part of the south sides, gave protection. A berm about 18 ft. wide flanked the front of the wall, followed by an inner ditch about 28 ft. wide and 11ft. deep, an inter-ditch berm of about 14 ft. and an outer ditch 19 ft. wide and 8 ft. deep, at least on the east side.

It was certainly provided with four gatehouses, one placed centrally in each side. The two surviving, on the east and south sides respectively, were almost identical, each being about 33 x 15 ft. in plan area, enclosing a single carriageway about 9 ft. wide and a single guard-room on one side. Both were well metalled and the east one later blocked. Wooden bridges here probably provided access across the adjacent defensive ditches.

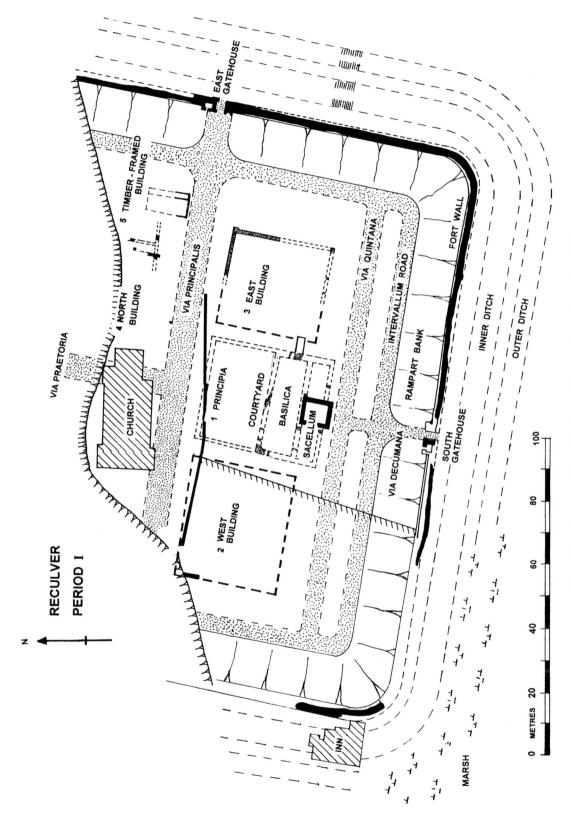

Fig. 70. *Reculver 1959–69. Plan of Roman Stone Fort (Period I).*

The fort wall was backed by a substantial Rampart Bank of dumped loams and clays, the material having been obtained from the fort ditches and from any terracing of the internal slope. The bank sloped up behind the fort wall and tailed back for a distance of mostly 40–45 ft., now reaching about 6ft. up the wall and probably higher originally. The tail of the Rampart Bank was bordered by a metalled *Intervallum* Road (elsewhere the *Via Sagularis*), mostly 12 to 15 ft. wide and located on all three surviving sides. This provided a perimeter road giving ready access from the interior and the gates to any part of the Rampart and thus the fort wall.

The *Intervallum* Road also defined the internal area, then reduced to about 480 x 455 ft. (149 x 139m.) This zone was sub-divided east-west across its centre by the *Via Principalis,* parts of which were located at four points. The southern half of the fort was further sub-divided by a parallel road, the *Via Quintana,* (extensively surviving), which separated the central and rear divisions of the fort. The former appears to have been about 150 ft. wide and the latter only about 44 ft. Another short road, the *Via Decumana,* joined the *Via Quintana* to the South Gatehouse. In the northern half of the fort a main north-south road, the *Via Praetoria,* must certainly have existed (though not touched by excavation and largely destroyed by sea erosion) which led to the North Gatehouse, certainly the principal gatehouse of the fort. A single east-west road about 15 ft. wide, found on the cliff-face in 1957 and 1966, ran north of the *Via Principalis* and helped sub-divide the northern half of the fort. This outlined an area about 95 ft. in width on its south side and left an area about 108 ft. wide on its north side.

With these internal divisions identified, it is possible to suggest what Roman linear measurements were involved in the overall layout of the fort. Certainly the *Classis Britannica* fort at Dover (Ref. 55) and the forts at Hod Hill, Dorset and Nanstallon, Cornwall were laid out to precise Roman dimensions. At Reculver, including the fort walls the north-south axis measures out at about 582 ft. and this converts into about 600 Roman ft., or exactly 5 *actus p.M.* Clearly, the military engineers set the fort out precisely and the east-west axis seems to be broadly similar. The north-south axis can also be sub-divided, with the north fort wall, Rampart Bank and centre-line of the *Intervallum* Road coming out at about 56 ft., or about 58 Roman ft., close to $\frac{1}{2}$ half an *actus.* Next comes an area from the centre-line of the *Intervallum* Road to the centre-line of the east-west dividing road found in 1957 at 121 ft. This converts into about 126 Roman ft. which is again close to 1 *actus*. From there to the centre-line of the *Via Principalis,* including another large space, is 118 ft., which translates into 122 Roman ft. which is again very close to 1 *actus*. Southwards from the centre-line of the *Via Principalis* to the centre line of the *Via Quintana,* is another 172 ft. which constitutes the Central Division. This converts into 177 Roman ft. which is again very close to 1$\frac{1}{2}$ *actus*. From the centre-line of the *Via Quintana* to the centre-line of the south *Intervallum* Road is another 58 ft. which is again about $\frac{1}{2}$ an *actus*, which defines the narrow rear division. Finally, from the centre-line of the *Intervallum* Road to the outside face of the south wall is another 56 ft. which converts to 58 Roman ft., again very close to $\frac{1}{2}$ an *actus*. Allowing for the difficulties in the area now lost to the sea, it seems clear that the north-south divisions of the fort were laid out with some precision.

The east-west axis is more difficult to assess due to the uncertainty of the precise sizes of the buildings involved. It is clear that the *principia* occupied the centre of the fort, which with a width of 104 ft. and conjectured roads each side (to centre-lines), produces a total of about 124 ft. This converts to roughly 1 *actus*. On the west side, the fort wall, Rampart Bank, *Intervallum* Road and open space to the west of the Earlier West Building, totals 111 ft. which converts to about 114 Roman ft., again roughly 1 *actus*. This leaves a space of about 132 ft. to the centre-line of the conjectured road on the west side of the *principia*, which converts to about 136 Roman ft., again very roughly 1 *actus*.

On the east side, the fort wall, Rampart Bank, *Intervallum* Road and open space total 132 ft. This converts to about 136 Roman ft., which is again roughly 1 *actus*. The remaining space for the

Earlier East Building to the centre-line of the conjectured road on the east side of the *principia* is 103 ft., which converts to about 106 Roman ft., rather less than 1 *actus*. Although these total 5 *actus*, the precision seems lacking, but this is probably due to the present uncertainties relating to the buildings and roads.

Within the fort, parts of at least twelve major buildings have been identified and it is now clear that two distinct periods of stone buildings are represented. In three cases the foundations of large buildings (Period I) underlay other large masonry buildings (Period II) of totally different plan. In addition, there is now strong evidence to suggest that some of the Period I buildings were never completed! In fact five large buildings relate to the fort-construction period, three in the central range and two north of the *Via Principalis* (Fig. 70, Nos. 1–5). The former seem generously spaced out with the central building, the *principia*, occupying the precise central north-south axis of the fort. Four of these were masonry buildings and the fifth timber-framed and all are described below.

(1) The *Principia*

Its overall width was 104 ft. and its north-south length is estimated at 130–140 ft. It contained three or five offices in its rear range, the central one of which was a cellared strongroom and *sacellum*, just 24 x 20 ft. internally. Its central basilica was about 104 x 40 ft. overall and the front courtyard is estimated at 104 x 70–80 ft. The building had been almost totally robbed, but its outlines were revealed by the broad pebble foundation, some 6 ft. wide for the large basilica (Plate XVII) and generally only 3 ft. wide elsewhere (see p. 42).

(2) The (Earlier) West Building

To the west of the *principia* was another structure, of which only the west wall, some 16 ft. in north-south length, was found. With a foundation width of 3 ft. 4 in. and clear traces of mortared masonry on it, another large building is indicated. Most of the remaining part of this building lay beneath the new Coastguard Station (built about 1885), and thus unavailable. The wall found lay 101 ft. from the inside face of the west wall of the fort which contrasted with the 122 ft. with the corresponding building on the east side of the fort. The apparent lack of symmetry here is not clear, but it may anyway not be significant. Either way, allowing for another nominal 20 ft. road between it and the *principia* a maximum width of 122 ft. is available. This seems excessive and it is likely that two or more structures were planned on the west side of the *principia*. A north-south length of 110–130 ft. seems likely. The function is unclear, but a pair of granaries here is not unlikely, as at Dover (Ref. 55).

(3) The (Earlier) East Building

To the east of the *Principia*, was another large structure, which had a north-south length of 110 ft. and a width of at least 55 ft. Allowing for a nominal 20 ft. road between it and the *principia* a maximum width of 93 ft. is available for this building. Its east wall lay 122 ft. from and parallel to the east wall of the fort wall and nothing was found in that area to indicate another structure. The outline of this building was detected on the three sides only on the evidence of the broad foundation pebbles, mostly 3 ft. 4 in. wide. No internal divisions were revealed (though these could exist) and there was no evidence that this building was ever completed. It was clearly superseded by one of the East Barracks (No. 2) which was constructed right over its east side. In addition, its foundation on the east side cut through a pit containing samian dated A.D.50–80 (p. 81) and its soil packing contained a stamped samian base (Stamp No.14) of Antonine date. The intended function of this building is not clear, but its large size and position in the central division of the fort suggests that it was intended to be the Commandant's House, or *praetorium*. The rear (south) wall of this structure appears to line up with the wall dividing the cross-hall and the offices at the rear of the *principia*. If so, this would have left a generous space between this building and the *Via Quintana*.

(4) The (Earlier) North Building

The pebble foundations of part of a fourth structure were found partly beneath both the Period II Bath House and the Officers Quarters (p. 59). No comprehensive plan could be produced due to the presence of the later structures and the limited excavation, but a building perhaps at least 30 x 25 ft. seems likely. The foundations, again of rolled beach pebbles, were only 2 ft. 8 in. wide and thus smaller than the three large buildings in the central division. A barrack-block on a north-south axis may be the most likely possibility. The general absence of demolition rubble and the presence of only one sandstone block from the wall, again makes it likely that this building was never completed.

(5) The Timber-Framed Building (p. 68)

The south end of the only timber-framed building found during the excavations, was revealed on the north side of the *Via Principalis* (in 1969) and about 100 ft. from the East Gatehouse. This had an overall width of 25 ft., a minimum length of 11 ft. and is very likely to have been laid out on a north-south axis. It appears to have been constructed on vertical wooden posts, placed in horizontal gullies which, in the apparent absence of laid floors, suggests it had a raised wooden floor. It thus resembles the posted structures found at nearby Richborough, where they are regarded as granaries of mid-1st century date.

Clearly, this Reculver building cannot be of mid-1st century date for it was constructed right across the progressively and well consolidated natural silt of the mid-1st century Fortlet ditches. Nor could it have related to the Period II construction programme, for it was cut through by the drain from the Period II Bath House. It thus must have formed part of the Period I programme, which agrees with the single samian sherd found in association. It could have served as a granary then, perhaps as a temporary structure serving the troops constructing the fort. Certainly, this could explain its contrasting timber form at a time when the permanent buildings were being built of stone. No trace of this building was detected in Trench C, some 50 ft. north of Trench A, so it is possible that its length was thus less than 60 ft. Nor was a replacement masonry building found here and one possibility is that the Timber Framed Building continued in use into Period II. What may be significant, is that the two large successive ovens found in and under the eastern Rampart Bank, were positioned about 120 ft. from this building. The ovens were probably for baking food-stuffs, perhaps those stored in the adjacent timber granary. If so, more ovens may await discovery along the adjacent section of the fort wall.

(6) General

The overall evidence from the various excavations seems to show quite clearly that some of the internal buildings within the fort were never completed as planned. The *principia* was certainly completed as the *sacellum* inscription shows (see below, p. 210) and it is likely that much of this formed part of the Period I programme. Clearly, the Earlier West Building and the Earlier North Building were started, but never completed. In addition, it seems that only the foundations of the Earlier East Building were laid. The probable wooden granary is likely to have been completed as a matter of urgency. The fort's defences, apart from the east wall repair, seems to be of a single build and it is likely that these and the Gatehouses were completed as originally planned. The internal road system also seems to date from Period I, for the *Via Quintana* was certainly repaired in Period II (p. 17) and part of the *Via Principalis* and also the *Via Decumana* were re-laid at a higher level, also in Period II (p. 49). The fort ditches, on the strength of a single section, are also likely to have been dug in Period I for the clay removed must certainly have helped form part of the Rampart Bank behind the fort wall (p. 22). In addition, the deep primary silt in the ditches, largely devoid of finds, but sealed by the likely Period II deposits, seems to reflect a substantial period of time when the ditches were not cleaned out.

(5) THE ROMAN FORT – PERIOD II (Fig. 71)

(1) General

The evidence from several of the excavations showed that substantial structural changes and alterations were made to the internal layout of the fort. These mostly form a broad pattern and seem to represent a major period of building, here regarded as Period II. The most dramatic evidence came from the East Barracks site in 1968, where Barrack No. 2 was found to overlay both the north and east walls of the Period I Earlier East Building and extending further north by some 12 ft. and also on a changed alignment (p. 81). In addition, the walls of both the Bath House and the Officers' Quarters, both regarded on circumstantial grounds as Period II, completely superseded the unfinished Period I Earlier North Building. Similarly, the ditch draining the Bath House cut through the south end of the Timber Framed Building, also identified as Period I.

   The plan of these later buildings, framed around the continuing *principia* and enclosed by the Period I fort walls and Gatehouses is only partially complete. Parts of eight more major buildings can be identified, six constructed of local sandstone blocks bonded in clay and probably supporting large, timber-frames. Their details are given in Table W below. The walls were nearly all 2ft. 2 ins. in width and rested on foundations of rolled beach pebbles mostly 6 to 12 ins. thick.

Building	Overall Length	Overall Width	Rooms	Wall Thickness
East Barrack 1	134 ft	24 ft	4	2 ft 2 in.
East Barrack 2	65 ft min	24 ft 6 in	3 min	2 ft 2 in.
South West Building	50 ft min	23 ft 10 in	1 min	2 ft 2 in.
West Building	32 ft min	25 ft	1 min	2 ft 3 in.
North West Building	?	?	1 min	2 ft 1 in.
North East Building	?	?	1 min	2 ft 2 in.
Bath House	39 ft	21 ft 6 in.	7	2 ft 2 in.– 2 ft 4 in.
Officers Quarters	55 ft	45 ft	6	2 ft 2 in.
Principia	130 – 140 ft	104 ft	3	3 ft 5 in.

Table W. Dimensions and wall thickness of the Period II Buildings.

(2) The Barracks

While none of the Period I internal buildings can be identified conclusively as barrack blocks, it seems certain that the pair of parallel buildings on the east side (East Barracks Nos. 1 and 2) were barracks and that these must relate to Period II. The overall widths were mostly 24 ft., but only one (East Barrack 1) was traced for its total length of 133 ft. 8 in. It is virtually certain that East Barrack 2, with which East Barrack 1 formed a matching pair, had been of the same length. As such it is clear that these can be identified as barrack blocks of familiar form. Both had been sub-divided internally by cross-walls, producing four rooms (A–D) of unequal size in the only complete barrack (East Barrack 1). Slight traces of painted wall plaster indicate that Rooms A and C, at least, were decorated internally.

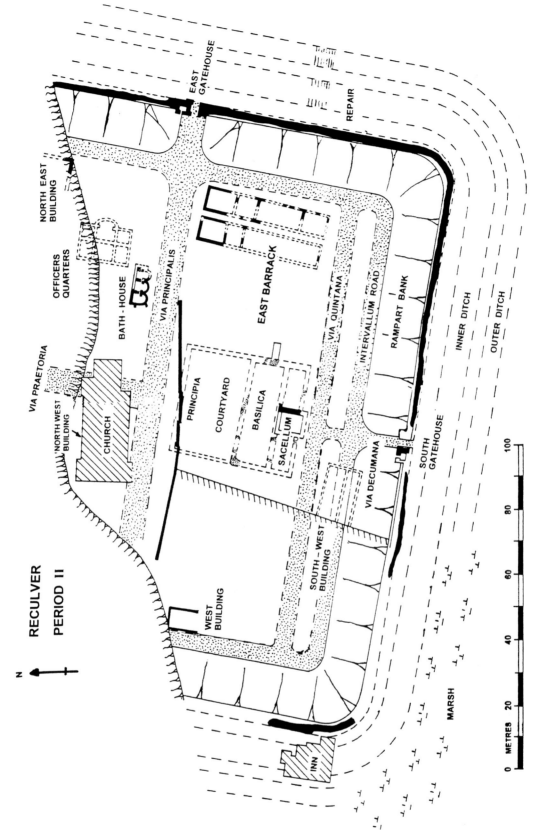

Fig. 71.　*Reculver 1959–69. Plan of Roman Stone Fort (Period II).*

Three of the other buildings are also likely to have been barracks, notably the West Building which to some extent resembles those on the east side. Similarly, the North East Building and the North West Building are by their locations also likely to have been barracks. The more certain South West Building is unusually wide, but seems to have been extended and thus may not have been a standard barracks. It had at least some painted walls, so is likely to have been domestic. No certain evidence for a building was found in the South East Area, but this could have contained a variety of minor structures, such as ovens, workshops or storehouses.

(3) The Reconstructed Plan (Fig. 72)

In overall spatial terms, the layout of the Period II fort, was predictably predetermined by the Period I arrangements. The central division of the fort, still framed by the *Via Quintana* and *Via Principalis* remained at 150 ft. It contained the *principia* and at least one pair of barracks. This left wide spaces on each side of the *principia* for other major buildings. These could have included the all important pair of granaries, as shown on the plan.

The rear division of the fort (nominally the *Retentura*) remained at a rather narrow 44 ft., framed by the *Via Quintana* and the *Intervallum* Road on the south side. This was itself sub-divided by the *Via Decumana* found in 1960 (p. 49), running from the rear of the *principia* to the South Gatehouse. This division included the South West Building, containing traces of painted wall-plaster and thus at least partly domestic. The South East Area, still shown open, could have contained a variety of minor structures such as workshops and stores.

There can be no doubt that the front division of the fort was still sub-divided by a major north-south road, the *Via Praetoria* leading from the front of the *Principia* to the main north gate of the fort (p. 38) in a manner employed in most earlier forts. This area north of the central *Via Principalis* (nominally the *Praetentura*) was clearly also sub-divided by an east-west road, leaving roughly 95 ft. on its south side and 108 ft. on its north side. The southern half was certainly occupied by a six-roomed Bath House (p. 54) and another large hypocausted building, regarded here as the Officers Quarters. Both these buildings necessarily had strong masonry walls, bonded with mortar in contrast to the clay bonding of the barracks. They sat at right angles to each other and could have flanked two sides of a wide courtyard, just possibly with a third building on the west side. The small Bath House, reminiscent of late-Roman military Bath Houses at the nearby forts of Richborough (Ref. 41) and Lympne (Ref. 42), seems too small for a large garrison and may have been provided for the officers alone.

The two certain barracks (EB1 and EB2) could not have stood alone and a total of five pairs of barracks seems both likely and reasonable. The available space would allow for another pair in the Central Division (here shown as E3 and E4) though it is possible that these could alternatively have been placed west of the *principia*. The North East Building (NE1), of which only two walls survive, was clearly flanked by the east-west road north of the Bath House complex. This only leaves about 108 ft. between this road and the north *Intervallum* Road and this is too short for the known length of the barrack blocks. If it was part of a barrack, as seems very likely, then the available space only allows it to have been on an east-west axis, but it does allow for the inclusion of a matching barrack (NE2). A corresponding pair (NW3 and NW4) also fit comfortably into the totally destroyed north-west corner of the fort. This then leaves the single wall found in the small trial-trench inside the Saxon church. It could again have formed one of another pair (NW1 and NW2), though this is again somewhat speculative. This reconstruction allows for a total of ten possible barracks, all arranged in pairs and well spaced around the fort.

The arrangement of rooms in the only complete barrack (East Barrack No.1) shows only four rooms, with Room C appearing nearly twice the size of the other three. If this room had been equally divided, then the building originally had five rooms of roughly equal size, say 22–29 ft. If valid, then each pair of barracks had ten rooms and thus ten barracks about 50 rooms. This could

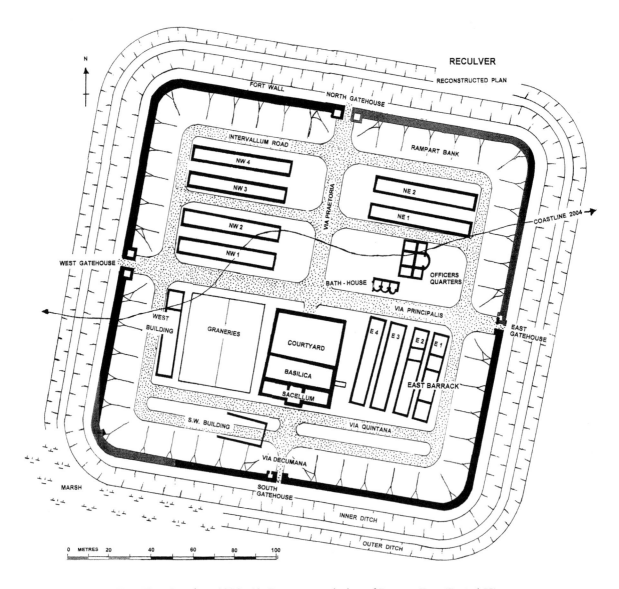

Fig. 72.   *Reculver 1959–69. Reconstructed plan of Roman Fort (Period II).*

have been sufficient for a garrison of a full infantry cohort of about 500 men, though the rooms vary significantly from the standard *contubernia* of the 2nd century.

What is of interest, though not necessarily highly significant, is the fact that the two East Barracks (Nos. 1 and 2), were not laid out parallel to the fort wall. The northern end of Barrack 1 was 73 ft. from the fort wall, whilst its southern end was about 81 ft., a variation of 8 ft. in a length of 130 ft. This swung the central axis about four degrees east from the overall Period I alignment. The corresponding structure on the west side of the fort (West Building) seems to have been laid out parallel to the fort wall, though this time only 65 ft. from it. The certain structure in the rear-division of the fort (the South West Building) was also laid out at an angle to the south wall of the fort. Its precise angle is difficult to gauge from the short sections of wall found, but again this seems to have been in the order of four degrees. Clearly, precision layouts were not important to the Period II garrison, but it is also possible that the fort wall was by then obscured by vegetation, or small trees, growing on the Rampart Bank.

(4) The Repair To The Fort Wall (p. 15)

It seems likely, at least on circumstantial grounds, that the repair to the east wall of the fort also relates to Period II. A cut about 12 ft. wide seems to have been made in the original (Period I) fort wall, which was then blocked off by a much narrower mortared wall and a large oven built in the recess so created. It is far from clear why the wall was breached, though several possibilities need to be considered. One is that an attempt was made here to attach an external bastion, exactly as at Burgh Castle (Ref. 43). No trace of this was found at Reculver and clearly the gap was later plugged and no bastion added. It is just possible that an access point was needed here, though just how this was achieved and why it should be needed is not clear. This feature remains a problem. Of some slight relevance is the evidence from the section across the fort's two ditches (p. 24) just 30 ft. north of the repair. This revealed two thick bands of clay dumped across the upper filling of both ditches. These must represent a deliberate attempt to infill the ditches here which, with post-Roman slumping taken into account, might have largely levelled them off. This seems an highly unusual operation and it is just possible that it relates to the equally unlikely (and adjacent) repair in some way. Such levelling is unlikely to have been carried out over the full circuit due to the scale of the work required and the impact on the external defences. Certainly no such dumped clay was detected in 1958 in the inner ditch near the south-west corner of the fort.

(6) THE ROMAN FORT – PERIOD III

The evidence for Roman structures after Period II is very slender indeed. It is certain that the East Barrack (No. 1) was partially burnt down and had collapsed by about A.D. 300 and was never rebuilt. It is also clear that a set of 12 substantial stone-packed post-holes had been cut through the deposits sealing it and also its twin barrack (No. 2) alongside. This is taken to be evidence of a late-Roman timber structure, but this remains inconclusive.

Perhaps of greater significance is the collection of 4th century coins and pottery which show occupation on some scale at least until about A.D. 370. If the collapse of the barracks was general, then some subsequent phase, with related structures, is very likely.

(7) THE BUILDING MATERIALS

(1) The Main Structures

Due to lack of resources no attempt has been made to provide a detailed study of the building materials recovered during the excavation. Considering the large size and number of internal buildings and structures, comparatively little building debris was recovered and clearly post-

Roman robbing must have been very extensive. The most conspicuous evidence is the largely ruined church of St. Mary's which seems to have been built almost completely from demolished Roman structures. In addition, many other buildings that had once formed part of the medieval settlement are likely to have used material from the fort. It may also have been used as a quarry for more distant buildings such as at the Archbishop's Palace at Ford, some two miles away and certainly for the church at Birchington in 1584 as the church-wardens accounts so clearly show (Ref. 44).

It is, however, useful to consider the materials used on the fort's construction. A pioneer survey of the materials used in most of the Roman shore-forts, was completed in 2002 and the actual quantities estimated (Ref. 45). This provides helpful confirmation for Reculver. The fort wall was largely constructed of courses of rolled flints set in a hard cream-white mortar, containing small grits. A small amount of Kentish Ragstone and Thanet Sandstone was incorporated within the core as well as occasional septaria nodules.

The external face largely consisted of neat ashlar blocks of grey Kentish Ragstone, varying between 4 – 8 in. x 4 – 6 in.(10–20 cm x 9–16cm.), to judge by the 60 or so that survive in small patches along the east wall. The internal faces were mostly constructed of large rolled flints with occasional ragstone. No tiles were incorporated in the fort walls, which still survive to a maximum height of 8 ft. 6in., though several tiles were built into the guard-chambers of the South and East Gatehouses.

The flint used in the fort wall was mostly large and water-rolled and is very likely to have come from storm-beaches below cliffs consisting of Upper Chalk. The nearest lie to the east on Thanet (3–12 miles), but considering the very large quantities involved the flint may have been collected from a much wider area, including from the White Cliffs of Dover. The ragstone came from the Hythe Beds, most likely from the Maidstone area, perhaps even from Boughton Monchelsea where very large and ancient quarries exist. The *septaria* probably came from the Isle of Sheppey (12 miles) and the Thanet Sandstone from the base of the cliffs immediately west of the fort.

With the walls of the fort totalling a length of about 760 yards, an average thickness of (say) 3 yards and an estimated height of (say) 5 yards, a volume of about 11,400 cu. yards is obtained. To this must be added the four large gatehouses, broadly an addition of 800 cu. yards, and a parapet perhaps another 400 cu. yds. In addition, the underlying foundation for the fort wall was at least 3 yards wide and consisted of small well-rounded pebbles, probably collected from the foreshore or storm-beaches such as exist today near Pegwell Bay. Whilst it was difficult to excavate beneath the fort wall, the exposed sections suggest a depth of only about 1 ft. and not 3 ft. as guessed in the 2002 study. These suggest that another 760 cu. yds. of material were needed for the foundations alone. A grand total of about 13,500 cu. yards for the fort wall and gatehouses results and this is likely to have weighed in the region of about 15,000 tons. This agrees, in broad terms, with the study of 2002. Of this total very roughly 65% was flint or pebble, 20% a lime-based mortar, 10% ragstone and 5% other materials. The chalk for the mortar would have been obtained from quarries, which still abound in Kent today, with again Thanet being the most likely source.

All these large quantities of rock had to be collected or quarried, loaded up, transported, offloaded, stacked and then used in construction. With these quantities, mostly from coastal or riverine sources, it is very likely that most of the raw materials would have been moved by ship. Here the *Classis Britannica*, already present in force in the Channel area is most likely to have taken a major role in the transportation of materials using its transport ships. With a nominal load of 50 tons per ship (estimates mostly vary from 50–100 tons) the total volume involved would have required about 300 ship-loads. Allowing for loading, sailing and offloading, perhaps 2–5 shiploads a day might be manageable. Given some bad weather, tidal considerations and several other limiting and logistic factors, many of which can only be guessed at this point in time, the whole operation could have been completed comfortably within one year.

To these quantities must now be added the materials used in the construction of the fort's internal buildings. This is very difficult to quantify as the Period I structures were never fully completed. Even so the *principia* might have needed another 1,000 tons, the Bath House another 100 tons and the Officers Quarters another 200 tons. The barracks might have needed another 200 tons each, which this time would have included a strong wooden frame infilled with daub and again on pebble foundations. Some ten barracks might thus require another 2,000 tons of materials. To this must be added the materials for minor structures, gravel roads throughout the fort and one or two larger buildings not found, hence perhaps another 1,000–2,000 tons. Whilst all these quantities are highly speculative, a grand total of (say) 4,000–6,000 tons for the internal buildings and roads might have been required.

Whatever the precise totals, the labour involved in collecting, quarrying, loading, shipping, offloading, stacking, mixing mortar, scaffolding and finally building, would have been very considerable. Allowing for the *Classis Britannica* to have provided the transport ships and sailors, the rest of the task is likely to have been carried out by the men forming the cohort building the fort. Here, about 500 men would have been available, conveniently divided up into six centuries of about 80 men each. Of these it seems likely that one century (perhaps in revolving order) would have been responsible for the daily domestic routines, whilst the others worked on the fort building programme. Each could have been allocated specific duties, such as quarrying and collecting; loading and unloading; carrying and stacking materials across the site; excavating foundation-trenches and external ditches and finally the building work itself.

The fort wall does not appear to have been built in obvious sections as at Richborough, but rather as a linear process between the Gatehouses. The mortared flint courses appear to be about 10 in. thick and to have been laid neatly between the facing stones, already in position, perhaps several days later. In this way a good working team of 80 men, properly supplied, could perhaps have completed 200 ft. of a linear course in a single day. With a height of 15 ft., consisting of about 20 courses and a circuit of 760 yds., a total of about 240 working days would be needed. Allowing for bad weather, delays with materials, the ever increasing height of the fort wall, the gatehouses and parapet, it still seems likely that the fort defences could have been built in no more than 1–2 years! To this must then be added the internal buildings, roads, the complete excavation of the fort ditches and the formation of the Rampart Bank. Even so, the whole process could have been completed within (say) 2–5 years. Whilst these calculations contain many imponderables the exercise is still worthwhile and to a small extent reflects the major building programme, managed throughout by the author, on the two-storey, large cover–building over the Painted House at Dover in 1976–7 (Ref. 46).

The excavations generally did not produce large amounts of building debris and this mostly took the form of random sandstone blocks and tile fragments. Many of the latter were *tegulae* and *imbrices*. Most of the debris was reburied at the end of the each excavation, though some 30 boxes are now stored at Dover Castle. Two areas that did produce substantial rubble and broken tiles were the *sacellum* in 1960 and the Bath House in 1965. All the tiles are of a sandy fabrics and none of the distinctive CL.BR. type. Clearly, some or all of the buildings inside the fort had tiled roofs. The few complete bricks are 15 x 10 in. Broken voussoir fragments were recovered from the Bath House area and the *sacellum* (Fig. 69, Nos. 475–9). Fragments of large bridging tiles were also recovered from the Bath House, but the only complete one was found set in the floor (Pit 25) of the East Barrack No. 1 (p. 75), which measured 22 x 22 x 2½ in.. Another, of similar size, can be seen in the north wall of the Saxon church where it joins the north tower.

(2) The Internal Construction

The evidence suggests that the *principia* and the Earlier West Building (both Period I), Bath House and Officers Quarters (both Period II), were the only structures so far known within the fort to have mortared masonry walls. The former was anyway the major structure of the complex, whilst the last two both had hypocausts with major heating elements. Otherwise, it seems that all the other buildings were constructed with timber-frames resting on clay-bonded sandstone sleeper walls. Timber must have been a major building element inside all these buildings, but due to decomposition very little evidence has survived.

A small amount of window-glass, mostly found in rubbish deposits, suggests that glazed windows did exist in at least some of the buildings (p. 189). The largest fragments were barely 2–3 in. (50–75 mm.) in length, whilst the colour is mostly pale green. A dozen show bevelled edges where the glass fitted into frames, whilst they ranged in thickness from 2 to 5 mm. The majority is matt on one side, some polished on both sides and some matt on both sides. None is really clear, the majority being just translucent.

The excavations recovered 1,708 fragments of wall-plaster (p. 183), the great majority from just four buildings and from a dump on the tail of the Rampart Bank close to the East Gatehouse. Only one small strip was found *in situ* in Room C of East Barrack No.1, where red had been painted at floor-level. The rest was found broken and scattered inside the fort structures and must represent very much larger areas originally plastered and painted.

The 392 fragments found in the ruined strongroom and *sacellum* of the *principia* show linear pattern, probably vertical panels, in white, green and yellow with borders of black, white, maroon and red. These suggest the form of internal decoration in this part of the building. The 98 fragments found in Room A at the North end of the East Barrack No.1 suggest decoration including white, red, blue and green. Trace of a possible dado of white with flecks of red, maroon and yellow was also found. The 52 fragments found in Room A and B of the Officers Quarters suggests linear patterns perhaps green, red or pink with bands of white, black or brown.

The 548 fragments found in the ruins of the Bath House form a distinct and separate group. This mainly consists of a thin layer of white plaster on thick, coarse *opus signinum* painted in black and orange-yellow. Of special interest are the fragments showing a second and sometimes a third layer of *opus signinum,* clearly indicating successive schemes of redecoration. The patterns are mostly unclear, but the second layer of fine *opus signinum* had been painted white and this decorated with double medallions, in red, enclosing possible floral motifs, also in red. A third layer of white-pink *opus signinum* had also been applied, following chisel keying, painted red, white and orange.

It seems clear from this evidence that at least four of the internal buildings were brightly decorated with painted designs. Indeed, it seems likely that most of the other buildings were also decorated, though the surviving evidence is very limited. Indeed, it seems likely that over 95% of the original plaster has now gone, either through early decay or later robbing. Small amounts of painted wall plaster were recovered from the Roman forts at Portchester (Ref. 51), Caister-on-Sea (Ref. 53) and Burgh Castle (Ref. 43).

(8) THE DATING EVIDENCE

The dating evidence for the site is generally good. The pottery from the prehistoric settlement at the north-east corner is sufficiently diagnostic to provide a date covering the late-Bronze and Early Iron Ages. Similarly, the 200 potsherds from the mid-1st century Fortlet ditches form a distinctive group, with its combed cooking pots, storage jars and platters. Taken with the "coins of Tiberius and Nero as being fresh and unworn", one or two Republican denarii and at least six British coins found in earlier centuries, these suggest a more extensive early-Roman site, largely in the area lost to the sea. The late-1st century material is limited, though the samian ware appears disproportionately more abundant than the coarse pottery.

The material from the Roman stone fort forms a considerable collection and can be studied under various headings. These include coins, mortaria, samian, inscriptions and stratified material (1–5).

(1) The Coins

A total of 816 coins is now recorded from the site since 1952, 67 from the 1952–8 excavations and the beach, 626 from the formal 1959–69 excavations and 123 unstratified from the general area. These are listed below and also compared with coins from four of the other shore-forts. Richard Reece has kindly examined all the coins from the 1959–69 excavations and unstratified sources from Reculver and his report appears in Chapter VI (p. 103).

The coins recovered must mostly reflect coin-loss across the sites and this cannot have been constant throughout several periods, nor even at a single location within a fort. In addition, some fortuitous circumstances may apply. The extent and depth of excavations often varied and the numbers and values of coinage in circulation must also have varied at different times. So, too, might variable inflation be reflected in the loss of coins, perhaps even due to size and value. In addition, there is always the slight risk of disturbed hoards being included in any total.

At Reculver the 1st century is largely un-represented, whilst the first half of the 2nd century shows a steady trickle. It is towards the end of the 2nd century that the numbers increase and the first half of the 3rd century is well represented. Very clearly the site was garrisoned during this period and here the Reculver list significantly matches the forts at Brancaster and Caister-on-Sea (both Period I). At the same time it so clearly contrasts with other Roman shore-forts such as Portchester (Ref. 51) and Lympne (Ref. 52), both accepted to be of later construction (Period II).

The dates given are anyway simply those when the coins were minted and it seems unlikely that most freshly minted coins reached the site promptly and were lost equally promptly. It seems highly probable that most coins in circulation were several, or many, years old when lost. These are the ones that must form the great majority of those recovered. There has been an ongoing debate about how long Roman coins were in circulation. One significant site is the battle-field in the Teutoburg Forest , where three Roman legions under Varus were wiped out by Germanic tribes in a two-day battle (Ref. 54) in A.D. 9. There, nearly 1400 coins have been found and listed and of the 550 low-value bronze coins, the everyday small change used by the soldiers, some 93% were between 12–17 years old when lost on the battle-field. The very few latest coins had been minted about A.D. 7, whilst the gold and silver coins tailed back 8–30 years. Indeed, but for the battle many of these coins would have remained in circulation for several more years. In addition, the Roman fort at Portchester, constructed under Carausius (A.D. 286–93) had no earlier settlement on the site. Yet it produced 56 coins (9%) minted in A.D. 259–86 and of these 22 were at least 20–30 years old when lost. Indeed, the published report (Ref. 51) readily accepted that "worn earlier radiates enter the site with the new coins of Carausius".

At Reculver, of the bronze coins of Marcus Aurelius (minted A.D. 161–80), the majority are mostly likely to have been lost about 165-onwards, whilst the bronze of Commodus (A.D. 180–92) are more likely to have been lost about 185-onwards. Similarly, the coins (including silver denarii) of Septimius Severus (A.D. 193–211) and Severus Alexander (A.D. 222–35) are likely to reflect losses some years later. As Richard Reece has confirmed, the coin losses at Reculver (on their own merits) favour activity inside the fort no later than the end of the 2nd century! What could also be significant is the absence of coins of Commodus at Maryport (out of 137), perhaps suggesting the absence of a garrison following its removal to Reculver, though coins of Commodus are less common.

The coins of the late-3rd century are much more numerous, as at other shore-fort sites, as are the coins of the first half of the 4th century. However, at Reculver the numbers of the late-third

Period	Date	Reculver 1952–58	Reculver 1959–70	Totals	Bran.	Caister	Lympne	Port.
I	–41	–	–	–	1	–	–	–
II (A)	41–54	–	–	–	1	–	–	1
II (B)	54–69	–	1	1	–	–	–	–
III	69–96	1	1	2	2	1	–	–
IV	96–117	1	1	2	4	–	–	–
V	117–138	3	5	8	8	3	–	–
VI	138– 61	4	5	9	6	2	1	–
VII (A)	161–180	6	7	13	9	26	–	–
VII (B)	180–193	1	8	9	4	–	–	–
VIII	193–222	9	12	21	29	22	–	–
IX (A)	222–238	2	16	18	12	11	–	–
IX (B)	238–259	4	14	18	6	11	–	–
X	259–275	11	194	205	76	157	22	43
XI	275–294	2	162	164	90	178	53	69
XII	294–317	5	11	16	44	52	10	75
XIII (A)	317–330	–	25	25	102	55	10	67
XIII (B)	330–348	3	68	71	253	256	54	188
XIV	348–364	2	32	34	31	51	1	31
XV (A)	364–378	2	17	19	32	41	2	78
XV (B)	378–388	–	3	3	14	2	–	5
XVI	388–402	–	3	3	1	2	–	14
	Sub-totals	**56**	**585**	**641**	**725**	**870**	**153**	**571**
Illeg.		**8**	**136**	**144**	**39**	**97**	**108**	**32**
Post-Roman		**3**	**28**	**31**	**–**	**9**	**–**	**–**
Final total		**67**	**749**	**816**	**764**	**976**	**261**	**603**

Table X.   Coins from Reculver (1952–70), Brancaster (Bran.), Caister-on-Sea, Lympne and Portchester (Port.)

century are disproportionately high against the 4th century coin losses noted at other sites. In addition, the very low coin losses at Reculver after those minted about A.D. 370 is significant and strongly suggests the absence of a garrison after that time.

(2) The Mortaria

About 150 sherds of mortaria were recovered during the excavation and these were sent to Mrs. K. Hartley for examination and comment. Her detailed report is included in Chapter VI. Of the sherds sent, about 90 rim sections have been classified by type (Types 1–32), of which 22 have been illustrated (Nos. 174–95). The remainder were wall sherds.

The whole collection has also been classified by fabric, of which 14 types have been identified. Two fabrics (F1 and 2) are from kilns at either Canterbury or Colchester and date from about A.D. 160–210. Three more (F3–5) are from either mid or East Kent and date from about A.D. 180–300. One fabric is from Northern France (F6) 1st–2nd century and another from the Rhineland (F7) A.D. 140–250. Two more (F8 and F9) are from Warwickshire A.D. 250–350 and the Lower Nene A.D. 230–400, respectively. Predictably, four more (F10–13) are from the Oxforshire region A.D. 240–400 and another (F14) is unknown and not dated. In terms of rims, 47 vessels (53%) were from the Oxfordshire kilns; 18 (21%) from east or mid-Kent; 10 (11%) from the Lower Nene; 5 (6%) from Canterbury/Colchester; 4 (5%) from the Rhineland; 2 (2%) each from Warwickshire and Northern France.

(3) The Samian Ware

A total of 673 sherds (13.60 kg.) of samian ware was recovered from the 1959–69 excavations and these have been examined by Joanna Bird. The total includes 16 stamps and these have been examined by Brenda Dickinson. The full reports of both of these studies are included in Chapter VI.

Even though the excavation only covered about 8% of the surviving area of the fort (or about 4% of the original enclosed area) the samian collection is unimpressive and is generally very fragmentary and worn. It contrasts with other large Roman sites, mostly civil, particularly those which developed in the 1st and 2nd centuries A.D. Only 25 vessels are illustrated (Nos. 206–30), including stamps.

Of the 673 sherds found, 116 clearly match or join other sherds and this reduces the total to about 550. This represents the maximum possible number of vessels, but many of the smaller plain sherds may join other vessels. The 14 separate excavations were, however, widely spaced across the site and this must reduce the likely number of matching sherds. Even so, a very broad estimate of say 250–400 vessels may be represented and this clearly suggests a large number of missing stamps. Of these possible vessels, 42 were decorated and the rest plain. For discussion purposes the sherds are listed under simplified date-ranges (Table Y), on the assumption that the adjusted sherd-count largely reflects the vessels represented. Hopefully, the percentages produced should act as a broad guide.

The single sherd of Tiberian-Claudian date fits well with the mid-1st century Fortlet and was found in 1962 (L.45). The Nero-Flavian samian, another 53 sherds (7%) in all, represent something of a problem, for apart from a single isolated pit, no other features of this date were located. Nor was there much corresponding coarse pottery, which would normally occur in greater quantities. Seven of the sherds came from the upper silts in the mid-1st century ditches, four from the isolated pit and the rest from the stone-fort levels and are clearly derived from earlier deposits. This early samian may represent a site now largely lost to the sea, or just possibly a small one removed by the likely Roman terracing and post-Roman ground reduction across the centre of the fort, by which time the Fortlet ditches were completely silted.

Even so, it has to be noted that a significant amount of Flavian samian was also found in the *Classis Britannica* forts at Dover (Ref. 55) where the main fort was not constructed until about A.D. 130. There, the Flavian samian was mainly found in association with coarse pottery and coins of Periods I–III (A.D. 130–208). Apart from a single ditch, no pre-fort structures or features were found. The 27 sherds (4%) of Hadrian/early-Antonine at Reculver are again somewhat premature across a site occupied from the late-2nd century, onwards. Again a focus for this could have been in the area now lost to the sea, but it seems more likely that it either represents pottery stocks held in warehouses, or else carefully retained in use, over many decades.

The much larger group of late-2nd to early-3rd century and later samian appears largely appropriate for a site principally occupied from the late-2nd century. The 333 sherds (51%) from

Period	Date A.D	Sherds	Percentages
Tiberian – Claudian	30–54	1	–
Neronian	54–68	6	1
Pre Flavian – Early Flavian	60–80	23	3
Flavian	70–95	24	3
Hadrian – Early Antonine	120–150	27	4
Antonine	140–180	123	18
Late 2nd – Early 3rd Century	175– 225	158	24
First half of the 3rd Century	200–250	175	27
Late 2nd Century – 4th Century (Argonne)	180–350	29	4
4th Century (Argonne)	300–400	17	3
Undated	–	90	13
Total		**673**	**100**

Table Y. Simplified dating of samian sherds.

these dates were found throughout the stone-fort levels, directly associated with corresponding coarse wares and also coins. The latest samian is mostly Argonne Ware (64 sherds in total) and this largely relates to the later occupation at Reculver.

The problem of earlier samian occurring on later-dated sites may need further consideration. In the shore-forts not only does this problem appear at Reculver and Dover, but it also appeared at Portchester (Ref. 51 p.276). There, the fort constructed under Carausius (A.D. 286–293), produced sherds from 22 samian vessels all of 2nd century date. The conclusion (in 1975), was that these vessels (mostly at least 100 years old) "represent old pottery brought to the site by the first occupants, possibly as treasured heirlooms or antiques".

In view of the information from these three sites it may be that some samian was stored, or remained in circulation, much longer than may reasonably be supposed. If so, this could have interesting implications for the evidence from samian ware across many sites. Significantly, the problem does not (now) appear at the shore-forts at Brancaster and Caister-on-Sea. At Brancaster the 501 sherds (13kg.), including 34 decorated and 16 stamped vessels, date from A.D.170 onwards and are thus largely appropriate for a site which can now be seen to date (as at Reculver) from the late-2nd century. At Caister-on-Sea the 1525 sherds (over 26kg.), including at least 27 decorated and 26 stamped vessels, are very largely dated to the late-Antonine period and later. This again accords well with a fort construction date in the late-2nd century and onward occupation, even though the samian came from the area of the obvious extra-mural settlement.

(4) Inscriptions

Parts of four monumental stone inscriptions were found on the site, but only one (p. 211) is of help as regards the critical dating evidence. Of the others, one (No. 442) has the poorly-cut letters PIA and was found above the *Via Quintana* in 1960 in a late-3rd century rubbish deposit. Clearly, this inscription had already been broken by then, and is thus likely to relate to Period I. Similarly, another fragment (No. 441) with a well-cut initial letter T was found at the East Gatehouse. This is likely to have been an inscription over the actual gate, much like that from the Roman fort at Carpow (Ref. 58). If so, then it too is likely to relate to Period I. Two more fragments (Nos. 443–4) were found in 1960 in the *sacellum* of the *principia* with mid-4th century coins. These displayed the well-cut letters V and NCI, and seem to have come from a large inscription, perhaps from the *sacellum* itself.

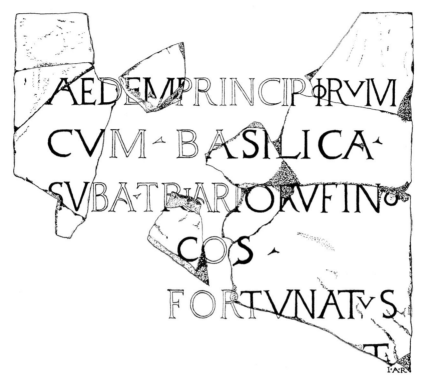

Fig. 73.   *The* Sacellum *Inscription (1/3).*

It is, however, the fourth inscription (Fig. 73) that is by far the most important. This was also found in the primary soil in the robbed *sacellum* in 1960 and eleven fragments reveal parts of at least 44 well-cut letters. This is the now-famous *sacellum* inscription and about 60% complete. It was cut on a slab of grey calcareous sandstone taken from the nearby Oldhaven Beds. Its front appears to have been ground, or polished, to create a smooth surface, whilst the back seems untreated. In section, it reveals at least three bedding-planes some of which have shredded due to the fissile nature of the stone. Originally, it appears to have been about 30 mm. in thickness. The sides and top seem to have been squared off, with tooling marks clear on the left side and a small bevel on the right side. There is no trace of mortar on the stone and it seems likely that the tablet was held in a frame. There are faint, but clear marking-out lines visible, including two vertical ones marking the intended side limits, which indicate that the original intention was to have margins about 32 mm. wide on each side. The space at the top was much larger at 52 mm. A series of faint horizontal lines marks out most of the tops and bottoms of the lines. These indicate that all the lines and interline spaces were meant to be about equal, at 22–23 mm.

It was between these lines that the letters were cut. These had been finely carved and there are slight but clear traces of red, or vermillion, paint inside several letters. The finished effect would have been a bright red inscription on a light grey ground. Parts of six lines survive, but in spite of the careful marking out it was clearly difficult for the stone-mason to fit in all the letters. The left-hand guide-line had to be ignored and a new position selected just 26 mm. from the edge, which the only surviving first three lines clearly indicate. Similarly, the right-hand line had to be over-ridden by single letters in lines 1, 3, 5 and 6. In addition, a ligature was needed in line 1(I and O) and also a small V. A small O was needed to end line 3 and a small V near the end of line 5. These changes created a new right-hand border just 14 mm. from the edge. Hence the finished inscribed area was off-centre of the tablet by about 12 mm. This is crucial to the identification of the missing letters for it helps to determine the correct overall width and thus the length of all the lines. The main control is provided by line 4, where the letters COS must have been centrally placed. The centre of the O to the surviving right- hand side is 167 mm. and thus the total width was 334 mm. However, with the text being off-centre of the actual tablet by some 12 mm. to the right the overall width is increased to 346 mm. with the lettering occupying about 306 mm. if the COS was centred on the lettering! Whilst either arrangement is possible, basic symmetry favours the latter.

The fragments were delivered to Professor Sir Ian Richmond of All Souls College, Oxford and his reconstruction of the text was published in 1961 in the Antiquaries Journal (Ref. 47) and is illustrated here (Fig. 73). He identified it as recording the construction of the shrine (*aedem*), of the headquarters (*principiorum*), cross-hall (*basilica*), under (*sub*) a consular governor (*cos*) whose cognomen was certainly Rufinus and with the work being carried out by the fort commander, one Fortunatus. In detail, Professor Richmond added:-

"The first line mentions *aedem*, followed by a masculine or neuter genitive plural of the second declension. The second contained the works *cu[m.b] asilica*, rather generously spaced, and giving the length of the line and thus a width to the stone of approximately 13 in. The third line is occupied by the preposition *su[b]*, followed by an official's names, of which *Rufino* is an intact *cognomen*, preceded by a rather short *nomen* ending in IO and containing an R towards its beginning. The title of this official is given by the word *co[n]s[ulare]*, 'consular governor', which occupies the middle of the fourth line and thus, by providing an axis, affords a second criterion for the width of the fragmentary stone, consonant with the first. The fifth line contains the *cognomen* *[For]tunatus*, while the sixth line ends with the letter . . . T, probably the final letter of a third person singular suffix belonging to a verb in the perfect tense, in a clause of which Fortunatus was the subject" . . . .

"Epigraphically, its importance lies in the fact that this is the first time the inscribed phrase *aedes principiorum* can be applied to and identified with the official shrine of the headquarters building, hitherto unmentioned in any inscription. It is also the first certain instance of the application of the name *basilica* to a military cross-hall, although the resemblance between these buildings and a civil *basilica* has often been stressed"

He added that the inscription could not have stood alone, for the obligatory imperial names and titles are missing and would thus have been on a corresponding tablet. He suggested that, as at several other named Roman sites, the two tablets would have been mounted on the narrow door-jambs, or piers, flanking the open front of the *sacellum* (shrine). He went on to examine the available space before the Rufinus cognomen and also the consular lists. From this he deduced that the best candidate was Aulus Triarius Rufinus, consul in A.D. 210 and thus governor of Britain in A.D. 210–16.

Subsequently, Mr R.P. Harper of the University of Durham, undertook a detailed study of the fragments and published his thoughts in 1964 (Ref. 48), but predictably failed to mention either the excavation or those who made the inscription available. Whilst not challenging the significance or meaning of the text, he contradicted Professor Richmond. He deleted Triarius and inserted one Q Aradius Rufinus, who is likely to have been governor of Britain after A.D. 225. It seems appropriate, if only on geographical grounds, that Kent should be the arbiter between Oxford and Durham, particularly after a pause of only 40 years.

Harper contradicted Richmond on three grounds. First, it was unusual for a consul *ordinarius* to be appointed as a governor of a military province. Unusual, but presumably not impossible, which weakens the point. Second, there was not enough space for three letters on either side of the floating R (in line 3). He then deleted the *praenomen* A, although there is ample room, on the grounds that this was optional in the third century. If correct, then there is an even chance that the A was included, which greatly weakens this argument. What must now be significant, as shown above, is that the text was off-centre of the tablet by some 12 mm. If the COS was centred on the text, rather than on the sides of the tablet, then another 12 mm is available on the left side of the Richmond reconstruction. This provides extra space for the *praenomen* A. However, the problem of the IAR remains and can be resolved by the creation of a small letter I, as Richmond suggests. Third, Harper states that Richmond's claim "that the name of Rufinus was not very common", was not true! True, or not, it alone cannot invalidate the Triarius claim. That said, much still hinges on the centring of the inscription.

In 1977, J.C.Mann added a note on the inscription (Ref. 82). In this he also challenged Richmond, claiming that the greater likelihood was that our Rufinus would have been a suffect consul. He offers any date in the 3rd century after the reign of Severus, but then admits our Rufinus could also have served in the late-2nd century. In 1981, A. R. Birley (Ref. 88) joined the debate and offered other possible candidates, but finally concluded that a wide range of dates was possible.

Whilst the measurements, given above, could be regarded as a complication two more considerations may be equally helpful. The first is that the central floating fragment, displaying the R and CO, could alternatively have formed part of lines 5 and 6. The R could have been part of the Fortunatus line, perhaps even the *nomen*, whilst the CO could just be part of COH in a not impossible position in line 6. Second, the verb (identified by others) at the end of line 6 and ending in T, could refer to either construction, dedication, or even re-construction. All this considered, Triarius and Aradius are no better candidates than several other Rufini, most likely in the period A.D. 185–240.

The inscription clearly relates to work on the *principia*, but the evidence in the ground shows that some of the original internal buildings were never completed as planned and that some were replaced by buildings of very different form. This major discontinuity shows that the Period I scheme was never completed and strongly suggests a hiatus in the occupation of the site. This in turn implies the withdrawal of the garrison. On its return a substantially new arrangement was adopted. Whilst it is possible that the inscription relates to Period I, it is equally likely that it commemorates the completion of the fort and *principia* during Period II. There is only one way to resolve this long-standing dilemma. That is to locate the missing fragments of the inscription, but clearly only someone with a detailed knowledge of the site will know where to look.

(5) The Stratified Material From The Site

Finally, it is important to consider the stratified dating evidence from the site itself, which includes well over 100 coins. At least thirteen areas (**a–m**) are of special interest.

(a) **The East Cliff Site 1957 and 1965–6** (p. 64)
Here, three coins are important. One (No. 66–8) of Marcus Aurelius (A.D. 150–60) was found with domestic rubbish sealed within the Rampart Bank. Another (1957–2) of Elagabulus (A.D. 218–22), was found with domestic rubbish thrown down over the tail of the Bank. The third (1957–1) of Commodus (A.D. 180–92) was found in the foundation-trench of the North East Building.

(b) **East Gate Site, 1967** (p. 25)
Here a coin (No. 67–23) of Commodus (A.D. 180–92) was found on the pre-fort land-surface and sealed by at least 5 ft. of dumped clay forming the Rampart Bank. This was almost certainly dropped when the fort was under construction, which accordingly could not have taken place before A.D. 180. Allowing for at least a short time in circulation, it seems

likely that this coin was probably dropped some years later. Its condition is not helpful. In addition, three more coins came from a large pit (F.3) dug into the top of the Rampart Bank. These were one (No. 67–52) of Severus Alexander (A.D. 222–35), a radiate (No. 67–49) of A.D. 270–90 and one (No. 67–48) of Allectus (A.D. 293–6).

(c) *Via Quintana* Site, 1959 (p. 15)

Here the Rampart Bank, again consisting of deep layers of dumped clay, contained two potsherds of special interest, both found in a layer of mussel shells inside the bank and thrown down by the builders of the fort. One was part of a decorated beaker (No. 176) of fine red ware, with a black metallic slip and often described as Rhenish ware. Such fine ware is regarded as a product of the late-2nd century. With it was a mortarium (No. 184) of a type produced in either Kent or Essex, between A.D. 170–210. It is likely that the rest of these vessels remain nearby.

(d) The South-West Building 1963 (p. 51)

A single coin (No. 63–13) of Hadrian (A.D. 134–8) was found in the east wall of this building.

(e) The Rear Division 1963 (p. 49)

Four dated coins were found in association with the *Via Decumana*. One (No. 63–27) of Antoninus Pius (A.D. 138–61) was found sealed by the first road and three more (Nos. 14, 20, 21), of Hadrian (A.D. 117–38) and two radiates (A.D. 270–300) were found in the silt between the two surfaces.

(f) The West Area 1966 (p. 85)

Here, six coins are of special interest. Two coins, one (No. 66–38) of Hadrian (A.D. 117–38) and one (No. 66–47) of Septimius Severus (A.D. 193–211) were found in the primary levels. Three more (Nos. 66–5, 34 and 39), all of Commodus (A.D. 180–92), came from three very adjacent features (Pit 25, Oven 8 and Gully F.24) and one (No. 66–13) of Caracalla (A.D. 201–6) came from Oven 1 nearby. Finally, one coin (No. 66–46) of Herennia E (A.D. 250–3) seems to have been trodden down into the underlying sands.

(g) Bath House Site 1965 (p. 54).

A coin (No. 65–2) of Julia Mamaea (A.D. 222–35) was found in the wall of the apse in Room 5. Outside the Bath House, sandwiched between the two separated metallings of the *Via Principalis,* was a coin (No. 65–17) of Carausius (A.D. 286–93).

(h) The East Barracks 1961–2 and 1968 (p. 73)

A single coin (No.61–92) of Aelius (AD 136–8) was found in the fort-construction levels near the east end of Trench B in 1961. Another 39 coins were found on the floor of Room A of East Barrack 1, under the remains of its collapsed walls. These all date between A.D. 244–90. Three more coins were found in Room D, two (Nos. 61–82 and 83) of Gallienus (A.D. 260–8) and Claudius II (268–70) under the burnt clay walls and another (No. 61–30) of Allectus (A.D. 293–6) came from the actual burnt daub layer. Nearby, another coin (No. 61–78) of Allectus (A.D. 293–6) was found in the *Intervallum* Road and two more (Nos. 61–31 and 33), both barbarous radiates (AD 270–90), were found in association with the probable veranda base.

(i) The *Via Quintana* Site 1959 (p. 18)

Two coins (Nos. 59–4 and 25) of Gallienus (A.D. 260–8) and Tacitus (A.D. 275–6) were found in the metalling of this road (L-3) in 1959. In 1961 another coin (No. 61–73)of Tetricus I (A.D. 270–3) was also found in this road. The deep grey loam (L-5) over the road, containing much domestic rubbish (perhaps from the adjacent East Barracks 1 and 2), contained another eleven coins all dating from A.D. 253–93).

(j)   The *Principia* Area 1960 (p. 45)

The fort-construction layers here contained a coin (No. 60–16) of Marcus Aurelius (A.D. 155–65) and the loam deposit covering both the *Intervallum* Road and the *Via Quintana* here contained two coins (Nos. 60–11 and 60–17) of Severus Alexander (A.D. 227) and Postumus (A.D. 260–8).

(k)   The *Sacellum* 1960 (p. 46)

The primary demolition deposit (L-19, 21) in the underground *Sacellum* contained 21 coins, two of 2nd century date, one early-3rd century, 14 dated A.D. 260–96 and two dated A.D. 320–25. The sealing rubble layer (L-3, 6, 20) contained four more coins all dated A.D. 270–336.

(l)   The South Gatehouse 1964 (p. 30)

One coin (No. 64–23), of about A.D. 270, was found in the loam over Road I. Six more coins (Nos. 16, 20, 21, 22, 27) were found in Road II and included two of the late-3rd century and one of Crispus (A.D. 317–26).

(m)   The East Ditches 1962 (p. 25)

A single coin (No. 287) of Gallienus (A.D. 258–68) was found in the outer east ditch, sandwiched between two substantial dumps of clay.

As regards the Rampart Bank, at two widely separated points, it sealed a coin of Commodus (A.D. 180–92), a mortarium dated A.D. 170–210 and a late-2nd century Rhenish beaker. Even allowing for an early loss of the coin a date for the Bank's construction much before A.D. 185, is unlikely. The greater probability is that these artefacts were lost or discarded no earlier than about A.D. 185 –200. The Bank itself contained a coin of Marcus Aurelius (A.D. 150–60) and mortaria, whilst it was in turn sealed by dumps containing a coin of Elagabalus (A.D. 218–22),with samian and mortaria.. The large pit, cut into the Bank near the East Gatehouse, contained coins of Severus Alexander (A.D. 222–35) and Allectus (A.D. 293–6). Clearly, the Rampart Bank was in place long before the end of the 3rd century and largely survives today.

The general soils associated with the Period I construction period, contained coins of Hadrian (A.D. 117 –38), Aelius (A.D. 136–8), Antoninus Pius (A.D. 138–61), Marcus Aurelius (A.D. 155–65) and Septimius Severus (A.D. 193–211). These fit comfortably as losses during the decades either side of A.D. 200. In, addition, coins of Hadrian (A.D. 134–8) and Commodus (A.D. 180–92) were found in the clay walls of two internal buildings (either Period I or Period II) and another coin of Julia Mamaea (A.D. 222–35) in the mortared wall of the Bath House (Period II). The latter apart, these fall in the earlier range of Reculver coins and help support the Period I construction date in the late-2nd century.

The soils over the Period I roads included coins of Hadrian (A.D. 117–38), Severus Alexander (A.D. 227), Postumus (A.D. 260–8), Carausius (A.D. 286–93) and three radiates (A.D. 270–300). It seems clear that these coin losses reflect the general 3rd century occupation of the site. The section of the relaid *Via Quintana* (examined in 1959) contained coins of Gallienus (A.D. 260–8), Tetricus (A.D. 270–3) and Tacitus (A.D. 275–6) and was probably laid down about A.D. 275–80. A single coin of Allectus (A.D. 293–6) was found in the metalling of the *Intervallum* Road and must relate to Period II.

As regards the internal structures, the final occupation soils inside the East Barracks No 1, actually sealed by the collapsed walls of Room A, contained 39 coins all dating from A.D. 244–80. Clearly, the collapse could not have taken place before about A.D. 280 and more likely sometime between A.D. 280–300. This is supported by the burnt and collapsed walls of Room D which sealed coins of Gallienus (A.D. 260–8), Claudius II (A.D. 268–70) and Allectus (A.D. 293–6). In addition, the soils covering the collapsed walls in Room A included coins of both the late-3rd and early-4th centuries, the latter entirely absent within the structure.

Finally, the demolition rubble in the *sacellum* of the *principia* produced 25 more coins. Whilst most date from A.D. 260–300, four coins date from about A.D. 320–335. The absence of later coins, still frequent on the overall site, suggest that the room had been robbed and was in serious decay sometime after A.D. 340 and perhaps in the period A.D. 340–60.

Summary of the Dating Evidence

The total evidence from the coins, mortaria, samian and main inscription, now needs to be summarised, but it is generally in good accord. Two critical coins of Commodus (A.D. 180–92), one under the Rampart Bank and the other from inside a wall of an internal building indicate that the fort could not have been constructed before about A.D. 180–5. Indeed, the significant numbers of coins of Marcus Aurelius (A.D. 161–80) and Commodus, on their own merits, support an initial occupation at Reculver before A.D. 200. This is supported by the samian ware, of which 18% of the sherds found have been identified as Antonine (A.D. 140–80) and another 24% as late-2nd to early-3rd (A.D. 175–225). It is also supported by the early mortaria which are dated A.D. 160–210 and include one vessel also found under the Rampart Bank. The accumulated evidence thus strongly suggests a fort-construction date of c. A.D. 185–200, with a preference for A.D. 185–95 and this allows for the coins of Marcus Aurelius still to be in circulation. This accords well with the date (*c.* A.D. 200) originally suggested by the author in 1959 (Ref. 3).

This then represents the Period I fort-construction programme, which was clearly well advanced, but not completed. The fort wall, gatehouses, rampart bank were constructed, the ditches dug and many internal foundations laid down. It is estimated (see above) that the whole programme could have been completed in 3–5 years and if so, then the stop came somewhere within this period. Just what caused such a major change of plan is open to debate, but clearly the circumstances must have been exceptional. It reflects the same pattern at nearby Dover where the earlier (Period I) *Classis Britannica* fort was started in about A.D. 117, but abandoned suddenly and not resumed until about A.D. 130 and to an enlarged plan (Period II). That sudden change is very likely to have related to military problems in the north whereby the fleet was urgently needed away from its permanent base at Dover (Ref. 55). Whilst several events, historically documented or not, could have been responsible for the sudden change of plan at Reculver, the most attractive is that of the expedition of Albinus in A.D. 197. In that year he transferred most of the garrison of Roman Britain to the Continent in his abortive attempt to seize the purple, against Septimius Severus. As a front-line unit, the *Cohors I Baetasiorum* at Reculver was well-placed to have been included in this cross-channel adventure. Afterwards, subject to its survival, it is equally likely to have been transferred north to help the new Emperor recover ground lost through the withdrawal of the northern garrisons.

Subsequently, a garrison (hopefully the *Cohors I Baetasiorum*) returned to Reculver and completed the construction of the fort, here described as Period II. This is likely to have been after A.D. 211 on the abandonment of the Scottish campaigns and thus after an interval of about 14 or more years, an interval that would help explain the change to the internal layout. Whilst the defences were retained intact at least four new buildings were constructed across the uncompleted Period I foundations, whilst the *principia* was retained. The new arrangements created the Period II scheme which is thus likely to have commenced *c.* A.D. 212–15 and continued throughout the 3rd century. This new phase is very likely to have seen the completion of the fort, a view substantially endorsed by the high coin-loss on the site which for the period A.D. 222–38 is four times above the British average. Period II is also well-represented by coin-loss and pottery until the very end of the third century and also saw the arrival of two rare coins from the east, perhaps reflecting Reculver's maritime connections, or just possibly the arrival of a small detachment of troops from

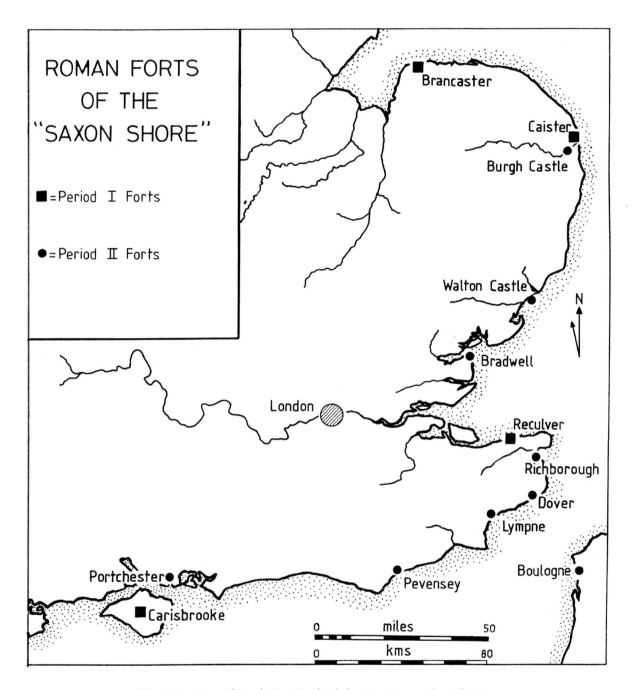

Fig. 74. *Map of South East England showing Roman Coastal Forts.*

Dacia, or beyond. Certainly, Aradius or Triarius, would have approved of the Period II completion! Eitherway, the *sacellum* inscription, with its published dating of A.D. 210–25 onwards, is now open for re-consideration. Certainly, the late-2nd century is not excluded. It could have related either to the uncompleted Period I arrangements, or the fort's completion under Period II, by one of several possible Rufinus candidates. The wider implications for the Shore-fort system are discussed below (p. 225).

What is also clear from the excavations is that at least the East Barracks No.1 was burnt down at the end of the 3rd century and never rebuilt. This is unlikely to represent events across the whole fort, but the coin-loss drops off in the earlier 4th century and the only trace of possible later Roman buildings are the post-holes over East Barracks Nos. 1 and 2. These are regarded as a possible Period III, from about A.D. 300 and ending perhaps at about A.D. 375 when the coin-loss falls right away and suggests minimal use of the fort thereafter.

(9) COMPARATIVE DATA (Fig. 75)

Of the twelve forts identified here as members of the Roman coastal defence system, popularly described as the Saxon Shore forts, it is now clear that Reculver is the only one which has so far produced significant excavated evidence of a planned layout. The only other forts where substantial internal areas have been excavated are at Richborough where about 60% was excavated in 1922–38 (Ref. 50) and Portchester where about 11% was excavated in 1961–72 (Ref. 51), whilst an air photograph of Brancaster provides important information. Three more forts, Lympne in 1850 (Ref. 52), Caister-on-Sea in 1951–5 (Ref. 53) and Dover in 1970–2002 (Ref. 55) have had their internal areas partly excavated. The very large-scale work at Dover, carried out at the centre of urban redevelopment, has produced spectacular evidence, but still awaits substantial funding for publication which was removed by English Heritage officals (GW and RT)without adequate explanation. Repeated attempts over three years (1998–2000) to re-establish English Heritage funding for the post-excavation programme, met with record official (PK) procrastination, feeble excuses and no progress Of the remaining five, the interiors are substantially unknown. Of these, Walton Castle has already gone into the sea, half of Bradwell has followed and Carisbrooke lies buried beneath a massive medieval castle. Only Pevensey and Burgh Castle seem open and largely accessible, both having had only a degree of excavation. Of all these forts, the immediate comparisons with Reculver are the air-photograph of Brancaster (Ref. 56), the excavated area of Caister-on-Sea and the defensive circuit at Carisbrooke Castle (Ref. 81).These are discussed below. Significantly, the large areas excavated at Richborough and Portchester revealed few internal structures relating to the masonry forts. At Lympne, however, way back in 1850 Charles Roach Smith located part of a very large masonry structure some 140 ft. in width and more than 30 ft. in length, consisting of at least three rooms, the central one projecting out beyond the others. From its size and central position there can be little doubt that this was the *principia* and that the projecting room was its *sacellum*.

Brancaster was another large, stone-built fort of very similar dimensions (584 x 574 ft.=178 x 175 m.) to Reculver (582 x 560 ft. = 177 x 171m.), again with rounded corners and no external bastions. The only meaningful excavation inside the Brancaster fort took place in 1935, when a long trench was excavated through each of the west and north defences. The work covered barely 0.06% of the internal area and thus as a sample is very unlikely to be fully representative and upon which definitive conclusions cannot be based. It did, however, reveal the fort wall (at 9 ft. = 3m. in width), a large external west ditch, a Rampart Bank (about 18–20 ft = 6m. in width) and also suggested two periods of construction, the later dating from the end of the 3rd century. Excellent post-war air photographs show two major internal buildings. The central one is surely the *principia*, facing north and fronting onto the *Via Principalis* which was accessed through east and west gates. A formal Reculver-style layout is clearly suggested with the main *Porta Praetoria* being the North Gatehouse and the rear-division being narrow as at Reculver In detail its *principia* can be scaled off

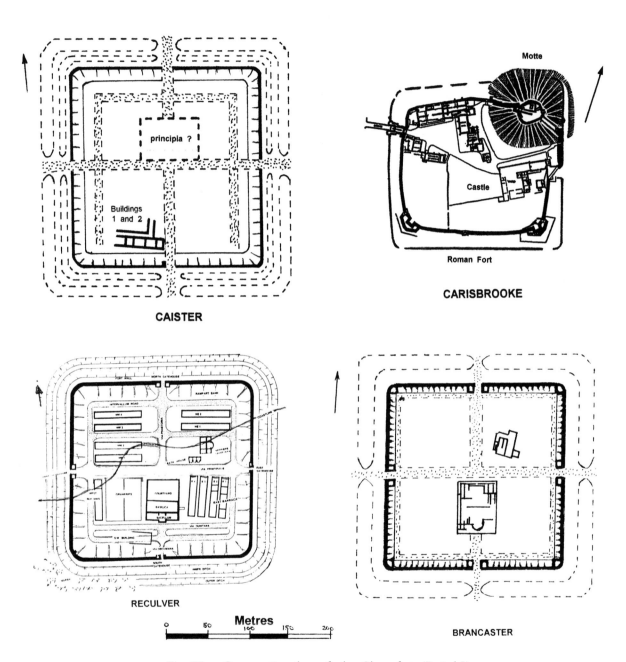

Fig. 75.   *Comparative plans of other Shore-forts (Period I).*

at about 125 x 122 ft. (40 x 37 m.) , strangely larger than that at Reculver, with a large projecting *Sacellum* at the rear, an obvious cross-hall about 115 x 39 ft.(35 x 13 m.) and a frontal courtyard about 65 x 65 ft.(25 x 25 m.). In the north-east sector of the fort is a middle-sized building, misaligned on the fort main axis (by about 10 degrees) and probably relating to a later phase, as at Reculver (Period II).

Excavations west of the Brancaster fort (Ref. 56) in 1974 and 1977 (ahead of housing development) located a complex system of small ditched enclosures, representing house-plots, which were multi-phased and flanked both sides of a wide ditched trackway leading to the west gate of the fort. These were matched by a larger group of enclosures on the east side of the fort, revealed by air photography, also flanking a wide ditched trackway though this time leading to the east gate of the fort. The large amount of Antonine samian from the west area strongly suggested a settlement starting earlier than A.D. 200, but not before about A.D. 170, a pattern largely supported by the coin evidence.

An helpful discussion, by author John Hinchcliffe, suggested that the early enclosures had formed part of a planned settlement. He did, however, identify the fort's construction-period as A.D. 225–30 and thus some 30–40 years later than the settlement immediately to the west. His resolution (clearly described as speculative) of this dilemma was to suggest the presence of another fort somewhere beneath the large stone-built fort. In support of this he emphasised the marginally different axes of the ditched enclosures on both the east and west sites to the known fort. He was further tempted to suggest that the mis-aligned building (marked A on his plan) in the north-east sector of the stone-built fort may have been the *principia* of the putative earlier fort!

His dating of the fort's construction to A.D. 225–30 was based on very slender evidence and in part on the Reculver inscription. The evidence from Reculver, now published here, indicates that the fort at Reculver was constructed at the end of the 2nd century. This must carry Brancaster with it for the two forts are very clearly matching members of the primary (Period I) short-fort system. In addition, the early Brancaster coins and samian ware largely match those at Reculver. This removes the problem of reconciling the artefactual evidence at Brancaster and there is now no need to introduce an unknown fort beneath it, nor to identify the north-east building as an early *principia*. Whilst the ditched enclosures at Brancaster are slightly mis-aligned on the fort, the all important trackways do in fact largely line-up on the east and west gates. Hence the mis-alignment here (only about 5 degrees in each case) may have little significance.

One final point is that the air photographs of Brancaster also show a rectangular, double-ditched enclosure, about 100 m. north of the fort. This appears military in character, but only measures about 90 x 80 m. (say 300 x 260 ft.). The most attractive solution is to suggest that this was a small Roman fort of the Conquest period, rather like that found under the stone-fort at Reculver. If so, this would help explain the presence of two mid-first century brooches and two equally early coins found inside the fort in 1935. Other early forts may await discovery elsewhere along the coast.

Caister-on-Sea. This Roman fort (at 620 x 615 ft. = 189 x 187 m.) also offers some useful comparative data. Like Reculver it, too, had a pair of defensive ditches and some evidence of an organised internal layout. The fort wall, robbed to below present ground-level, had been about 9 ft. 6" (3m.) wide at the base and there was evidence of a supporting Rampart Bank. Like Reculver, the latter also sealed an extensive mortar-mixing layer. An area roughly 180 x 180 ft. (55 x 55 m.) was excavated by Charles Green in 1951–5, which, with other minor trenching, represents about 9% of the internal area. This early excavation revealed parts of two large buildings (described as Buildings A and B) containing at least ten rooms and incorporating part of an earlier structure. It is just possible that the two buildings formed two sides of a larger courtyard building at one time. With clear evidence of hypocausts and painted walls the buildings are not typical barracks and are more likely to have served as officers' quarters, or even a *mansio*. The buildings were not exactly aligned on the fort wall and a variation of about 3 degrees seems clear. This misalignment matches, in principle, the variations at both Brancaster (10 degrees) and the Period II barracks at Reculver (4 degrees).

The east side of this building was flanked by a metalled road which passed through the South Gatehouse. Whilst only the west side of this Gatehouse was excavated it contained a small guard-chamber identical to those in the South and East Gatehouses at Reculver. The site is now largely covered by private houses and it is difficult to work out the original layout of the fort. On analogy with Reculver the South Gatehouse is likely to have been the main *Porta Praetoria*, or just possibly this lay on the east side. Either way, on this slender evidence, the *principia* is likely to be under the west side of Brooke Avenue, though probably damaged during construction-work in 1935.

A good discussion, by Margaret Darling and David Gurney accepted an early-3rd century date for the fort's construction, partly on the coin-evidence with high-values for A.D. 192–222. The pottery was also considered. About 30% (over 200 sherds) of the samian was from Central Gaul and dated to the later-second century. Of special interest was that 15 of the 24 dated stamped vessels and 15 of the 23 dated decorated vessels, dated from A.D. 160–200. This presented the authors with another dilemma for this dating was generally too early for an early-3rd century construction. They reconciled this with the suggestion that Roman military warehouses had retained stocks of 'quality' pottery. With Reculver now known to have been constructed at the end of the 2nd century, the dilemma is removed for Caister can be re-dated back to the same period. Hence the samian from Caister need not have been stockpiled in the manner suggested, but simply arrived in the normal course of events.

Carisbrooke Castle, Isle of Wight.

Here, a major rectangular, stone-walled enclosure (at least 480 x 450 ft = 146 x 137 m.) is sealed beneath both the 11th century motte and also the great 12th century castle. A limited excavation of the internal area found only a few Roman artefacts. Long lengths of its defensive walls on the east, south and west sides are visible, but only slight traces of the north wall are known. The north-east and north-west corners appear rounded, as at Reculver, Brancaster and Caister, but the central East Gate appears inturned. The wall is clearly several feet thick. The coursing is neat, some in herring-bone style and set in a hard pebbly mortar, as at Reculver, though few facing stones are clear. No trace of tile coursing can be seen, but a small integral bastion is visible roughly midway between the East Gate and the north-east corner. Slight traces of a possible matching bastion exists on the west side just north of the main castle gatehouse. The east one seems to project about 3 ft. from the fort wall and is clearly very much smaller than the massive bastions of the later shore forts. This may in fact be evidence of a prototype, marking the transition from the earlier unbastioned forts to the later ones found bristling with fully developed external bastions of large size. Indeed, it is even possible that Carisbrooke may have been provided with eight such vestigial bastions roughly evenly spaced around the circuit. If so, a careful search at Brancaster and Caister may one day reveal similar structures. Any at Reculver are likely to have been robbed away with the external facing stones and any deeper foundations destroyed by the considerable vertical ground reduction around the fort. Even so, it may not be a total coincidence that the unexplained repair in the east wall at Reculver (p. 20) occurs roughly midway between the East Gatehouse and the south-east corner, thus largely matching the certain arrangement at Carisbrooke (!) Of the internal (Roman) arrangements at Carisbrooke, nothing is known for any trace of these is likely to be deeply buried. No clear evidence of a west gate has been recorded, but as the west wall appears to re-align each side of its centre, some structurally significant point seems to be indicated. The curious and unsubstantiated suggestion that this massive masonry fortification was a late-Saxon construction can be dismissed.

Beyond the coastal Shore-forts the majority of comparisons can be made with 2nd century forts, mostly in Northern Britain. It is at once clear that Reculver (3.026 hectares) was substantially bigger than most of those, whilst Newstead (Ref. 57–5.3 hectares)and Malton (3.4 hectares) were two of the few that matched its size. Its square shape is also mostly at variance with the earlier forts which generally adopted a more oblong arrangement. With them, however, it shared external defensive ditches, multiple gatehouses, an internal Rampart Bank and a well-ordered internal layout comprising a *principia,* barracks and a rectilinear system of roads. Its defensive wall (at 9 ft. = 3m.) was considerably thicker than most of those built in the 2nd century, but thicker walls were already being introduced later at Malton (Ref. 59) and Castle Cary (Ref. 60), which can be considered as intermediate stages in the process of creating more massive defensive walls.

It also shared the same broad layout with a central *principia* fronting the main *Via Principalis* and closed at its back by a parallel *Via Quintana.* In terms of area, the front *praetentura* occupied about 50%, the central range about 30% and the rear *retentura* only 20%, half of which was taken up by the Rampart Bank and Intervallum Road. The rear division, with a width of just 13m., was thus unusually narrow. The *principia,* at 32 x 40m., was larger than most, but occupying 4.22% of the internal area it was in proportion to the large size of the fort. This does not take into account the possibility of a forehall. Its projecting *sacellum* follows some 2nd century forts such as Gelligaer, Mumrills, Balmuildy and South Shields, whilst its underground strongroom reflects those at Chesters, Segontium and Brough-by-Bainbridge. A site of useful comparison is Carpow on the River Tay (Ref. 58), where a large 25 acre (10 hectares) fort was constructed in Severan times and largely abandoned about A.D. 211. Its principia, regarded by the excavators as of legionary size, was 155 x 133 ft.(47 x 41m.) and thus only about 50% larger than that at Reculver. At Carpow, the rear-range contained nine offices, the central one (clearly the shrine) measured 20 x 18 ft.(6 x 5m.) and projected 4½ ft.(1m.) behind the rear wall of the *principia.* This is also the arrangement at Reculver, where the *sacellum* was actually larger (by 26%), but combined the functions of both strongroom and shrine. The similarity here must surely reflect the largely contemporary dates.

The only complete barrack found at Reculver was East Barrack No.1 (p. 73), which was 134 x 24 ft. (41 x 7m.), but this clearly formed one of a matching pair (with East Barrack No.2) with a generous gap of about 6 ft.(2m.) between them. It is assumed that the N.E. Building and others were also paired and the reconstruction (Fig. 72) allows for a total of five pairs. The internal divisions in East Barrack No.1, of four or five large rooms, immediately contrasts with the normal 2nd century arrangement of ten small *contubernia* (Ref. 40) and seems to suggest that Reculver represents a 3rd century (Period II) type evolving from the earlier form. Reculver also contrasts with a later form as at Housesteads (Ref. 61) and Wallsend (Ref. 62), where the "accommodation" seems to have been in so-called "chalets" laid laterally across the line of the earlier barracks. It also contrasts with the mid-3rd century examples of five *contubernia* as recently revealed at Wallsend.

The location at Reculver of a small Bath House (39 x 22 ft. = 12 x 7m.) within the fort is only occasionally matched in earlier forts where such buildings were normally large and outside the defences. Notable examples of large external bath-houses occur at Chesters (29 x 24 m.) and Vindolanda (about 20 x 20m.). Clearly, the Reculver Bath House was very much smaller and as this formed part of the Period II arrangements it raises the question of the siting of any Period I Bath House. If completed, it seems probable that it lay outside the fort in the traditional manner and indeed the "foundations" recorded by Battely about 1700 (p. 12) are clearly the best candidate. Locally, at Richborough and Lympne, the Bath Houses were inside the forts and both of these forts were also part of the late-Roman coastal system. The Reculver Bath House compares well with Richborough at 11 x 7m., but was smaller than that at Lympne which was about 15 x 9m. The plan of each was substantially different (Fig. 75). However, at Reculver, the linear arrangement of three heated rooms, each initially provided with an apsidal hot-bath, contrasts with most arrangements elsewhere. Presumably, these served as tepid and hot rooms of which the hot-baths were often an integral part. A broadly similar layout occurs at Newport, Isle of Wight (Ref. 63), itself not very far

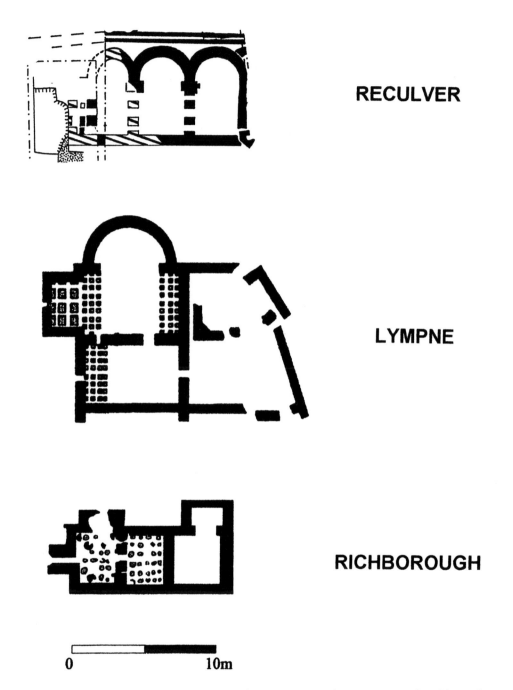

RECULVER

LYMPNE

RICHBOROUGH

0   10m

Fig. 76. *Comparative plans of Roman Bath Houses at Reculver, Lympne and Richborough.*

from the corresponding fort at Carisbrooke (!) What seems likely is that another room (or rooms) could have existed at Reculver on the west side, now buried beneath the churchyard. Indeed, a single butting wall was just detected at the south-west corner and the corresponding north-west corner was outside the excavation. If extra rooms did exist here, then a dressing room and/or a cold room are possible. This would then increase the length of the building by 10–20 ft.(3–6m.). Finally, the deep cistern found outside the east wall of the *basilica* at Reculver, resembles the tank found at the corner of the *principia* at Fendoch (Ref. 64).

By tracing what survives of the foundations of the *principia*, an absolute overall width of 104 ft. (32m.) was obtained. The north-south length of 130–140 ft. (say 41m.) has been estimated by placing the north wall on the side of the projected line of the *via principalis*. This length-width ratio fits well with many other known principia. Its rear division, with an overall width of 25 ft.(8m.) and a central *sacellum*, can be identified as a normal office-range. It seems likely that there was just one large office each side of the *sacellum*, though a total of five rooms is just possible. The central room measured 24 x 20 ft.(7 x 6 m.) internally, was sunk about 4 ft.(1m.) below Roman ground-level and projected about 5 ft. (1½ m.) behind the main rear-wall of the *principia*. This partially surviving structure represents a cellared strongroom, as noted elsewhere, with the actual shrine (*aedes*), above it and reached by steps. This office range was probably largely of one storey, with only the *sacellum* likely to have been two-storey in height. The presence of broken box-flue tiles in the ruins of the *sacellum*, only otherwise found in the Bath House, could indicate that at least one of these rooms was heated. Significantly, perhaps, no trace of a sub-structure that could indicate a hypocaust was found in the limited area excavated. Certainly, clear evidence of a hypocaust was found in the rear offices of the *principia* at Housesteads (Ref. 61).

The outline of the *basilica* was partially traced on its west, north and east sides, only through its surviving pebble foundation, which were mostly 6 ft. (2m.) in width. From these it seems to have measured 95 x 31 ft. (29 x 9m.) internally, largely in proportion to the large size of the *principia*. The large size of the foundations suggests that this cross-hall (*basilica*) was a two-storey structure probably with a central ridged roof. The generous width is likely to have needed extra roof support in the form of internal piers, either in one or two rows, thus creating one or two aisles, respectively, in true basilican form. A useful comparison can be made with the well-known *principia* at Housesteads, where the cross-hall had a width of about 28 ft (9m.), perhaps about 3–4 ft. less than at Reculver. At Housesteads a single line of six large piers created an aisle on the courtyard side and reduced the hall-span to about 18ft. On balance, a broadly similar arrangement is likely to have been used at Reculver, but with more piers to reflect the greater length. A *tribunal* may, or may not, have been included. The internal area was not examined in the 1959–69 excavations.

The front courtyard, at about 104 x 70–80 ft. (32 x 23m.) overall, seems in proportion, but its exact form and detail are not known due to the poor survival caused by later, substantial ground-reduction here. The stone-lined well, at its north-east corner, may relate to the *principia*.

(10) THE GARRISON

The only reference to any Roman garrison at Reculver occurs in the *Notitia Dignitatum* (p. 11). This clearly identifies the *Cohors I Baetasiorum* as the garrison under a tribune. It seems likely that this cohort was raised in Lower Germany and that it was in Britain from at least A.D. 103. Diplomas record it for the years A.D. 122, 124 and 135. It was the garrison of the Roman fort at Bar Hill on the Antonine Wall, during the reign of Antoninus Pius (A.D. 138–61). It is recorded on an inscription there where it used the title *c(ivium) R(omanorum)*. This title is likely to have been awarded for exceptional services in Southern Scotland in about A.D. 140. Another inscription mentioning the cohort, this time from the Roman fort at Old Kilpatrick also on the Antonine Wall, is dated to the second Antonine period (A.D. 158–63). This was on an altar dedicated by centurion Julius Candidus of the First Italic Legion, who had been given command of the cohort. It was certainly the garrison at the Roman fort at Maryport (Cumberland) from about A.D. 160 to at least the early 180s when there seems to have been a major reorganisation in the location of the frontier regiments.

It was whilst at Maryport that it dedicated five altars, either to Military Mars (3) or to the Emperor's Victory (2), which were soon buried and remain in excellent condition. These were recovered from deep pits with twelve others in 1870, some 350 yards north-east of the fort. Their burial may have been part of a re-organisation of the site, or equally to prevent their desecration, which was certainly achieved. Two of these altars were erected by Ulpius Titianus and three by Titus Attius Tutor, both commanders of the cohort with prefect status. The latter, at least, had a fine career. Initially, he served as a *decurio* (town councillor) of Solva, Noricum; next as prefect of the *Cohors I Baetasiorum*, followed by the post of tribune of the *legio II Adiutrix* stationed at Aquincum (Budapest). His next appointment was as prefect of the *ala Tungrorum Frontoniana* (Dacia) and finally as prefect of the *ala I Batavorum milliaria* (Dacia). All these details were recorded on his career inscription at his home town.

It now seems highly likely that the cohort was moved from Maryport directly to the north coast of Kent, as part of a large scale re-organisation. The evidence of the tiles stamped C IB from the oven in the East Cliff section (p. 64) suggests that the cohort actually built the fort at Reculver. So far seven tiles with this distinctive stamp (and no other) have been found at Reculver and it is not impossible that its name was also on the missing fragments of the *sacellum* inscription. If so, the Fortunatus name on that inscription could have been another one of its commanding officers. How long the unit stayed at Reculver is not known, but a stay of about 150 years seems highly improbable. The coin-loss evidence suggests only a minimal occupation of the fort after about A.D. 375. Hence, the entry of the *Notitia* (dated by others to about A.D. 400) must relate back to a much earlier period.

Apart from the garrison, there is some evidence that there may have been civilians also living within the fort at some stage. This takes the form of beads (Nos. 401–2) and in particular bracelets (Nos. 304–313, 404–407), with one complete child's bracelet (No. 304) coming from the rubble in the strong-room under the *sacellum*. It has also been suggested that civilians were living within the fort at Portchester. Another factor worthy of comment is the discovery of at least ten infant burials inside the fort. Of these, six clearly relate to the Roman structures. Three were found associated with the foundations of the West Building (p. 86), another in the corner of Room A of the East Barrack No.1 (p. 75) and one more inside the east wall of the same building. These are most likely to represent the ritual burial of still-born, or newly born, infants. In addition, two water-pipe collars found on the West Area strongly suggest that the fort was provided with water supplied through wooden pipes. This in turn suggests these were in adequate supply, either from somewhere inside the fort, or from the adjacent extramural settlement.

(11) THE ROMAN COASTAL DEFENCE SYSTEM (Fig. 74)

The construction of a large stone fort on the north coast of Kent at the end of the 2nd century, in an otherwise totally civil zone, is clear evidence of a major change in military strategy. This is reinforced by the transfer of a front-line auxiliary unit, the *Cohors I Baetasiorium*, nearly 300 miles and away from its coastal defence duties on the Cumberland coast at Maryport. That coastal defence, covering some 40 miles and consisting of major forts and mileforts, was a vital extension around the west end of Hadrian's Wall (Ref. 65). It now seems clear that this cohort actually constructed the fort at Reculver which, at 177 x 171m. internally, enclosed about 7½ acres (3.026 hectares).

What is now very clear is that Reculver formed part of an initial chain of forts (Period I) covering some 350 miles of coast and extending from the Wash to the Isle of Wight. Three other forts were clearly part of that chain and it is likely that others have been lost to the sea. It is thanks to the recent excellent publication of Brancaster, Norfolk (Ref. 56) and Caister-on-Sea, Norfolk (Ref. 53) in East Anglian Archaeology, that their data is now finally available. Both forts a were very similar indeed to Reculver (see above) and it must be that they were constructed as part of the same overall scheme. The third fort is at Carisbrooke, Isle of Wight, so often missed (S. Johnson 1977; P. Salway 1981; D. Mason 2003) or dismissed (S. Johnson 1979, Ref. 66 and A. Pearson 2002, Ref. 45) by students of shore-fort studies. The major stone-walled enclosure (at least 146 x 137m.), sits sealed by both the great 12th century castle and also the late-11th century motte. It clearly cannot be post-Norman Conquest, nor even looks like it. The only explanation by others is that it was a late-Saxon masonry fortification in spite of the fact that these seem unknown elsewhere! The fact that the Carisbrooke fort occupies a hilltop close to the centre of the Island and not a specific coastal site, as with most other forts in this series, cannot be used as evidence to dismiss what is so clearly visible on the ground. The forts' function was anyway to guard a small island and not a long stretch of coastline. It also had access to the island's largest inland waterway, the River Medina, which flows to within one mile of the fort. It seems likely that a Roman quayside installation awaits discovery here, perhaps buried beneath more recent silts.

In terms of spacing, the forts at Brancaster and Caister are about 65 miles (100 km.) apart, whereas Reculver lies about 100 miles (160 km.) to the south of the latter. On purely numerical and circumstantial grounds at least one more fort between these two sites may have existed and has been destroyed. Certainly, the later Roman fort at Walton Castle, on the Suffolk coast has been removed from its cliff-top position by the sea. Hence another fort in the Period I Reculver series, perhaps in the general Felixstowe area, is quite possible and its massive broken walls could yet lie submerged just off the coast hereabouts (see footnote). Certainly, fragments of Walton Castle still survived beneath the waves in 1957 when they were photographed at low tide by this author. A further measure of the extensive erosion hereabouts is evidenced by the total destruction of the documented town of Dunwich well before 1800 (Ref. 67).

Looking westwards, the Reculver-Carisbrooke gap appears to be an alarming 150 miles (240 km.). Surely at least one more fort must have existed here and if regular spacing was an important factor, then two more could have existed. Again most of the Sussex coast has been subjected to sea erosion, notably at Selsey Bill, so otherwise unknown Roman sites could certainly have existed. Whilst the location of such a missing fort (or forts) is highly speculative, sites nominally near Eastbourne and Worthing are mathematically suitable locations. This produces a theoretical total of at least seven early coastal forts and no doubt this will not be the end of an interesting debate! Not least this should include a detailed study of missing harbours, some no doubt deeply buried (as at Dover) under very extensive layers of silt. So, too, must further consideration be given to the role of the defences at Brough-on-Humber (Period VI– Ref. 85) another 75miles (120 km.) to the north-west of Brancaster, where a naval base has been suggested, but awaits confirmation.

What is now abundantly clear is that the original (Period I) group of coastal forts, certainly four but probably more, were later supplemented by further forts. Of these, eight can be identified with certainty and again others may have been destroyed by sea erosion. The new forts were all

Footnote. Ten months after this was written Howard Davies (Somerset) and John Fairclough (Suffolk) incidentally drew the writers attention to a letter written by a local Suffolk man, William Myers, in 1762 (Ref. 70 p. 448). This mentions "large ruins....brickwork, square stones etc.," at West Rock, in the sea 3–4 nautical miles east of Walton-on-the Naze and identified as possible Roman masonry. This certainly deserves another survey.

distinguished by their thicker walls, frequent external bastions, mostly variable circuits and frequent tile or stone coursing. Strangely, before about 1960 this clear distinction was mostly missed, or dismissed, by early writers. Even the good evidence from our 1957 excavation at Reculver and its subsequent publication and discussion on the matter in 1959 (Ref. 3), received a poor reception and was actively discouraged (though with little effect).

From the west, the new forts included one at Portchester, Hants (Ref. 51), perhaps replacing the one at Carisbrooke and also another at Pevensey, Sussex (Ref. 68), under construction about A.D. 295–300. Three more appeared in Kent, including one each at Dover, *c.* A.D. 270 and Lympne, where they each replaced *Classis Britannica* forts of the 2nd century. The new fort at Dover partly overlay the ruins of the naval fort, abandoned about A.D. 208, selecting a site marginally nearer the harbour. Large-scale excavations by the Kent Archaeological Rescue Unit across the two forts from 1970–2002 (Ref. 55) showed that some 60 years separated the two events. The construction of the later fort had also destroyed much of the *mansio*, now known as the Roman Painted House, thus ensuring the unique survival of large areas of painted wall-plaster.

A third Kent fort was added at Richborough about the same time, destroying another *mansio* and superseding a small triple-ditched fortlet, constructed around A.D. 250. The latter had enclosed the ruins of the great tower-like monument, built in Flavian times, which had clearly been utilised as a signal-station. Two more forts were constructed, one at Bradwell, Essex (Ref. 69) and the other at Walton Castle, Suffolk (Ref. 70), the latter perhaps replacing the putative Period I fort in that general area. Finally, another new fort was built at Burgh Castle, Norfolk, to reinforce the existing Period I fort at nearby Caister-on-Sea.

Most of the eight new forts are likely to have been constructed between about A.D. 270–300 and thus represent a major new period of construction (here regarded as Period II). The interesting claim that all these forts relate to the Carausius-Allectus episode of just eight years, is not supported by the total dating evidence. Nor is it likely that any imperial invasion force sailing from Boulogne to recover the province would enter the North Sea and thus require new forts as far north as Walton Castle and Burgh Castle. Later still, in the fourth century, a series of five signal stations was constructed along the Yorkshire coast (Ref. 71) and these are mostly regarded as an extension of the coastal defence system. In addition, the settlement at Bitterne received its masonry defences at about the same time. The masonry tower at Shadwell, east of London, originally identified as a signal-tower, has since been described as a Roman mausoleum.

Even further afield, along the west coast at Anglesey (Ref. 72), Cardiff (Ref. 73) and Lancaster (Ref. 74) new forts were appearing and demonstrate the need for extensive coastal defence there. Across the Channel at least 15 more Roman forts (Ref. 75) are either recorded or known along the French and Belgian coasts, or at the mouth of the River Rhine. Most of these are listed in the Gallic section of the *Notitia Dignitatum* (chapters 37 and 38), with ten under the Duke of the Armorican and Nervian frontiers and three more under the Duke of *Belgica Secunda*. The fort names and garrisons are given, the latter mostly under prefects (10) or tribunes (2). In addition, there was even a small fortlet at Alderney in the Channel Islands (Ref. 76) and familiar looking forts at Oudenburg (163 x 146m) and Brittenburg (160 x 150m). More excavation and precise dating is still needed at several of these sites.

The *Notitia Dignitatum*, dating from about A.D. 400, is one of the few surviving documents for the period. It also includes details (chapter 28) of a *Comes Litoris Saxonici* (the Count of the Saxon Shore) with a list by name of nine coastal forts under his command. Eight of these can be reconciled with some of the twelve known Period I and Period II forts on the British side of the Channel. One is problematical and three (or more) are clearly missing. The compilation of this document, perhaps based on earlier lists and also itself later copied, is predictably unlikely to be totally comprehensive, or fully reflect a changing situation over a span of about 200 years. More forts certainly existed and more may yet be found.

The *Notitia* also lists the garrisons of the nine forts covered and this includes the *Cohors I Baetasiorum* at *Regulbium*. No scholar in the last 400 years has doubted the identification of *Regulbium* with present-day Reculver and our discovery of tiles stamped C IB, makes this totally conclusive. It also confirms the accuracy of the *Notitia* in this respect. Indeed, the evidence now suggests that this garrison actually built the fort at Reculver at the end of the 2nd century. It seems rather unlikely that this garrison remained at the site for nearly 200 years and suggests that the *Notitia* was incorporating much earlier material. Indeed, the coin loss at Reculver suggests comparatively little activity there after about A.D. 375 and a military withdrawal about then seems a strong possibility. The same document lists the *Cohors I Aquitanorum* at Brancaster, where tiles stamped by that unit have more recently been found. The list also includes the *Legio II Augusta* at Richborough, but this is likely to relate to a detachment rather than the total legion. The presence of a large amphitheatre at Richborough, however, often associated with legionary bases elsewhere, could indicate that the detachment was a very large one. If so, it need not have been packed into the six acre fort, but largely housed in a much wider area around the fort, where there is clear evidence of extramural settlement.

The reason for this long period of fort building along some 350 miles of the South-East coast of Roman Britain has attracted much discussion in recent decades. Taken with newly fortified bases on the Gallic side of the Channel, the external military threat must have been substantial. The enemy is now generally accepted as being the Franks, Friesians and Saxons, mostly from the lands north of the River Rhine (Ref. 77). They were clearly mobile and in significant numbers to demand a major military response over a long period of time. Indeed, it seems likely that they operated in small fleets descending on any part of the various coastlines and across much open sea. There would be little chance of direct interception, particularly at night or in poor visibility. The many vulnerable shipping and coastal targets could be picked-off at will and in a very short time. They were, in effect, a naval 'guerilla' force.

The view is that they initially raided the shipping lanes in the Channel, along parts of the East Coast and river estuaries, such as the Thames and Wash. These raids may initially have been dealt with by Roman naval squadrons. The deployment, however, of good infantry cohorts and the construction of so many large forts strongly suggests that the Channel and North Sea had become a new frontier. It is likely that the scale of the raids had been badly under estimated by most scholars, largely due to the limited historical data. The significant number of new forts and new defences for some established towns on both sides of the Channel must surely be highly indicative. The number of coin-hoards from East Anglia dating from the end of the 2nd century suggests insecurity in depth, whilst the provision of a town wall for Rochester, Kent at about A.D. 200 must surely be significant. Indeed, it seems likely that one day the town walls of Canterbury, Chichester and London may be found to date from about this time. This all suggests that the raids were also hitting the mainland and were not confined to the shipping lanes. In addition, the need for four large forts on the Kent coast, all within a span of only 45 miles, strongly suggests that this became the front-line sector, as in the 19th–20th centuries! Perhaps, too, the famous Roman wreck on the Pudding Pan Sands with its large cargo of samian ware, was an early victim of raids on the shipping lanes. The view that the new coastal forts were supply bases for northern campaigns is now largely contradicted by the lack of multiple granaries on the South Shields scale (Ref. 78) and the certain inclusion of Carisbrooke far along the south coast.

Even so, the role, function and occupancy of each fort, is likely to have varied over a span of some 200 years. Each fort must certainly have been served by an adjacent quayside, or small harbour, but the suggestion that each fort was a fully fledged port is not yet supported by much evidence, other than at Dover. The greater probability is that the local harbour installations at each fort also simply represented convenient havens. In addition, the movement of ships both merchant and military in these dangerous waters is very likely to have created the need for convoy arrangements. Thus naval units attached to the forts would have been well placed to offer such protection along most of the British coastline and their attached harbours some additional safety when needed.

Accordingly, there must have been a very substantial threat already before the end of the 2nd century when Reculver and the other Period I forts were almost certainly built. Such a threat from the sea must certainly have involved the *Classis Britannica* squadrons, based mainly in the Channel. Their main base at Dover, as evidenced by a substantial fort, developed harbour and two large masonry light-houses, was abandoned about A.D. 208 and never re-occupied by them. It is highly likely that the whole fleet moved north to service (with other fleets) the major campaigns in Scotland led by Septimius Severus himself from A.D. 208–11. These campaigns involved the construction of a new legionary fort at Carpow on the banks of the River Tay, which was itself largely abandoned in A.D. 211 after the death of Severus and the end of the campaign, following a treaty with the enemy (Ref. 79).

The *Classis Britannica* never returned to its Dover base and it now seems clear that part, or all, of it was re-deployed. In view of the major new threat from across the North Sea, reflected in the construction of the Period I forts, it seems likely that its squadrons were now spread along over 350 miles of coastline. It must be that these squadrons were working in close collaboration with the auxiliary units in the forts and very reasonable to assume that they were based in the harbours attached to them. It is equally possible that they shared barracks within these large forts, as suggested by Richmond in 1963 (Ref. 47). Indeed, at Reculver, some 50 Roman tiles, incorporated into the later Saxon and medieval church on the site, are of the distinctive Fabric 2 type, directly associated with large-scale tile production by the Roman fleet at some unknown site in the Weald. This suggests a direct link between the *Cohors I Baetasiorum* and the *Classis Britannica* at *Regulbium* and this could indicate that they shared the fort. The tiles in the East Gate at Reculver are not of Fabric 2, contrary to claims made elsewhere (Ref. 80). So, too, should be dismissed the suggestion (Ref. 86) that the Reculver Fabric 2 tiles are from a unique nearby source. Clearly, if such tiles could reach Richborough they could certainly have been transported the extra ten miles to Reculver along the tidal channel between Thanet and the mainland.

Whereas the fleet had a largely support role in the 2nd century, it seems likely that by the 3rd century its role had changed to that of patrol and defence. The apparent disappearance of it after about A.D. 250, when the Arles inscription (dated to Philip II A.D. 244–9) shows it still to exist, could reflect a total reorganisation of the fleet in the second half of the 3rd century, or later, although the absence of evidence may not be evidence of absence! Indeed, Carausius is identified as admiral of the fleet in about A.D. 285, which suggests that it survived at least up until then. Perhaps it was this short-lived adventure that showed the dangers of such a centrally organised fleet and that it was re-deployed thereafter. In addition, it is highly likely that the fleet and its men would have been employed in the collection and transport of much of the stone and other materials employed in the construction of the forts, both in the early (Period I) programme and the later one (Period II). It is even possible that its marines actually built one, or more, of the forts for it had considerable building skills as evidenced at Dover and along Hadrian's Wall.

REFERENCES

Ref	Subject	Author	Reference
1	Reculver Exc. 1952–4	Philp, B.J.	Arch. Cant. LXXI (1957), p.167
2	Reculver Exc. 1955–7	Philp, B.J.	Arch. Cant. LXXII (1958), p.160
3	Reculver Exc. 1957	Philp, B.J.	Arch. Cant. LXXIII (1959), p.96
4	Reculver Exc. 1958	Philp, B.J.	Arch. Cant. LXXIV (1960), p.182
5	Reculver Exc. 1960	Philp, B.J.	Arch. Cant. LXXVI (1961), p.lii
6	Reculver Exc. 1965	Philp, B.J.	K.A.R. No.2 (1965), p.24
7	Reculver Exc. 1965	Philp, B.J.	K.A.R. No.3 (1966), p.41
8	Reculver Exc. 1966	Philp, B.J.	K.A.R. No.6 (1966), p.7
9	Reculver Exc. 1967	Philp, B.J.	K.A.R. No.10 (1967), p.6
10	Dover Exc. 1970	Philp, B.J.	K.A.R. No.23 (1971), p.74
11	Dover Exc. 1971	Philp, B.J.	K.A.R. No.28 (1972), p.236
12	Dover Exc. 1971	Philp, B.J.	K.A.R. No.29 (1972), p.260
13	Dover Exc. 1975	Philp, B.J.	K.A.R. No.45 (1976), p.119
14	Dover Exc. 1978	Philp, B.J.	K.A.R. No.53 (1978), p.64
15	Dover Exc. 1984	Philp, B.J.	K.A.R. No.78 (1984), p.187
16	Burials Reculver	Philp, B.J.	K.A.R. No.136 (1999), p.123
17	C.I.B Maryport	Wilson, R.J.	Roman Maryport and its Setting, (1997), p.80
18	C.I.B Barhill	Breeze, D.	Proc. of Soc. Ants of Scotland, Vol. 102, (1993), p.109
19	C.I.B Balmuildy		Brit. Vol. I (1970), p.310
20	Early Records	Swanton, M.	Anglo-Saxon Chronicles, (2000), p.34
21	Early Records	Smith, C.R.	Richborough, Reculver & Lympne (1850), p.221
22	Early Records	Ragg, F. W.	V.C.H. Kent, Vol. III (1932), p.211
23	Early Records	Leland, J.	Iter. VII (1530–7), p.136
24	Early Records	Battely, J.	Antiquitates Retupinae (1711)
25	Early Records	Boys, W.	Bibl. Topogr. Brit I (1781), p.83
26	Early Records	Dowker, G.	Arch. Cant. XII (1878), p.1
27	Early Records	Home, G.	Arch. Jnl., LXXXVI (1929), p.260
28	Early Records	Thompson, F.	Arch. Cant. LXVI (1953), p.52
29	Early Records	Freeman, R.	Regulbium, (1810), poem.
30	Mansio, Dover	Philp, B.J.	Roman House with Bacchic Murals, Dover (1989)
31	Corn Drying Oven	Philp, B.J.	Arch. In the Front Line (2002), p.205
32	External Road	Chenery, M.	Kent Minor Sites Series No.9 (1996), p.1–35
33	Richborough pre-historic	Bushe-Fox, J.P.	The Exc. Of the Roman Fort at Richborough, Kent, IV (1949), p.8
34	Faversham Enclosure	Philp, B. J.	Excavations at Faversham 1965, (1968), p.65
35	Keston Enclosure	Philp, B. J.	The Roman Villa Site at Keston, Kent (1991) p.29
36	Lenham Enclosure	Philp, B. J.	Kent Special Subject Series No.7 (1994), p.5
37	Roman Forts	Jones, M.J.	B. A. R. No. 21 (1975), p.108
38	Richborough Fort	Cunliffe, B (Ed)	See Ref. 33, Vol. V(1968), p.232
39	Early Coins	Wheeler, R.E.M	V. C. H. (Kent) Vol. III (1932), p.22
40	Roman Barracks	Bidwell, P.	Roman Forts in Britain (1997)
41	Richborough Bath House	Bushe-Fox, J.P.	See Ref. 33. Vol. II (1928), p.24
42	Lympne Bath House	Smith, C.R	Ant. of Richborough, Reculver and Lympne (1852)
43	Burgh Castle	Johnson, S.	Burgh Castle Exc. by C. Green 1958–61 (1983), p.6
44	Stone to Birchington	Barrett, J.	A History of the Ville of Birchington (1893), p.61
45	Pioneer Study	Pearson, A.	The Roman Shore Forts (2002), p.62
46	Painted House	Ruck, G.	K.A.R. No.47 (1977), p.157
47	Triario Rufinus	Richmond, I.	Arch. Jnl. Vol.41 (1961), p.224
48	Aradio Rufinus	Harper, R.P.	Anatolian Studies (JBIAA), XIV (1964), p.163
49	Maryport Fort	Wilson, R.J.	See Ref. 17
50	Richborough Fort	Bushe-Fox, J.P.	See Ref. 33, Vol.IV (1949)

51	Portchester Fort	Cuncliffe, B.	Excavations at Portchester Castle, Vol. I (1975), p.75
52	Lympne Fort	Harrison, J.	Britannia Vol. XVI (1985), p.209
53	Caister-on-Sea Fort	Darling, M. & Guerney, D.	Caister-on-Sea. Excavation by Charles Green 1951–55 (1993), p.106
54	Roman coins	Philp, B. J.	K.A.R. No.143 (2001), p.64
55	Dover Fort	Philp, B.J.	The Excavation of the Roman Forts of the Classis Britannica at Dover 1970–77 (1981), p.118
56	Brancaster Fort	Hinchcliffe, J.	Excavations at Brancaster 1974 and 1977 (1985), p.1
57	Newstead Fort	Curle, J.	A Roman Frontier Post and its People (1911)
58	Carpow Fort	Dore, J. & Wilkes, J.	Proc. of Soc. Ants. Scot. 129 (1999),481
59	Malton Fort	Corder, P.	The Defences of the Roman Fort at Malton (1930)
60	Castle Cary Fort		Proc. of Soc. Ants. Scot. 37 (1902),p.291
61	Housesteads Fort	Crow, J.	Housesteads (English Heritage –1995)
62	Wallsend Fort	Hodgson, N.	Brit. XXXV (2004), p.148
63	Newport Villa	Rook, A.	Roman Baths in Britain (2002), p. 53
64	Fendoch Fort	Collingwood, R. & Richmond, I.	Arch. of Roman Britain, (1969), p.30
65	Maryport Fort	Wilson, R.J.	See Ref. 17
66	Survey	Johnson, S.	The Roman Forts of the Saxon Shore (1976), p.143
67	Dunwich	Rigold, S.E.	JBAA 127 (1974), p.97
68	Pevensey Fort	Fulford, M.	Antiquity 69 (1995), p.1009
69	Bradwell Fort	Wilkinson, T. & Murphy, P	The Archaeology of the Essex Coast, Vol.I (1995), p.
70	Walton Castle	Fairclough, J. & Plunkett, S.	Proc. Suffolk Inst. Archaeology, Vol. 39 (2000), p.419
71	Signal stations	Pearson, A	Roman Britain and the Roman Navy (2003), p.182
72	Anglesey Fort	Putnam, W.	Roman Frontier in Wales (1967), p.135
73	Cardiff Fort	Webster, P.	Cardiff Castle Exc. 1974–81 (1981), in Morgannwg 25, p.201
74	Lancaster Fort	Jones, J.	Brigantia Mon. I (1988), p.21
75	Gallic Coast	Mason, D.	See Ref. 67, p.163
76	Alderney Fort	Brulet, R.	In Roman Frontier Studies (1989) p.155–69
77	Rhine Area	Pearson, A.	See Ref. 45 p.133
78	South Shields Fort	Bidwell, P. & Speak, S.	Soc. Ants. Newcastle, Mono. 4 (1994)
79	Treaty	Richmond, I	Roman Britain (1955), p.59
80	Tiles in East Gate	Pearson, A.	See Ref. 45, p.51
81	Carisbrooke Fort	Young, C. J.	Rome and her Northern Provinces (1983), p.290
82	Inscription	Mann, J.C.	The Saxon Shore, C.B.A.No.18 (1977), p.15
83	Coastline	So, C. L.	Arch. Cant., LXXXVI,(1971), p.93
84	Baptistry	Rigold, S.E.	See Ref. 82, p. 72
85	Brough-on-Humber	Wacher, J. S.	Excavations at Brough-on Humber 1958–61, Soc. Ants. Reports XXV (1969), p.3
86	CL BR Tiles	Peacock, D. P.	Brit. VIII (1977), p.235
87	Small Finds	Crummy, N.	Colchester Archaeological Report No. 2 (1983)
88	Inscription	Birley, A. R.	The Fasti of Roman Britain (1981), p. 172
89	Name	Rivet, A. & Smith, C.	Place-names of Roman Britain (1979), p. 446

INDEX

Plate I.   *Reculver. The foreshore west of the fort (mid-summer).*

Plate II.   *Reculver. The foreshore north of the fort (mid-winter).*

Plate III. *St. Mary's Church, from the south-east.*

Plate IV. *The south wall of the Roman fort from the west (2004).*

Plate V.   *The east wall of the fort, detail showing facing stones (2004).*

Plate VI.   *Repair in the East Wall of the fort (exterior), 1964.*

Plate VII.   *Repair in the East Wall of the fort (interior), 1964.*

Plate VIII.   *East wall of fort (interior)* Via Quintana *section (1959)*

Plate X. *Stone boulders in Via Quintana, from east (1959).*

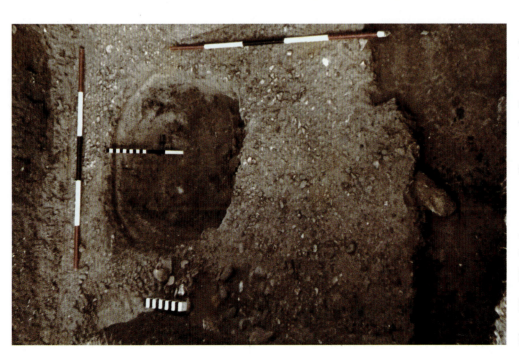

Plate IX. *Via Quintana metalling, cut by Roman pit, from the north (1959).*

Plate XI.   *South Gatehouse, showing metalling & stone blocks, from south-east (1964).*

Plate XII.   *South Gatehouse, detail showing metalling and stone blocks (1964).*

Plate XIII.   *South Gatehouse, detail of stone pecking on stone blocks (1964).*

Plate XIV.   *East Gatehouse, showing Rampart Bank & edge of Guardroom (1967).*

Plate XV. *East Gatehouse, showing Guardroom, from the north-west (1967).*

Plate XVI. *East Gatehouse, showing Guardroom and fort wall, from the east (1967).*

Plate XVII.   *Central Area, pebble foundations of cross-hall, from the east (1960).*

Plate XVIII.   Sacellum, *showing east wall and rubble infill, from the east (1960).*

Plate XX.   *Water Cistern & cross-hall foundations, from the west (Box GC 1963)*

Plate XIX.   *Sacellum east wall, from the south (1960).*

Plate XXI.   *South Area, showing evaluation trenches, from the west (1963).*

Plate XXII.   *South-west Building, detail showing east wall, from the east (W3 Box J 1963).*

Plate XXIII. *South-west Building, detail showing south wall (W4), from the south (1964).*

Plate XXIV. *Bath House, showing Rooms 1–6, from the north-east (1965).*

Plate XXV.   *Bath House, detail of Plunge Bath in Room 4, (1964).*

Plate XXVI.   *Bath House; apsidal baths (Rms 5 & 6) and external drain, from the east 1964).*

Plate XXVII.   *East Cliff; fort wall, Rampart Bank and mortar spread, from north-west (1965).*

Plate XXVIII.   *East Cliff, showing corner of North-east Building, from the east (1966).*

Plate XXIX.   *North East Area, Trench A, showing Bath House Drain cutting early features, from the east (1969).*

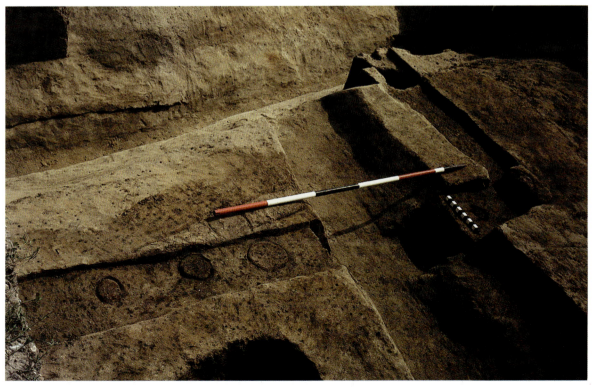

Plate XXX.   *North East Area, detail showing wooden post outlines, from the north (1969).*

Plate XXXII. *East Area, Trench B, showing walls and floors of the East Barracks Nos. 1 & 2, from east (1961)*

Plate XXXI. *East Area, general view of Trench D, from the east (1961).*

Plate XXXIV. *East Area, general view of Trench A, from the south (1961).*

Plate XXXIII. *East Area, Trench B, with rubble over Intervallum Rd, from the east (1961).*

Plate XXXV.   *East Area, showing Period I foundations beneath East Barracks No.2, from the west (1968).*

Plate XXXVI.   *West Site, general view, from the east (1966).*

Plate XXXVII.   *West Site, showing east wall of West Building, from the south (1966).*

Plate XXXVIII.   *West Site, showing infant burials at north-east corner, from the south (1966).*

Plate XXXIX. *Corn-drying Oven, south-east of fort, from the north-west (1963).*

Plate XL. *Corn-drying Oven, south-east of fort, detail of wall-flues, from south-east.*

Plate XLII. *Fortlet, South Area, Trench A, showing Palisade Trench and ditches, from the north (1963).*

Plate XLI. *Fortlet, South Area, Trench B, showing Palisade Trench and Ditches, from the north (1963).*

Plate XLIII.   *Fortlet, South Area, Ditch Junction (Box JH), from the north-west (1963).*

Plate XLIV.   *Fortlet, South Area, detail of Ox Skull in ditch (Box JH), (1963).*

Plate XLV.   *North-east Area, Trench A, showing ditches, from the south (1969).*

Plate XLVI.   *Extramural Settlement west of fort, showing wells on foreshore (simulated).*

Plate XLVIII. *Reculver, the foreshore west of the Fort (The Great Freeze 1963).*

Plate XLVII. *St. Mary's Church, showing Saxon* opus signinum *floor, from the west (1969).*